Cazenove & Co

The eight senior partners, painted by Simon Elwes in 1957:
Geoffrey Akroyd, Derek Schreiber, Peter Kemp-Welch,
Antony Hornby, Philip Cazenove, Ernest Bedford, Frank Holt
and Albert Martin.

Cazenove & Co:
A History

David Kynaston

B.T. Batsford Ltd, London

© David Kynaston 1991

First published 1991

All rights reserved. No part of this publication may be reproduced
in any form or by any means without permission from the Publisher.

Typeset by Servis Filmsetting Ltd, Manchester
and printed in Great Britain
by Butler and Tanner Ltd, Frome, Somerset
for the publishers
B.T. Batsford Ltd
4 Fitzhardinge Street
London W1H 0AH

A catalogue record for this book
is available from the British Library.

ISBN 0 7134 6059 8

CONTENTS

PREFACE

This book builds on the written work of several people.

The first historian of Cazenove's was Albert Martin, a partner who in 1955 (over half a century after he had joined the firm) wrote a brief, privately-published booklet. It contains certain factual errors, especially about the firm's origins, but overall provides a valuable framework.

Then in 1971, shortly after retiring as senior partner, Sir Antony Hornby wrote an account of his long career with the firm, again privately-published. A most readable book, it furnishes much important material not available elsewhere.

Thirdly, in 1980, Nicholas Lyster, the son of a partner, carried out much detailed research into the firm's history. His account provides a fuller, more reliable chronology than in Martin's book and in general was a notable effort by a university undergraduate.

Finally, in 1982, the firm commissioned the late Dr S.R. Cope, a distinguished banker-scholar, to undertake a full-scale history. Over the ensuing years he did much archival work and produced a substantial body of material, mostly relating to the nineteenth century; but in 1986, handicapped by illness and physical disability, he was unable to continue his work.

The following year I accepted an invitation to bring the long-nurtured project to fruition. Drawing greatly on the work of my four predecessors, as well as on the notes of another former partner, Godfrey Chandler, this I have done. I owe much to their endeavours and I hope to have written a book worthy of them.

London, June 1991

ACKNOWLEDGEMENTS

The following kindly gave me permission to consult and reproduce material in their possession: the Bank of England; Baring Brothers; John Foster & Son and the Brotherton Library, University of Leeds; Morgan Grenfell; N. M. Rothschild & Sons; Schroders; and University College, London.

I would like to thank the following people: Lady Freyberg for her help in establishing the date of the brokers' medal struck for her ancestor Philip Cazenove and thereby the date of the founding of the firm; Pat Buchanan, the former librarian at Cazenove's, for her careful research on behalf of both Raymond Cope and me; Judy Slinn for conducting various interviews during Raymond Cope's illness; Robert Bruce, formerly a partner of Laurence Prust, for his assistance on the Laurence Cazenove & Pearce period; John Patchett for his help over the records of John Foster; John Orbell, the archivist at Barings, for his encouragement and help both to Raymond Cope and me; J. G. Baird of the Royal Bank of Scotland and G. F. Miles of Barclays Bank for guiding me (if fruitlessly) through the archives of Glyn Mills and Martins Bank respectively; Richard Roberts for his critical comments on chapters five to seven; and a cluster of other historians, Kathleen Burk, Philip Cottrell, Martin Daunton and Philip Ziegler, for guidance on specific questions.

I interviewed many present and former partners and members of the firm, and the book could not have been written without them.

I would like also to thank five relatives of former partners for their help: Sylvia Barnett; Michael Ingram; Gelda James; Evelyn Micklem; and Lady Page.

Finally, I must thank the many others who kindly gave me their insights not only into the history of Cazenove's, but also into the history of the City as a whole: Sir John Baring (Lord Ashburton); Eddie Binks; Teddy Butler-Henderson; Raymond Cazalet; Tim Collins; John Craze; Nigel Davey; Jack Durlacher; Jeremy Edwards; Albert H. Gordon; Henry Grunfeld; Nicholas Herald; Sir John Hogg; Eric Hollis; Sir Simon Hornby; Lord Keith of Castleacre; John Kinross; Paul Ledeboer; Daniel Meinertzhagen; Sir Jeremy Morse; Angus Murray; Sir John Prideaux; Eddie Ray; Lionel Rolfe; Sir David Scholey; Sir Philip Shelbourne; Peter Smith; Tim Stock; Sir Charles Troughton; Michael Verey; James Wannan; Donald Wells; Richard Westmacott; Richard Wilkins; Sir David Wills; Sir Hugh Wontner; and Ben Wrey.

Responsibility for all errors of fact and judgement rests, as ever, with the author.

This book would not have been possible without the unfailing patience and support of Harry Cazenove over a period of almost ten years. Above all, his scrupulous attention to detail proved invaluable to both the author and the publisher. It is a cause of great sadness that he died while the book was in its final stages of being prepared for publication.

CHAPTER ONE

A Huguenot partnership
1823–1835

The evolution of the stockbroking business of Cazenove & Co has been a long process. For almost 170 years it has involved successive partnerships, each including in its title the name of Cazenove and each following what might be called 'the Cazenove tradition', entitling the firm to be regarded as not only one of the oldest houses on the Stock Exchange, but also one of the most highly respected. Its origins lie deep in European history, in that small group of Huguenot financiers, brokers and merchants which, held together by closely-knit family relationships and Calvinistic faith, played an important role in the larger community of Huguenots who sought and found, in England, economic opportunity as well as religious freedom.

Among them were descendants of Pierre de Cazenove, one of the thousands of Huguenots who, in the wake of the Revocation of the Edict of Nantes, left France at the end of the seventeenth century to settle in Geneva. There, at the age of twenty-seven, he married Marie Plantamour in 1697 and six years later was admitted into the Bourgeoisie of the Republic of Geneva. Pierre had four sons, including Théophile, who himself emigrated to Holland, married and had seven sons. One of them was John Henry, who came to England with his father around the middle of the eighteenth century. He decided to stay, became naturalised in 1762, and set up a merchant banking business in the City of London, where he combined dealing in 3% Consols and East India Company stock with trading in Indian piece goods.

Another son of Pierre de Cazenove was David, who was born in Geneva in 1711. David's third son, James, emigrated to England and, like his cousin John Henry, went into business as a merchant. By 1775 he was established in St Martin's Lane and three years later, at the age of thirty-four, became a naturalised Englishman. The ties of background and family remained strong: in 1789 he opened a drawing account at the Bank of England, to whom James declared that he was in partnership with his brother, Charles Henry, and two other Huguenots, Amy Gidion Bourdillon and Peter Reliet. Four years later, City directories show the business of James Cazenove & Co to have been at the Old Pay Office in Old Broad Street, less than 400 yards from the offices of James's cousin.

James's business involved a wide range of activities and, like many other merchants of the period, he seems to have been as much a banker as a merchant. Thus, for example, his firm opened acceptance credits for V. du Pont de Nemours & Co of New York in favour of Biedermann of Paris; it was involved in American stocks that were dealt in on the London market, working in tandem with the important New York brokerage house of Le Roy Bayard & McEwers and probably also the Bank of the United States; and it dealt from time to time in Government funds, especially 3% Consols. It was not, however, especially prominent in subscribing to new issues, despite a close association with Barings, and its subscription of £10,000 to the war loan of 1797 seems to have been exceptional. Nor was the firm a member of the London Stock Exchange, although on occasion it did act as a broker or dealer. Overall it appears to have been a broadly prosperous concern, if not spectacularly so. And soon after his death in 1827, James received the following tribute: 'No brilliant talent – universal good name – example to his sons – provided generously for his wife – left his house of business in a prosperous condition.'

The tribute was the more notable for being paid to him by his widow. Marie-Anne Sophie Houssemayne du Boulay, daughter of the pastor of the French church in Threadneedle Street, had married James in 1781, James at that time dropping the 'de' of de Cazenove; and over the following two decades she bore him four sons and five daughters. They lived in Hackney and later at Grosvenor House in Hoe Street, Walthamstow (then an attractive wooded area), where Marie-Anne presided as a devoted mother and capable manager of the household. 'Madame Cazenove,' wrote one French visitor, 'est l'âme de tout.' Glimpses of their family life give the impression that it was happy, and there exists from the same source a charming sketch of a children's party that Marie-Anne arranged in 1802: the girls are in white, hair *à la grecque*, and two of the boys are providing the music. After dinner the same evening, according to the visitor, there was 'répétition en famille d'un quatuor de Mozart, délicieux'.

James's two oldest sons were Henry, born in 1782, and James, born two years later. Soon after leaving school, they set out together in April 1803 to make a Grand Tour of France, Austria and Switzerland. The aim was, in their own words, 'to make acquaintance with the friends and correspondents of our father's commercial house, and to perfect the good education we had received by seeing a little of the world.' They saw more than they had bargained for: within weeks Britain was once more at war with France, and Napoleon had issued a decree forbidding all British subjects to leave the country. The upshot for the two brothers was enforced exile, first in France and then in Geneva, until during the winter of 1810–11, showing much courage and resource, they escaped back to British soil via Bosnia, Greece and Malta. In Athens, as they later recalled, they were entertained by Lord Byron, who gave them a supper and dance 'that we might have an opportunity of seeing an assembly of Grecian ladies'. However, 'we were not particularly struck with their beauty' and 'were much better entertained with a dance by one of Lord Byron's Albanian servants, who had formerly belonged to a band of robbers in the mountains of Albania'. Finally back home, Henry and James spent most of 1812 writing up their adventures for anonymous publication, and then in 1813 took the natural course of joining their father's merchant house of James Cazenove & Co.

Also in that year the third son, John, born in 1788, followed the same path. He was to emerge as an indifferent businessman but genuine intellectual, whom modern scholarship is beginning to rescue from relative obscurity. On the business side, he devoted much of his attention to insurance, becoming a member of Lloyd's in 1819 and then in later life, from 1843 to 1858, serving as Secretary to the Family Endowment Society. The Society was modelled on the theories of a French pamphleteer, Francois Corbeaux, and sought to provide endowment on the issue of marriage, but it lacked any sound actuarial basis; in 1861 it was forced to abandon this line of business. John meanwhile had established quite a considerable reputation in the field of political economy, the so-called 'dismal science' of Carlyle's famous phrase. An early member of the influential Political Economy Club, he published in 1822 a pamphlet entitled *Considerations on the Accumulation of Capital.* Other works followed, including *Questions respecting National Debt and Taxation, Outlines of Political Economy* and, towards the end of his life, the modestly-entitled *Thoughts on a few subjects of Economics.* But perhaps John's greatest achievement was his responsibility for editing (as scholars now believe he did) the second edition of Malthus's *Principles of Political Economy,* a seminal work of economic thought. His other great interest was chess, and as early as 1817 he published for fellow-aficionados *A Selection of curious and entertaining games at Chess that have been actually played.*

Our chief interest, however, lies in James's fourth son, Philip, the founder of what is now Cazenove & Co and arguably the single most important person in the history of the firm. He was born on 23rd November 1798; and like his three brothers before him, he went to school at Charterhouse, which was then in the City and quite close to the family counting house in Old Broad Street. Philip was there from July 1813 to December 1815 and, taking his place in Watkinson's house in Charterhouse Square, endured the fairly Spartan conditions of the still unreformed English public school system. The general reputation of the school was high: old Carthusians included Joseph Addison, John Wesley and the Prime Minister of the day, Lord Liverpool, while the Duke of Wellington, a few years after Philip had left, described Charterhouse as 'the best school of them all'. The Duke, however, was possibly unaware of recent developments under the youthful and vigorous, but ultimately misguided, Dr John Russell, headmaster since 1811. Attracted by the economies of scale involved, Russell mistakenly employed the so-called Bell or Madras System, justly described by one of his successors as in essence 'a glorified system of pupil teaching'. By 1818 there were five masters for 238 boys, by 1821 still only five for 431 boys. Academic standards inevitably suffered, the school went into decline, and by the 1830s the experiment was abandoned. Philip himself was there only at the beginning, and his own education was perhaps not significantly affected, but it cannot have been the best time to go to Charterhouse.

What sort of person was Philip when he ventured into the great world at the start of 1816? We can only guess on the basis of later habits and characteristics, principally as described by the *Guardian* (a weekly church paper) in the fullest of his obituaries in January 1880. The writer was at pains to stress that Philip had not been an uncultured businessman:

> He was somewhat early removed from school to enter into business. But he retained through life his literary tastes, and many playful Latin epigrams issued from his pen on passing events in his family or in the world. He delighted in the company of a genial scholar, with whom he could cap quotations, and the pocket of the brougham in which he drove to town always contained a Greek Testament and a small edition of Horace.

This is a portrait of the mature man, but clearly the young Philip was not, to use Matthew Arnold's later abusive term about the Victorian middle class, one of life's Philistines. He also had the inestimable advantage of a sound business brain and sober working habits. In the brief but telling words of the same obituary: 'In business he was methodical, and what he advised was always to the point.' As to the more general character of a man who in later years would emerge as one of the great Christian philanthropists of the age, it was said:

He was simple in his habits, and somewhat reserved, perhaps, in exhibition of his feelings. Whenever he could, he avoided letting his good deeds transpire. In general society he was full of cheerfulness, and keenly appreciated telling or hearing a pleasant anecdote. He was remarkable for his gentle playfulness in his family circle, and given to a genial hospitality.

The fullest expression of these characteristics lay in the future. Meanwhile, one can perhaps imagine the Philip Cazenove of about 1816 as somewhat shy, possibly rather intense, well read and well spoken, and already determined to make the most, for the benefit of others as well as himself, of the unforgiving minute.

What Philip did during his first three years after school is not known – perhaps he spent some time in the family business learning about the ways of the City of London. What we do know is that on 3rd November 1819, in the words of the minutes of the Committee for General Purposes of the London Stock Exchange, 'J. F. Menet by letter 2nd inst desired leave to introduce Philip Cazenove as his Clerk' and that this was 'allowed'. Granted that he had presumably decided to take up – or at least try – stockbroking as a career, it was a natural move for Philip to make. John Francis Menet too was descended from a line of Huguenot refugees; his father had also been a merchant in Old Broad Street; and, what no doubt clinched the association, since 1805 he had been Philip's brother-in-law, having married Louisa, one of his elder sisters. He was already in his late forties when Philip became his clerk and had himself been a member of the Stock Exchange for only two years. Moreover, his business was probably fairly small, for he had no partner and shared premises at 7 Old Broad Street with three other stockbrokers and three merchants. Little else is known about Menet, apart from the fact that he lived in Shacklewell Lane, Hackney, and a few years later was one of 'Twenty-Six of the substantial Inhabitants of the Parish of West Hackney' who were appointed to be a select vestry for the newly-built West Hackney Church. Hackney was then a prosperous village, so by the early 1820s he was probably becoming a man of some means.

Philip, meanwhile, was doing well during his apprentice years on the Stock Exchange. In 1821 he was authorised by the Committee to do business for time on behalf of Menet, thereby enabling him to go on to the floor of the House and transact bargains to be settled at the end of the fortnightly account. The following year he was also authorised to do business for money on Menet's behalf, thereby involving cash settlement. Also in 1822, at quite a young age, he took the step of getting married. Philip's chosen was Emma Knapp, younger sister of Susan Knapp, whom Philip's brother James had married in 1820. The Knapps were a well-known banking family in

Winchester, but the girls' father, Edward, had died relatively young and their mother, Mary-Ann, had married Thomas Bridges, a merchant in Mark Lane, and taken up residence in Homerton, just to the east of Hackney. The Cazenove family itself had been living since 1817 at Crouch End, Hornsey – making a rather easier journey to the City for the father James – and it was there that Philip took his young bride prior to finding a home for themselves.

Before that happened, there was the small matter of the founding of a historic firm. On 19th March 1823 (at the start of the Stock Exchange year) Philip was elected a member. His two sureties were Andrew Mieville, who had earlier sponsored Menet, and Henry Patteson; for his bankers, he gave the name of Willis, Percival & Co, an old-established firm who were bankers also to John Henry and James Cazenove as well as to Menet. Then, just over a fortnight later, the Committee minutes for April 4th record that 'J. F. Menet and Philip Cazenove, by Letter dated April 1st, gave notice of their Partnership'. The stockbroking firm of Menet & Cazenove was thus in existence and there was everything to play for.

––––––––––

The 1820s were a propitious time to launch a business in the City of London, which after a long period of rivalry was by now conclusively supplanting Amsterdam as the main international centre of finance. A complex chain of causes lay behind this, and probably none was more important than the ability of Britain during the eighteenth century first to establish and then to sustain herself as the world's dominant commercial and naval power. It was a dominance confirmed by spectacular colonial gains in Canada, the West Indies and India which more than offset the loss of America. On the back of this immense trading muscle, itself further strengthened by Britain's emergence as the first industrial nation, and benefiting greatly from its pioneer development of the method of discounting bills of exchange, the City by the early nineteenth century was uniquely placed to finance not only Britain's trade, but also much of the world's trade, especially once that trade began to burgeon following the end of the Napoleonic Wars. Nor was this all. Ordained to be as good as gold since 1717, sterling and its rise as a world currency had been rudely interrupted by the war with France. Now, in 1821, with the resumption of gold payments by the Bank of England, sterling could reassert its claim to be the indispensable currency of international finance and commerce. Over the ensuing nine or so decades, probably the meridian period in the entire history of the City, it began to seem inconceivable that Britain had once been without the gold standard, or indeed would ever be persuaded to relinquish it.

There was one more crucial dimension to the larger dispensation that was taking shape at the time that Philip Cazenove went into partnership with his brother-in-law, and this was the dimension that touched most closely on their particular business. It is difficult to condense in a few sentences the already rich history of the London stock market prior to 1823, but a brief sketch is essential. It was a market that had begun to take organised shape in the 1690s, and for the next century and beyond dealt primarily in British Government securities ('the Funds'), as Britain spent most of those years at war and her National Debt steadily grew. For some years this market took place at the Royal Exchange, but for most of the eighteenth century it resided in the coffee houses of Change Alley, most famously Jonathan's and Garraway's. Then in 1773, with space increasingly at a premium despite the emergence of the Rotunda of the Bank of England as a temporary alternative place for dealing in the Funds, the brokers and jobbers abandoned their coffee houses and moved to a building at the corner of Threadneedle Street and Sweetings Alley. It had the words 'The Stock Exchange' inscribed above the door, and an entrance fee was levied of sixpence a day. However, this soon proved excessively crowded, and perhaps also unruly, so at the beginning of the nineteenth century the decision was taken to construct a new Exchange and to make it a closed market, thereby effectively sorting out the prosperous and respectable from any less desirable elements. The first stone was laid in May 1801 at the chosen site of Capel Court, still the location of the Stock Exchange almost two centuries later.

Such are the bare bones of the origins of the modern stock market – but alone they tell one relatively little about its inner spirit. For at the heart of Stock Exchange history, and crucial to any understanding of its overall development, there lie strong and abiding notions of on the one hand mutual trust amongst members, and on the other independence from outside interference. These were notions that took firm root in the specific circumstances of the eighteenth century. They were partly a reaction against the more or less ineffectual attempt of the City authorities to exercise a system of licensing over the brokers. But above all, they were a necessary response to the parliamentary legislation of 1734 that, in the eventual wake of the infamous South Sea Bubble, sought severely to reduce the range of stockbroking business. In particular, the legislation introduced that year by Sir John Barnard attempted to outlaw the highly profitable but speculative end of the business known as 'time bargains', somewhat akin to modern-day 'options', by which 'bulls' and 'bears' in effect gambled on future prices without actually buying or selling stock when the bargains were struck. Confronted by this hostile legislation, the brokers and jobbers of the day simply ignored it and concentrated instead on developing their own self-regulating mechanism, in which the wish to control their own affairs, and above all to impose an absolute sanctity upon the completion of bargains of whatever sort, became paramount. 'My word is my bond' now emerged as no idle boast but the very premise of commercial survival – a fiercely autonomous, indeed almost outlaw mentality consummated by the establishment in Capel Court of a self-contained, purpose-built closed market. It was a physical fortress that few outsiders would breach until the creation in 1953 of a long-overdue Visitors' Gallery.

'A neat, plain building fronted with stone to the attic story, which is of brick. In the interior, under the clock, at the south end, is a tablet exhibiting the names of such defaulters as have not been able or willing to make their payments good.' Such was a contemporary description of the new Stock Exchange, which was opened to business – though only to its initial 551 members – early in 1802. Upon the keystone of the principal entrance sat a bust of Mercury, a perhaps ironic touch by the architect Peacock. Business during the first decade was dominated by the continuing need to fund the Napoleonic Wars, involving the flotation on the Stock Exchange of a series of massive loans to the British government. After 1815 the picture changed, and increasingly it was the governments of other countries that came to the London market. In the early years of peace Baring Brothers made a fortune out of placing French rentes, as well as floating loans in silver roubles for Russia; while in 1818 Nathan Rothschild issued a sterling loan of five million pounds for Prussia and then in 1822, after the Congress of Laibach, floated loans of forty million roubles for Russia, one hundred million florins for Austria and forty million thalers for Prussia. By the early 1820s there was also a rising tide of London issues on behalf of Latin American borrowers, including Peru, Mexico and Guatemala. Traditionally, foreign stocks had been dealt in on the Royal Exchange – indeed, the foundation stone of the Capel Court building had explicitly stated that by contrast it was 'for the transaction of business in the public funds' – but inevitably this changed along with the changing pattern of investment. After 1815, dealing in foreign stocks greatly increased in Capel Court, until in February 1823 (shortly before Menet and Cazenove entered into partnership) a Foreign Room was established, separately organised and managed but physically connecting with the main Stock Exchange. It was a cumbersome arrangement and did not last very long; but was nevertheless a clear harbinger of the extent to which the nineteenth-century stock market was to export capital to all quarters of the globe.

Apart from its bust of Mercury, what was the new Stock Exchange like during these first two or three decades? From the various fragmentary sources that exist, it is reasonably clear that there was a functional distinction, as there probably had been during most of the eighteenth century, between the jobbers, who specialised in holding particular types of securities, and the brokers, who bought or sold these securities on behalf of either themselves or members of the public. It is also clear that right from the start the domestic life of 'the House' (as the Stock Exchange was familiarly called) was dominated by the jealously-guarded authority of its Committee for General Purposes, a body of thirty elected each year by and from the membership. In the uncompromising words of the first edition of the *Rules and Regulations*, issued by the Committee in 1812: 'Every member, who may be guilty of *dishonourable* or *disgraceful conduct*, or who may violate any of the fundamental laws of the Stock Exchange, shall be liable to *expulsion.*' In practice, expulsion almost invariably meant total ruin for the dishonoured party.

In the context of broadly favourable market conditions and opportunities, it was a life-risk that an increasing number of people were prepared to take, including of course Menet and Philip Cazenove. Unfortunately, not much is known about their first generation of fellow-members, although a browse through the annual election and re-election forms shows well-known Stock Exchange names like Mullens, Capel and de Zoete already beginning to crop up. The only surviving contemporary estimate of the ability of these early members is a somewhat unflattering one from the pen of the famous political economist David Ricardo. Replying in 1814 to a fellow-student who wanted to know which members of the Stock Exchange might be able to help him over the question of the circulation of currency, he wrote: 'The Stock Exchange is chiefly attended by persons who are unremittingly attentive to their business, and are well acquainted with its details; but there are very few in number who have much knowledge of political economy, and consequently they pay little attention to finance, as a subject of science. They consider more, the immediate effect of passing events, rather than their distant consequences.' It was an informed assessment, for Ricardo himself had done very well as a jobber, being especially skilful in arbitrage dealings, besides coining an axiom of permanent worth: 'Cut your losses and let your profits run'. A later generation of political economists would know his critique of the Stock Exchange by the name of 'short termism', but it is worth pointing out that in it he laid an equal stress on the dedication and attention to detail on the part of those early inhabitants of Capel Court.

However, it was not all work and no play, as one of the Committee's enjoinders of 1812 made eloquently clear:

The Committee earnestly recommend, to the several members, that *order and decorum* which is so essentially necessary to be observed in all places of business; and that they forbear on their own parts, and discourage as much as possible in others, those rude and trifling practices which have too long disgraced the Stock Exchange in the estimation of the public; which would not be tolerated in any other place; and which, it is seriously apprehended, may have been injurious to the best interests of the House.

It was a vain appeal, for during the rest of the century the Stock Exchange consolidated its reputation as the unrivalled home of practical joking, ranging from the throwing of paper balls and making of 'butter slides' to a variety of incendiary practices that naturally much alarmed the authorities. Such joking was especially the preserve of the jobbers, who spent all day on the floor of the House, but it is unlikely that all brokers eschewed the practice.

As for the atmosphere of the 1820s themselves, a lively description was given many years later by a veteran member:

> We had some fine games in the old days. At 2, Capel Court, Mendoza had a boxing booth, where instead of knocking prices about, a member could go and knock somebody about or get knocked about himself, if things did not suit him *inside*. An old woman had a stall inside the House, close to Capel Court door, where those who had not quite outlived their earliest tastes could feed on buns, cakes, etc. A gallery ran round the House; seats and desks were fitted up for clerks and members. It was very convenient, because if a man wanted a book he simply called up to his clerk, who would throw it over. Some of the funny ones used to drop things over on unsuspecting members. Sometimes, in the afternoon, a jobber used to give us a tune on a cornet, and I reckon we had plenty of fun when things were dull. We used to buy our own chops and steaks in those days, and take them to a cook-shop or chop-house and have them cooked, paying a penny for the privilege. Almost over every bargain a glass of sherry used to be drunk. "Who pays?" was a very common expression.

Intensely clubbish, oscillating between bursts of feverish activity and lengthy periods of dullness punctuated only by rumour and schoolboy japes, and keenly conscious of the collective honour of its membership, the Stock Exchange of the early nineteenth century possessed an ethos and way of life entirely and unmistakably its own.

The reaction of the outside world to it ran the entire gamut of emotion. There was no more hostile critic than William Cobbett, who wrote scathingly of how the war and concomitant growth of the funded debt had brought to social and economic power a whole class of undesirable 'contractors, pensioners, sinecurists, commissioners, loan-jobbers, lottery-dealers, bankers, stock-jobbers'. He particularly disliked those 'great parcels of stock-jobbers' who lived in Brighton with their families, though 'they skip backwards and forwards on the coaches and actually carry on stock-jobbing in "Change Alley"'. Rather more measured was the response of the celebrated clergyman and wit Sydney Smith, who asserted that 'the warlike power of every country depends on its Three per Cents' and went on in a fine conceit: 'If Caesar were to reappear on earth, Wetenhall's list [of Stock Exchange prices] would be more important than his Commentaries; Rothschild would open and shut the Temple of Janus; Thomas Baring would probably command the Tenth Legion, and the soldiers would march to battle with loud cries of "Script and Omnium Reduced! Consols and Caesar!"'. But the last word, entirely unironic and revelling in the sheer 'buzz' of the square mile, of which the Stock Exchange had become the very essence, should perhaps go to Lucy Snowe, heroine of Charlotte Brontë's novel *Villette*:

> I have seen the West End, the parks, the fine squares, but I love the City far better. The City seems so much more in earnest: its business, its rush, its roar, are such serious things, sights and sounds. The City is getting its living – the West End but enjoying its pleasure. At the West End you may be amused, but in the City you are deeply excited.

At the time that Menet and Cazenove began their partnership, the City was dominated as never before or since by the influence of a single man: Nathan Meyer Rothschild. 'Short and fat, with blue eyes, reddish hair and a strong German accent' (in the words of a descendant), he exercised an extra-ordinary degree of influence over most parts of the City, and above all the Stock Exchange. His scale of operations was enormous, his judgement usually excellent, and his access to private sources of information seemingly uncanny. There were several different main strands to his business activities, but setting aside his famous *coup* in the wake of the battle of Waterloo, none caught the eye as much as the enormous loans which he arranged on behalf of governments, including in 1819 contracting for a £12 million loan to the British government. In general, so ubiquitous was his market presence that if ever business was flat in Capel Court, the brokers and jobbers of the day never doubted who was the one man necessary to make things hum again. He himself always employed several brokers at any one time, thereby ensuring that it was impossible for anyone else to be sure precisely what position he had taken. As for his supremacy as a manipulator of markets, his brother-in-law Moses Montefiore said no more than the truth when he told Rothschild in 1818: 'You have beaten your antagonists so frequently that I am surprised there are any so hardy to be found in the Stock Exchange to oppose you in any considerable operation'. Universally acknowledged as the leviathan of the stock market, 'NM' could make or break the fortunes of not only the princes of Europe but also the humbler players nearer to home.

Curiously enough, it was Rothschild who almost bought Grosvenor House when James Cazenove decided in 1817 to move the family from Walthamstow. After expressing an initial interest, he was told by James junior (entrusted with the negotiation) that the house, with its outbuildings and estate, was worth almost £20,000. Rothschild pondered the matter and after a few weeks sent James a letter dated Friday, 27th June 1817, conveying an offer of £15,750 'payable in cash immediately' and demanding an answer 'by Monday at 11' – a typical Rothschild touch. James countered with a figure of £19,000 and Rothschild let it drop. Relations between the two families, however, were not significantly impaired, and it seems reasonably clear that a few years later the patronage of Rothschild was an important – perhaps the decisive – element in assuring the early viability of the stockbroking firm of Menet & Cazenove. Indeed, from as early as 1821, even before Philip became a partner, letters survive indicating a fairly busy working relationship. Interestingly, Menet emerges from the correspondence as the sort of person who was not prepared to kowtow, even to the great Rothschild. Thus on 20th August 1821 he wrote to him: 'I am desired by my principals to express their surprise that the Neapolitan Bonds purchased for them on the 6th August, and paid for, are not yet delivered, and to request that they may be, with as little delay as possible.' By October 1823 the firm had begun doing substantial business on behalf of Rothschild, including on one day selling Russian stock amounting to £17,612 and purchasing £8,584. In 1824 the turnover in French stock was more than £200,000 on both sides of the account, worth some £10 million in present-day terms. Activity then declined somewhat over the next two or three years, but what was important was that a connection had been established, even though for the time being it was limited to transactions in foreign government stocks: it was a connection that many other stockbroking firms would have given much for.

Suitably emboldened, and further fortified by knowing that he now had a capable partner, Menet by 1823 was advertising himself as 'Agent for the Purchase and Sale of Russian, French, Prussian and American Stocks'. It was a useful, and fairly conservative, specialist niche to have found, for over the next two years there took place on the Stock Exchange one of that institution's most spectacular booms and crashes, inevitably leaving a trail of victims in its wake. It was a boom characterised partly by a rash of ill-advised South American loans, but above all by the flotation of more than 600 joint-stock companies, of which less than one-quarter achieved any sort of permanence. Among those which speedily collapsed were companies designed – at least on paper – to promote such worthy ventures as Bognor New Town, Tropical Free Labour, Westminster Fish, and Economic Funeral. One contemporary, in an inquest published soon afterwards, blamed influences outside the Stock Exchange: 'In most instances the projector was either an attorney, who by the concoction of a scheme availed himself of the advantage which it afforded by a bill of costs; or some unprincipled person actuated solely with a view to pecuniary profit.' However, the writer added about an indispensable part of any Stock Exchange new issue boom: 'Premiums were obtained by an artificial value being created by manoeuvres, and by the aid of individuals, who, for the sake of a commission, lent themselves to the fraud so committed; thus reflecting disgrace by their acts, on a body of whom many are of the first respectability, and hold in society a character for probity and honour worthy of example.' Rothschild himself steered well clear of the mania, and it is likely that most of his 'pet' brokers, including Menet & Cazenove, would have followed suit. Indeed, when there was total panic in December 1825 and it seemed likely that the Bank of England would have to stop payment, it was Rothschild who saved the day, thereby adding further lustre to his house and, by reflected glory, his intimate circle of City associates and subordinates.

In the midst of this mania, Philip and his wife left the family home in Hornsey and moved into a house in Upper Clapton, which he bought from a fellow-broker, James Capel. It was a substantial property and included, according to the lease, not only outbuildings and gardens, but also 'pleasure grounds'. To the rear was an open area known as Springfield (now Springfield Park), which fell sharply to the River Lea and afforded wide views towards his parents' old home of Grosvenor House. A hamlet of Hackney and contiguous to Stamford Hill, where Rothschild lived, Clapton in the mid-1820s was an attractive residential neighbourhood that was warmly commended by *Pigot's Commercial Directory*: 'There are many very elegant houses inhabited by wealthy and respectable persons, and the situation of the place is particularly pleasant.' The same directory, in its 1826–7 edition, published a list of fifty-six 'gentry and clergy' living in the area and these included Philip Cazenove. It was therefore an entirely suitable move for an aspiring young stockbroker and his prospective family, in that last era before the growth of a suburban railway system entirely changed the residential patterns of the metropolis.

It was as well that Philip settled when he did, for there now loomed, for the Cazenove family as a whole, a difficult period. In October 1827, James senior died, leaving a comfortable fortune of almost £48,000. As planned, the business of James Cazenove & Co was continued by the remaining partners, but they did not last long, and at the end of 1831 the firm was dissolved, with all three sons bankrupt. John at least had his insurance and political economy to which he could turn, but for Henry and James, the more active partners, it was a major disaster. The reason for the failure of the business is obscure. Perhaps, despite appearances and the testimony of James's widow, the firm had been undermined by the credit crisis of 1825; perhaps they had losses as a result of the political convulsions in Europe in 1830; or perhaps it was just bad management on the part of the younger generation. But whatever the main cause, it was an astonishingly rapid demise after the death of the firm's founder. Menet & Cazenove itself does not appear to have been involved financially, but not surprisingly Rothschild was, to the extent of £2,400, on which he received from the liquidation only 1s 11d in the pound.

Philip and his partner, meanwhile, continued during the late 1820s and into the first half of the 1830s to consolidate their position as brokers on the Stock Exchange. Documentation is frustratingly thin, but it is possible to obtain some idea of the type of business they were conducting at this stage. In particular, there survives a price list issued by them to customers on the first day of 1828. The front side of the list was devoted to foreign funds and included twenty-two issues: eight were Latin American bonds, most well below par; while the other fourteen were European issues of widely differing quality, ranging from French 5% rentes and Prussian 6% sterling bonds, both around par, to Greek and Spanish bonds at 16½ and 10¾ respectively. On the reverse side of the list were prices of not only the funds, but also various miscellaneous securities, nearly all with a heavy unpaid liability. These included insurance companies like the Alliance Fire and Life Assurance, banks like the Provincial Bank of Ireland, and concerns ranging from Anglo Mexican Mining to the company controlling St Katharine's Dock. Taking the list as a whole, it is clear that even if Menet & Cazenove was conservative enough to have avoided burning its fingers seriously in 1824-5, it could not afford to ignore the basic fact that a prime engine of the Stock Exchange was speculative business. To quote the disarmingly frank words of one broker, defending his profession in *Fraser's Magazine* about half a century later: 'A Stock Exchange restricted to investment business would be as useful and as popular as a public-house licensed only for ginger-beer'.

The odd snatch of surviving correspondence with Rothschild further creates a more vivid impression of the firm's day-to-day activities. That of the spring of 1829 distinctly conveys the world of the back office as opposed to the more rarified ambience of *haute finance*. Thus on April 14th the firm wrote to Rothschild:

> Enclosed we beg to hand you 37 Certifs and power for the transfer of 258,769 Rtes to Benjamin Heywood – according to the terms agreed upon – and shall be obliged by having in return 25 Certifs of F. 10000 Rtes each and 1 of 8769 Rtes. You will observe that the death of B.A. Heywood and all testamentary documents have already been registered thro' your house in the case of two sales of five per cts made to you last month.

The transaction proved complicated, and on May 2nd Menet & Cazenove wrote again:

> We are sorry that there should have been any thing to prevent the transfer of the French 3 Per Cents to Benjamin Heywood, and hope the French Treasury will yet allow the transfer to be made, with some clause for the Inscription, as has been occasionally done. If however this should not be feasible, and you had no objection to request Messrs de Rothschild to transfer the amount into B. Heywood's name we would immediately give you a fresh power in blank, as required.

The overall connection with Rothschilds remained fairly lucrative, and an inspection of that house's ledgers for 1830 and 1833 shows that each year it transacted business through Menet & Cazenove worth over £1 million. The stocks of foreign governments continued to dominate, including those of Brazil, Denmark, Portugal, Spain, Greece, France and Russia, while in November 1833 the brokers were entrusted with a purchase for £7,880 on behalf of Mrs Rothschild. By 1834 the business done for Rothschilds in foreign stocks amounted to over £2 million, presumably earning for Menet & Cazenove a commission income somewhere in the region of £2,500. It was a tidy enough sum and must have provided the firm with the sound financial basis it needed.

Another merchant banker furnishing useful business was Frederick Huth, one of several German merchants to have followed the example of Rothschild by moving to England during the Napoleonic Wars and establishing a major commercial house there. There may well have been a Huth connection with Menet & Cazenove during the 1820s, but there is no doubt that there was a profitable one during the first half of the 1830s. In particular, there survives not only a bundle of slips recording purchases and sales of 3% Consols on behalf of F. Huth & Co, for the most part in the £5,000–20,000 range, but also a certain amount of correspondence from principal to broker. Four examples from 1831 give something of the flavour of the relationship: on January 14th a letter from Huth enclosed two bonds of £150 each of the Mexican Loan of 1825, 'which please to sell at the best market price of the day for Cash & account to us for the same'; on July 13th, Menet & Cazenove was asked to sell for Huth's account eighteen bonds of the Prussian Loan of 1818 'at the most favourable price you can obtain'; on November 2nd a note asked the brokers to sell a £100 Danish bond, 'if it can be done at 65 or above'; and finally, on December 8th, the request was to sell two Mexican bonds of the 1825 Loan 'to our best advantage', that most time-honoured of phrases. Huth at times could be quite clear about what he wanted. Thus he wrote on 30th September 1833: 'We hereby authorise you to sell for our account 1 Bond for 1000 Fr French 5 per Cent Rentes if between this and the end of October you can obtain $102\frac{1}{2}$ per cent for the same. Should you not be able to sell at this price, our limit for said bond is 103% in all November, or $103\frac{1}{2}$% in all December, of which please take note.' Usually something was left to the professional judgement and expertise of Menet & Cazenove, but on this occasion at least nothing was left to chance.

Meanwhile, what of life in 7 Old Broad Street during these pioneer years? The sources allow only one glimpse, and that a rather oblique one. The Stock Exchange Committee minutes for September 1833 open the window:

> Menet & Cazenove by letter desired to introduce Thomas Price as their clerk, not authorised to do business for money or time.
>
> It appeared by the admission of Mr Cazenove (who was called up) that Mr Price had been a considerable number of years in their employ, during several of which he had been in the constant practice of officiating for Messrs Menet & Co unsanctioned by the Committee; and that those gentlemen had never paid for his admission; the terms of which however, Mr Cazenove did not recollect.

Two days later Price was summoned, and he told the Committee:

> That he had been in the employ of Mr Menet, and subsequently Messrs Menet & Cazenove, 15 or 16 years, during the last 9 or 10 of which he had been in the habit of frequenting the Stock Exchange as their clerk; and he admitted that for the latter 5 years he had occasionally transacted business for them. He said he had some time since mentioned to Mr Menet the propriety of his being regularly introduced through the Committee, but in consequence of the pressure of business (as he believed) which engaged Mr Menet at the time, no further notice was taken of the subject.

Price then withdrew, and:

Mr Cazenove was now again sent for, and the impropriety pointed out to him, of having neglected for so long a period making the proper application for their clerk's admission; he declared that they never knew until very recently, that it was required so to do, unless the clerk were authorised to transact business for his employer; which had never been permitted, although Mr Price might occasionally have done some small transactions when Mr Menet and himself were temporarily absent; all which transactions certainly passed through their books, although they were done for the friends of Mr Price himself, to whom they had given leave to receive such commissions for himself; expressly stipulating that every such transaction should be known to them.

After some deliberation, the Committee decided to allow the application, but insisted that Menet & Cazenove should pay not only for the admission but also for the arrears, totalling £75 15s. A rather embarrassing episode thus ended, reflecting the case of a young firm whose business was growing somewhat faster than it was properly equipped to cope with. Philip for one, after his double appearance before the Committee, would undoubtedly have resolved that in future everything was to be done by the book.

Protocol was certainly observed a year later, as the Committee minutes record: 'Menet & Cazenove, by letter dated 22nd September 1834, desired to introduce Henry Cazenove as their clerk, authorised to do money business only. Allowed.' The employment of Philip's oldest brother was no doubt a sign of the firm's expansion, but it also served to give him a new field of activity three years after the shattering collapse of James Cazenove & Co – a collapse that had also meant that Henry had had to relinquish his directorship of the Royal Exchange Assurance Company. Almost exactly a year after Henry began his association with the firm, however, a much more fundamental change took place. A sombre Philip wrote to the Committee on 1st October 1835: 'I beg to inform you that the death of my brother-in-law, the late John F. Menet, necessarily terminates our partnership, and that my brother, Henry Cazenove, is authorised to do business for me for money and time.' Menet's death at the age of sixty-four was perhaps not entirely unexpected, for he had only very recently made a will, but it must still have been a heavy blow to Philip, who in a sense owed him everything.

For three months he pressed on alone as P. Cazenove & Co, but soon knew it could only be a temporary solution. With his brothers recently bankrupted and his partner dead (having quite properly left his property to his wife and family), Philip would have to look elsewhere to raise the capital he needed in order to continue in business. In effect this meant that he had to find new partners whose Stock Exchange connections would not disturb the valuable relationship which he now had with Rothschild. The future was uncertain, with the untimely death of Menet clearly marking the end of the first chapter of the firm's history.

CHAPTER TWO

Expanding horizons
1836–1854

On 18th January 1836 the partnership was announced, as from New Year's Day, between Joseph Laurence, Philip Cazenove and C. T. Pearce: thus record – as usual baldly and without explanation – the minutes of the Stock Exchange Committee. This new venture was to be known as Laurence Cazenove & Pearce. Its offices were in the north gallery of the Auction Mart in Bartholomew Lane, and in the event it was to survive as an entity for almost two decades, until the end of 1854.

It was on Philip's part a well-considered and entirely logical move to turn to solid men like Joseph Laurence and Charles Pearce in his hour of need after Menet's death. Prior to 1836 they had been two-thirds of the Stock Exchange firm of Laurence Whitmore & Co, already based in the Auction Mart. It was a firm that had been founded in 1827 and was well known for the considerable scale of its business and the soundness of its credit. Even in the generally anxious year of 1831, following revolutions in Europe and amidst agitation at home for Parliamentary reform, it had frequently obtained from the Bank of England loans for fourteen days or longer periods, for amounts sometimes as large as £60,000. Moreover, it also enjoyed a strong and profitable connection with the house of Rothschild, in 1835 handling for it some £1.4 million of foreign stocks. It is entirely possible that it was with the tacit or even active support of Nathan Rothschild (in the last year of his life) that Philip Cazenove was now able to make an advantageous deal and clinch the new partnership. John Whitmore himself agreed to go into business on his own, leaving Laurence and Pearce to join forces with Philip.

Relatively little biographical detail survives about Joseph Laurence, who was originally called Joseph Levi. His family firm had been produce brokers before becoming stockbrokers and he himself had been a member of the

Stock Exchange since 1824. Two years later the firm of Levi Brothers failed, along with several others; and in December 1826 he changed his name to Laurence. At the time of the new arrangements in the 1830s he lived at Blackheath, but some years afterwards moved to the district of Beddington, where he was to die in 1878 at the age of eighty-seven. The obituary in the *Sutton Herald and Mid-Surrey Advertiser* was warm in its praises:

> The deceased gentleman was closely identified during his life with all objects of public charity connected with his own or neighbouring parish of Wallington, and was a generous and unwearied friend and supporter of the Wallington church. He took also a deep interest in the welfare of the working classes and was the founder of the South Beddington Coffee-house, an institution with which his name will long be recognised.

Joseph was not the only Laurence connected with the firm of Laurence Cazenove & Pearce. In July 1843 his son Sydney was introduced as a clerk, authorised to do business for money and time, and at the beginning of 1846 he became a partner. Simultaneously, Philip's brother Henry, who had become a member in 1839, also became a partner, taking the total to five, more than almost any other firm on the Exchange. Happily there survives the new partnership deed, drawn up in June 1846. It reveals the firm's capital as standing at £26,000, with £10,000 put in by Philip Cazenove, £8,000 by Joseph Laurence, £6,000 by Pearce, £2,000 by Sydney Laurence, and none by the presumably impecunious Henry Cazenove.

As for the third of the original partners, Charles Thomas Pearce, we know that he became a member of the House in 1819, lived at Peckham, and was sufficiently well respected to be elected Chairman of the Stock Exchange Committee in 1842. He remained so for over five years, and during his term of office presided over the no doubt popular move that henceforth the Exchange would close on Saturday afternoons. In November 1847 he died unexpectedly at his new home in Camberwell, having been ill for only two days. In performing its 'very painful duty' of communicating to the House this 'melancholy and sudden decease', the Committee took comfort in the knowledge that every member would 'bear testimony to the upright and dignified feelings by which that excellent man was pre-eminently distinguished, and which tended so effectually to elevate and sustain the character of the Stock Exchange'. It was, almost certainly, a deserved tribute. Pearce too, like Laurence, had a son who joined the firm, though in his case posthumously. This was Charles Pearce, who was elected a member in 1851 and at the start of 1853 became a partner.

Philip himself moved home during this period, in August 1846 at the age of forty-seven. His new family home was in Clapham, where he obtained from Thomas Potts, a window-glass and white-lead manufacturer in the City, the lease of a large country house standing well back from Clapham Common and overlooking Battersea Rise. Built around 1827, it stood in twelve acres on the south side of the road from Wandsworth to Clapham. The rent was £300 a year and it turned out to be Philip's last home. It was no doubt a desirable and pleasant residence, but to some extent he was bucking the trend by moving where he did, at least to judge by the words in 1845 of D. Morier Evans, a leading financial journalist:

> Regent's-park, and the rows of villas that stud the neighbourhood of Kensington, Brompton, Hammersmith, and other places tending to those points, are thickly inhabited by City men. Clapton, Hackney, Islington, Peckham, and Clapham, were, at one time, considered very convenient distances by these people. Their taste has, however, even changed in this respect; and these spots have been denuded of a number of their former occupants. Clerks, instead of principals, now reside in these localities, all short walks or rides from the City being filled with the habitations of this class of persons.

The least brash or pretentious of men, Philip Cazenove was perhaps not entirely typical of what was becoming an increasingly assertive and self-confident Victorian middle class. It was a well-justified self-confidence: by 1848 this middle class had received the vote, secured the repeal of the Corn Laws and thus the triumph of free trade, and repulsed the threat of the working class in the Chartist movement. Britain as a whole was about to move into a period of unparalleled prosperity, and in 1851 the splendours of the Great Exhibition in Hyde Park amply vouched for the permanence of the new social compact. Not surprisingly, the relatively humble abodes of Hackney and Islington no longer held the allure they once did.

On the Stock Exchange itself, with the Official List of prices being published daily from 1843, these were years of a generally favourable context in which Laurence Cazenove & Pearce could operate, though not without some severe and testing fluctuations. In particular, two markets now grew rapidly, offering many opportunities for making (and losing) money. One was in lending money to the eastern states of the United States, busy constructing canals and the start of a railway network. As with South America in the 1820s, these foreign bonds did not always prove a reliable investment for the lenders, but their growth certainly helped to generate market activity. The same was even more true of the notorious domestic railway boom of 1845 – notorious because of the many bubble companies, ruthless market-rigging and collapsed hopes that characterised a few heady, ultimately nightmarish months. It was a boom that, as far as one can tell,

31

Laurence Cazenove & Pearce wisely eschewed. Out of it, however, came permanent benefits: a railway system for the country at large and, for the Stock Exchange, a new and large market (familiarly known as 'Home Rails') that before long settled down to become a principal focus of both steady investment and less certain speculation. This it was to remain right up to the Second World War, thanks in no small part to the pioneering activities of the much-maligned 'Railway King' of the 1840s, George Hudson.

Inevitably, numbers continued to grow in Capel Court, so that by 1850 membership was up to 864. The Committee had been complaining for many years about the lack of space, and in 1853 the Trustees (who controlled such matters) decided that the only practical course was to pull down the original 1801 building and construct an entirely new Stock Exchange. This was duly done – in the astonishing (to modern eyes) time of nine months – and in March 1854 the new building was open to business. Charles Duguid, the financial journalist and turn-of-the-century historian of the Stock Exchange, later described it thus: 'It was, and is, a structure of brick, roofed with wood, with ironwork in the piers and some of the beams, and the whole of the interior was plastered with somewhat elaborate ornament.' Testimony to past expansion as well as future aspirations, this new Stock Exchange, although needing to be supplemented, would stand until the 1960s.

A new partnership naturally encouraged a larger scope, and there is little doubt that the stockbroking business of Laurence Cazenove & Pearce was more ambitious than that of Menet & Cazenove. In particular, it embraced (probably carrying on from the days of Laurence Whitmore & Co) a substantial element of 'money broking' in the overall composition of the business. This was a technically demanding activity, volatile and sometimes dangerous, and was pursued by relatively few stockbroking firms. One firm that did indulge, and had been doing so since the late eighteenth century, was Spurling & Skinner, on whose behalf Percival Spurling in 1877 gave to the Royal Commission on the Stock Exchange almost the only contemporary description that survives of this specialised activity:

> We can lend at times almost any amount which is given into our hands, on short loans. The ordinary run of loans for bankers goes from Tuesday to Friday and from Friday to Tuesday, and if the rate of money in the Stock Exchange is a fraction above what it is in the bill market we find an inexhaustible supply from large capitalists who live about the area within half a mile of the Stock Exchange. If the money is cheaper in the Stock Exchange than it is in the bill market, and if a profit is to be made out of it,

then we find capitalists ready to avail themselves of it in order to lend money in the outside market: that is an enormous business.

Supposing that a capitalist had in his hands £100,000 which he might employ in short loans upon bills or in any other transaction out of the Stock Exchange, he might sometimes employ it so as to get a better percentage in the Stock Exchange? – Yes. We will assume that the rate of money upon the Stock Exchange is 3 per cent, and that the rate of bill brokers is 2½ per cent; it would be more for the banker's advantage to lend his money at 3 per cent than to take it to a bill broker.

How is the lending on the Stock Exchange carried on? – As far as I am concerned it generally begins by a jobber coming to me and saying, "Borrow money." There are two different classes of loans, fortnightly loans and the loans in the English [i.e. Consol] market, chiefly from Friday to Tuesday and from Tuesday to Friday; they may be from day to day. The jobber, in making prices, has bought on Tuesday a quantity of stock which he wants to pay for, and he has not sold it for money; he will borrow of me a sum of money to pay for, say, £100,000 Consols, which he has bought for money; he puts those Consols in the names of my employers, for whom I have lent the money. On the Friday, if he has then sold the stock, he will pay me off the loan and the stock will come out of my bankers' names.

Essentially a form of arbitrage, relying on different interest rates in different markets, it was a type of business that demanded good faith from all concerned but could be very profitable.

As practised by Laurence Cazenove & Pearce, this money broking seems mostly to have taken the form of borrowing from the bankers Barings and re-lending to jobbers on the Stock Exchange at slightly higher rates. The amounts and frequency of the operation varied greatly during the lifetime of the partnership, with much depending on the state of the larger money market and the attitude towards it of the Bank of England. In the autumn of 1844, for instance, the Bank adopted an aggressive discount and lending policy, taking the money market by surprise, and among the casualties was the Laurence Cazenove loan account with Barings, which was temporarily closed. But both before and subsequently the firm borrowed large amounts, most spectacularly in 1850 when the total amount borrowed from Barings during the calendar year was a massive £13,550,000. The type of security on which Laurence Cazenove obtained these loans varied. Often it was the unimpeachable security provided by Consols, but on occasion it was rather more speculative, perhaps typified by the Paris-Lyons railway shares on which the firm borrowed over £32,000 at the end of December 1846.

Likewise varying was the length of time for which Laurence Cazenove received these loans in order to re-employ the money. Sometimes it was on a day-to-day basis, but at other times it was for as long as a month, the latter being the settlement period in Consols. Ultimately, all depended on market conditions. But precisely how profitable such business was, it is impossible to say, largely because of inadequate documentation. For 9th June 1840, however, the records of Barings show that on that day Laurence Cazenove took a loan from the bank of £20,000, for four days at 5 per cent. In the relevant ledger, the loan carries the notation '£10.19.2 less Com. £1.1.11,' with the amount charged to Laurence Cazenove being the difference, namely £9 17s 3d. Almost certainly this means that the jobber paid 5 per cent, that Barings received only 4½ per cent, and that Laurence Cazenove received the difference of ½ per cent. At the very least, it was a side-line to the main stockbroking business that must have been 'a nice little earner'.

In one unfortunate episode of this period, however, Laurence Cazenove lent money and found itself coming somewhat unstuck. This was the Villiers case. The Hon Charles Pelham Villiers was born in 1802, 'belonged by birth and family to the aristocratic order' (as the historian Justin McCarthy later put it), and in 1835 became MP for Wolverhampton. Over the next decade he became renowned in Parliament and the country as a whole for his annual motion demanding the repeal of the duties on corn. He was no orator but, again in the words of McCarthy, 'had a marvellous power of arraying telling arguments, and of compelling the attention even of the most listless and the least sympathetic audience', while according to the *Dictionary of National Biography*, 'in conversation he had few superiors'. The only problem was that he had no money. Indeed, it was lack of funds that lay behind his decision in 1847, when chosen for South Lancashire, to continue to sit for Wolverhampton. As the *DNB* tactfully described it: 'He felt that his means did not enable him to undertake the representation of a great county constituency, and he preferred to trust the tried loyalty of his borough constituents.' Impecuniosity also lay behind his unhappy relations with the Auction Mart.

The story began in 1841 (a year of a general election and thus expensive), when Villiers decided it was time to do something about his parlous financial position. He was heavily involved in the stock market, being caught, apparently, in the already incipient mania for speculating in railway shares. Needing £5,000 to pay for calls on shares of newly-formed railway companies, he was accordingly lent that sum by Laurence Cazenove & Pearce, with the loan being secured on shares. By 1848 only £2,000 had been repaid, and, becoming understandably impatient, the firm fixed the end of March that year as the deadline by which the rest of the loan had to be repaid. Villiers failed to oblige, and on April 4th the firm unceremoniously sold the shares, without having told him what it was about to do.

Villiers was furious:

> He did not consider Mr Laurence had the right to sell the shares without his authority, he knew he was making exertions to raise the money, and he had no idea that he would have sold them without giving him further notice. When he called on Mr Laurence on the 14th or 15th of April and offered to pay the money, and proposed that the shares should be replaced, Mr Laurence hesitated some time, and seemed to be looking at the prices. At last he declined, but offered to refer the matter to Baron Rothschild [son of the great Nathan], and if he should decline that, he would refer him to their solicitor. Baron Rothschild was applied to, but being on terms of intimacy with both parties he advised its being decided by the Committee of the Stock Exchange.

Thus record the minutes of the Committee, before whom Villiers and the partners duly appeared. Having had their say, they retired, whereupon 'considerable discussion took place' between the members of the Committee. Finally, by a 12–4 vote, they decided 'That Messrs Laurence Cazenove & Co having allowed the period of notice for the 31st of March to expire, without calling upon Mr Villiers for his authority to sell the shares in question, had no right to sell them without further notice, and that Mr Villiers is entitled to claim his shares upon payment of the money due from him, on or before Tuesday 16th May.' That date lay only five days hence, and it is improbable that Villiers ever recovered his shares, or indeed that the firm had been fully covered by the proceeds of the sales of those shares, granted the nervous state of the markets just before the big Chartist demonstration on Kennington Common on April 10th. Villiers himself continued with a Parliamentary career that proved to be one of remarkable longevity, paying his last visit to Wolverhampton in 1875 and remaining member for that constituency until his death in 1898.

A more orthodox stockbroking activity – especially as the century progressed – was a close involvement in the provision of capital. From the point of view of the history of Cazenove's, this mostly awaited the next partnership, but a handful of examples do survive from the Laurence Cazenove & Pearce period. One occurred in October 1839, after the Stock Exchange Committee had declined to allow the 'marking' (i.e. quoting) in the Official List of the prices of bonds of the New Mexican 5% Consolidated Fund and Mexican Deferred Bonds, apparently because of 'the application having been made by Messrs Lizardi & Co only, and not by The Committee of Bondholders'. As a result the Committee received communications from not only Lizardi & Co but also Laurence Cazenove & Pearce, whose letter read as follows:

> An arrangement having been made with the Mexican Government, for the conversion of the Bonds, and the funding of the arrears of Dividends, which appears to be satisfactory to the majority of the Bondholders, we take the liberty of requesting you to direct the prices of the New Bonds to be quoted on the authorised list.
>
> A very large amount having been already converted, by English holders, as well as for foreign account, it becomes important that a market price should be established by a regular quotation of the new stock.

Modestly but firmly put, it was an argument of decisive appeal, and by a unanimous vote the Committee decided to quote the prices. The Stock Exchange of the nineteenth century never forgot that its underlying *rationale* was as a market-place where it was left to the free and unhindered judgement of the investors themselves to decide on the merits of individual securities, whether new or old. An official 'mark' therefore implied no official judgement on what those merits (if any) were.

In this bracing atmosphere, it was not only outsiders who could misjudge the market situation and lose substantial sums of money, though undoubtedly outsiders tended to be at a disadvantage. Early in 1847, for example, the Treasury offered a loan of £8 million at 89½ for the relief of the terrible Irish famine, and Barings and Rothschilds, as the great merchant bankers of the day, each took one half. The loan attracted much attention, and Barings, who offered part of their share to banks and others likely to be interested, encountered such lively response that they cut down allotments drastically – to such an extent that, although Barings' participation was £4 million, they allotted only £1,739,200. The remaining £2,260,800 they no doubt expected to sell at a profit, and in April 1847 they duly decided to sell. For this purpose they worked through four stockbrokers, one of whom was Laurence Cazenove. It was a clear indication not only of the firm's good relationship with Barings but also of its reputation as substantial dealers in the funds. For some months the price remained between 86½ and 88, but when sellers outnumbered buyers the market slipped to 85. By April of the following year, when all their stock had been sold, Barings found themselves with a loss of £45,848. Sometimes it could be safer to be a stockbroker, picking up a steady flow of commissions, than a celebrated loan contractor.

Few concerns needed capital as much as those of the new railways. From 1842 the Bank of England, keen to expand its avenues of private lending in the context of great ease in the money market and thus drastically declining discount business, supplied such capital. This took the form of loans up to

£250,000 upon debentures of the particular railway company. The Bank might have been expected to choose a firm that specialised in railway issues to act as intermediary in these transactions, but in fact it chose Laurence Cazenove & Pearce, who do not appear to have been active in the railway market. The explanation no doubt lies in the firm's already good relationship with the Bank, dating from the early 1830s, before Philip's partnership with Laurence and Pearce. Moreover, in the year that Charles Pearce became Chairman of the Stock Exchange Committee, he must have been well known to the Governor of the Bank. But whatever the reason, it was through Laurence Cazenove & Pearce (and in effect probably through Laurence personally) that the Bank purchased railway debentures for well over a decade. The usual procedure was for the firm, having been in touch with a railway that needed short-term money, to make a specific proposal by letter to the Governor of the Bank. The amount of stock offered at any one time was usually £100,000, always at par, and the Bank either accepted or rejected the offer, with little negotiation of the terms. For their services, Laurence Cazenove & Pearce charged the company $\frac{3}{16}$th per cent. By 1852 one or two of the bigger railways, such as the London & North Western, were starting to deal directly with the Bank, thereby avoiding payment of a commission. Smaller and less well-placed lines, however, like the South Eastern & Dover, still found it best to go through Laurence Cazenove. Not long afterwards, at the end of 1854, the partnership ceased, and predictably it was Laurence who inherited this useful line of business.

The earliest record we have of Cazenove's formally acting as brokers to a company floating a new issue on the Stock Exchange dates from July 1852, when Laurence Cazenove & Pearce performed that role on behalf of the North of Europe Steam Navigation Company. It was a role that Francis Lavington, author of a pioneering study of the pre-1914 capital market, later summarised as essentially fourfold: namely, that the responsibilities of brokers were to 'lend their names to the prospectuses, assign the underwriting on payment of an "overriding" commission, carry through many of the technical formalities, and open up a market among their clients'. By the 1850s the underwriting function had not yet fully developed, but otherwise those were the salient duties. As far as 'technical formalities' were concerned, none was as important as effectively representing the company (or foreign government) before the Stock Exchange Committee, usually to secure not only a 'special settlement' that ensured a free market for the shares, but also an official 'mark' or 'quotation' that meant they would be quoted on the pages of the Official List. Altogether, acting as broker to a new issue could be a demanding business, but over the rest of the century it was one that increasingly became a *forte* of Cazenove's and did much to establish the firm's reputation by the end of that century as being a cut above most of the rest of the pack.

In 1852 itself, the North of Europe Steam Navigation Company flotation was a relatively minor affair, comprising 25,000 shares of £20 each. The same was not true the following spring, when Laurence Cazenove & Pearce, in conjunction with William Chapman of Leadenhall Street, acted as brokers to the ambitious issue by the Grand Trunk Railway Company of Canada of 72,460 shares of £25 and £1,811,500 6% convertible debentures. A project famous in railway history, the intention was both political and economic: to unite the disparate elements of a far-flung country and to handle the ever-larger quantities of American grain, carrying them to eastern Canadian ports for trans-shipment to England. Some illustrious names lay behind the railway as now presented to the British investing public – Robert Stephenson (son of George) as civil engineer, Peto, Brassey, Betts & Jackson as contractors, Baring Brothers and Glyn, Mills & Co as bankers in London, the entire cabinet of the Province of Upper Canada on the board of directors, not to mention Thomas Baring and George Carr Glyn – and the tone of the accompanying prospectus was euphoric: 'A conviction of the great benefits of unanimous action has provided a combination of railway interests probably never before seen, and ensuring such an energetic and harmonious working of the entire line, as cannot but produce the most satisfactory results.' It was a notable *coup* for Laurence Cazenove & Pearce to be chosen as co-brokers, a choice probably determined not only by the close relationship in this period with Barings, but also by the fact that Glyns had become the firm's bankers. It was a well-established bank, founded in 1753, and its customers were almost entirely commercial, including by this time a large number of railway companies. An excellent bank to have in one's corner, its connection with Philip Cazenove and his descendants was to survive the split with Laurence and Pearce in 1854.

The Grand Trunk Railway, however, proved an unhappy venture for its financial supporters. Launched on the London market at a rather difficult time, with other schemes strongly in competition with it, and the diplomatic situation in the Balkans deteriorating, it managed to raise £2.78 million of the projected £3.6 million largely on the strength of the high reputation of its principal backers. But within weeks the shares were at a discount, and by 1855 the railway was in great financial difficulties. When, in 1859, the contractors triumphantly completed the line by building the Victoria Bridge in Montreal, the finances of the Canadian government together with those of the railway were hopelessly compromised. It remained an uphill, largely unrewarding struggle at the London end, as was reflected by a letter in March that year from Glyn to Baring: 'Laurence says now is the time for a pot of fire in the Grand Trunk Bonds and that very little will bring them up to par.' Joseph and Sydney Laurence had now split from Philip Cazenove, and, when in 1860 a further Grand Trunk issue was made, Cazenove's was not connected with it nor indeed participated in it. This new issue proved an almost unqualified failure, so it is unlikely that the Laurences' erstwhile partner felt much regret.

Inevitably, though, the 'bread-and-butter' for Laurence Cazenove & Pearce, as with any nineteenth-century stockbroking firm, was the mundane buying and selling of existing securities on behalf of clients, whether private or institutional. How much those clients paid could vary greatly, for throughout the century there obtained in the sphere of brokers' commissions a state of *laissez-faire*. In 1838 over a hundred members and firms did unsuccessfully petition the Committee to introduce a fixed scale, while later, in 1860, in the wake of public complaints that charges were too high, another attempt to introduce a fixed scale also foundered. It is impossible to be sure how the rates of Laurence Cazenove compared with those of other firms; what is likely, however, is that the firm shared in the increasing tendency for brokers (as mentioned by Morier Evans in 1845) to reduce their usual commission by 50% when they were executing speculative business. It was a reasonable differential, granted that speculators were constantly in the market or carrying-over, thus providing regular revenue at little inconvenience, whereas investors on their relatively rare interventions usually wanted their securities either taken up or delivered, in either case involving a fair amount of office-work. To what extent this differential acted as an unwarrantable incentive to rash speculation is another matter and by definition almost impossible to judge.

Meanwhile, in the 1830s and 1840s, business continued to be done, though probably on a declining scale, for the two main institutional clients of the Menet & Cazenove epoch, namely Huths and Rothschilds. The Rothschild connection in particular does seem to have become less close, even though for some years the firm acted as that bank's principal brokers for American securities. In particular, there survives a ledger for 1843, showing that during that entire year Rothschilds had only some twenty-five transactions outside the American market executed by Laurence Cazenove & Pearce, totalling a turn-over of less than £300,000. It is possible (though perhaps unlikely) that a letter received by Rothschilds from the Auction Mart in February 1840 had occasioned some coolness:

We regret to inform you that our friends for whom you have received the divids due the 1 Nov last on New York City Water Stock are hard in their complaints of the high rate of Exchange at which you have paid those divds, since they have received divds due the same day on the same kind of stock at the exchange of 105½ & 106 through other houses . . . They therefore conceive themselves entitled to be paid by you at the same exchange & presume there must be some mistake about the remittance which differs so widely from the exchange which rated at that period.

By contrast, the connection with Barings now flourished during the 1840s, so that between July 1840 and July 1841, for example, Laurence Cazenove bought for that house £1,030,000 of 3% Consols and sold £820,000. With a commission of ⅛th per cent applying for buying and 1⁄16th per cent for selling, these transactions probably earned for the firm an income of some £1,800, although if a transaction was being done ultimately on behalf of a client of Barings, then that particular commission would have to be split with the bank. This division of the spoils would over the years be a perennial grievance on the part of almost all stockbrokers, who felt, not without some justification, that they earned their half of the commission rather more than the banks earned theirs.

An equally perennial stockbroking complaint would concern clients (usually private) who did not settle their accounts promptly, or indeed sometimes at all. At least one such trying episode afflicted Laurence Cazenove & Pearce during the 1840s and featured another MP, this time William Bulkeley Hughes, member for Carnarvon since 1837. The episode was brought to the attention of the Stock Exchange Committee in November 1849, when there appeared in the *Globe* a detailed report of a case heard in the Bail Court between the firm and Hughes. In the court, counsel for Hughes stated in the strongest terms that his client had been consistently cheated by Laurence Cazenove, who had not only pushed unwanted shares on him but had also charged him, in the counsel's words, '2s 6d per share higher than the highest quoted price'. Consequently, he argued, the award of the arbitrator between the two parties should be set aside. Six days later, Joseph Laurence was summoned to the Committee room and told that 'the affair in question having been bruited in the Stock Exchange and given rise to some unpleasant comments, the Committee felt bound to take some notice of it'. The Committee, however, 'left it entirely to the discretion of Mr Laurence, whether he deemed it expedient to offer any explanation, or to await the issue of the law proceedings.' Declaring himself 'most thankful to have been afforded the present opportunity', Laurence chose the former course. The ensuing statement was a vivid guide to the trials and tribulations of dealing for an unscrupulous client:

Some time ago [about 1845 during the railway boom?] Mr Hughes was introduced to them, by a mutual friend a solicitor, who he believes was also, at that time, interested in Mr Hughes's speculations. In the first instance, they effected very large operations, not by written orders, but by Mr Hughes or this solicitor coming in with orders, to buy or to sell hundreds of shares at various hours of the day. They got into a very extensive account, but everything done in the most straightforward way that it was possible to be, and not a murmur heard, on any point, until after they were compelled to take legal proceedings; they had repeatedly pressed him to close his accounts, but it went on for a year and a half, and the result was a large loss which they had to pay, together with calls on shares held for him.

During that time they had been pressing him for a settlement for two years, during which period they received numerous letters from him, always thanking them for their forbearance, but never expressing a single objection to the account, or a hint of any fault to be found in any way. The amount of their claim is between £3,000 and £4,000, and when they threatened to take law proceedings, his solicitors came and offered to pay down £2,500, pressing them to take it, saying he defied them to make good their claim at law. They offered to strike off the commission amounting to between £300 and £400, but refused to make the large reduction proposed, as it might be inferred by so doing that they were conscious of fraud, and they challenged him to put his finger on a single item in the account that they could not substantiate and verify.

The result was they commenced an action, and after having the trial postponed in every possible vexatious way, term after term, it at last came on, and they got a verdict subject to a reference to an arbitrator to go into the detail of the accounts. When they appeared before the arbitrator, they were met and opposed by two counsel, and compelled to give legal proof of every item in the account, they [i.e. the counsel] refusing to take the jobbers' accounts, or admit cheques given for differences as proof, but requiring to show how the money was actually paid. They had to prove above one hundred items by calling the several jobbers with whom the business was done, but they could not detect an inaccuracy of a single penny throughout the whole of the transactions. An accountant was sent to examine their books, who was four or five days at their office, and this person did not confine himself to the accounts in which Mr Hughes was concerned, but pried into all their other transactions.

With respect to what was said of selling their own shares, and recommending him to buy them, the transaction occurred at a time when Mr Hughes was chairman of the York & Lancashire Railway, and as such was aware of some important arrangement being about to be made, which would affect the price of the shares. He came to them and said if they would lend him the money he would sweep the market of every share in that railway. A few days afterwards, they wrote and offered him a certain lot of those shares, not as brokers, but a certain number at a certain price, and after two days' consideration he came and took them. They charged him no commission, and he knew to a penny what they were worth, they gave him no advice in the matter.

The matter was kept a year and a half before the arbitrators, delay being promoted by every legal artifice, extending even to perjury. However, it has resulted in their having obtained an award for the whole of their claim, less about £20, about which there was some legal difficulty in the proof. But not one single instance could they prove, where any irregularity or discrepancy occurred, in the notes of purchase or sale, and the actual transactions with the jobbers. Nor is there a fact connected with the whole affair that either himself or partners are conscious to deserve shame or regret beyond that of having had to deal for a person of such a character as Mr Hughes had proved himself to be.

It was an exhaustive explanation, accepted as 'quite satisfactory' by the Committee, and at the end of it Laurence again expressed his thanks for 'the opportunity of saying this much', adding: 'It was the more satisfactory to him, being as it were taken by surprise in the matter, without a moment's premeditation.' The final vindication, and closing of the episode, came the following June, when the Committee received a letter from the firm, accompanied by a press report, 'wherein is recorded the result of the law proceedings that had been pending between them and Mr Hughes MP and showing that the charges urged by Mr Hughes's counsel against Messrs Laurence & Co had been fully refuted'.

On occasion, usually through an unfortunate combination of circumstances, dealings on behalf of a client or group of clients could lead to a dispute with a fellow-member of the Stock Exchange. One such regrettable dispute was settled by the Committee on 2nd July 1840, when the memorably-named Solomon B. Worms brought a complaint against Laurence Cazenove & Pearce. Worms told his story. It hinged on an incident that had taken place two days earlier at about a quarter to four in the Hercules Passage, close to one of the four entrances to the House. There he had met by chance Philip Cazenove, who had asked him whether he felt inclined to buy some North American stock, 'if he could offer it at a very low price'. It had to be sold that afternoon, said Philip, 'in order to send the Account of Sale [i.e. the contract note] to America by the night's mail by the *British Queen.*' The stock consisted of £10,000 5% bonds of the State of Indiana, which Philip was selling on behalf of principals. The price was 75, including the interest, which was payable on the following day, July 1st.

Worms hesitated, but later in the afternoon called at the Auction Mart, where he saw Pearce, Philip not being there, and left a note reading, 'I buy £10,000 Indiana Sterling at 72½ ex div, payable 15 July.' The next day, however, complications arose, for the market was firmer and the parties involved, other than Worms, were now saying that they did not understand that there had been a conclusive sale but merely a 'bidding', and that some of them were entering into fresh negotiations to sell at 73½. Moreover, a foreign holder of the stock claimed that, all along, he had intended to sell at 75 ex div. Philip himself now asserted that he had not contemplated a positive sale, but merely a bidding.

In the Committee room, the decisive moment came when Worms pointed out an inconsistency between Philip's claim that there had never been a conclusive bargain and his insistence on sending out a contract note immediately. He asked: 'What would have been my situation in the event of a declaration of war? Could I have backed out if the Stock had fallen 20 per cent?' To these very fair questions, no answer was forthcoming. Where-upon, after the parties had withdrawn, the Committee, after some discussion, resolved 'that a specific contract was made between Mr Cazenove and Mr Worms'. On the basis of the evidence presented, it was not a verdict with which Philip could reasonably have quarrelled.

There was more, however, to the day-to-day relationship of stockbroker and client than the execution of buying or selling orders, central and indispensable though that function was. There was also the whole area of the giving of advice, for which by tradition no charge was made. Such advice was not always about specific investments, as is shown by a letter of August 1848 that survives from Huths to Laurence Cazenove & Pearce.

> Some friends of ours in Holland wish to form a company in London with a Capital of £300,000 for the purpose of carrying on a refinery of sugar at Amsterdam which promises very satisfactory results.
>
> Would you be kind enough to inform us whether, supposing the probable advantages of the plan to be clearly demonstrated, you believe that parties could be found in this country willing to invest their capital in such an undertaking?

Unfortunately there is no reply extant, but the very fact of the enquiry anticipates rather suggestively the way in which company finance was to be such a major growth area in the history of Cazenove's. Five years later, however, on an altogether different subject, we do know what advice the firm gave. The occasion was the decision by the Chancellor of the Exchequer, William Gladstone, to wind up the moribund South Sea

Company, which had been founded in 1711 and long since lost its original purposes. Existing stockholders were given the right to have their holdings converted into cash, which almost overnight led to up to three million pounds being available for reinvestment and thus needing to find a new home. Accordingly, many stockbrokers now wrote to their clients in order to make suggestions, including Laurence Cazenove & Pearce to Barings on 7th November 1853. After referring to the plethora of enquiries the firm had received for such suggestions, the letter appended a list of sixteen of them, giving for each the name of the security, the price, the interest or dividend dates, and the price of the security six months previously, which for most was much below the current price. Reflecting the predominance of railway stocks in most investment portfolios, twelve out of the sixteen suggestions were for railways: eight at home, two in North America (including the Grand Trunk Railway of Canada) and two in Europe. The remaining four were 3% Consols, 3½% annuities, Bank stock and Canada 6% debentures, an eminently conservative choice. But as the letter modestly added: 'We have selected a few only of each class of securities, but we shall be happy to give more precise information respecting these, or any others which you may prefer, out of the general price list.' Anxious to oblige, but not wishing to pre-judge the wishes of such an important client, the role of the stockbroker was still essentially that of passive intermediary, with the art of stockbroking research not yet even a distant gleam in the eye.

By the early 1850s the signs were becoming apparent of change in the offing at Laurence Cazenove & Pearce. One clue to possible internal strain lies in the firm's accounts that, unlike for most of the century, survive for these years. They show that profits should have been substantial – granted that commission income for 1851–4 averaged almost £39,000 per annum, while annual business expenses were only about £3,000 – but that in practice, as far as one can tell, they were not. This was largely for two reasons. Firstly because, in the context of a market that was still (in Clapham's later phrase) 'deep in the railway jungle,' there were some highly disappointing results produced by the firm's own trading in stocks and shares. For 1851 this trading produced a profit of £1,193, but over the next three years losses accrued of £32,860, £4,887 and £3,237 respectively. Secondly, and equally damagingly, there was the sizable provision that had to be made in the accounts for bad and doubtful debts, coming over the four years to a net amount of £36,253. Such a figure can only be attributable to poor judgement in making advances and, together with the losses on the firm's own trading, possibly led to a certain degree of friction in the partnership.

There was also the whole issue of the rising younger generation. As we have seen, Joseph Laurence's son, Sydney, had been a partner since 1846, while C. T. Pearce's son, Charles, became a partner in 1853. The new partnership deed shows a capital increased to £52,000, with £18,000 each put in by Joseph Laurence and Philip Cazenove, £12,000 by Sydney Laurence and £4,000 by young Pearce. Already in 1852, Philip's older brother, Henry, had decided to retire as a partner, thus ending a lengthy, rather chequered business career. Philip himself was by now in his mid-fifties, so the question naturally began to arise: what did the Cazenove side of the partnership have to offer in the way of young blood, to match that of the Pearce and Laurence families? It was at this stage that two members of the family came to the fore. One was Edward Cazenove, eldest son of another of Philip's brothers, James. He had been born in 1825 and become a member of the Stock Exchange in 1849, apparently going into partnership elsewhere. The other was Henry Cazenove junior, Philip's eldest son, who had been born in 1829 and, like his father, was educated at Charterhouse. He became a member of the Stock Exchange in 1851. Two years later, both he and his cousin Edward married. By 1854 Henry was living at Orsett Terrace, Hyde Park, and Edward at Weybridge, Surrey. In the face of all this upward mobility, would there be room for everyone – or rather, profitable business for everyone – at the Auction Mart?

By definition this is a guess. It is entirely possible that the decision to end the partnership had been taken several years earlier, irrespective of the aspirations or otherwise of the younger generation. But either way, the basic facts are clear. On 30th December 1854 the partnership of Laurence Cazenove & Pearce was dissolved and, almost simultaneously, two new Stock Exchange partnerships were formed. One was that of Laurence Son & Pearce, comprising Joseph Laurence, Sydney Laurence and Charles Pearce junior. Ultimately this firm would become Laurence, Prust & Co, which eventually reformed into two separate broking firms under the names of CCF Laurence Prust & Co (dissolved in 1990) and Laurence Keen & Co. The other new partnership formed was P. Cazenove & Co, whose three partners were Philip Cazenove, Edward Cazenove and Henry Cazenove junior. Whatever the different motives involved, it is hard not to feel that Philip had reached the stage where he felt the need not only to have a stockbroking business in his own hands but also to prepare the way for younger members of his family eventually to take over that business. He had gained much through his connection with Laurence and Pearce, but the time had come for a further culminating phase of a remarkable career.

CHAPTER THREE

A *new issue broker*
1855–1884

T he new firm of P. Cazenove & Co temporarily based itself at Edward
Cazenove's former offices at 39 Lothbury, but by 1859 at the latest
it had found a much more permanent home at 52 Threadneedle
Street. The likelihood is that these early years were difficult ones for the
new enterprise, with a substantial amount of the traditional business of
Laurence Cazenove & Pearce (including the selling of railway debentures
to the Bank of England) being retained from 1855 by Laurence Son &
Pearce. Such anyway is the impression given by the drawing account
ledgers of the Bank itself for the second half of the 1850s, revealing the
balances at the disposal of P. Cazenove & Co, and the volume of money and
stock passing through the account, to be fairly paltry in comparison to that of
Philip's former partners. It was as well that he was still on friendly terms
with Rothschilds. This was clearly shown in May 1856, when that house,
seeking on the government's behalf to raise £5 million in Consols in order to
fund the Crimean War, looked to P. Cazenove & Co to locate a significant
part of that sum. The firm obliged to the extent of returning to Rothschilds a
list of forty-six applicants for £857,000, including P. Cazenove & Co itself
for £50,000, Henry Cazenove senior for £20,000, and his brother James for
£9,000. Rothschilds would simultaneously have employed several other
brokers, but its inclusion of Cazenove's is early evidence of a certain
'placing' reputation.

There remained plenty of work to be done if the firm was to establish
itself as one of the Stock Exchange's leading brokers. It is likely that within
the partnership much of the running was increasingly made by Henry
junior, who during this first decade of the new partnership's existence
lived with his young family in a series of town houses with fashionable
addresses (Gloucester Terrace, Upper Hyde Park Gardens, Lancaster

Gate) and, for the moment, resisted the temptation to become a country squire. All the evidence suggests that Henry was a highly capable man, that he had a distinctly worldly streak and, for all his own charitable activities, perhaps lacked something of his father's piety; and that in general he was someone who in his professional life did not question the assumptions of an increasingly vigorous and (to modern eyes) largely unregulated market place. As such he had, from the point of view of the firm's history, excellent qualities with which to consolidate Philip's pioneering achievement.

Sadly, Philip's other new partner, Edward Cazenove, was unable to make a similarly decisive contribution, for early in 1857, quite unexpectedly, he died of a brain tumour at the age of only thirty-one. It must have been a heavy blow to the firm as well as his family, but fortunately an effective replacement was at hand to fill the gap in the partnership. This was in the person of Peter Reid, who became a partner at the beginning of 1858. He was then in his thirties, having been born in Perth about 1825, before coming to London at an early age and being elected to the Stock Exchange in 1853. Interestingly, one of his three sureties was Joseph Laurence. Little enough is known for certain about Reid's character, though again all the evidence is that he was a thorough and efficient stockbroker who by the 1870s increasingly made a speciality of the exacting task of bringing new issues to the market. By all accounts a modest and unassuming man, he appreciated art and was a close friend of Millais. His qualities complemented those of the more extrovert Henry, and together they made an effective team.

Philip Cazenove himself remained indisputably the head of the firm, but, confident of the abilities of his partners, he now increasingly devoted his main energies to manifold works of goodness and charity. These instincts had always been present – typified by his habit of devoting May 1st and November 1st, when by tradition the Stock Exchange was closed, to the task of auditing the voluminous accounts of an important Church society – but it was not until this stage of his career that they came to the fore, probably hastened by the sudden and untimely death of his wife while on a visit to Great Malvern in 1860. Some twenty years later, Philip's obituaries were to pay full but not exaggerated tribute:

His face, the very ideal of refined benevolence, was one of the most familiar to those who frequented the board rooms of the S.P.G. [Society for the Propagation of the Gospel], the S.P.C.K. [Society for the Propagation of Christian Knowledge], the National Society, and the Additional Curates' Society. Of these, and not a few other church charities, he acted

47

as treasurer, and took an earnest interest in their proceedings; while he was a large contributor to their funds. At the same time he was an active member of the governing bodies of Guy's Hospital, of the Ophthalmic Hospital, of the Evelina Hospital for sick children, and of many other philanthropic institutions. Appeals for the building of churches, schools, and parsonages, not only for London, but for the country, day by day found their way to his hand, and were never disregarded. In the parish of Battersea, in which he lived, he gave the most liberal aid in churches, schools, and good works; while he set a notable example of devout and simple piety and self-forgetting personal service.

The words of *Church Bells* were matched by those of the *Guardian*:

Every day in Lent, and frequently at other seasons, he found time to join the 'two or three' who were gathered together in some quiet City church. His office was the well-known resort of those who were distressed, and many a hard-working and ill-remunerated clergyman who sought relief from him obtained not merely counsel but substantial help in the way of gift or loan (which was never asked to be repaid), and was thus sent away rejoicing. To aid in church building, to provide living agents for evangelising the masses, to promote education, and to alleviate bodily suffering, were the great objects which he had ever before him.

It was entirely in character that one of the hospitals to which he lent his closest support, as a governor from 1861 and later vice-president, was St Luke's, a hospital for the insane. In the 1860s the care of those deprived of their reason had little popular appeal and indeed was only just emerging from a period in which treatment of the insane was harsh and unsympathetic. Again, it was a mark of his deep interest and sustained committee work on behalf of another hospital, Guy's, that the first lecturer there, John T. Dickson, should dedicate a volume of lectures to him. Frequently asked if he would allow himself to be proposed for a seat in the House of Commons, Philip Cazenove always declined. As one obituary explained: 'His reason for doing so was not generally known. But his family were fully aware of it. He felt that he had no time to spare from the works of benevolence and charity which he had undertaken.' And the obituarist added, with what cannot have been overstatement: 'To these he devoted almost every hour that he could snatch from his business.'

The basic constituents of that business, under Philip's overall rather than detailed direction, remained familiar. One such, after an interval of nine months at the outset of the new partnership's existence, was the resumption of 'money broking', again taking the form of borrowing from Barings, usually for fortnightly periods, in order to re-lend elsewhere, often in the Stock Exchange itself. The volume of this borrowing was well down on the peak year of 1850, and indeed was not continuous, with little occurring during the late 1850s and early 1860s. Nevertheless, it provided a useful if not major part of the firm's business, and was also an important point of continuity with the Laurence Cazenove & Pearce era. Moreover, a further sign of the working relationship (if not a particularly close one) that now existed with Barings is shown by a letter from P. Cazenove & Co to the bank on 23rd July 1861, markedly critical of the official whose family for several generations had been responsible for the Stock Exchange's Official List: 'Chilian 4½ per cent ought to have been quoted by Wetenhall in his list of the 17th inst: 81½. He cannot now tell us how he got the price of 80⅜ – the only traceable bargain besides one at 81¼, was one for £300 at 81. They are quoted 81½ today.' With the system of 'marking' bargains wholly voluntary on the part of members, and the relay of continuous 'tape' prices not yet in operation, the initial complaint by Barings, which presumably was what elicited the letter from Cazenove's, was merely part of a widespread grievance about the latitude and often plain inaccuracy of the market's official prices.

One way of countering this problem was through the daily price list of selected securities that the firm by this stage was sending out to clients. One that survives was for Friday 23rd December 1859. It comprised a single sheet, gave the closing prices for nineteen stocks and shares, and at the foot provided the briefest of summaries of the day in question (one notoriously susceptible to pre-Christmas japes): 'Business has again been dull and prices have not experienced any material variation. Mexican and Turkish Stocks are a fraction lower. French Rentes after receding to f.70.25, close the same as yesterday, f.70.50.' The recipients were John Foster & Sons, important Bradford textile manufacturers although not quoted on the London Stock Exchange until after the Second World War. On the same day Fosters also received from Cazenove's a letter revealing the most natural of stockbroking roles, that of seeking to encourage new business:

If you decide on taking any San Paulo shares please send us a telegraph to that effect tomorrow as the subscription List will be finally closed tomorrow afternoon. Applications have already been received for considerably more than the entire capital.

We have £5,000 Virginia State 5 pCt Sterling Bonds for sale at 88. The dividends are payable in London at Messrs Baring Brothers, and the price *includes* the dividend due next month of 2½ pCt.

The reference to sending a telegraph is interesting: public telegraph lines had linked London and the main provincial centres since the late 1840s, resulting over the next decade in a much more integrated British securities market.

Fortunately, there exist (though often in rather illegible form) not only a major tranche of correspondence from Cazenove's to John Foster, but also, covering a longer period, letters from Fosters to Cazenove's. From this valuable archive it is possible to build up a composite picture of the evolving relationship between broker and an actively investing client, one that apparently began at about the time of the pre-Christmas letter of 1859. The following day, Christmas Eve, Fosters gave a fairly dusty response to the firm's suggestions: 'We have concluded to do nothing in the San Paulo railway, nor do we like American State Bonds.' The year 1860 was quiet, but the pace of communication began to pick up in 1861. 'We think that the following will tempt you', Threadneedle Street wrote to Black Dyke Mills in March:

> Some Friends of ours hold an amount of Buckinghamshire Ry Ltd (guaranteed 4% in perpetuity by London & No Western and therefore first class) & being pressed for money have commissioned us privately to sell it, having had a temporary loan upon it. This stock is firm at 96, but for an amount of £10,000 stk, we could get it for you at 93 & perhaps get it transferred *stamp free* into your name. This is a chance thing of a high character that we are not able to offer very often thus cheap & is well worth your consideration. An answer by return of post will oblige.

The answer, sent with due promptness, was at best lukewarm: 'We do not particularly like the Buckinghamshire Stock, as, at the present time, the interest to us is only very small. At the same time if you could do it at 90 for Cash, you can do so.' Probably no purchase was made. By early summer, imminent civil war in America loomed large, and Cazenove's on June 4th correctly informed Fosters that 'there seems no reason to doubt that both sides are in earnest', soon afterwards trying to persuade its client to make some cheap purchases in such American stocks as Maryland, Virginia and North Carolina. But Fosters appear to have preferred to play safe and inquired at the beginning of July: 'Do you know of any Railway Debentures to be had at $4\frac{1}{2}$%?' The firm replied that it could indeed obtain 'some London & South Western (first class) Debs 3 years to run at $4\frac{1}{2}$%', only to receive from Fosters a mildly tart reprimand: 'We should have thought $4\frac{3}{4}$% would have been given, in the present state of the money market.'

Despite such occasional notes of discord, broker and client were by 1862 in almost daily correspondence. In particular, the spring of that year saw a flurry of activity. That Cazenove's could offer properly cautious advice was shown in a letter on March 15th about the possibility of a further purchase by Fosters of Victoria 6% stock: 'We think it might answer very well for a temporary investment or speculation, as Colonial securities find great favour with the public, but we should not recommend a *permanent* investment in the Bonds of a Colony where the public debt has grown so rapidly and the democratic element so largely prevails.' Five days later attention had turned to an imminent new Turkish loan: 'The terms will be as favourable as to ensure success. We think you might safely take a large stake in it either as a temporary or permanent investment. We shall make up our usual List which we have been requested to do by the Agents for the Loan.' The firm duly applied to Messrs Butterfield Bros for £120,000 on behalf of Fosters, but could not promise success. Fosters itself decided that stoicism was the best course: 'We are afraid with so many applications for the Turkish Loan we shall not have a very large amount allotted, we must however take our chance, & hope for the best.' To which Cazenove's replied encouragingly the following day, the 28th:

> You may depend on us using every exertion to secure as large an allotment as possible. We have already pressed two of the gentlemen on the Committee of allotments on the subject and have no doubt you will be placed on the best footing. The List closed today and the total amount applied for is about 35 millions. Our own List reached nearly 4 millions. The price of the Scrip is 2½ ⅝ pm [i.e. premium].

Early in April the allotment was made, and Fosters wrote to Cazenove's: 'We think perhaps under the circumstances we have been fairly treated, having received an allotment of £30,000.' The firm could not resist replying: 'We are glad you got so large a slice of the Turkish Loan, which is due no doubt to our energetic representations in your favour. The allotments have not been made pro rata and very few have been made of so large an amount as your own.' And the letter added in a way so characteristic of the nineteenth-century new issue process: 'If you should be disposed to take the profit on all or part of the allotment the price now obtainable is 2⅜ ½ pm.'

By April 5th, Fosters was wondering about the next big thing to reach the London market: 'Will you oblige us with your best information with reference to the New Egyptian Loan? If the terms are favourable & the investment moderately safe, we shall probably apply for a quantity.' This time the textile manufacturers received little encouragement: 'With regard to the Egyptian Loan, we think it follows too closely on the Turkish Loan being somewhat of a kindred security . . . There are so many new Securities now coming forward that we think the supply will prove much in excess of the demand and lead ultimately to a general decline in prices.' A further warning followed soon afterwards, and Fosters on the 12th April, seemingly eschewing the Egyptian loan, concurred: 'We perfectly agree with you, in your opinions with regard to the rage for New Schemes, & we fully intend keeping clear of them. There will no doubt be plenty of work for the legal gentlemen shortly.'

Nevertheless, in a buoyant capital market opportunities kept coming forward, some of them sober enough to be worth recommending. 'We think', Cazenove's wrote at the end of April, 'the Russian 5 Per Ct stk cheap & good at 92 – but it will not be a "sporting" thing like Turkish nor the amounts asked for nearly as large, so you had better apply for what you would like to have & let us know please on Friday morning.' The firm was making up a list of subscribers on behalf of Rothschilds (which was offering £10 million to the public) and on May 2nd wrote again to Fosters, which had decided to apply for £60,000: 'There has not been the same eagerness for the Russian as was shown for the Turkish Loan, but the applications are of a bona fide character.' And again, equally reassuringly, on the 5th:

> The Russian Loan is a decided success in spite of the opposition of the *Daily News* [the prominent Liberal organ] and other papers. The amount applied for in London and in the Continent is upwards of £15,000,000 and the closing price is ¾ 1 pm. We have specially requested Messrs Rothschild to attend to your application, and have reason to believe you will receive an allotment of nearly the whole amount applied for.

Three weeks later, there arrived another offer difficult to refuse:

> We beg to enclose a prospectus of an issue of Bonds for the Lausanne & Fribourg Rwy, forwarded by the Canton of Fribourg, which will be published in the newspapers tomorrow morning. We had £100,000 or a Third of the whole issue placed in our hands privately this afternoon, all of which we have taken for friends in London. The subscription List will be closed tomorrow at 3 o'clock. If you agree with us in thinking well of the security and should wish to engage in it please send us an early telegraph tomorrow stating the amount you desire to subscribe for.

With a certain Yorkshire caution, Fosters confined themselves to applying for £5,000, perhaps mindful of those legal gentlemen sharpening their pens.

From the point of view of Cazenove's, all this was sound and fruitful investment on behalf of an increasingly valued client. However, taking place more or less simultaneously, secret speculation by one of the firm's own clerks was quite another matter. The clipped minutes of the Committee for General Purposes for 16th January 1863 intimate at what was an all-too-familiar tale on the nineteenth-century Stock Exchange, though one that usually befell other firms:

> Letter read from P. Cazenove & Co saying that their late clerk James Woods had entered into numerous speculations with Mr Henry Bateman [a member] extending over a lengthened period without their knowledge or authority, and finding that at least one difference was settled by means of a cheque of theirs fraudulently obtained they begged the Committee would institute a thorough investigation.

Much complicated evidence then ensued, including details from Henry Cazenove and Peter Reid, the latter of whom 'said the clerks were never allowed to speculate, but if they ever wanted to make an investment the firm did it without charging any commission.' As to how these forbidden speculations had occurred, 'Woods deceived the head book keeper by making false entries to balance his frauds. Their clerk, Edwards, unfortunately lost his health. They had been robbed of £650.' Among others giving evidence was Bateman, who said 'he did not know that Woods was not authorised, he thought it was all done for Cazenove & Co, he could see very well now after the fact had occurred'. At this point the Committee stayed its hand, having been told by Henry Cazenove that further allegations were pending.

Three days later, when it met again, another letter was duly read from the firm: 'It stated that their chief clerk Henry Dore [a member, unlike Woods] had been engaged in speculative transactions in conjunction with their late clerk James Woods and also on his own separate account.' Dore was then summoned and he gave the names of members (five in all) with whom he had dealt. Over the following week, the Committee brought the case to its conclusion. Further evidence came from Reid, who stressed that 'when they found out that Dore had been speculating they pressed him for all particulars'. He added that although Dore 'had paid for stock with their money', that money 'was all restored, they had lost nothing by Dore'; and he went on: 'He [i.e. Dore] kept no books and disclosed the facts with considerable reluctance.' But even if he had not been reluctant to disclose these speculative transactions, which seem to have taken place over five years from 1857, Dore's fate would have been the same: expulsion. Thus the Committee decided on January 26th, as well as suspending for periods of three to six months most of the members who had dealt for him or Woods. Cazenove's itself was recognised as an entirely innocent party in what must have been a highly upsetting episode in the small, tightly-knit world of 52 Threadneedle Street.

Woods and Dore, however, would not have been the only small men to have succumbed to what by the mid-1860s was becoming, as hinted at in the Foster letters, an increasingly feverish, speculative climate. Various factors created this atmosphere, but probably the most important was the recent coming into existence of legislation permitting limited liability, of which the cornerstone was the Joint Stock Companies Act of 1856, subsequently codified in 1862. The upshot was a rapid growth in the number of new companies, with inevitably a fair number of them being floated on the London Stock Exchange. During the late 1850s and early 1860s some of this welcome business came the way of Cazenove's. Flotations for which the firm acted as broker included those of the Atlantic Royal Mail Steam Navigation Company, the Thames & Mersey Marine Insurance Company, the Commercial Copper Smelting Company, and the Bank of Hindustan, China & Japan. By the mid-1860s, when things were starting to overheat, the firm developed a series of connections with various institutions closely connected with the new issue market – institutions not all of equal worth and probity. There were, as in all overheated phases of the market, many rogue operators about, and Cazenove's at this stage did not always show the best judgement of men and matters.

An honourable exception was the International Financial Society, which was successfully established in 1863 as part of a wider phenomenon appearing during the 1860s boom: namely, in the words of the Society's historian, 'a new form of issuing house – the finance company, an English version of the continental investment bank'. Most of the IFS's board comprised merchant bankers, and its main focus in the 1860s was on promotions of foreign companies rather than domestic industrial. Its relationship with Cazenove's was close and continuous.

Altogether less happy was the firm's involvement by the mid-1860s in the intricate, enmeshing network of finance companies that came to centre around Overend, Gurney & Co. Gurneys was a long-established and, by tradition, infinitely respectable discount house, but it was now under new, highly imprudent management, a change with disastrous consequences not only for the house itself. Among the finance companies formed by the new management, with grandiose ambitions but flimsy finances, was the Contract Corporation, for which Cazenove's acted as brokers. One of its subsidiaries was Smith, Knight & Co, a contracting firm with on paper a capital of £4 million divided into 80,000 shares of £50 each. Of these, however, only 20,000 shares were subscribed, and the directors stated in the prospectus in 1863 that they did not contemplate calling up more than £10 a share. Therefore, £4 million of theoretical capital would bring in initially only £200,000 in hard cash. Again, Cazenove's were the brokers. Another company in this connection was the high-sounding Bank of London, founded in 1855 and by the mid-1860s the cause of much bullish but ill-founded speculation. It was its building in Threadneedle Street that provided Cazenove's with an office, and Philip was sufficiently enamoured not only to quote the shares in lists such as that of December 1859 but also to make it one of the firm's bankers. Perhaps he was unaware of how intimately involved the Bank of London was in the whole Overend Gurney scheme of things, but if so his eyes were soon to be opened.

Prior to the inevitable crash, the years 1863 to 1865 were particularly active in the London capital market, even though not each issue went to the entire satisfaction of its promoters. As it happens, we have for these years some fairly good documentation for a handful of flotations on whose behalf Cazenove's acted as broker. Together they give a good idea not only of the type of issue with which the firm associated itself in this period but also something of the perennial complexity and problems involved, from a stockbroking point of view, in the new issue business as a whole. Indeed, many brokers tended to eschew such business (profitable though it might be), for reasons that the *Statist* eloquently explained some years later:

> They prefer good steady everyday work which involves no special responsibility and only a reasonable amount of brain labour. To turn over familiar stocks like Trunks or Eries by the thousand day by day and week by week is the ideal existence of a prosperous broker. His morning letters and his afternoon cables are quite excitement enough for him. Surrounded by a circle of well-to-do clients, who can be trusted to take up their stocks or meet their differences without a murmur on pay-day, he is happy in his small world. From his office to the House, and from the House back to his office, is an ample round of existence for him. When he feels seedy or wants diversion he can have his Saturday to Monday at Brighton or the Isle of Wight. What could a well-endowed citizen wish for more? Such a man has no inherent love of novelty, and his predisposition is to suspect everything in the way of originality. Whatever might throw the big machine out of gear finds in him an avowedly prejudiced critic.

Thus, the *Statist* declared, 'company accoucheuring is not particularly popular in the House'. The partners of Cazenove's liked 'well-to-do clients' and weekend diversions as much as the next stockbroker, but it was greatly to their credit, then and later, that their horizons were much broader than those of most and they did *not* 'suspect everything in the way of originality'. It was an openness of mind that repaid them well, but inevitably it involved some hard knocks on the way.

The first of these flotations, putative as well as actual, involved the expansively-named Asia Minor Company, which in April 1863 applied to the Stock Exchange Committee for settlement and quotation of its shares. However, 'A letter addressed to the Committee signed by several members was read. It stated that, on the strength of the opinion of the Solicitor General, they had demanded that the company be wound up and their money returned. They requested that the consideration of the appointment of a settling day be deferred till they had received a reply.' Several then attended the Committee, including Henry Cazenove: 'Mr Cazenove said that one of the directors of the Bank of London asked his firm to be brokers for the company and they consented. There were several respectable names among the directors – but there were points on which they wanted explanations and could not get them. He understood that a manager of the company had taken 1,000 shares and borrowed the money. He was now in Asia Minor.' After another member had pointed out that in the articles of association 'the objects of the company were not those described in the prospectus', Henry added: 'Mr Mason, one of the directors, seemed to be a man of immense means. The company had not treated them [i.e. Cazenove's] properly and after the settlement they meant to withdraw.' Having heard the evidence, the Committee ordered that the shares 'be not marked' – a wise decision, because a few days later it was revealed that the directors had decided to wind up the company. Philip himself was called in to offer an explanation: 'He said they had received no satisfactory information, they understood the company was to be dissolved. Mr Joyce, who introduced the company to them, applied for 500 shares and they were all allotted to him.' And he added, with what perhaps was wry understatement: 'He supposed the directors would rather return the money than risk a Chancery suit.'

The following January the prospectus was published of the Australian & Eastern Navigation Company, a combination of three Liverpool shipping firms whose aim was to start a steamship line that would compete with the sailing ships that had hitherto dominated the Australian trade. There were 40,000 shares of £50 each to be issued and there were four brokers, two in Liverpool supplementing Cazenove's and Helbert & Wagg [subsequently Helbert, Wagg] in London. Allotment was made of 39,965 shares on 5th February 1864: just over 15,000 to directors, and the rest, in theory, to the public. Before allotment was complete, certain directors had bought through the company's brokers, mainly those in Liverpool, a total of 19,630 shares, and various partners of the directors had also bought shares. As a result the shares went up to 7 premium by February 4th, and the public clamoured for allotments. Not only the public clamoured: many Stock

Exchange bears now found themselves badly squeezed and facing acute difficulties. Consequently, 159 members sent in a memorial, 'praying the Committee not to grant a settling day on the score of the statements in the prospectus being incorrect and the shares being allotted in an exorbitant proportion to the directors, their relations, friends and dependants, and that certain shares being also tied up by conditions [i.e. not to sell], speculations were entered into to such an extent as to make the fulfilment of bargains impossible.'

During March the Committee attempted to cut what had become a veritable Gordian knot. Amidst a welter of detailed evidence that it took, Henry Cazenove related, in connection with the shares going to such a steep premium prior to allotment, 'that he had seen so much suffering and distress that he had told some of the directors if they did not do something to relieve it, his firm would withdraw from being brokers to the company'; while the next day, both he and his father stated that they had endeavoured to persuade the directors to put some of their shares on the market, Henry adding that he believed his persuasions had had some effect. For their part, the directors argued strongly to the Stock Exchange Committee that other shipowners had made a dead set against steamships, and that therefore it was necessary to 'make a price' in order to float the company. There may well have been some truth in the defence, though it is unlikely that they objected to the many shares that they had been allotted at par already being quoted at a substantial premium. Whatever the larger economic implications, the Committee declined to buy the directors' argument, and on March 21st it formally refused the request for a set-tling day, resolving that the mode of allotment had been 'highly objectionable'.

It was an episode that played a significant part in Stock Exchange history, for in its immediate aftermath the chairman of the Committee, F. L. Slous, successfully persuaded the majority of his colleagues, against the opposition of S. H. de Zoete, to impose a ban on dealings in the market prior to allotment. The long-serving secretary to the Committee, Francis Levien, later recorded the aftermath:

It soon became apparent that the view taken by Mr de Zoete was a correct one, for the attempted restriction proved worse than useless. Some of the dealers [i.e. jobbers] saw that by offering facilities for indulging in the proscribed dealings, they had an opportunity of creating business of so profitable a nature as to enable them to disregard the risk of losses through bad debts irrecoverable under the rules. The result proved that they were right. Large sums were made, and the object chiefly aimed at by the Committee – namely, an efficacious check to the tricks of the company promoters – was defeated.

And as Levien added, those members who had obeyed the new rules, and in so doing had turned down business, naturally lost patience, with the result that, in the spring of 1865, the Committee was forced to lift the ban. For many years thereafter there would be no further attempt to clamp down on pre-allotment dealings, which, in accordance with the cardinal principle of the inviolability of the bargain, were held to be 'good' even though, by definition, a special settling day could not be granted until after allotment. Nor was this surprising: dealing before allotment was undoubtedly a valuable source of income to many members, *caveat emptor* remained the underlying philosophy of the markets, and no annually-elected governing body was going to tamper a second time in that particular area, at least until the general climate of opinion in the House and elsewhere had much changed.

Early in 1865, Cazenove's was involved at an early stage in the construction of London's underground, acting as joint brokers (with George Seymour & Co) for the issue made by the Metropolitan District Railway Company. No documentation survives about the precise role that the firm played in the flotation, but presumably it would have had an early sight of the prospectus, which described how the proposed line was to run 'from Kensington, through Brompton, Belgravia, Westminster, along the Thames Embankment, skirting the Strand to Cannon Street, City'. The prospectus waxed strong about the project's financial prospects:

> The existing Metropolitan Railway from Paddington to Farringdon Street has been open two years, and although it is still incomplete and the traffic imperfectly developed, pays four per Cent dividend, and its shares are at a premium of £30 per £100 . . . It is intended to proceed vigorously with the immediate construction of the portion of the line between Westminster Station and Cannon Street, so that it may be opened to the public contemporaneously with the Thames Embankment . . . It must be remembered that this line will practically enjoy the advantage, which is possessed by few others, of being protected against any competition.

These were plausible hopes, but in practice the response to the issue was rather sluggish, especially once it became clear that construction costs were significantly exceeding original estimates. Nevertheless, the line was eventually built, and in years to come the Forsytes would be able to travel with ease and gratifying cheapness from their homes in Belgravia to their company meetings in the City.

Similarly subterranean was the new issue made in the summer of 1865 by the Metropolitan Sewage & Essex Reclamation Company. In August the

Committee considered the settling of the shares, of which 17,395 had been applied for but only 15,940 allotted; of these, 10,000 had been given to eight persons connected with either the company or the International Financial Association. In person, Henry Cazenove defended his firm's role as brokers to the issue: 'As for the allotment, the brokers had nothing to do with it. It was made by the International Financial Society.' Presumably there was a connection, though he did not mention it, between the Society and the International Financial Association. And Henry added, about the narrowly-spread allotment of 10,000 shares, that 'surely it must be admitted that it was to responsible parties'. The Committee allowed the settlement, but in its minutes there was a sequel to the episode, one not unlike the 'Australian & Eastern' saga of the previous year, with its cornered bears and sub-sequent attempts to redress the situation. It now came to the Committee's attention because of a written complaint lodged against Cazenove's by a member, Robert Baily:

> About three weeks since, Messrs Bristowe Bros [an important firm of jobbers] were deputed by Messrs Cazenove & Co to compromise The Metropolis Sewage Company's dealing with the jobbers in the House, and to supply any such, who furnished their names, with whatever shares they subscribed for at 5 pm.
>
> Messrs Bristowe asked him – Mr Baily – how many he required, to which he replied, '35 shares', and his name was put down for that amount. Two days afterwards he asked Mr Henry Cazenove to make his number 50 shares, wishing to have 15 to protect his list; stating that the 35 he had already put his name down for were for a bear, a member of the House, who wished to buy back his shares through him, Baily. Thereupon Mr Cazenove struck his name off the list, and on his calling upon Mr Cazenove the next day at his office to represent the injustice of the case, Mr Cazenove said he should not have the shares because he [i.e. Baily] was not a bear himself.

Inevitably, the parties concerned were requested to attend:

> Mr Cazenove detailed the instructions given to him by Mr Bate of the International Financial Association to supply such jobbers who had been 'caught out' in making prices [i.e. during pre-allotment dealing], with shares at 5 premium, and said that he, Cazenove, accordingly told Mr Bristowe to make out a list. A list for 1,300 shares was thereupon sent in, and Mr Baily's name was on it. On the same day, Mr Baily spoke to him, and having said he had not sold a bear, he, Cazenove, told him that he was not one of the parties entitled to have the shares, and his name was consequently struck out.

Mr Baily said that he went to Messrs Cazenove's office on the day following that on which the list was made out.

Mr Cazenove insisted that it was on the same day, and that when he told Mr Baily that he was not authorised to let him have the shares, Mr Baily made no objection.

Bristowe then corroborated Henry's account, but by five votes to four the Committee decided that Baily was entitled to the 35 shares (if not the 50) claimed of Cazenove's at 5 premium. In fraught circumstances like these, caused as much as anything by an inequitable allotment, it was not an easy life acting as the honest broker.

The truth of this was forcibly confirmed within weeks. The flotation in the summer of 1865 of the Peruvian Railway Company, with Cazenove's and George Seymour & Co again sharing broking duties, was from the first a disreputable affair. Behind the new company, and calling all the shots, stood a recently-formed, inadequately-financed concern called the International Contract Company, whose theoretical purpose in life was to construct railways and participate in their financing. In this case, the ICC took participation to an excess: subscriptions were invited for 66,890 shares; over 120,000 were applied for, but only 53,400 were allotted; and of these, 47,148 went to the ICC. Moreover, not content with these, it then bought over 6,000 shares in the market, leaving everyone else with barely 100 shares between them. Hardly surprisingly, the shares soon went to a premium of almost £10, with many jobbers being unable to obtain them and thus fulfil their commitments to sell. At this point, under considerable jobbing pressure, the two broking firms intervened and, as it subsequently emerged before the Committee, told the company at the end of August that unless 'a liberal supply of shares came to market' they would withdraw their names from the issue. In front of the Committee, Henry Cazenove stressed that the allotment had been made at the office of the company, before strongly defending his own role in making terms between the company and the jobbers.

> There was no compromise in the matter – the case was precisely the same as that of the Metropolis Sewage Co. Mr Pickering [the managing director] allowed the shares a matter of liberality, he, Cazenove, having explained that there was no vindictive feeling in the case, and that it was better to be on good terms with the jobbers . . . He [i.e. Cazenove] had acted throughout from motives of pure good nature, Barry [one of the jobbers] having come and pleaded 'ad misericordiam' . . .

Henry also 'narrated the circumstances under which he became one of the brokers to the company, saying that as there were ill-natured remarks made on the subject, he wished it to be known that his firm received £2,500, the same amount as that received by Messrs Seymour & Co and by each of the two firms of solicitors employed by the company.' In the event, the jobbers received their shares at the prices at which they had previously sold. As for the Peruvian Railway Company itself, by April 1867 it had been wound up and creditors were being invited to put in their claims to the liquidator at 16 Tokenhouse Yard, future premises of Cazenove's.

Many other ventures, including the Bank of London, had by then already hit the buffers, for on 10th May 1866 there came the dramatic news that the house of Overend, Gurney & Co had closed its doors. And, 'with the fall of the institution which next to the Bank of England was the mainstay of British credit', as one historian was to put it, 'the whole brood of finance and contracting companies were swept into the court of chancery'. The extent of Overend Gurney's failure was a colossal £5 million, so that by May 12th not only had the Bank of England raised its rate to 10 per cent, but the Bank Act itself had been suspended – 'a shock', according to *The Times*, 'that would be felt in the remotest corners of the Kingdom'.

Nowhere, however, was the shock felt more than in Capel Court, where the mood was black and several firms went under. Cazenove's itself does not seem to have been directly affected, but clearly this was the end of the firm's relationship with the various appendages of Overend Gurney. In fact, the worst phase of the crisis passed surprisingly quickly, though as *The Times* again remarked, in a retrospective piece: 'For some months after the panic, English credit fell into entire disrepute on the Continent.' That credit would recover, and the nineteenth-century City would again continue to flourish and expand, but undeniably the Overend Gurney collapse marked the end of the first, indiscriminate phase of the age of limited liability.

Irrespective of the occasional serious crisis, such as that of 1866, it was clear by this time that the central purpose of the London market had undergone a fundamental change since the eighteenth century. Morgan and Thomas, the historians of the Stock Exchange, offer a succinct perspective, though the precise numbers remain a matter of some debate:

By the mid 1850s British overseas investments were probably rather over £200 million; during the next twenty years they increased more than five-fold. It was this great upsurge of foreign lending in the third quarter of the nineteenth century which made London the undisputed financial centre of the world, and brought a vast increase in business to the Stock Exchange. Between 1860 and 1876 more than a hundred and fifty foreign government loans were issued in London with a nominal value of more than £720 million.

During the late 1860s and early 1870s, a particularly prime area for these burgeoning foreign loans was South and Central America, and the relatively new (in London at least) merchant banking house of Bischoffsheim & Goldschmidt was especially to the fore in placing a series of loans for states there. Broker on occasion to these often impecunious states was Cazenove's, performing a well-paid but risky role that was potentially open to criticism and misunderstanding.

The project for the construction of an inter-oceanic railway in Honduras, in the financing of which Cazenove's played only a minor part, had a particularly long and unhappy history of mismanagement and fraud. The issuing house was Bischoffsheim & Goldschmidt, which on behalf of the government of Honduras published in 1867 a prospectus for the issue in London and Paris of a loan equivalent to £1 million, P. Cazenove & Co acting as London brokers. The prospectus boldly claimed that the line would 'effect a saving of time, as compared with the Panama route, of not less than five days between the Atlantic and Pacific ports of the United States'; but the issue itself was received with, in the words of one commentator, 'perfect indifference and profound contempt', and the public applied for only £48,000. In 1869 the Honduras government tried again in Paris, but with little more success, and then in 1870 again in London, where Bischoffsheim & Goldschmidt issued a prospectus for a loan of £2.5 million. Once again, Cazenove's were named as brokers. It was third time unlucky, because within days the Franco-Prussian war had broken out, and it proved impossible to place the issue as planned, although extraordinary efforts were made to do so. It was later said that 'between fifty and one hundred people were in the market making prices in the stock, and were dealing with each other and the brokers all round'. Indeed, one jobber bought and sold the entire loan once over. Whether Cazenove's was involved in this phase is not clear. Despite all this, there was yet one more effort made, and it came about when a resourceful engineer, James Brunlees, persuaded the Honduras government and its contractors to convert the projected railway into a so-called 'ship railway', by which ocean-going ships would be raised from the sea by hydraulic lifts, transported across the Isthmus on fifteen parallel tracks that would carry a giant cradle, and slid into the water on the other side. This new and fantastic scheme (in which Cazenove's probably was not concerned) came to the market in May 1872; but it was so comprehensively criticised – not only by the press, but also by the recently-founded Council of Foreign Bondholders – that it was soon abandoned.

Even more minor, but worth recording, is the part that the firm played in the more or less concurrent 'San Domingo' scandal. The key figure, with whom Cazenove's had little or nothing to do, was the greedy and unscrupulous Edward Harzberg Hartmont, who was Special Commissioner for the government of the Republic of San Domingo, and who was contracted to pay the proceeds of the flotation, after expenses, to that government. Working on his behalf was the highly reputable merchant firm of Peter Lawson & Co, which in July 1869 issued a prospectus for a 6% loan of £757,000 for San Domingo. Brokers to the issue were Mullens, Marshall & Co, long-standing brokers to the British government. The loan, however, was badly received, and by late October only £179,000 had been subscribed, over half by Lawsons themselves. Not long afterwards, an appeal for help was made to 52 Threadneedle Street. Several years later, in front of a Parliamentary Select Committee in April 1875, Henry Cazenove told how his firm had become involved. The evidence is interesting in itself, as an early example of a broking house in effect forming a syndicate to carry through a large-scale and delicate operation, while it also affords the opportunity of hearing directly the voice of Henry himself:

> Your firm, I believe, have had large experience on the Stock Exchange in transactions relating to loans and other matters? – Yes.
>
> Had you cognisance of this San Domingo Loan of 1869 at all? – Not originally.
>
> Were you employed to effect a sale for the disposal of the San Domingo bonds? – Yes, we were. About December 1869 or January 1870, Mr Sharp, solicitor to Messrs Peter Lawson & Son, asked us whether, in our capacity of brokers, we could effect an arrangement for the disposal of about half a million nominal of San Domingo Six per Cent Bonds. We looked into the matter, and put ourselves in communication with several of our friends and clients. After a considerable amount of discussion, and a great deal of time being occupied, we finally brought together at the office of one of our clients, Messrs J. S. Morgan & Co, all the parties, and put them in direct correspondence with each other.

The details of the resulting agreement, reached after several meetings and dated 31st January 1870, were then read out and confirmed by Henry. They showed the buying syndicate to be fivefold: Bischoffsheim & Goldschmidt; the Anglo-American houses of J. S. Morgan & Co and Morton Rose & Co; Charles Morrison, a City financier; and the London merchant banker Julius Beer. The questioning continued:

> You do not object to your commission being stated, do you? – Not the least in the world. I am much obliged to you for the suggestion.

'On the acceptance and ratification of the contract by the parties thereto, Messrs Peter Lawson & Son shall pay to Messrs P. Cazenove & Co the sum of £2,000 as commission on the transaction. This commission may, at the option of Messrs Peter Lawson & Son, be paid in cash or in bonds of the loan, reckoning each bond of £100 as £60 cash.' – That commission was afterwards paid us in bonds.

I believe it was a very troublesome transaction to you? – It took a great deal of our time, and of course time is money with us; nearly six weeks. It would be the ordinary usual commission, would it? – For such a transaction as that it is a lump sum by a mutual agreement to be made between the parties; what they consider your services are worth.

Notwithstanding Henry's rather tart reply, it does not seem to have been an extravagant commission for the services provided. Moreover, Lawsons must have been satisfied, for between February and May Cazenove's sold on that firm's behalf some £70,000 of the bonds for which it had originally subscribed. It was not the easiest of tasks, for as Henry recalled, 'just about that time there was a little excitement in the market, caused by the idea that San Domingo was going to be annexed to the United States'. Overall, however, the efforts of Cazenove's availed the young republic little for, according to a statement to the Select Committee prepared by Hartmont, only £50,000 ever reached San Domingo directly. A total of £176,700 was used to make the first six half-yearly service payments, and the rest seems to have disappeared in the hands of Hartmont. The loan itself went into default in January 1873.

From these and also from other episodes in no way involving Cazenove's, it was abundantly clear by the mid-1870s that there was something wrong – in the eyes of most outsiders at least – about the whole process of issuing foreign loans on the London market. Following Parliamentary pressure, the result was the Select Committee on Loans to Foreign States, which gathered its evidence in the course of 1875. Henry Cazenove appeared twice, first to relate his firm's part in the San Domingo story, then to offer his more general thoughts on the subject of such loans. On the second occasion, many of the exchanges focused on the undesirability or otherwise of the continuing norm of pre-allotment dealings. Henry did not deny that the effects of such dealings were sometimes pernicious, nor indeed that the public had 'lost a great deal of money in the five or six loans that this Select Committee have investigated', but he argued that taken as a whole they were beneficial and even necessary. In particular, he instanced the two French loans which had been issued after the Franco-Prussian war to provide funds for the payment of the indemnity to Germany. The amounts were large and, because of their size, each loan was handled by a syndicate of bankers in Paris, London and Germany, who skilfully 'worked up' the market price to a premium of about one per cent. Henry was insistent that this operation would certainly not have been successful if there had been no dealings before allotment: 'Day by day the Loan grew in favour, and people beginning to see that it would be very largely applied for, bought in the market, and gave a higher price than the price it was offered at; as one talked to the other, so the feeling of success pervaded everyone, and the subscription became enormous in consequence.'

About another much-touted remedy, Henry was not merely sceptical but positively hostile, namely towards the suggestion that, in his own words, 'the public should be made better acquainted than they are with the contracts, that they should be published in the prospectus':

> With that I do not hold at all. It is a matter of impossibility that a mercantile firm should publish in the prospectus all their contracts and all that concern themselves alone. Very likely the foreign government itself would interfere to prevent it; but as regards the contractors, although they might not have anything to conceal, they would not be willing to make the contracts public.
>
> You mean the contracts between themselves and the Government ought not to be made public? – Certainly not . . . I do not admit that the affairs of a Government and a contractor, if honestly and properly arranged together, should be made public to the public. I do not see why they should be.

Henry was, however, prepared to suggest two specific reforms. One was that prior to the Committee considering an application for settlement and quotation, advertisements should appear in the press for a week announcing the impending decision, so that the public should have a better chance to express any grievances or reservations. As he explained, 'at present notice is given by the Stock Exchange Committee, but only to their own members'. For his other suggestion, he first put forward the notion that the contractors themselves should come before the Committee instead of the broker doing so, but then discounted it on the grounds that they would refuse to do so. As he revealingly put it, 'questions might be asked, especially where a body of men are assembled, which gentlemen of high position would not choose to answer'. So, instead, Henry more modestly suggested that, 'if a statutory declaration or notarial certificate is given in to the Committee' rather than 'the simply formal letter that has hitherto been given', that 'would be a much stronger and more decided case of proof' about the truth of the details submitted by the contractor. However, he characteristically added when asked if he really had such great faith in statutory declarations: 'Well, I have greater faith in them than in simple letters; although, perhaps, if what is not the case is told in the latter, what is not the case might be put down in the former.'

Henry's evidence as a whole was eminently quotable, but perhaps one should end with a sequence that brought into question the very concept of a regulated market, at least in terms of the new issue process:

> What do you consider the use of giving settlement and quotation at all; why should not every kind of stock have of itself settlement and quotation? – I can see no reason why it should not, except of course, that you would then have no protection whatever. It may be urged that the Stock Exchange Committee have given no protection whatever, and that it has been proved that they have not; and I think it very likely that is the case, and if it was an understood matter that the Stock Exchange was, as it were, to be thrown open, and that everything brought out might be dealt in and quoted, and that the Stock Exchange Committee had not one iota, either of authority or responsibility, I do not see why it should not be so.

> Does not the present system lead people to suppose that they have a protection when they have not? – It does not lead people in the City to suppose it; it leads the outside public perhaps to suppose it.

> The burden of these things does not fall on gentlemen in the City; it falls on curates and old ladies, does it not? – I have known it fall sometimes on the gentlemen in the City; they do not always get off.

Deal honestly and look after yourself – it was a robust, highly practical philosophy to which Henry Cazenove and the great majority of his fellow-members in Capel Court fully and unashamedly subscribed.

The trend of opinion elsewhere, however, was moving in the other, more interventionist direction. The Select Committee of 1875 led within two years to a full-blown Royal Commission on the Stock Exchange, which reported in 1878. This latter body made much of what it regarded as the pernicious practice of making 'false' markets and thereby creating artificial premiums, and it trained its heaviest guns against the pre-allotment dealings that permitted, even encouraged, this practice. It argued that if such dealings were permanently abolished, it would be far harder for fraudulent loans and companies to come successfully (from their contractors' point of view) to the market. It was a wholly cogent argument, supplemented by various specific suggestions about how the Committee might improve the quality of its supervisory function, yet for the time being the fortress that was the Victorian Stock Exchange was able to continue repelling these and like-minded invaders. It did so partly because City opinion as a whole – supported by an influential minority outside – was firmly on its side. The words of the *Economist*, the most respected organ of the financial world, were entirely typical in this respect. Addressing itself in March 1877 to the inquiry likely to be undertaken by a Royal Commission, it strongly condemned the frauds exposed by the work of the Select Committee, but went on: 'The more this market is left to itself, the better for the dealers in it, for each will be responsible for his own acts only. And the better for the public too, for then they will not be, as now, misled by trust in unreal help and by the belief that, as someone else is taking care of them, they need take less care of themselves.' *Those* were the standards of the age, and the men who lived in that age must be judged by them, not those of a later, altogether unimaginable century.

Meanwhile, significant changes were taking place at 52 Threadneedle Street. As we have seen, Philip's day-to-day involvement probably diminished during the 1860s, and in 1873 he formally retired from business, though remaining titular head of the firm. Thereafter his main connection with the City was probably through his work on behalf of the Council of Foreign Bondholders, of which he had become a member in 1869. Designed to protect the interests of individual holders of foreign bonds in default, it was to have a long and interesting life ahead of it. Otherwise, Philip continued as before to devote the greater part of his time, while his energies remained, to the many charities and good works so close to his heart.

With Philip retired, there were three partners to carry on the activities of his firm. One was George John Coulson, who became a partner on Philip's retirement. Apart from the facts that he was admitted in February 1866 as authorised clerk to Cazenove's (probably when in his forties) and became a member the following month, and that he lived at Forest Hill, we know very little about him. The other two partners remained Peter Reid and Henry Cazenove. It is likely that, with Henry increasingly out of town, much of the burden of day-to-day responsibility fell on Reid's very capable shoulders, even though it is clear enough that overall Henry remained the pivotal figure. The new focus for Henry was a country house near Aylesbury in Buckinghamshire known as 'Lilies': destroyed a few years earlier by fire, it was rebuilt by him when he acquired the property in the mid-1860s. He entrusted the work to the well-known architect George Devey, and it was completed by 1870, Henry and his family moving in two years later. It was a magnificent house, surrounded by a well-timbered park and replete with stabling for twenty-two horses, and Henry threw himself into his new life with enthusiasm and much generosity. On his death in 1894, the obituary in the *Bucks Advertiser & Aylesbury News* conveyed something of its range and spirit:

> The poor of the parish, his servants, his tenants, the neighbouring farmers, the local tradesman, with all these he was quite as much a favourite as with any of the county magistrates. Although most attentive to his duties as landlord and magistrate, and taking great interest in philanthropic institutions, such as the Aylesbury Infirmary, he entered with thorough zest into lighter matters, such as farmers' dinners after Agricultural Shows, &c, where his genial presence was always most welcome. He was also prominent in the hunting field, and greatly enjoyed that truly national sport. Of his open-handed liberality to the poor, to churches, to hospitals, and to charitable institutions of every kind, he always spoke with the utmost modesty. He had been brought up, he said, to these ideas of duty, and was simply acting as his father's son.

In short, Henry Cazenove was a Tory country squire of the old and best school, even though he was 'first generation' in that way of life. It was, in its way, a remarkable achievement to combine that role with being a powerful, much respected member of the turbulent, on occasion even cut-throat, London Stock Exchange.

In that institution itself, the rapid development of communications during these years was further expanding both the range and the quantity of business. As early as 1853 there had been direct telegraphic communication with Paris, while in 1866 the successful laying of the first transatlantic cable meant that henceforth there could be a market in London in American stocks based on that day's New York prices. The following year saw the invention in America of the ticker-tape teleprinting machine, able to make prices and other news almost instantly available to the financial community; and from 1872 the Exchange Telegraph Company was allowed to collect up-to-the-minute prices from the floor of the House and to send them out on the tape to subscribers, which included banks and other outside institutions as well as member firms. Then of course there was the telephone, which met with a certain initial resistance in the City, but ultimately had advantages that could not be gainsaid, whatever the innate preference for talking with someone face-to-face. By 1884 there were some 200 Stock Exchange firms connected, including the successor partnership to Cazenove's. Taken as a whole, all these changes led to a perceptible quickening of pace, greater mobility of capital, and the rapid development of highly sophisticated arbitrage dealing, taking advantage of often tiny price differentials around the world. The membership of the Stock Exchange grew inexorably (to over 2,500 by 1883), while no market flourished more than the American or

'Yankee' market, which after the House closed at four o'clock defied the weather by assembling outside in Shorter's Court for several more hours in order to continue dealing while New York was still open. No one yet talked about 'global trading', but in a sense it was happening a century before the term was invented.

Meanwhile, the basic routine of stockbroking life went on, and as ever its economic base was the day-to-day garnering of small but regular commissions. It was a reality well expressed in the 1869 edition of *Practical Hints for Investing Money*, a small treatise written by Francis Playford, himself a broker on the Stock Exchange. In it, he observed of the broker's commission that this was something

> . . . which the public should cheerfully pay to ensure for themselves the proper execution of the business with which they entrust him, which consists in seeing that all bargains made through his agency are effected at a fair price, exercising his experience in conducting transfers of property in a secure method, and taking care that none but legitimate documents are passed from seller to buyer – an operation which calls in many cases for an amount of shrewdness and experience that can only be gained by long and regular training from early youth.

Playford then added pointedly:

> We do not make this observation in disparagement of more highly-educated men, who have attended our colleges and universities, and entered the business at a later period of life – for they may be, and some of them are, equally sound and judicious Brokers. The fact, however, is beyond dispute, that a great number of our present Brokers most thoroughly conversant with the details of the business and most reputed on the Stock Exchange, have entered as clerks in Stock-brokers' offices at very early ages.

As far as remuneration itself was concerned, the author not only stressed the preponderance of 'small commissions that give an immense deal of trouble with but little reward', but also went on:

> Let it be observed, moreover, that in office-expenses and clerks' salaries, many Stockbrokers expend upwards of £1,000 per annum – some few [including probably Cazenove's] even expending twice or thrice that amount – though a moiety of the sum mentioned would suffice for the majority.

And Playford concluded: 'In fact, few Brokers have ever been known to amass fortunes, though most of them, with a moderately good connexion, make fair incomes, while there are of course many who hardly cover their office-expenditure.'

To judge by the life-style at Lilies, the business activities of P. Cazenove & Co probably did continue to cover expenses. Fortunately, there is the correspondence with John Foster to shed further valuable light on these activities; and it is clear from reading it that, although ultimately an executant, a stockbroking firm of the period like Cazenove's could not afford to ignore the advice-giving and information-giving functions if it was to generate adequate commission. A letter of December 1868 (written, as usual at this time, by Coulson) was fairly typical:

> We have just completed the Sale of a large amount of Metropolitan District Railway Stock at the low figure of 61 ex div. The Sale has been distributed amongst our own clients who think well of it at that price & there is a sum still of £30,000 – if you should care to have it . . . Part of the line will be open for traffic this week, and its future is thought very promising.

Nevertheless, the firm was scrupulous about what it could or could not offer advice. This particularly applied, as shown by a letter of May 1869, to American railroad securities, which by this time were starting to become the great speculative 'counters' for the London stock market as a whole:

> Erie shares opened this morning 19½ to 20½ & close 19 to 19½. They have not been so low as this for some time & at the price of your present holdings it would seem the proper period for you to average [i.e. buy more at the lower price]. We are not in possession of any information however to guide you, & the security as you are aware is so very speculative & open to so many influences that one cannot exercise any judgement.

The firm was similarly honest in April 1870 about another foreign railway in which Fosters was interested:

> We cannot give you any definite information respecting the coming dividend in Lombard & Venetian shares but it is very currently rumoured that instead of 13 pCt paid last year the amount this year will not exceed 5 pCt. The riddle will be solved at the meeting which will be held at Paris on the 28 inst. If we get any *reliable* information before then we shall give you the benefit of it.

However much a client might wish to be put on the inside track – in an era when the concept of 'insider dealing' was hardly formulated, let alone censured – Cazenove's had the good sense never to forget that precipitate or misleading information was worse than useless.

The year 1870 itself was to be a traumatic one, though it began well enough in Capel Court, as Coulson reported to Fosters on January 3rd: 'The new year opens with considerable animation in our Markets and the prospect of a run of active business. The public are at last getting over the panic of '66 and taking fresh courage for both investment and speculation.' But by July the mood was very different, as the diplomatic difficulties between France and Prussia threatened to turn into full-scale war. 'We have been in a fine panic again today', Coulson wrote on the 11th. 'All parties here think it is only a question of time. Jealousies like the present must be ventilated sooner or later.' Two days later, however, and the markets were up: 'It was never reasonable that two such powers could fight on such a pretext.' But then, as the news from the continent worsened, came three terrible days, as successive despatches from Coulson reflected:

We have had a day of continuous panic. Yesterday we were all in the stirrings for peace. Today we have every ugly rumour that fact or fancy can create . . .

We have had numerous failures. Not of any amount but still large enough to be unpleasant . . .

The darkest gloom we are told is before daybreak, so we have only to keep up good cheer & await the turn of the tide . . .

With bank failures and suicides rife in the square mile, it was not a time for faint hearts. But mercifully, for the Stock Exchange if not for Napoleon III, the conflict itself proved much shorter than had been anticipated. A letter from Coulson on August 8th caught the more hopeful tone: 'It is now generally expected that the Continental War will not be of very long duration. We have rumours at the close of business today that the Prussians have concentrated their forces & that severe fighting is going on before Metz.' Showing a certain Bismarckian realism, the London market does not seem to have minded who won, so long as someone did and quickly.

From the early 1870s, the correspondence between Cazenove's and Fosters becomes more fragmentary (in terms of what survives); but in July 1871 there was an interesting letter from the London end, in effect about the mechanism to underwrite new issues that then obtained:

In reference to the £5,000 Northampton & Banbury Railway 5% Debenture Stock which you took in Syndicate. You have to apply for that amount of Stock in the ordinary way, but only such amount will be allotted to you, & all others in Syndicate, that the public have not applied for out of the £113,000 Stock. As the List closes on Wednesday, if we do not hear from you, we will make application & pay the deposit for you, the same as we do for ourselves.

In the event, Fosters was allotted £3,650 of stock, in effect as sub-underwriters taking their share of the 'stick'; while in terms of unloading that share, the syndicate was to be entirely in the hands of the International Financial Society until the end of August, 'when the real position & profit will be finally ascertained', Coulson assured the rather anxious Fosters. Similarly of wider interest was a letter that Cazenove's wrote in March 1873:

We think it a very favourable opportunity for the purchase of English Railway Stock which has been suddenly depressed & we have no doubt that it will be found much more by heavy bear operations than by any Sales on the part of the public, Speculators having taken a very gloomy view of the future & of the influences of the Coal, Iron & Labour questions . . .

It was an implicitly sharp distinction between market operators and the investing public at large, revealing also that Cazenove's seemed to think the latter influence the more important. Over the next decade we have only letters from Fosters and they are mostly of a very routine nature. Nevertheless, that advice from Cazenove's continued to be important was clearly demonstrated in April 1884: 'As we have some trust money to invest which must be invested in Preference or Debenture Stocks of Railways in this country or India, we shall be glad if you can recommend a sound 4 per cent at 102 to 4.' Fosters then suggested three possibilities, before concluding: 'Do you know anything better than these; and if not, which do you consider preferable?' A few days later the partnership of P. Cazenove & Co was wound up, but the connection with John Foster continued into the next phase of the firm's history.

Overall, however, setting aside foreign loans, the activities of Cazenove's are but sparsely documented from the late 1860s to the early 1880s, though it is clear that the valuable relationship with Barings persisted. Thus borrowing from this bank continued on a regular if not enormous scale, for example totalling about £138,000 for the year from May 1868. Similarly regular but not spectacular was the participation by Cazenove's in loans issued by Barings: in 1882 for instance, when the Russian 3% Loan for almost £9 million was floated, the brokers Campion Pawle & Co took £20,000, J & A Scrimgeour took £15,000, and Cazenove's was among a handful of brokers taking £10,000. Another lingering attachment, if of an altogether less weighty nature, was with the International Financial

Society. Following the financial crisis of 1866, the Society was a pale shadow of its former self; but from 1868 it not only made regular loans to Stock Exchange firms, including Cazenove's, but also through the auspices of Cazenove's regularly participated in new issue allotments. Moreover, in 1880 the Society received a series of proposals from its brokers: to buy for £20,000 the engineering works of Messrs May & Mountain of Birmingham, which it declined; to take debentures of the languishing London Financial Association, which it agreed to do to the extent of £150,000, with Cazenove's itself taking £50,000; and finally to take debentures of the Railway Debenture Trust, which again the Society agreed to, this time to the extent of £50,000. There must have been a residual association, for at the 1892 general meeting of the Society, one of the three shareholders nominated by the shareholders as a whole to liaise with the board was Henry Cazenove, by then long retired from active business.

In general, the firm was busy enough in this period on the new issue front. This was so not only in the high-profile area of foreign loans, although in addition to other activities there, it was Cazenove's who in May 1878 successfully acted on behalf of Rothschilds in persuading the Stock Exchange Committee to agree to the quotation of the United States Funded 4% Loan, which was already quoted on the New York Stock Exchange. However, it was in the sphere of railway issues that the firm now began to make something of a speciality, particularly of foreign railways, where there was still considerable scope for expansion. In the early 1870s the firm, in association with the American house of McCalmont Bros, was involved at least twice in issuing gold bonds of the Philadelphia & Reading Railroad Company, including in 1872 organising a syndicate that featured a £30,000 participation in them by the International Financial Society. These operations seem to have gone smoothly, but the role of new issue broker still remained a potentially invidious one, as the case in 1879 of the 8% first preference and 6% second preference £20 shares of the Mexican Railway Company clearly showed. On July 7th the Committee considered an application to mark these shares and, after examining the report of its Share and Loan department and other documents, summoned the broker, who was to find it tough going:

Mr Henry Cazenove said that the application originated from members of the House who had dealt largely in these particular shares, as well as in the ordinary shares already quoted in the List. Under these circumstances he undertook that the company should supply the Committee with full particulars, and he appeared, as the company's representative, to show that it stood before them as an old company, of sufficient importance for the quotation of the large number of dealings that had been, and would in all probability be, entered into. He should say that at least 5,000 shares had been dealt in since the papers were first deposited with Mr Slaughter [of the Share and Loan department]. There had been no attempt on the part of the directors to seek quotation for the purpose of getting rid of their property. He could not at the moment explain how it was that 50,598 shares only of the second portion of 60,000 shares had been distributed, nor say whether 35,500 odd of that amount were still in the hands of two holders. He would make enquiries on this point, and also as to other large holdings of the 8% shares.

Enquiries made, Henry reappeared on the 24th and 'repeated statements previously made by him, adding that since the matter had come before the Committee, 190 1st Preference shares and 126 2nd Preference shares had passed into fresh accounts.' Unconvinced, the Committee deferred further consideration for three months, but in December they did finally grant the application. Their doubts were perhaps not so surprising, given both the evidence and the fact that Mexican Railway ordinary shares were already long renowned as highly speculative counters. On the other hand, bankers to this new issue were Glyn, Mills, Currie & Co, while the company's directors included the eminent merchant banker Henry Hucks Gibbs. From a broking point of view, perhaps the moral was simply that in the new issue business one never could tell.

Pleasantly less controversial were the Indian Railway issues, with which the firm was now becoming especially associated as brokers. Probably the first was the issue in 1875 of £500,000 6% guaranteed stock of the splendidly-named His Highness the Nizam's State Railway Company. The railway, which connected the Great Indian Peninsula Railway to Hydera-bad, had been opened for traffic the previous year, and the prospectus emphasised that 'the State of H. H. the Nizam has, under many years of enlightened administration, become a highly prosperous and well ordered country'. The issuing house in this case was the Railway Share Trust Company, but in the summer of 1881 it was the houses of Rothschilds and Barings who acted jointly to float the £1 million issue of the Bengal Central Railway Company, employing Cazenove's as brokers. 'The Line', the prospectus explained, 'will traverse the rich and populous districts of Nuddea and Jessore, serving numerous important trade centres hitherto for the most part dependent on slow and uncertain communication by boat and bullock-cart.' The following year, the same historic issuing houses were to the fore, this time asking Cazenove's to share broking duties with Helbert, Wagg & Campbell, in the similarly-sized issue of the Bengal & North

Western Railway Company. Again, the prospectus entertained few doubts: 'Hitherto the trade of this extensive district has been chiefly carried on the rivers Gogra, Gunduk and Raptee – conveyance on which is so tedious, uncertain and costly that, in the opinion of the local authorities, the proposed railway will obtain a practical monopoly of the traffic.' The spread of civilisation and 'a practical monopoly': together they made an irresistible combination.

It was a proposition with which the firm's founding father would no doubt have agreed. Philip Cazenove had continued during the 1870s to pursue his many beneficent activities, but early in 1879 he fell ill and, 'after a year of weariness and languor, and the depression incident to his illness, he entered into the rest for which he yearned.' Philip died in his Clapham home on 20th January 1880, at the age of eighty-one. The funeral was held at St Mark's Church, Battersea Rise – 'one of the churches,' the *South London Press* reported, 'which Mr Cazenove was mainly instrumental in having built' – and as one would expect, 'the attendance was very large, the sacred edifice being almost filled'. The interment was in the family vault in Hornsey churchyard. The year after his death saw the consecration of St Michael's Church in Battersea, built as a joint memorial to Philip and the curate of Battersea, the Rev. H. B. Verdon, who had died in 1879. The entire cost was met by friends of the two men, and the noted architectural historian Goodhart-Rendel was subsequently to commend the church in the apposite phrase, 'everything very honest and thoughtful'.

But perhaps the last words about an extremely able businessman, who even after all his charitable activities left an estate worth about a quarter of a million pounds, should go to G. E. Cokayne, the chronicler of an interesting but little-known institution known as 'The Club of Nobody's Friends'. The club had been founded in 1800 by William Stevens, a hosier of Old Broad Street and notable philanthropist, and derived its title from the name of 'Nobody' by which Stevens called himself in his publications. There were at any one time some sixty members, comprising an equal number of church and laity, and by the mid-1870s its members included the Bishops of London, Rochester, Winchester and Lincoln, the Dean of York, the Lord Chief Justice, and many other worthies, including Henry Hucks Gibbs, who became vice-president in 1880. Philip himself was elected in 1872 and before his death was able to attend thirteen meetings, which were held at the Freemason's Tavern and included the passing of a loving cup. When Cokayne came in 1885 to write the club's history, he wrote of Philip in the warmest terms and stated that, with perhaps one exception, he had 'more nearly resembled the founder of this club than any other member'. Granted the membership of the club, past as well as present, it was a remarkable, even extraordinary tribute, but it was no more than a great man deserved.

If the death of Philip marked the end of an era in one sense, so in another did the decision by Henry relatively soon afterwards to retire from active business, though retaining his membership of the Stock Exchange. He was in his fifties, comfortably situated and with no need to make more money, and not unnaturally he preferred the life of a country gentleman to the bustle of Capel Court. It was also decided – and perhaps had been a long time before – that neither Reid nor Coulson would remain with the firm once Henry retired. Both were getting on in years and both likewise decided to retire from business, Peter Reid in later years achieving justifiable renown as the single-handed founder of the Hospital Convalescent Home at Swanley, Kent. It was characteristic of him that, as his obituary in the *Financial Times* was to put it in 1917, 'Mr Reid desired above all things that the home should be self-supporting in order to avoid any appeal for public support.' Henry and his partners retired at the end of April 1884, and the firm of P. Cazenove & Co was thus formally dissolved.

Waiting in the wings since at least the late 1870s, and through his person ensuring that the Cazenove presence would continue, was Philip's grandson Arthur Philip, son of Canon Arthur Philip Cazenove, who himself in 1856 had married a sister of Henry's wife. Canon Cazenove had been educated at Exeter College, Oxford and from 1859 was vicar of St Mark's, Reigate for thirty years, becoming Rural Dean of Reigate in 1879. His eldest son, Arthur Philip, born in 1857, likewise went to Exeter College and in July 1877 was admitted as an unauthorised clerk to P. Cazenove & Co. Two years later he was elected a Stock Exchange member and in 1880 was admitted as an authorised clerk to the family firm, henceforth able to deal on its behalf. He was still very young, and on 25th April 1884 the merchant banker Alban Gibbs wrote tellingly if somewhat inaccurately to his brother Vicary in New Zealand: 'Read and Cazenove retire from active business leaving things to their nephews &c. This is a bore.' There was in fact only one nephew – Arthur Philip – and it was obvious that much would depend, in terms of capital and connections as well as expertise and experience, on the '&c.'. As with Philip's predicament almost half-a-century earlier after the death of Menet, the decisive question was who would now form a new partnership with the young Cazenove.

CHAPTER FOUR

Careful consolidation
1884–1918

The Akroyd family originally came from Scandinavia, the name meaning 'a dweller in an oak clearing'. The first Akroyd to be connected with the Stock Exchange was John, who became a member in 1848. From 1865 he was in partnership with John Smithers in the stockbroking firm of Akroyd & Smithers, and during the early 1870s he took into partnership two of his sons, John and Swainson, who had become members in 1870 and 1872 respectively. Soon afterwards, a third son, Bayly, entered into a jobbing partnership with Alfred Smithers (younger brother of John), this firm being B. N. Akroyd & Smithers. There the mildly confusing situation remained for a few years, until in about 1879 John Smithers left and the broking firm took the title of Akroyd & Sons. It was this firm that at the end of April 1884 merged with P. Cazenove & Co, with the new firm henceforth calling itself Cazenove & Akroyds. John Akroyd senior now retired, and for almost the next twenty years the three sole partners in the firm were Arthur Philip Cazenove, John Bathurst Akroyd and Swainson Howden Akroyd.

History relates frustratingly little about the Akroyd brothers. They were in their thirties when they joined forces with Arthur Philip and seem to have been known to their friends and associates as 'Jack' and 'Swinny' respectively. They were brought up in South London, educated at Radley College, and as adults lived until the 1880s in the family home at first Croydon and then Broadwater Down, Tunbridge Wells. Like his brother Bayly, Swinny Akroyd played cricket for Surrey in the 1870s and was described by *Wisden Cricketers' Almanack* as 'a sound batsman with excellent style, and a good field anywhere'. He appeared twenty-three times for the county and scored 622 runs at an average of 15.55, not discreditable in the era before The Oval wicket became a batsman's paradise. Both he and Jack led somewhat peripatetic existences once they had left the family home, failing to put down roots in one place. Around the turn of the century Jack built a handsome residence in the modern style at Chalfont Park, Gerrard's Cross, and by 1909 he had moved to Birdingbury Hall, Rugby. Swinny's homes included 36 Portland Place; Wavendon House, Woburn Sands; and Thorpe Satchville, Melton Mowbray.

Overall, the firm impression of the two men is that they were keen sportsmen, congenial company and capable operators, if not perhaps from the first flight. They were more than adequately equipped to ensure that Cazenove's remained well above the reaches of mediocrity, even if the truly transforming take-off awaited a future generation of partners. Moreover, the Akroyds brought to 52 Threadneedle Street not only their experience and their connection, but also, just as importantly, their capital. There survives a balance sheet from August 1887 which shows their having contributed a sum of almost £60,000 between them, compared with Arthur Philip Cazenove's sum of less than £20,000. This latter figure, however, was supplemented by £12,000 provided between them by Henry Cazenove and Canon Cazenove. Taken as a whole, the new firm was thus amply supplied with working capital, granted the continuing low level of office expenses, and as well positioned to respond to the opportunities of the time as the energies and talents of the partners allowed.

If in the event the firm did not respond altogether brilliantly – if by no means poorly – that must have been due in some measure to the third of the partners, Arthur Philip himself. The probability is that he was very much a representative stockbroker of his period: genial, easy-going, and disinclined to desert a steady routine, whether mental or physical. He was a life-member of the MCC (inheriting a love of the game from his father and thus enjoying an affinity with his new partners); while after leaving the City, and before returning home to Cadogan Place, he would spend most of the afternoon in his West End club. It was not for nothing that (following the Russo-Japanese war) he was known as 'Port Arthur', and in general his presence seems to have been as comforting and comfortable as the name suggests. Yet at the same time he was also, unlike most late-Victorian or Edwardian stockbrokers, a genuinely pious man, who was a churchwarden at Holy Trinity in Sloane Street and a devoted friend of the London Orphan School, serving for many years as a prominent member of its board. He also possessed a certain original, even mischievous intelligence, even if it was rarely exercised in the stockbroking field. The story goes that shortly before the First World War, when his daughter was due to come out and he found himself temporarily low in funds, he resigned his membership of the prestigious Ranelagh Club and instead joined the Royal Zoological Society.

This action did not exactly make him the flavour of the month amongst his family, but in its way it was a telling practical joke directed against all the fuss of the London 'season'. Unassuming, solid, and certainly no fool, Arthur Philip Cazenove provided the vital element of ballast during what was in many ways a time of consolidation in the history of his family firm.

Britain's industrial supremacy began to be challenged, especially by Germany and the United States, during the three decades before the Great War, but for the City of London these were the halcyon years. Lying at the centre of the liberal and highly integrated international economy – an economy characterised by the freedom of its capital flows and to a large extent its trade flows – the City prospered as never before and perhaps never again. It was during this period the eldorado of the western world, attracting a large number of talented immigrants (from Ernest Cassel downwards) eager to employ its resources in the pursuit of individual fortune. Francis Hirst, a respected financial commentator and Edwardian editor of the *Economist*, tried to encapsulate what the City was:

> It is the greatest shop, the freest market for commodities, gold and securities, the greatest disposer of capital, the greatest dispenser of credit, but above and beyond, as well as by reason of all these marks of financial and commercial supremacy, it is the world's clearing house.

Hirst was writing in 1911, but his bucolic description was as applicable twenty or even thirty years earlier.

This is not to pretend that the square mile did not continue to have its alarums and excursions, not to mention its periodic crises. Indeed, the Baring crisis, which beset it in 1890, was arguably the most severe, at least in terms of its potential implications, of the entire nineteenth century. The City had been palpably overheating in the late 1880s, typified by the sudden rash that appeared at this time of investment trusts, one of which, the London and New York Investment Corporation, featured Jack Akroyd as a founder. It was also clear to perceptive observers that Barings was dangerously over-committed in the Argentine. No one, however, anticipated the depth or intensity of the crisis, memorable in the annals of the City, that was played out during November 1890. By Saturday the 15th, against a background of plunging markets and rising Bank Rate, the recently-established *Financial Times* was evoking what it could only call 'The Agony':

> The City is becoming enveloped deeper and deeper in a baleful, mysterious crisis. Day by day thick clouds gather over the Stock Markets,

and where they come from, and who is responsible for them, no one has a definite opinion. All who have financial interests at stake feel as if they were standing on the brink of a volcano which at any moment may open up and swallow them. This slow-killing agony has been going on now for about two months without coming to a head. The worst kind of fever would reach its climax in less time.

Succour, however, was at hand, for over the weekend it emerged that the Bank of England had arranged a guarantee fund to stand behind Barings, thereby solving the bank's acute liquidity problems. 'Saved' was the bald but graphic title of the *FT*'s profoundly relieved leader on the Monday, the paper declaring that, if Barings had gone under, 'what might have happened on the Stock Exchange is a prospect too fearful to contemplate', and that 'not a living man in the House has witnessed anything approaching the catastrophe which would have been inevitable'. A few weeks later the Chairman of the Stock Exchange presented Governor Lidderdale with an address of thanks, and among those who subscribed capital to the new limited company of Baring Brothers & Co that succeeded the old partnership was Cazenove & Akroyds.

The Stock Exchange inevitably suffered several sluggish spells in the ensuing years, including one in the immediate aftermath of the Baring trauma, but broadly speaking the trend until 1914 was ever onwards and upwards. Membership figures alone told their story, going up from 3,233 in 1890 to 5,567 by 1905, from which high point the total declined somewhat as a result of additional entrance qualifications. This new stringency had several causes, but well to the fore was the intense physical overcrowding in the House by the turn of the century, with square footage per member going down from 4.07 in 1885 (the year of a major extension) to 2.36 by 1902. Dominating this elusive space were the jobbers, who by the eve of the Great War divided themselves into some 600 firms, a figure all the more startling to modern eyes for being exclusive of the many one-man jobbing operations also in existence. The markets that these jobbers manned on behalf of some 300 broking firms, and ultimately a burgeoning investing-cum-speculating class in the outside world, were many and varied, but none during the 1890s was as busy or eventful as the so-called 'Kaffir Circus', which rose to a fever pitch of activity, spilling out onto Throgmorton Street for 'after hours' dealing, during the South African gold mining boom of 1895.

Inside, the atmosphere of the House remained a uniquely boisterous one. Paper balls continued to be thrown (often with unerring accuracy), 'butter slides' continued to be made, and the newspapers of unsuspecting readers (including that of Arthur Philip on at least one occasion) continued to be set alight. Wearily the late-Victorian and Edwardian Committee posted warning notices, or even made the occasional example of an offender, but to little effect: if newspapers were temporarily left unburnt, there were always coat-tails to turn to. It is almost impossible to exaggerate either the intense clubbishness of the Stock Exchange of this period or the unequivocally shared nature of its norms or code. For instance, a member who during the Boer War refused to guarantee the place of a clerk who had gone to fight found himself literally on the floor of the House being mercilessly assaulted. Soon afterwards, the press reported that a broker who had gone into the American market on the morning of Queen Victoria's death and asked the price of Milwaukees 'promptly got his hat smashed for daring to think of business'. In the 1890s a prominent Liberal sympathiser, A. L. Leon, who was a member of the London County Council as well as of the Stock Exchange, was forced to flee from a mob of howling jobbers on his first appearance in the House after having abetted Mrs Ormiston Chant's moralistic campaign against renewing the licence of the Empire Theatre, a favourite place of entertainment.

Yet beneath this shared code – muscular, patriotic and resolutely middle-brow – there lay the uncomfortable fact that ultimately it was each man for himself, and that in the event of failure there would probably be no way back. Nor was this an idle possibility, granted that the sheer weight of numbers alone made for an intensely competitive market-place. An average of over twenty members were declared defaulters each year, always by means of a dramatic ceremony in which the Stock Exchange 'waiters' or attendants brought down a hammer three times and then, amidst a deathly silence, read out the names of those who had been unable to 'comply with their bargains' and had therefore failed. The fear of failure was never more graphically described than by John Braithwaite of the brokers Foster & Braithwaite, in a letter to his father in 1911 at the height of their firm's troubles: 'It has been before my mind like a nightmare day and night more or less continuously for the last month and more – I have suffered it all mentally over and over again – when the hammer has gone in the House it has sounded like a knell in my ears – I have thought of the long list of our names and the awful staggering hush afterwards.' The Stock Exchange was no place for weak nerves, and it was little wonder that its residents tended to find relief in less than cerebral ways.

Yet whatever the intense and dramatic fluctuations in the House at large, it is probable that life in 52 Threadneedle Street during these years continued on an unambitious but more or less even tenor. It must have been a fairly profitable existence, to judge by not only what we know of the partners and their life-style, but also the surviving Profit and Loss account of

1887. This shows that over a six-week period the firm earned £5,104 in commission and interest (worth some £190,000 at present-day values), yet operating costs were only £255. It is also likely that the firm was not particularly affected one way or the other during the 1890s by the enormous speculative boom engendered by West Australian as well as South African gold mining securities: in 1892 it was employing three unauthorised clerks, in 1896 one authorised and one unauthorised clerk, and in 1901 one member-clerk and two unauthorised clerks, figures suggestive of considerable continuity of scale of operation. By the turn of the century there were probably not many more clients than the fifty or so listed in the 1887 account; as for the money-broking side of the business, the records of Barings suggest that this continued only in a relatively minor way. It is in this light that one should perhaps view a small but indicative anecdote dating from 1899. That year a fourteen-year-old was interviewed for the job of office boy, given some sums to do, and performed so well that he was told by Swinny Akroyd that he was 'too good for us'. The boy, however, insisted that he wanted the job and was eventually given it. His name was Albert Martin, and apparently his first task was the less than glamorous one of emptying the chamber pots kept by the Akroyds in the partners' room.

Meanwhile, the firm continued to deal on a regular basis for John Foster of Bradford. That this particular client still followed the market keenly is shown by a letter of February 1886:

> With reference to your Contract Note of the 9th for the sale of £3,000 East Argentine Ry Deb Stock for our Mr Herbert, will you have the Kindness to inform us how it was you could not obtain a better price than $106\frac{1}{4}$, as we notice that the only two transactions recorded in 'Wetenhall's' were done at $107\frac{1}{2}$ and 108?

A week later, with a satisfactory explanation presumably received, Fosters wrote again:

> Our Mr F. C. Foster desires to thank you for your telegram of this morning, but he does not feel disposed to sell Bombay & Baroda Stock under $152\frac{1}{2}$. Please wire if you can get that, also what you can buy three or four thousand New Zealand 4% Inscribed Stock at? Kindly wire at the same time the selling price of Great Northern Ry Ordy?

Towards the end of 1886 there took place the famously oversubscribed Guinness issue. Various members of the Foster family applied for shares, having been sent a prospectus and application forms by Cazenove's, but to judge by a letter of November 11th they seem to have fared as poorly as most people: 'As Mr Robert's Allotment of Guinness Deb Stock is so small, he thinks of disposing of it, will you please say what price you can obtain for it?' From all this it might appear that Fosters increasingly looked to its broker solely for information and execution, rather than advice as well. However, ten years later, in February 1896, a request suggests otherwise: 'Please wire in the morning price at which you could buy £1,100 N.Zealand 4% Ins Stk, or Victoria 4% Ins 1885, & say which of the two you would prefer.' Overall, the impression (from what is only a partially surviving correspondence) is that by this time Fosters thoroughly knew its way about the course, but that on occasion the firm still looked to Cazenove's for specific market guidance.

In general, the probability is that it was increasingly toward company finance and in particular new issue business that the firm turned – though by no means exclusively – during the late-Victorian and Edwardian epoch. This of course did not necessarily involve acting as broker to the company or government concerned. Instead, it could often involve participation in a syndicate. Such participation was often lucrative – especially granted the sometimes rather unscrupulous way in which these syndicates were operated – though was not invariably so. The syndicate arranged jointly by Rothschilds and Barings at the time of the flotation of the Manchester Ship Canal in July 1887 was a case in point: less than one-fifth of the £4 million issued was subscribed for by the public, almost entirely in and around Manchester; the £410,000 of unattractive preference shares landed on Cazenove's was second only to the £1,025,000 of shares picked up by the brokers to the issue, Greenwood & Co; and the payment of 1% commission for taking part in the syndicate, in this case amounting to £4,100, was thin compensation. By the 1890s it was becoming increasingly common practice (although not formally legalised until the Companies Act of 1900) to underwrite new industrial issues, which increasingly replaced the old syndicate methods. Thus, in 1895 at a Board of Trade inquiry into the Companies Acts, the prominent stockbroker H. Rokeby Price, giving evidence on behalf of the Stock Exchange Committee, categorically stated that 'many most profitable and useful undertakings have been established which, without underwriting, would not have been in existence'. Cazenove & Akroyds seems to have played a full part in underwriting as a whole, typified by a letter to the firm in 1895 from Rothschilds: 'The issue of the Brazilian Government 5% Loan having been successful, we have the pleasure of informing you that you are released from your liability with respect to the £40,000 underwritten by you.' The commission paid for this potential service was £800, at a relatively modest rate of 2% befitting the relatively safe nature of the issue.

As for the role of actual broker or co-broker to new issues, Cazenove & Akroyds maintained the firm's tradition, established since the 1850s, of being well to the fore, though in no sense staking a claim as market leader. During the three decades before the Great War it was involved in this sense in at least fifty flotations on the London Stock Exchange and probably many more. They ranged from major issues like Burma Railway's £1.25 million 3% debenture stock in 1902 or the City of Bahia's £1.6 million 5% loan in 1913 to more modest affairs like Hammersmith Distillery's offer in 1889 of 20,000 ordinary shares of £1. Breweries and suchlike were a growth area in terms of coming to the market, hitherto having usually been in private ownership; and in 1895 and then 1896 the firm acted on behalf of Cannon Brewery, whose managing director, William Musgrave Wroughton, had married one of Henry Cazenove's daughters. The firm in 1903 also represented a small company of port wine shippers, Martinez Gassiot, in which it enjoyed a certain financial interest. It was indicative that in this case Cazenove's underwrote the shares, something for which it was increasingly willing to take the responsibility for arranging when it acted as brokers to an issue, though often farming out a large part of the sub-underwriting and thus risk to other firms or individuals. The *Economist* in 1913 described who in general such people might be:

> There are brokers and jobbers always on the look-out for cheap stock; there are market dealers, not only willing, but anxious, for stocks likely to stimulate business . . . Amongst the brokers' clients will be found banks, insurance companies, trusts, and financial houses, besides the smaller individual customers, and a little army of provincial Stock Exchange members who have ready channels for the absorption of good stock at relatively low figures. Foreign banking houses, too, possess keen appetites for such things.

Contacts were everything, and evidence suggests that Cazenove & Akroyds was as adept as anyone at utilising them in this key area of the new issue business.

Within this field, if some brokers (like Greenwoods) were known as railway brokers, the particular speciality of Cazenove's in these years was to act as what one might call armament brokers. This role began in 1888 when the firm was co-broker (but sole representative before the Committee) to an issue of shares, sponsored by Rothschilds, in the Naval Construction and Armaments Company based at Barrow. A piece of correspondence to Barings, dated 20th February 1888, shows how keen Cazenove's was to ensure that the issue would be fully subscribed, while avoiding the still illegal procedure of making an actual underwriting contract: 'We have arranged for you to receive a firm allotment of 5000 shares . . . It is understood that in order to secure this allotment you will make an application for a larger number of shares if required by Messrs Rothschild.' Nine years later the company was taken over by Vickers, who also took over Maxim Nordenfelts and thus emerged as the only company in Britain able to manufacture a battleship complete with armour, engines and guns. The Vickers, Sons & Maxim issue of 1897 was a major one, involving £2 million of capital. Cazenove's acted as brokers, as it again did eleven years later when Vickers raised further capital. It was hardly surprising that the company returned to the market, for by then Europe was a continent virtually divided into two armed camps, with the popular cry soon to be heard about the dreadnoughts, 'We want eight and we won't wait.' Moreover, by the 1900s Vickers had a serious competitor in William Beardmore & Co of Glasgow, which in 1904 issued £½ million of debentures. Cazenove's was the broker and it also underwrote the issue for a commission of 3%, with the right to underwrite a further £½ million, which it did the following year at 3¼%. The firm was again the broker (with A. G. Schiff & Co and two other firms, including one in Glasgow) in 1913 when Beardmore's issued £1 million of preference shares, in this case underwritten by the issuing house Emile Erlanger & Co. The prospectus had a mildly chilling but no doubt effective tone:

> In 1904 the works were transferred to Dalmuir, where the Company established one of the largest and best equipped shipbuilding and engineering works in the United Kingdom. The Company has thus been placed in a position to construct and fully equip from its own establishments war vessels of every type up to the largest and most powerful battleships . . .

The chance to test that power came soon enough.

––––––––––––

Our knowledge of Cazenove & Akroyds during this period extends somewhat beyond these rather bare, unsatisfactory bones. That this is so is entirely due to the survival of the records of the merchant banking house of Antony Gibbs & Sons. The firm, founded in 1808, was best known for its activities in Spain and South America and during the middle of the nineteenth century enjoyed a highly lucrative guano monopoly in Peru. By the 1880s it was moving increasingly away from merchanting and towards banking, a shift of focus that inevitably involved closer relations with various Stock Exchange brokers, one of whom was Cazenove's. Largely (though not wholly) running the business were four Gibbs brothers – Alban, Vicary, Herbert and Henry – and on any one day the custom was for whoever was manning the Bishopsgate offices to write to at least one of the other brothers who was elsewhere, putting him in the picture and often asking for his opinion or advice. These letters, especially helpful between the late 1880s and mid 1890s, were often hastily scribbled and in trying conditions, and definitely not written for posterity, but they give a better idea than from anywhere else of the relationship then between merchant banker and broker.

The probability is that the Gibbs partners occasionally dealt with Arthur Philip Cazenove and sometimes Swinny Akroyd, but usually with Swinny's brother Jack. The first reference to Cazenove & Akroyds, from Herbert to Alban in September 1888, is glancing and imprecise but already suggests a certain degree of initiative-taking on the part of the broker: 'We have bought a lot more converted at 40 and £75,000 at $40\frac{1}{16}$ which Akroyd did on his own responsibility & I accepted'. This impression of being more than merely a passive executant was confirmed in April 1890, when the question arose of syndicating a large number of preference shares. 'Vicary and I have been carefully through the proposed Cuban business,' Herbert wrote to Alban, 'calling in Akroyd at the end of the conference.' The conference decided it would be impossible to form a syndicate, and the question was then considered of whether or not to put up all the £200,000 themselves: 'Is it worth while to risk this £200,000 & wait for better times? Vicary & I think this very doubtful . . . and Akroyd is quite clear that he will not risk his share.' That summer Gibbs issued a Mexican government loan of £6 million; Cazenove & Akroyds acted as brokers; and on September 1st, just days before the issue was to be launched and beset by questions of allotment and pricing, Vicary in some exasperation wrote to Herbert: 'J. Akroyd is away partridge shooting. I am met at every turn by these sacré holidays.' He could perhaps have used the help, for the issue proved a massive success and was three times over-subscribed.

Soon the mood of the City started to darken, presaging November's Baring crisis. On the evening of November 19th, shortly after Lidderdale's crucial intervention, Henry Gibbs wrote to Vicary in Athens:

> I am glad to report to you a slight but distinct rise in prices all round. The general feeling also is better. Akroyd thinks everyone had been preparing for some great disaster for the last two months and though now it has come, it is an unexpected one and even a more alarming one than they dreaded, yet they are at last beginning to feel that the worst is over and that after all the Bank has stopped any actual panic and perhaps after a few more days of gloomy rumours etc, things will gradually right themselves, though of course they can't come round in a moment.

It was on Jack Akroyd's part a conventional enough but roughly accurate assessment, though in the event it would take the City years rather than months to recover fully from the crisis. Indeed, such was the nervousness in its immediate wake, especially in relation to anything connected with the Argentine, that in January 1891 Herbert wrote to Vicary:

> The Market has been full of rumours & we have been freely talked about . . . The story was that we were under contract to finish the Arg.N.E. [the Argentine North Eastern Railway, which had unsuccessfully come to the London market three years earlier, with Cazenove's acting as brokers], that we had not been able to sell a third of the Stock & we could not finish the railway, & that we had been selling large blocks of Consols & Mexicans. We authorised Akroyd to say that we were not under contract to finish, that we had only a small interest in the line, part of which we had sold, that we hadn't sold any Consols, that we hadn't got any Mexicans & finally that we & our friends intended to finish the line . . .

Akroyd seems to have convinced the market about the soundness of Gibbs, and it was perhaps as a reward that, when Herbert wrote to Vicary a few days later that 'Tuesday is settled for the Shoot', he added: 'I have told Akroyd 9.15 from Euston.'

Over the next few years, as the Baring crisis gradually receded, Cazenove's tried to interest Gibbs in a variety of schemes. One such was related by Henry to Herbert in December 1892:

> Akroyd has been in, he wanted to know if we would join a syndicate, if he got one up, to buy the Uruguayan bonds from The Midland Uruguay Coy at price, I am not sure if he said 36 or 38, but I suppose the former. He said the price would go up directly it was known the bonds had been taken off the market, & he thought there was money in it. I said I didn't think we should much fancy it . . .

Henry, however, promised he would consult his brother, and the following day he wrote to Herbert again: 'I received your telegram this morning & accordingly told Akroyd we would not join the proposed syndicate . . . It seems he had thought of giving 37 for them, they are only quoted at $36\frac{1}{2}$!' Unabashed, Akroyd the following March asked Herbert if Gibbs would underwrite part of the forthcoming Greek 5% Funding Loan, which was being issued by Hambros with Cazenove's acting as brokers. Herbert, however, rather brusquely declined, saying that they would have nothing to do with the issue until their own account with the Greek government had been settled.

There was also a certain implicit resentment when Henry wrote to Herbert in September 1895 about how on his morning train that day he had heard from a fellow passenger, a broker called Hodgson, that Bechuanaland Railway was a good thing. This was a fairly new company that had Cecil Rhodes and Alfred Beit as two of its directors, Cazenove's as its co-brokers and that, according to its prospectus issued two days before Henry's letter, proposed to take its existing line from Mafeking and press on towards Bulawayo. Henry, writing on a Friday, told Herbert how he had followed up his railway tip:

> Cazenove said that he was getting a lot of applications, so I applied for £100,000 Debs.
>
> The list will be closed at 11 am Monday. I should think there would be a good rush for it, and I thought it better to follow the public's example and apply today. The Debs are 2 to 3 premium. Akroyd, who told *us* Monday would do, told *Hodgson* today would be better.

Henry was perhaps over-anxious, for it is hard to believe that Akroyd would not have set aside a goodly quota for what after all was one of his more important clients.

Meanwhile, as in previous decades, Cazenove's continued during the 1890s to take a keen interest in Peruvian securities, especially those of the Peruvian Corporation. 'I have sent for Akroyds,' Vicary Gibbs reported in August 1891 about securing debentures from the Corporation, '& told them to see what they can do in the way of getting up a syndicate to buy £250,000 now.' And the following day: 'Akroyd is continuing to arrange his syndicate to buy these bonds from the company at about 5% below market quotations, & seems pretty sanguine of succeeding.' And eventually, twelve days later: 'We have today after continued struggles concluded the Peruvian Deb deal ... We get the debs at 65, they are quoted today 80 or less dividend 77 & the buyers have to provide some interest but altogether there is a very handsome margin.'

Finally, three years after this gratifying experience, it was Cazenove's who took the initiative in bringing Gibbs into a syndicate to buy £200,000 more of Peruvian debentures. It was a complicated episode, involving leverage on the Corporation itself, but as Herbert wrote to Vicary: 'I have not given you all the arguments that were used by Akroyd but I must say that on the whole I am inclined to do the business, for I think that we shall be able to get something out of the Directors in the way of economy, and I also think that, if we don't do the business some one else will without producing the same satisfactory effect on the bonds. Also I think there is money in it.' The decision was thus made to participate, though in the event, as Herbert reported on 29th January 1894: 'The Akroyds' Father is dead so I had to deal with Cazenove.' John Akroyd senior had indeed died that day, at

Bournemouth in his seventy-fifth year, leaving behind a notable trio of Stock Exchange sons.

———————

After almost twenty years as sole partners, Arthur Philip Cazenove and the Akroyd brothers decided in 1903 that it was time to broaden and also rejuvenate the partnership. The person they now brought in was Claud Pearce Serocold, who in time would become one of the great names in the history of Cazenove's. After being educated at Eton and New College, Oxford, he had joined the stockbroking firm of Rowe & Pitman, becoming a member of the Stock Exchange in 1901. Soon afterwards, while still in his mid-twenties, he moved to Cazenove & Akroyds. It is likely that his principal 'backers' within the firm were the Akroyds, with whom he now became very friendly. Indeed, the story goes that when Serocold, soon after becoming a partner, began regularly to call on the Rothschilds at New Court, he was always announced as 'Mr Akroyd', and they only learnt his surname after four years. By August 1908, with the Akroyds no doubt away shooting, he was also calling on the Gibbs partners in Bishopsgate, as Brien Cokayne reported to Herbert:

> Serocold has just been in to say that Shanois [?] are up to 11s 6d/12s 6d & to ask whether we would care to sell any of those we bought last year at 8s 9d. I told him I had absolutely no view of my own & asked him for his advice & the reason of the rise. He said the rise was being made in Paris & had nothing to do with the state of the business, regarding which no one in Europe knows anything nor can know anything as no reports from the place [?China] can be believed. He thinks we ought to begin selling at about this level & so follow the market up if it goes.

As baffled by 'Shanois' (presumably a nickname for a stock) as the historian is, Cokayne asked for Herbert's advice, though with what result we do not know.

Shortly before the war, Cazenove & Akroyds further expanded with the addition of a fifth partner. This new recruit was Charles Micklem, who was to become the other paramount figure (with Serocold) of the inter-war years. Micklem, born in 1882, had been educated at Wellington and Hertford College, Oxford; and he had entered the Stock Exchange in 1904 as an unauthorised clerk to the brokers Billett, Campbell & Grenfell, becoming a member five years later. By 1912 he had moved to Cazenove's on a half-commission basis, before in 1913 becoming a partner on a salaried basis of £400 a year, a manifest sign that at this stage his ability outran his capital. By March 1914, however, he was entitled to 10% of the profits, with

Jack Akroyd taking 33% of the remainder, Claud Serocold 22½% (showing how well established he had become), Swinny Akroyd 18½%, and Arthur Philip Cazenove 16%. It was an important acquisition on the part of the firm; and in later years Micklem would recall how, on first coming to Cazenove's, he was given by the Akroyds a list of clients and told that they had been neglected and that he was to do what he could about it.

One client, however, that almost certainly received proper attention throughout was John Foster. 'Mr Herbert A. Foster desires to thank you for your favour of yesterday, relative to the Pekin Syndicate Shares', ran a typical letter to Cazenove's in November 1904, though adding in somewhat coals-to-Newcastle fashion: 'You will find a favourable reference to the subject in today's *Financial Times.*' Or again, in February 1905, another member of the family thanked the firm for a telegram which apparently had stated: 'Should be inclined to wait a bit before selling Mexican First Prefs.' So it continued down the years, with the likelihood being that it was Arthur Philip himself who handled the Fosters account. Undramatic, uncontroversial, based on mutual trust and interest, the abiding relationship is well caught in a letter to Cazenove's of October 1908: 'Mr Robert J. Foster will be much obliged if you will kindly inform him what premium (if any) there is on the Allotment letters of the Buenos Ayres Western Ry New Issue, and if you recommend a purchase.' Fosters in due course acquired 80 shares, so presumably Arthur Philip recommended a 'buy'.

In the wider world of the Stock Exchange as a whole, one major theme and one major episode stand out during the Edwardian period. The theme was the triumph of the small firm over the large firm, a triumph of immense significance in the long run of City history. The crystallising issue was that of capacity, and in 1908 the Stock Exchange Committee introduced rules (coming into force the following year) that hardened the distinction between broker and jobber, which had tended to become blurred in recent years on the part of the larger broking and jobbing firms. Then, in 1912, capacity was further rigidified with the introduction of a minimum scale of commission, again supported by the much more numerous smaller firms and unavailingly opposed by the larger ones such as Cazenove's. As a result of these measures, taken together, the distinction between the two capacities was artificially preserved, in the event for another three-quarters of a century, when otherwise it might well have dissolved naturally much sooner.

As for the stand-out episode, ensuring plenty of work for firms of all sizes, this was the phenomenal rubber boom of 1910, which was stimulated by the widespread conviction that there would be an ever-expanding demand for rubber, especially on the part of the rapidly growing motor and electricity industries. During the first five months of that year, the public not only subscribed to more than £16 million of new rubber shares, but also speculated prodigiously on existing concerns. Many of these shares were of a two shilling denomination, compared with the usual £1 or even £5 share, and the inevitable consequence was a considerable broadening of the social base of the investing class. The financial press began to pitch its appeal to a new type of reader, while on the Stock Exchange itself the scenes at times were akin to a rugby match – so much so that on one celebrated day a member fainted at eleven o'clock and was not picked up until four, when the crowd that had been unwittingly supporting him all day began to drift away. Cazenove's probably did its fair share of the business; and many years later, when such rip-roaring booms seemed to have become a thing of the distant past, old-timers would fondly recall how the firm during the rubber mania had destroyed over a thousand dividend claims, of which only a handful were reclaimed because the brokers' back offices were so overworked.

As it happens, profit figures for Cazenove's survive for the last two full Stock Exchange years before the war. In the year ending 31st March 1913 the firm made a profit of £24,430 (worth now about £1 million), in that ending 31st March 1914 a sum of £18,961. These were probably pre-tax figures, but that was hardly a critical factor, granted that in February 1914 the income tax payment for the year 1912–13 was only £1,157. Office salaries ran at little more than £100 a month, sometimes less, and the firm could amply afford in these years to give one hundred guineas to the *Titanic* Relief Fund or twenty guineas to the Scott Antarctic Fund. Cazenove & Akroyds was by no means making staggering profits but they were comfortable enough, with the great bulk of the income coming from the commission (as opposed to interest) account. Certainly these profits soon came to seem enviable to a degree.

'No company was ever issued with a more timely title than this morning's "J.M." Shock Absorbers. The market ought to have a large supply.' So declared the *Financial News*, in a moment of mordant humour, on 29th July 1914 as the City of London helplessly watched Europe move towards the brink of its first major war for almost a century. That day seven firms were 'hammered', mainly because of defaulting clients on the Continent; but according to the same paper's market report, 'the calm and dignity with which the Stock Exchange comported itself will probably become historic'. A dramatic chain of events ensued: on the 31st the House was closed until further notice; on 4th August, Britain declared war on Germany; and over the following week, intensive high-level negotiations restored the machinery of credit that had been in a state of crisis-ridden suspension since the end of July. For the Stock Exchange as a whole, though, there was no immediate redress. Even when it was allowed to reopen on 4th January 1915, the restraints under which it operated were considerable, including a system of minimum prices for eighteen months and increasingly tight Treasury control over new issues, which were reduced to a trickle. Moreover, the House during the war became not only a moribund place in terms of business, but also a rather unpleasant one, with the institution's not unjust reputation for 'fair play' being besmirched by a series of attacks, physical as well as verbal, on any member with an even faintly German name who now dared to show his face.

As with all stockbroking firms, activity at Cazenove's ground to a semi-halt for these four years. Serocold and Micklem were engaged in war work (Naval Intelligence and the Royal Marines respectively); Jack Akroyd retired in 1916 and died three years later, fittingly while shooting in Scotland; and, with Swinny Akroyd also getting on in years, it seems to have been principally Arthur Philip Cazenove who held the fort. Profits inevitably slumped, averaging less than £4,000 a year. As for what life was like in the office itself during the war, we have an account by Kathleen Cross, who for half a century was to work for the firm in a clerical capacity:

I first visited 52 Threadneedle Street as a guest in August 1915. Mr Arthur Cazenove had sponsored my entry into Parr's Bank. They owned the building at 52 Threadneedle Street and this was their City branch. The bank did not use for themselves a small portion of the building at the side and this was leased to Cazenove's.

It consisted of a ground floor divided into a fairly large room for the partners, a small box-like room for an interview room, and a very small general office with a counter. Here a junior sat and received stock and transfers that were delivered; he was a messenger and general 'dog's-body'.

At the back of this office was an iron spiral stairway which led to a room above where most of the work was done. There was little in the way of comfort. The desks were very high with sloping tops and they [i.e. the staff, whom Kathleen Cross had not yet joined, though working in the same building] sat on high stools. The staff consisted of Mr Francis Bernard Neal, known as 'the Governor' or 'F.B.N.', who was virtually manager and authorised clerk. George Hanneford kept the clients' ledgers and accounts. Each of these wore morning dress. Victor Warren was on transfers. Albert Martin made out contracts and managed inscribed and bearer stocks – he was also an authorised clerk in the House. Harry Young was on journals and jobbers' ledgers – he had been discharged from the Army with a bad war wound in the leg. There was little in the way of toilet accommodation, which made it unfit for female staff. Albert Martin's married sister, Mrs Unthank, came in the afternoons to type letters on an almost pre-historic typewriter and she did the filing. The staff on war service were Bertram Crosse (no relation), who was in the Rifle Brigade, and John McLaren who was normally a dealer and half-commission man, and Albert Martin's young brother Ernie – he was normally the typist.

With the end of the 1914/1918 War the staff returned and Mr Serocold and Mr Micklem came back. The accommodation had become very cramped.

These recollections were written in June 1985 – a remarkable and invaluable feat of memory about a different world.

The situation to which Serocold and Micklem returned at the end of 1918 demanded early action and not just in relation to the cramped accommodation. They themselves, for all their ability, were still relatively inexperienced stockbrokers. One of the partners had retired, while the other two were both in their sixties. There was no younger Akroyd yet ready to come in as a partner. As for Arthur Philip's two sons, Bernard and Arnold Cazenove, both decided that a career in the City was not for them. In short, what was needed was a fresh injection of outside blood – or, put another way, those essential qualities of capital, connection and talent. It was becoming a recurrent pattern in the firm's history, as on each occasion a major transfusion sought to defeat those ancient enemies, time and decay.

CHAPTER FIVE

A *triumvirate emerges*
1919–1932

On 1st January 1919 the partnership was dissolved between S. Brunton, J. E. Tomkinson and G. A. Barnett; on the same date, Tomkinson and Barnett joined the partnership of Cazenove & Akroyds. The firm of Tomkinson, Brunton & Co thus merged with Cazenove's, whose name however remained unchanged as Cazenove & Akroyds.

Tomkinson Brunton was itself the result of a merger, which took place in 1907 between R. E. Tomkinson & Co and Brunton, Bourke & Co, both firms having been in existence since the 1880s. Brunton Bourke was closely connected with Barings and earned a small but secure niche in City history when in October 1890 Sidney Brunton was the first member of the money market to warn Glyn Mills (which subsequently headed the rescue team) that Barings required a large sum of money and that it would be difficult for that troubled house to appear in the market as borrowers. As a separate entity, not much is known about Tomkinson, Brunton & Co during its brief existence, apart from the crucial fact that it made the mistake of lending money to the Canadian Agency, which when it failed shortly before the war left the firm in an extremely difficult position. The moratorium on bank loans, following the outbreak of war, gave some breathing space; and in 1918, on returning from military service, J. E. Tomkinson managed to settle his firm's debts. The firm itself was left with nothing, but salvation came in the form of Claud Serocold, who, on the suggestion of a mutual friend, agreed to take Tomkinson and Barnett into partnership, as well as absorbing Tomkinson Brunton's remaining three senior clerks. It was an act of generosity on the part of Serocold, but also thoroughly sensible: in the two specialised areas of gilt-edged dealing and money broking, Tomkinson Brunton had something distinctive to offer; and it was these two particular strengths that from 1919 it imparted to Cazenove's.

On the gilts side the key figure was James Edward Tomkinson (Palmer-Tomkinson from the 1930s, on inheriting an estate from an aunt). His uncle was the founder of R. E. Tomkinson & Co, and it is clear that there was no great family wealth at his disposal when, in his mid-twenties, he became a member of the Stock Exchange in 1905 and a partner in his uncle's firm the following year. There was, however, a long-standing connection with the City: many years before a Tomkinson had come from Cheshire (where the family still resided) to be general manager of the Sun Insurance office. Jimmy Tomkinson himself was educated at Eton and Balliol College, Oxford; and after the merger in 1919 he became not only the third most important person at Cazenove's throughout the inter-war period, but also a major presence on the Stock Exchange Committee (later the Stock Exchange Council) for twenty years from 1927.

He is remembered as a very strong character: proud and obstinate, even to a degree; independently minded; exceptionally generous; and straight as a die. He was also a humanist (in the broadest sense of the word) who took much more interest in the welfare of the staff than most partners of the time. In private life he was the keenest of sportsmen, enjoying fishing and golfing. He was also an early convert to the mixed blessings of Alpine sports and indeed, as a friend of Sir Arnold Lunn, was one of Britain's original skiers. But, having as a boy represented Eton at rackets, his greatest passion was for squash, which he more than anyone else was responsible for transforming from a haphazard, ill-regulated game called 'Baby Rackets' into one of the most popular and established games with courts all over the world. He was chairman for many years of the Squash Rackets Association, was instrumental in standardising the court and codifying the rules, and in particular strongly supported the introduction of the slower ball intended to help the stroke player against the rackets player. As a player himself he won the amateur championship in 1926 at the age of forty-seven and was to be remembered by his obituarist for his 'forehand reverse angle shot, played unexpectedly, which scored many winners, and his unfailing courtesy in the court.'

Jimmy Tomkinson was equally dominant in his working life, being one of the biggest dealers in gilts between the wars. The sums involved were usually enormous, and he dealt for many of the leading companies and institutions, including the Great Western Railway, most of the other home railways, Martins Bank and the Prudential. His approach towards the business seems to have been a telling combination of the old and new. He sublimely ignored the precepts of actuarial science, preferring instead to rely on simple arithmetic to calculate the values of gilts; and in general he conducted his affairs on a highly personal basis, which involved intimate relations with the key jobbers in the Consol market. Yet at the same time he was a systematic exploiter of the effects of taxation on gilts and in particular was one of the pioneers of the then-accepted practice of so-called 'washing' – selling stocks full of dividend from high taxpayers to those who wanted their dividends gross and then buying the stocks back for those taxpayers when they were ex dividend. His skill at performing this lucrative manoeuvre, in order to make an untaxed capital gain, undoubtedly attracted a large amount of commission-earning business. Another reminder that it was then a different world lay in the fact that – astonishing as it may seem – he was simultaneously both joint broker *and* joint auditor (even though he was not an accountant) to the Great Western Railway, and indeed had a gold medallion giving him free travel on all railways. Such was Tomkinson's palpable integrity that no one would have thought to question the arrangement.

As for the money-broking input in 1919 (an area with which Cazenove's had had little to do since the mid-nineteenth century), this business lay firmly within the hands of the Brunton family. Sidney Brunton, who had joined the Stock Exchange in 1876, enjoyed a great reputation in his highly specialised field. On one occasion he stalked to the Bank of England to demand 'extra help', and when it was refused moved slowly towards the door saying, 'That's a pity because Consols will fall heavily in the morning!' Help was forthcoming before he reached the door. Now in 1919, as an elderly man, he did not formally join the new partnership, but did have his own room in the office and cut a striking, long-remembered figure with his thick white silver hair, goatee beard, black jacket, check trousers and small red tie. Moreover, he had an equally colourful and extrovert son who was learning the business and in 1925 became a partner, allowing Sidney to semi-retire. This was Miles Brunton, who loved cricket, billiards and shooting, ran the local Working Men's Club near his home in Hertfordshire, and adored all practical jokes, whether by or against him. His language could be more quarter-deck than partners' room (let alone drawing room), he bullied all the banks to lend him money, and his connections with the discount companies were unique. A story captures something of the flavour of the man. One day a cashier of the Union Discount who liked to appear alert was offered by a clerk from Cazenove's a parcel of securities wrapped in the usual fashion as collateral for a loan. The cashier glanced at it quickly, noticed the dollar sign on one of the items and said in a serious voice, 'I'm sorry, but we can't accept dollar collateral.' It was only when he looked again that he saw that the collateral consisted of $1 million of Confederate currency, which Miles Brunton had kept for years as a curiosity.

What was the nature of the money-broking business, which in time

Cazenove & Co, 1823–1939

Philip Cazenove in 1829

7 Broad St. 26 June 1[821]

N M Rothschild Esqre
            Sir

        Enclosed I beg to send you 2 6[...]
No 36371. for 2600. Rentes ⎫ in the name of
   37525. – 3480.   ─ ⎬ Richard, Pusey
      ⎰ 6080. together, which I reques[t]
you will have transferred to the name of
Caroline, Pusey, Widow of Richard
Pusey – for this purpose I send you
her power of Atty as Extrix of her decea[sed]
Husband – the Certificate of his burial
& an extract of the Will –
When the transfer has been effected I w[ill]
repay you your expenses with thanks,
      and remain meanwhile Y[our] [obt] H[umble] [Servant]
            for P. F. Menet &
                  P Cazenove

Letter in Philip Cazenove's hand to Rothschilds, 1821
(by permission of the N.M. Rothschild archives)

Medal struck in 1823 licensing Philip Cazenove as a stockbroker

FOREIGN FUNDS.

London, January 1, 1828.

	Price.	Exchange.
AUSTRIAN Metallic 5 per Cent. Bonds in Florins, Dividends payable 1st May and 1st Nov	*91*	10 Florins per £ Ster:.
BRAZILIAN 5 per Cent. Bonds, in £ Sterling, Dividends payable 1st April and 1st October........	*59 7/8*	
BUENOS AYRES 6 per Cent. Bonds, in £ Sterling, Dividends payable 12th January and 12th July ..	*45*	
CHILE 6 per Cent. Bonds in £ Sterling, Dividends payable 31st March and 30th September		
COLUMBIAN 6 per Cent. Bonds in £ Sterling, Dividends payable 1st May and 1st November		
Ditto ditto, Divs. payable 15th January and 15th July	*26 1/2*	
DANISH 3 per Cent. Bonds, Div. payable 31st March and 30th September...........................	*59 1/2*	
FRENCH 5 per Cents. or Rentes, Dividends payable 22d March and 22d September...................	f. *107 1/4 . 1*	f. *25·20*
Ditto 3 per Cents. Divs. payable 22d June & 22d Dec. f.	*67 1/2 . 7*	f. *11*
GREEK 5 per Cent. Bonds in £ Sterling, Dividends payable 1st January, and 1st July		
Ditto, 1825.............................	*16 1/2*	
GUATEMALA 6 per Cent. Bonds, in £ Sterling, Dividends payable 1st February and 1st August ..		
MEXICAN 5 per Cent. Bonds, in £ Sterling, Divs. payable 1st Jan. 1st April, 1st July, 1st October ..		
Ditto 6 per Cent. Bonds, Dividend ditto ditto	*45 1/4*	
NEAPOLITAN 5 per Cent. Bonds in Ducats, Dividends payable 1st January and 1st July..........		Fcs. 4: 40 per Ducat. Do.25 : 65 per £ Ster:.
Ditto 5 per Cent. Bonds, in £ Sterling, Dividends payable 1st February and 1st August		
PERUVIAN 6 per Cent. Bonds in £ Sterling, Dividends payable 15th April and 15th October	*25.*	
PORTUGUESE 5 per Ct. Bds. Dividends payable 1st June and 1st December......................	*71 1/2 . 2 .*	
PRUSSIAN 5 per Cent. Bonds in £ Sterling, Dividends payable 1st April and 1st October..........	*100*	
PRUSSIAN..Ditto.. new, of 1822, Dividends payable 1st January and 1st July	*99*	*£o.:.*
RUSSIAN 6 per Cent. Paper Ruble, Dividends payable 1st January and 1st July...............	*82*	*13.* per Ruble.
Ditto 5 per Cent. Metallic or Silver Ruble, Dividends payable 1st March and 1st September............	*88.*	3s. 1d. Ditto.
RUSSIAN 5 ⅌ Ct. Cert: of £111, £148, £518, & £1036 in £ Ster:. Divs. payable 1st March and 1st Sept. ..	*91 . 90 3/4*	
SPANISH Bonds of 1821, Dividends payable from 1st Nov. 1823	*10 3/4.*	
Do. of 1823, Dividends payable from 1st Nov. 1823 ..		

Prices of French Funds, in Paris, the 29 Dec.

		Exchange on London,
5 per Cent. Rentes.................f. *104. 60.*		1 Month ..f. *25/15.*
3 per Cent. Rentes.................f. *67. 30.*		

JOHN F. MENET & P. CAZENOVE,
No. 7, Broad Street, and Stock Exchange.

[Turn over.

Menet & Cazenove 1828 price list
(by permission of the Stonor archives)

Auction Mart, Bartholomew Lane, c. 1830: interior and exterior
(by permission of Guildhall Library, Corporation of London)

Joseph Laurence
(by permission of Jack Laurence)

Philip Cazenove in 1848
(by permission of Lady Freyberg)

Henry Cazenove

Peter Reid

John Akroyd

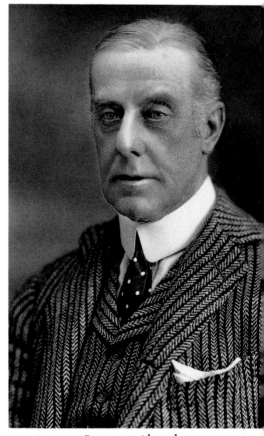

Swainson Akroyd

Arthur Philip Cazenove with
his mother and elder son
(by permission of Charlotte
Parry-Crooke)

Threadneedle Street, 1910,
showing Cazenove's office on
the right
(by permission of Guildhall Library,
Corporation of London)

Claud Serocold

Charles Micklem

Jimmy Tomkinson
(by permission of the Squash Racquets Library)

Garden party at Hurst, home
of Jimmy Tomkinson, 1925

Lord Faringdon

Algy Belmont

The former Huth banking hall

The firm's Christmas card, 1939

Garden party at Long Cross, home of Charles Micklem, 1934

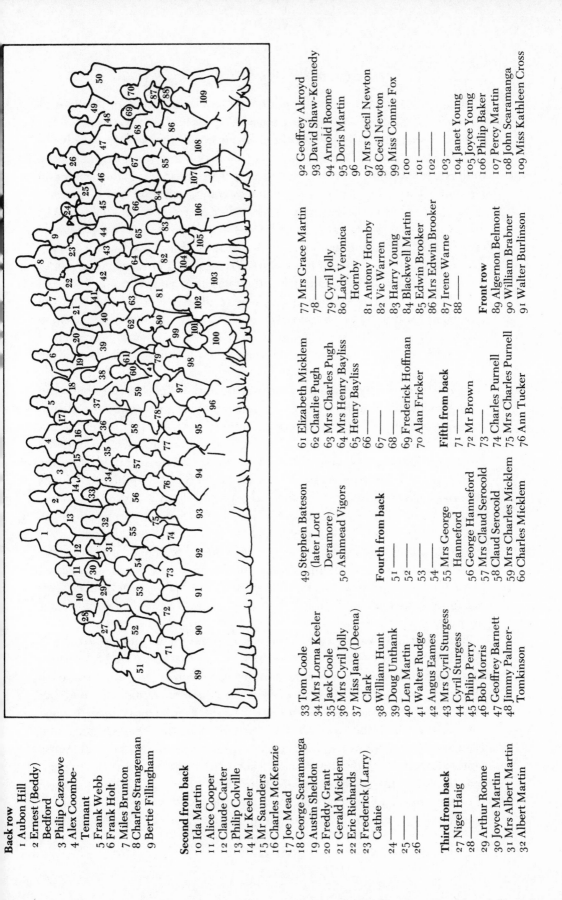

Back row

1 Aubon Hill
2 Ernest (Beddy) Bedford
3 Philip Cazenove
4 Alex Coombe-Tennant
5 Frank Webb
6 Frank Holt
7 Miles Brunton
8 Charles Strangeman
9 Bertie Fillingham

Second from back

10 Ida Martin
11 Alice Cooper
12 Claude Carter
13 Philip Colville
14 Mr Keeler
15 Mr Saunders
16 Charles McKenzie
17 Joe Mead
18 George Scaramanga
19 Austin Sheldon
20 Freddy Grant
21 Gerald Micklem
22 Eric Richards
23 Frederick (Larry) Cathie
24 ——
25 ——
26 ——

Third from back

27 Nigel Haig
28 ——
29 Arthur Roome
30 Joyce Martin
31 Mrs Albert Martin
32 Albert Martin

33 Tom Coole
34 Mrs Lorna Keeler
35 Jack Coole
36 Mrs Cyril Jolly
37 Miss Jane (Deena) Clark
38 William Hunt
39 Doug Unthank
40 Len Martin
41 Walter Rudge
42 Angus Eames
43 Mrs Cyril Sturgess
44 Cyril Sturgess
45 Philip Perry
46 Bob Morris
47 Geoffrey Barnett
48 Jimmy Palmer-Tomkinson

49 Stephen Bateson (later Lord Deramore)
50 Ashmead Vigors

Fourth from back

51 ——
52 ——
53 ——
54 ——
55 Mrs George Hanneford
56 George Hanneford
57 Mrs Claud Serocold
58 Claud Serocold
59 Mrs Charles Micklem
60 Charles Micklem

61 Elizabeth Micklem
62 Charlie Pugh
63 Mrs Charles Pugh
64 Mrs Henry Bayliss
65 Henry Bayliss
66 ——
67 ——
68 ——
69 Frederick Hoffman
70 Alan Fricker

Fifth from back

71 ——
72 Mr Brown
73 ——
74 Charles Purnell
75 Mrs Charles Purnell
76 Ann Tucker

77 Mrs Grace Martin
78 ——
79 Cyril Jolly
80 Lady Veronica Hornby
81 Antony Hornby
82 Vic Warren
83 Harry Young
84 Blackwell Martin
85 Edwin Brooker
86 Mrs Edwin Brooker
87 Irene Warne
88 ——

Front row

89 Algernon Belmont
90 William Brabner
91 Walter Burlinson

92 Geoffrey Akroyd
93 David Shaw-Kennedy
94 Arnold Roome
95 Doris Martin
96 ——
97 Mrs Cecil Newton
98 Cecil Newton
99 Miss Connie Fox
100 ——
101 ——
102 ——
103 ——
104 Janet Young
105 Joyce Young
106 Philip Baker
107 Percy Martin
108 John Scaramanga
109 Miss Kathleen Cross

developed into a permanent Loans department that earned for Cazenove's a regular, steady income that, according to a perhaps slightly exaggerated tradition, would usually pay for the firm's overall expenses? It was always something of a world apart from the main body of the firm, and little understood by those not working in it, but in fact what it did was quite straightforward. Essentially, the business comprised a service to the gilt-edged jobbing firms, of which there were then half-a-dozen leading ones. A jobber might be short of stock that he had to deliver the next day, in which case Cazenove's would lend him stock that it itself had borrowed from the institutions, such as Martins Bank or the Prudential. Conversely, the jobber may have been bullish – standing in the market 'with his buying boots on' and filling up his book – and in that case he would need money the following day to pay for the stock (the following day because of the daily settlement in gilt-edged). This money Cazenove's would lend, having borrowed it originally from the banks or the discount market. But whether borrowing and lending stock, or borrowing and lending money, it was all done by men walking about the streets in top hats, buying and selling Treasury bills, and taking a view in gilt-edged stocks. Conviviality was a necessity as well as a pleasure and, in the accurate words of Antony Hornby, a subsequent senior partner who came to Cazenove's in 1927, 'it was a business which consisted largely in "passing the time of day" and making friends so that when the crunch came it was easy on the "old boy" net to find £5 million to balance the books in five minutes.' Until the early 1970s, only two other stockbroking firms, Laurie, Milbank & Co and Sheppards & Co, were permitted by the Bank of England to borrow and lend government securities in this way. Over the years Laurie Milbank was usually reckoned to be the leader of the trio, while Cazenove's and Sheppards alternated in second place. In such an intensely personal business, much depended on how energetically it was being pursued at any one time by the partners involved, and inevitably this fluctuated.

The other new partner as a result of the merger in January 1919 was Geoffrey Barnett, who had been a member of the Stock Exchange since 1906. In his Tomkinson Brunton days he had been active preparing each afternoon a daily list of gilt-edged yields for which the jobbers queued, but after the war the main qualities he brought to Cazenove's were good connections (his father was on the board of both Alliance Assurance and Lloyds Bank), intense rectitude and an immaculate sartorial sense epitomised by his trousers always being adorned by spats with pearl buttons. In time he had a room of his own where, swathed in a huge travelling rug, and protected in the winter by kid gloves and a fur muff as well as a foot warmer, he would complete *The Times* crossword, then call for a cup of Bovril ('lukewarm again') and get on with his main task, which was signing the firm's contract notes on behalf of the partnership as a whole. In front of him was a huge blotting pad, which he never used unless completely clean ('always the danger of forgery'). Later in the morning he would leave his room and walk over in his top hat to the Bank of England office in Finsbury Circus in order to act as the clients' 'attorney' for all the gilts inscribed there, a habit that ceased in the 1930s when 'inscription' was converted to 'registration'. Tall, thin and distinctly reactionary in bent ('Unit trusts are *not* Stock Exchange securities' was a favourite saying of later years), he may not have been a dynamic business-getter; but quite apart from all the tedious and necessary contract-signing, it was he who held at his home in St Albans the firm's first garden-party on behalf of the staff. Partnerships need many varying qualities, and Geoffrey Barnett, a man of his time, provided his share.

––––––––––

Taken as a whole, the Tomkinson Brunton infusion in 1919 was undoubtedly important, but alone it does not explain why Cazenove's between the wars moved from somewhere in the middle of the first division of stockbrokers to a position at or near the top of the league. To understand *that* achievement, based essentially on company finance, one has to turn to the two men who had been junior Cazenove partners before the war and who now returned to become not only the dominant figures within the firm, but also major presences in the City at large. Lionel Fraser, chairman in the 1950s of the issuing house Helbert Wagg, provided in his memoirs the classic description: 'I always thought the partnership of Claud Serocold and Charles Micklem was the ideal one . . . They brought something new to stockbroking. One, shrewd and charming, opened the door, and the other, detailed and able, did the work. They laid the foundations of a fine business.' Complementing each other to an almost uncanny degree, Serocold and Micklem emerged in the 1920s as the two most important people in the history of Cazenove's since Philip himself.

Claud Serocold was born in 1875, the fourth son of Charles Serocold of Taplow, Buckinghamshire. Exceptionally slow in growing as a schoolboy, he achieved the distinction of coxing the Eton crew for three successive years and he was still in jackets (because not tall enough for a tail coat) when elected to 'Pop'. Generally known as 'harum-scarum', he became president of that august body before he left. Popularity followed him to Oxford, where he coxed the winning Boat Race crew of 1895 even though he weighed nine stone – he could play the piano after supper, and that apparently won him the berth. No scholar, he left New College without a degree after only a year and soon joined Rowe & Pitman, moving to Cazenove's a few years later. His father had given him £10,000 to start his business career and already he had the outgoing personality and range of contacts to suggest that it would be a successful one.

All the signs are, however, that before 1914 he was a relatively minor figure in the City and concentrated more on the fun aspects of life, being indeed something of a playboy. His haunts varied from Cannes to the Empire in Leicester Square; he spoke French well; he appreciated music and art; and in general he seems to have been considered (at least by his somewhat staid family) as slightly raffish. His abiding passion was the sea, and he had already become a member of the Royal Yacht Squadron. What, however, turned him into a figure of substance was the Great War and in particular his role in it. There were few more crucial parts of the war effort than Naval Intelligence, where, in the legendary 'Room 40' of the Old Building of the Admiralty, Captain (later Admiral) Reginald Hall and his small band of code-breakers succeeded brilliantly in reading (and distracting) the mind of the enemy. In 1915 Serocold became one of Hall's two personal assistants, made an enormous success of the job and also made many new and important connections. It was a rather different man who returned to Threadneedle Street at the end of the conflict.

What were the qualities that he now brought to bear? Physically he was slightly under average height and indeed was known in the Serocold family as 'the little Butler', because he was always neat, well-dressed and a quick judge of circumstances. With his crimped, marcel-waved hair, he looked more pompous than he was. He was in fact marvellous company: quick, entertaining and generous, he made throughout his life a host of friends. He was also a safe confidant and a born diplomat, capable of cracking the hardest nuts. In business terms, he was ambitious and wanted to make money yet at the same time remained wholly agreeable in all his doings. He had a lot of practical-based knowledge, possessed the invaluable knack of sizing someone up, and perhaps above all was able to make a decision and then sell it on the basis of what he had been told by a technical person, even though he was no technician himself. He may (as the Lionel Fraser passage suggests) indeed have been the perfect front man, but there was rather more to him than that.

Undeniably the 1920s was his great decade, when he used his considerable charm and flair to make or remake many fruitful connections for Cazenove's. None was more crucial than the link with Barings, which had rather faded by the turn of the century. In particular, it seems that soon after the war Serocold became personal broker to Lord Revelstoke, the autocrat of 8 Bishopsgate and a giant in the City. He called there each day and probably became the Stock Exchange 'ear' for Barings as a whole, as a snatch of correspondence from Arthur Villiers of Barings to Revelstoke in September 1926 suggests:

> Serocold told us yesterday that his stock-broking friends who are in touch with the Chartered Company informed him that Rothschilds had approached the Chartered Company and said that they would be happy to study the issue of Rhodesian Railway Bonds. Serocold quite appreciates the fact that we are under no obligation to him. My feeling is that Erlanger will do the business, but it might be worth telling New Court a little of what has happened.

Infinitely tactful in these delicate areas, Serocold in the 1920s also became friendly with Schroders and Morgan Grenfell, where he had Abel Smith cousins. A solicitous letter to him in February 1928 from Michael Herbert of Morgan Grenfell, concerning the Cairo Bus Company, suggests that a good working relationship had already been forged:

> We have looked over the papers you kindly left with us but I fear it is not quite in our line, though we appreciate having had the opportunity of looking at it . . . Merely unofficially, would you not be well advised, if you go on with the business, to be on the same side of the table as Baron Empain, who of course runs all the trams and who I suppose must have some sort of a pull in getting concessions.

Serocold's connections were not confined to the great merchant banks. His brother Oswald was chairman of Watneys and much business resulted. He himself became friendly with Richard D'Oyly Carte and from 1921 was on the board of the Savoy Hotel. He was a neighbour and friend of the Hambledens (of W. H. Smith) at Henley and was well-connected in society generally. At a time when the private client was still more important than the institutional this was indispensable, and in particular Serocold made two friendships that stood Cazenove's in excellent stead. One was with Major M. E. W. Pope, whom Serocold enabled to make a fortune through the sale of the coal-mines owned by Pope and his brother. The other was with Sir Connop Guthrie, a Suffolk landowner whom Serocold got to know so well that in later years he persuaded Guthrie to finance the private wing of Kings College Hospital (of which Serocold was treasurer) in thanksgiving for the safe return of his son Giles (the subsequent chairman of BOAC) in the London to Melbourne Air Race. During the inter-war years, if ever Cazenove's needed to fill a hole in a syndicate or an underwriting, the firm could turn to Pope or Guthrie with confidence. The same was also true of the Prudential, by now starting to emerge as a major investment force. Serocold was especially friendly with Percy Crump, the Pru's Secretary (i.e. investment manager) from the early thirties. The two of them would sometimes play threepenny bridge in the Claridge's penthouse with Connop Guthrie and the film magnate Alexander Korda. *That* was how the world worked then, if perhaps not now, and Serocold was a supreme exponent.

Great stockbrokers (like fast bowlers) hunt in pairs, and between the wars Charles Micklem proved the perfect person to capitalise on the Serocold connections, while bringing some important connections of his own. He was born in 1882, the fifth son of Leonard Micklem, who had married Dora Weguelin; her father, a former Governor of the Bank of England, was described by Disraeli to the Prince of Wales in 1875 as 'a man of considerable abilities'. Leonard for some years had lived the life of a country gentleman near Twyford in Berkshire, but by the time his fourth son was born he clearly felt the need for more lucrative employment and became a company secretary in the City. The 1884 prospectus for the Bahia and San Francisco Railway Company reveals Leonard Micklem as secretary. He must have possessed certain qualities, for of his eight sons almost all rose to the top of their respective professions. Charles himself was always intended for the Army and in 1896 he went to Wellington College, the natural choice of school. He was then supposed to go to the Royal Military Academy at Woolwich ('The Shop') but did not do so, perhaps because he was not yet tall enough but more probably on account of his colour blindness. Instead he went to Oxford and then, in about 1904, into the City, following his elder brother Hugh on to the Stock Exchange. With relatively little money behind him, he served a lengthy Edwardian apprenticeship with Billett, Campbell & Grenfell, before moving to Cazenove's in 1912. Two years later the war broke out and he was able to achieve the military distinction that had been denied him. He served with the Royal Marine Artillery, Howitzer Brigade, in Gallipoli and France, was twice mentioned in despatches and was awarded the DSO. While in the trenches, he also successfully read for a law degree. In 1919 he returned to the City determined to reap the reward for those long years spent learning the nuts and bolts of the business.

Major Micklem remained in some sense an Army man for the rest of his life: with his tall, upright bearing, grey moustache and rather stern expression, he created a presence of which most of the staff and not a few partners felt somewhat in awe. Indeed, his standards were of the very highest and his sense of duty and of justice were unimpeachable. He was a man of few words, he was not a socialite like Serocold, and his resolution in all aspects of life was unwavering. He did much public service, and it was entirely characteristic that he was a Justice of the Peace, taking a particular interest in juvenile delinquents. Outwardly severe and usually reserved, he was in fact charming once he relaxed and did possess a quiet sense of humour. A handful of anecdotes or glimpses have been passed down that bring out some of his qualities. The personal austerity was exemplified by the fact that he always travelled third-class to and from Waterloo, an occasional source of embarrassment to junior partners in more exalted carriages on the same train. If asked (as he often was) for an opinion of doubtful characters within the City, his invariable reply was an unyielding, 'We do not know them in business'. When a fellow partner was being divorced in highly public circumstances, Micklem's likely disapproval was such that the other partners tried their hardest to hide from him that day's *Daily Mail*. Such was his thoroughness in everything he did that, for over twenty years, an office manager at Cazenove's was deputed to keep detailed accounts about the cows on his farm at Long Cross near Chertsey, where he built a house in 1930 and with the support of his wife, Diana Lloyd, raised their family of six children. But perhaps the last word on Charles Micklem's character should go to his obituarist in *The Times*, who recalled how 'in his youth he was a fine athlete and had a charming way of defeating you at squash, tennis and golf as to leave the impression in your mind that you had won after all.'

But if his ultimate strength was his character, Micklem in the 1920s also developed his own connections, although on a less ambitious scale than Serocold. He established a particular closeness to the investment trusts, which after the war enjoyed not only a new wave of formation but also greater stability than had been the case before 1914. It is perhaps easy now to forget what a great force these trusts were, especially in the equity market, at a time when most insurance companies eschewed ordinary shares and the pension funds had not yet emerged as an important factor. Another *forte* of Micklem's was industrialists, with whom he forged (especially in the 1930s) appreciably wider links than Serocold did – though again there was the fraternal connection, in this case Micklem's half-brother Robert, chairman of Vickers-Armstrong. Significantly, he was also a particular friend of Alfred Wagg of Helbert Wagg, which in these post-war years differed from most merchant banks in that it began, essentially as an out-and-out issuing house, to specialise in the finance of British industry rather than trying to recover the international business that had been lost to the City. In addition, there were three other issuing houses (none of them merchant banks) towards which Micklem's relationship was absolutely crucial in the attainment of what would soon become the firm's paramount role in the sphere of company finance.

The first was the Power Securities Corporation, formed in 1922 by the utility engineering firm Balfour Beatty, which between the wars was the largest private enterprise grouping in the British electrical industry. Power Securities sponsored many issues in these years, specialising in electricity supply undertakings; it invariably turned to Cazenove's to act as broker, a relationship cemented by Micklem's close friendship with the managing director William Shearer, whose eldest son subsequently married one of Micklem's daughters. The second issuing house was Selection Trust, formed in 1914 by the mining entrepreneur Chester Beatty in order to finance and develop new mining ventures, a task in which it was especially successful between the wars in relation to the copperbelt of Northern Rhodesia (now Zambia). It may have been Serocold who made the initial connection with Selection Trust, but it was certainly Micklem who assiduously fostered it – particularly as he had not just one but two brothers on the board. One of these brothers was Hugh, and it was through him that Micklem established the close connection with the third and perhaps most important issuing house, itself intimately connected to the Chester Beatty mining empire. This was Cull & Co, a so-called 'finance house' which was created by four ex-partners (including Hugh Micklem) of a leading oil jobbing firm who had made a fortune shortly before the war when Burmah Oil shares were introduced to the Stock Exchange. 'Never fail to give the public the shares they want' was reputedly Hugh's dictum, and between the wars Culls operated as a formidably effective outside house. It formed Ultramar, acted for AEI and Courtaulds, did an enormous business in mining, celanese and oil shares (running huge positions in companies like Shell) and made itself 'the shop' (thus controlling the market) in all Chester Beatty securities. Although almost entirely ignored in City literature, no doubt because it was neither a merchant bank nor a member-firm of the Stock Exchange, Culls was an immensely valuable client for Cazenove's to have.

Yet neither Victorian rigour nor personal connection quite goes to the heart of explaining why Charles Micklem was the outstanding stockbroker of the inter-war Stock Exchange. The answer surely lies in the combination of his attributes, which included not only an acute financial brain, creative as well as shrewd, but also extremely sound judgement, of both people and situations. At a time when most brokers were still not much more than glorified tipsters, it was as if he had come from a different planet. We are fortunate that there exists from the early 1930s, covering the second half of his career at Cazenove's, a wealth of documentation which shows him at work creating on behalf of the firm a marvellously successful and ambitious new issue business. His incisive but always constructive letters to company chairmen, together with his highly succinct memoranda for internal purposes, speak louder than any generalisations can. The only shame is that these records were not being kept in the 1920s.

Of course, there were other partners at Cazenove's in these post-war years apart from Micklem, Serocold and the Tomkinson Brunton intake. Arthur Philip Cazenove took life more easily after the war but he still came to the office each Thursday and was in partnership when he died at his home from pneumonia in October 1921. The tributes in the press were warm, and one correspondent recalled how 'he was the most generous and kind-hearted of men, and was never heard to say an unkind word of anyone'. For the next four years Swainson Akroyd was senior partner. After a prolonged illness, he died in December 1925. The news was 'learned with regret by a wide circle in the City', *The Times* reported, and indeed he had had a distinguished if not glittering career. With his brother he had made a significant contribution to the firm's prosperity.

Most of the new partners of the decade were not major business-getters. The splendidly-named Ludlow Ashmead Cliffe Vigors, who became a partner in 1922, was equally splendid in appearance, his aristocratic looks completed by a monocle. He had come over from Java and his main interest as a stockbroker was in the Rubber market. His real passion, however, was for hunting and country life in general, and at Christmas he gave each of the male staff a turkey. Three years later, in 1925, Jack Akroyd's son Geoffrey became a partner. He developed useful connections with Glyns and Hambros, and he had a convivial disposition that made him very popular with clients, partners and staff. But over the years he was relatively inactive and brought little substantial new business to the firm. Also lesser figures, in the broad sweep of the history, were Cecil Breitmeyer and John Scaramanga, who both became partners in 1928. Breitmeyer was the son of a South African mining magnate and was expected to bring business from Central Mining and other houses, but after only two years a tubercular condition compelled him to retire. Scaramanga was a more important force. He had been with at least two other firms before coming to Cazenove's and had a very quick, mathematical brain. He joined in order to do arbitrage with the Paris market on behalf of Seligman Brothers, established an important relationship with the merchant bank Singer & Friedlander, and was able to converse on equal terms with the more professional investors, such as some of the Scottish investment trusts. His background was Anglo-Greek, and he brought a distinct new dimension to the firm.

Of those becoming partners in the 1920s, however, the major presence undoubtedly was Algy Belmont. He had been at Berlin University learning German when the war broke out and was thus consigned to spend the war in Germany, though he twice escaped as a prisoner. A few years after the war he went to Cazenove's and became a partner in 1925. His father-in-law was Sir Robert (later Lord) Kindersley, the effective creator of Lazards, and it was a connection that brought Belmont a lot of business. He was popularly known as 'Electric Whiskers', a reference to not only his enormous black moustache but also the fact that his temper tended to be on a rather short fuse. He could indeed be most severe in his punishment of inefficiency, but beneath his apparent fieriness lay a kind heart and a keen sense of humour. He was a great dealer in wine and usually had suggestions for both wine and shares when he called each morning on the houses for which he was responsible. Indeed he was in general extremely active, showing a capacity for hard work and sticking at things that in time made him particularly useful on the new issue side. It was soon clear within the firm that he was the leading member of the younger generation.

Certainly there was no cult of youth. 'No one in the City will listen to what you have to say for twenty years', Serocold was wont to remark to his junior partners. To a quite astonishing degree Micklem, Tomkinson and he *were* Cazenove's during the inter-war period, determining the size and direction of the business and taking between them well over half the profits. Within that omnipotent triumvirate, Tomkinson remained slightly to the side. He continued to regard the Tomkinson Brunton element as almost a firm within the firm, gave his former staff a substantial cash present each Christmas from his own pocket, and in general rather ploughed his own furrow, partly because he was the last Cazenove's partner to have a share of commission, thus giving him a direct interest in what he did. He was however a major figure, not only because of the enormously profitable business that he did, but also because in a sense he provided the indispensable human 'oil' or lubricant that ensured that Cazenove's was popular in the Stock Exchange at a time when it might have been much disliked for becoming increasingly powerful. Serocold and Micklem were often on the floor of the House but they did not carry quite the weight there that Tomkinson did through his uniquely close relationship with the still all-important gilt-edged market.

Nevertheless, in terms of the key decisions and actions as well as taking the leading share of the profits, Serocold and Micklem were the main men. They trusted each other implicitly and played their cards close to the chest, prompting an exasperated Algy Belmont to remark once that their secretary knew more about what was going on in the firm than their fellow-partners did. One of their great combined qualities was their decisiveness, in addition to the soundness of their decision-making, and in this respect Hornby tells a salient story from these years. Sir William Aykroyd, chairman of T. F. Firth & Sons, the carpet manufacturers, came to the office one morning on the introduction of Martins Bank and said he proposed to spend only that day in London and wanted to raise £1 million partly for the company and partly for his family by the sale of shares. Neither Serocold nor Micklem had ever seen his figures before, but Aykroyd caught his afternoon train home with issues of debenture, preference and ordinary all safely arranged.

Within that overarching duumvirate, the ultimate force was Micklem, even though Serocold was for many years senior partner. The City knew that in the end it was Micklem's opinion that really counted; and it was also Micklem, a truly great man, who created an ethos that was to last far beyond his lifetime and make Cazenove's somehow different from other stockbroking firms. What was that ethos? It is not easy to find the precise words, but its inner core perhaps comprised the qualities of solidity, reliability and also pride, a determination to build something to last. When the young Godfrey Chandler came to the firm during the Second World War, he was told by a staff veteran, Arthur Roome, that there were two office rules: that they did not discuss outside the office what they did inside it; and that Cazenove's only did business with those with whom it wished to do business. It was an ethos, a usually unspoken and certainly unwritten code, that permeated directly from the example of Charles Micklem.

Nevertheless, it is important to remember that the triumvirate was not building from scratch. In later years Palmer-Tomkinson would recall how, when he came to the firm in 1919, Serocold had told him that 'a partner in Cazenove's can walk into any business house in the City and get a hearing, and if he has anything to say which is worth saying, he can get business'. Or in the apposite words of Antony Hornby, looking back to the immediate post-war situation: 'The ground was fertile and just needed cultivation.' That was so, yet the fact remains that in 1919 no one could have guessed the profound transformation that the business of Cazenove's would soon undergo, mostly in the 1930s but also to a degree in the 1920s. It was a transformation that owed almost everything to the people at the top of the firm and was one of the most fascinating episodes in the history of the modern City.

The City itself was a battered place on 1st January 1919: New York had replaced London as the world's leading international financial centre and now had far more capital at its disposal to be invested internationally than London did; the mood on the Stock Exchange was pessimistic and its membership a thousand less than five years earlier; and the overall state of the British economy, particularly its traditional export industries, was dire. For a time it seemed that the City might be able to blow these problems away, as there took place a hectic and mainly ill-judged new issue boom, focusing partly on the expanding motor industry. But by 1921 markets were falling sharply, the world economy was on a downturn, and it was becoming clear to some of the more thoughtful people in the square mile that the golden, pre-1914 days of unfettered international capital flows and the world as the City's oyster had gone for ever (or at least for the foreseeable future) and that instead the City would have to look more closely than it had ever done before to the needs of domestic industry. It was an inexorable reorientation masked only briefly by what was the nostalgic and unrealistic decision in April 1925 to return to the traditional glories of the gold standard.

By the time that Winston Churchill as Chancellor of the Exchequer announced this move, widely welcomed in the City as a restoration of the natural order of things, the markets had begun to recover. Indeed, the summer of 1925 provided a rubber boom fully the equal of that of 1910. The *Financial Times*'s very popular Stock Exchange correspondent, 'Autolycus' (the stockbroker Walter Landells), offered a vivid description in the middle of July, incidentally reflecting the more gentlemanly hours of business that then obtained:

> Well before ten o'clock in the morning business was being done on the telephones, though many jobbers refused, naturally enough, to make prices until the market opened properly. A little before half-past ten, when prices were developing rapidly, there came a perceptible series of rushes from half-a-dozen parts of the House. They converged upon the Rubber market. It had the extraordinary effect of making business well-nigh impossible to execute, for the simple reason that around the principal dealers, there surged and shouted such a crowd as the market has not seen for a decade or two. You could not get near the man you wanted.
>
> I dropped a pencil, and wasted ten minutes to get out of the market in order to replace it, for to pick it up was impossible. In previous booms, one has heard stentorian bidding for shares going on all the time; but now there is no time for bidding. It is only occasionally that a buyer breaks in to such lusty song. Everyone is far too busy to bother about anything except to book bargains as fast as possible.

The following summer saw another event that entered Stock Exchange mythology. This was the General Strike, on the first day of which 'Autolycus' confidently predicted that 'the Stock Exchange will not be closed on account of the crisis', and added: 'The very idea of closing the House is scouted as being a sign of weakness, which, if adopted, would be construed as a concession to the forces of disorder.' The markets indeed remained open throughout, with 'Autolycus' on the third day noting how 'passing from one market to another in the House, I hear a good deal of surprise expressed at the extreme moderation with which the Government are treating the ring-leaders and the rioters.' In the early afternoon of May 12th, after nine days, a waiter mounted the rostrum in the Consol market and through a mega-phone announced that the strike was over. Cheers rolled round the House, while according to a rather breathless 'Autolycus': 'So general was the bidding that the volume of sound became welded on to a single note which rose, strident and triumphant, above all the uproar caused by the rushing feet, the staccato snap of the pneumatic telegram tubes, the shouting of the waiters, the electrified enthusiasm in the air, and the intense relief . . .'

By 1927 markets were rising rapidly and there began a spectacular new issue boom, reaching a climax in 1928 and declining somewhat in the first half of 1929. The economic activities that attracted this capital were on the whole legitimate enough – the gramophone and the radio, artificial silk, cinemas and colour photography were all becoming necessities to twen-tieth-century man – but many of the companies now brought into existence to produce these blessings were little more than 'shell' affairs. Moreover, the methods of promotion were often extremely dubious, with the company promoters of the day especially favouring the ploy of 'parent-and-offspring financing'. In the words of Alec Grant, author of the authoritative study of the inter-war capital market: 'Companies engaged in producing something sold the right of producing it somewhere else to companies specifically formed for the purpose at the expense of the public – often before the parent company had effectively commenced operations on its own account.' 1928 was in many ways the last of the old-style, nineteenth-century booms, producing a few good companies but also a lot of rubbish that quickly perished once the market had turned. It gave the Stock Exchange a thoroughly bad name and is still remembered by a few survivors with affectionate disgust.

What did Cazenove's itself do during this first decade after the war? Unfortunately, we know very little about the firm's day-to-day activities during this period. The money-broking side seems gradually to have expanded, while presumably the tenfold increase of the National Debt as a result of the Great War was beneficial for a specialist gilt-edged dealer like Tomkinson. As for the broking business as a whole, a certain oblique light was thrown by a letter sent in December 1922 from Serocold to the Stock Exchange Committee, in the context of a sub-committee having recently been appointed to consider the question of commissions, which since 1912 had been regulated according to a minimum scale and which Cazenove's continued to oppose. The letter also reflected that strong tradition within the firm, going back to Henry Cazenove, of dislike of excessive regulation:

In the ordinary course of everyday business, I meet business men of high position in the City of London, both Bankers, Merchants and others who are accustomed to dealing on the Stock Exchange, and I find them of the opinion that if the Stock Exchange is to remain the chief centre of dealings in Securities, there will have to be a radical alteration in the existing Rules and Scale of Commission.

It is generally recognised that there should be a minimum commission, but it should be at a considerably lower scale than that which at present obtains, and the rules which deal with commissions should be greatly modified where large lines of stock are concerned. The latter modification of course applies mainly to the market in Government and Colonial Securities.

The present scale of commissions between the provinces and London also needs revision in order to attract more business to London.

It is pretty obvious that with a lower minimum commission and *in certain cases* a greater freedom permitted to Brokers to charge their clients what they think right and deal where they think right, a much greater volume of business will come to the Stock Exchange, and after all that is the result which must benefit the House in general.

In view therefore of the many opinions which I hear day after day from various important quarters in the City of London I feel that it is my duty to write and urge that it is not *more* legislation that we want, but much less and say, that it is most desirable and very urgent that the Stock Exchange should return to the very freest possible trade, and an end put to the present restrictions.

It is with great reluctance that I write this letter but it has been brought to my notice so forcibly lately that the Scale and Rules of Commissions under the present laws of the Stock Exchange cannot continue without seriously endangering the position of the Stock Exchange as the free market for the Securities of the World, that I feel bound to bring these opinions to your notice.

I beg to add that these observations are solely personal and not on behalf of my partners.

Over the following weeks a campaign to liberalise the commission rules was waged by the nine broking firms that were probably the largest: namely (in order of signature to a petition), Mullens & Co, Cazenove & Akroyds, Cohen Laming Hoare, Grieveson Grant & Co, Heseltine Powell & Co, R. Nivison & Co, Rowe & Pitman, J. & A. Scrimgeour and J. Sebag & Co. In the course of 1923, however, the campaign petered out – partly because of the implicit opposition of the much more numerous small firms, partly as markets improved – and the matter was left in abeyance to await future attention.

Meanwhile, there is some evidence that in its regular everyday business (i.e. in the secondary market) Cazenove's was by the mid-1920s becoming increasingly partial to the practice of initiating and then managing syndicates that over a specified period would buy and sell particular lines or types of securities. One senses the hand of Micklem, but unfortunately the evidence does not allow us until the 1930s to know more precisely how these syndicates operated and who the participants were. Otherwise, for the 'regular' broking activities of the 1920s, we have to rely on the memories of Antony Hornby from 1927. Happily, he has much of interest to say:

Stockbroking was very different in those days. Partners obtained more or less all their business by visiting banks and queuing up for orders outside the investment managers' offices. Claud went every day to the parlour of Barings, Schroders, Morgans, Flemings and probably Martins and told them any market gossip, discussed what we as a firm were doing and picked up scraps of information. It was also necessary to know the latest market prices and for this purpose partners went through the House fairly frequently to check them. This led to a much closer liaison between jobber and broker and to know what was going on and do big business needed a close personal relationship. Claud could be constantly seen in intimate talk with Sanyer Atkin, Gordon Anketell, Jack Russell and the like.

There was no statistical department, no intelligence department, no settled policy of the firm. If letters came from private clients or country brokers asking for suggestions or an opinion on a specific share they were handed to our partition to answer if no partner felt inclined to do so. We just asked a jobber what he thought! Nevertheless we didn't seem to lose our business altogether by some miracle. But it is true to say that Claud and Charles did more than 50 per cent of the firm's business between them.

I suppose on an average day there were only about 25 to 30 bargains done and the bargain book often didn't turn over the page. When one got an opportunity one went to see what had been entered. I used to be very impressed at entries by Claud in his hasty handwriting of £100,000 Consols and fascinated by complicated deals by Charles selling 5,000 shares at 5s with call of further 5,000's at 5s 3d and 5s 6d.

Claud had some very speculative clients but he managed never to get his fingers burnt. He dealt for Count Loewenstein, a mysterious Belgian speculator who suddenly appeared in the financial firmament with his two holding companies – Hydro's and International Holdings. Schroders were his London contact and enormous dealings took place. He had a private aeroplane and one morning we heard when we arrived in the City that he'd fallen out of it over the channel. The bottom fell out of the market – everyone imagined he was bankrupt but his estate turned out to be solvent with assets of more than £2 million. One of the few people who must have known whether he committed suicide was his secretary, Miss Clarke, who was with him in the plane and who subsequently came to Cazenove's as Claud and Charles' secretary. But she could never be persuaded to talk.

Although books continue to be written about the man who fell from the sky in July 1928, it will probably never be certain what happened and why.

Turning to the new issue business, it was in general a very fragmented picture that the London capital market presented during the 1920s. The merchant banks continued to rule the roost on the lucrative foreign issues. But, in terms of the increasingly numerous domestic issues, they were on the whole less active as 'sponsors' or issuers than the various company promoters who persisted in their often dubious activities, specialist issuing houses like Power Securities, and a dozen or more stockbroking firms, including Cazenove's. The pre-war Companies Act was still in force; most prospectuses were only four pages long and relatively easy to write; the control over these prospectuses exercised by the Stock Exchange's Share and Loan department was fairly lax; and there was no need to get a timing or Bank of England consent for the making of an issue. Granted such conditions, it was not surprising that cowboys continued to appear, especially in boom times. The demand was clearly there, for many private companies, faced after the war by high surtax and estate duty, now wished to get a quotation for their shares so that the families could raise capital for their own or their company's needs. Acting as either issuer-cum-broker or broker on behalf of the issuer, Cazenove's was one of many intermediaries that sought to meet that demand, somewhat tentatively in the 1920s but full tilt thereafter.

At the heart of the operation were of course the mutually complementary skills of Serocold and Micklem, who between them possessed the gift of gaining the confidence of both the borrowers and the lenders of money. An important but unsung figure, however, was Albert Martin, the former office boy who had emptied the Akroyds' chamber pots. It was now that he made himself into a master of the mechanics of new issues, becoming in time such an acknowledged expert that the Share and Loan department (forerunner of the Quotations department) regularly asked his advice. Even then, decades before 'Chinese walls', the new issue business was shrouded in secrecy: Serocold and Micklem would rarely tell the other partners about an issue in advance, while at the beginning of each underwriting Serocold would make a tour of the office and remind the staff that the work was confidential. A high premium was placed on discretion throughout the business – typified by the fact that for many years the staff were not allowed to have private bank accounts and instead had to bank with the firm – but in the new issue sphere it was of the absolute essence.

Caution appears to have been the keynote at the outset. There are gaps in the records, but even during the new issue boom of 1920 the firm seems to have been associated with only four issues made that year. One was for Sheffield Steel Products, which was a recent amalgamation of ten local companies and claimed to be the world's largest manufacturers of table cutlery. The *FT* was confident enough, asserting that 'the company is able to compete successfully in foreign markets, even where high protective tariffs are imposed'. But in the event the company failed to pay a single dividend during the decade, a reflection of the intense difficulties faced by the British steel industry as a whole. Another issue in 1920 was the successful offer for sale of £2.8 million 7½% preference shares of the British Cellulose and Chemical Manufacturing Company. During the war it had received major contracts to manufacture, from cellulose acetate, non-inflammable water-proof covering for aeroplanes and airships. Now the company was preparing to turn to the mass manufacture of artificial silk, while also being the largest British producers of calcium carbide and aspirin. The directors included the already well-known Swiss chemist-cum-financier Dr Henry Dreyfus (together with his brother Camille), the issue was sponsored by Dunn Fisher & Co (with James Dunn at the helm), and Cazenove's acted as sole London broker.

Over the next few years, it was Barings who emerged as the dominant issuing connection. In conjunction with Rothschilds and Schroders, that house proceeded to sponsor a series of major foreign loans, and almost invariably Cazenove's secured a place on the ticket as one of the London brokers. One of the earliest in the sequence was the £7 million 7½% Coffee Security Loan of 1922 to the Brazilian government, with Barings responsible for arranging the sub-underwriting of £1 million of the sterling bonds. It kept £½ million for its own list and the other £½ million was allocated to three brokers, including Cazenove's, who had to arrange the sub-underwriting of £125,000 in return for an over-riding commission of ¼%. Cazenove's similarly had to place the sub-underwriting for a further £125,000 of the loan allocated to it by Rothschilds. The Cazenove sub-underwriting list for the total of £250,000 survives and it shows thirty-five names, including well-known houses like Hambros and Brown Shipley, particular connections like Cull & Co, Glyns and the International Financial Society (a name from the past), and a handful of individuals, one of whom was Granville Bromley-Martin, a director of Martins Bank and a particular friend of Serocold. These sub-underwriters each received an underwriting commission of $1\frac{1}{2}$%. It was presumably easily-earned money, because within a day or two of the sub-underwriting letters being despatched London Trust felt moved to complain to Barings about being omitted from the lists. A reply was sent on behalf of Lord Revelstoke: 'He thinks that you may not be aware that the underwriting in question was entrusted to an influential number of stockbrokers, whose co-operation would ensure, he had hoped, the distribution of the underwriting over a reasonably wide area. The stockbrokers who were employed in this instance by the three issuing firms were Messrs Greenwell, Messrs Panmure Gordon, Messrs Sebag, Messrs Cazenove & Akroyds, and Messrs Messel'. The letter considerately added that 'he would like you to know that no participations were ceded by his firm direct to any Trust Company'.

Other substantial loans organised by the consortium and involving Cazenove's followed over the next few years, including in 1926 a £$1\frac{1}{4}$ million 7% Sterling Loan for the pleasingly-named Counties of Hungary and also the more politically-charged Stabilisation Loan of £$7\frac{1}{4}$ million 7% Sterling Bonds to the Kingdom of Belgium, which after fourteen years was relinking her currency to gold and raising various loans for the purpose, amidst much domestic controversy. That same year saw a £2 million 6% Loan to the State of Hamburg that included a revealing episode during the preliminary dispositions. Frank Tiarks of Schroders (which led the way in the consortium over this loan) early in September thought that a price of 94 or 95 would be appropriate, but on the 22nd Villiers of Barings reported to Revelstoke:

> Tiarks is very anxious not to underwrite the Hamburg loan but to issue it at 93 and pay $\frac{1}{2}$% brokerage. He says that if there is underwriting they will have to give £400,000 to their Hamburg friends; from £250,000 to £500,000 to Whigham [of Robert Fleming]; something to his Trust Company; and that after allowing for intimate friends of the three firms there will only be a paltry sum for the brokers and that it will consequently cause more heartburnings to underwrite than not to do so.

The next day, however, at a meeting of the consortium and others at Schroders, the decision was announced by Baron Schroder that each of the five brokers, including Cazenove's, would receive £100,000 underwriting to place, whereupon, according to Villiers' report of the conference: 'Serocold was asked his opinion and he was very definite that, however small the participation, the stockbrokers would much prefer to have some underwriting.' The prospectus appeared the following week and the issue (done in the event at 93½) was successful, with over £35 million applied for.

By the mid-1920s, it was an impressive range of connections that Cazenove's was starting to draw upon in its new issue business. Taking the years 1926 and 1927, there were at least seventeen other flotations (i.e. apart from the foreign loans organised by the consortium) with which the firm was associated. Of these, it acted as sponsor or co-sponsor in six and was broker or co-broker for the other eleven. Issues that Cazenove's sponsored included those for the Brazil Land, Cattle and Packing Company, the Rhodesian Land, Cattle and Ranching Corporation, the Second Alliance Trust Company, and the giant northern department store chain Lewis's. Issuing houses that employed Cazenove's during these two years included Schroders, for the Soc. Internationale d'Energie Hydro-Electrique; Cull & Co, for Selection Trust and also British Celanese, which in 1927 Henry Dreyfus wrested control of from Loewenstein; Power Securities Corporation, for the Buenos Aires Central Railway and the Buenos Aires Lacroze Light and Power Company; the Whitehall Trust (of which Kindersley was chairman), for Debenhams Securities; and Erlangers, for the City of Santos 7% Loan and the International Sleeping Car Share Trust. Combining diversity with solidity, it was already an array that few other stockbrokers could match.

One noteworthy episode was the issue by Ford Motors in December 1928 of 2.8 million shares of £1 each at par. In the words of the prospectus: 'The Company will erect on its 300–acre site at Dagenham a motor manufacturing factory which will be the largest in the world outside the U.S.A., and will be equipped on the most modern lines, based on the unique experience of the Ford organisation.' On the day the prospectus was published, the *FT* in its comments looked back on the success of the old 'T' model and ahead to the new 'A' model: 'Assuming that the new company [i.e. Ford of England] does as well with the new model as has been done in the past with the old, the shares should prove an excellent industrial investment.' The issue was handled as a placing by Morgan Grenfell, with Rowe & Pitman and Cazenove's as brokers. Hornby recalls the aftermath:

In those days there were no rules to speak of covering placings and one could distribute the shares as one pleased. We divided them around favoured clients, mostly in smallish amounts of a few thousands or even hundreds. On the first day of dealing New York came in a buyer at £1 premium (Kemp-Gee had an unlimited order and bought a million shares from us on that day). On the second evening they closed at £2 premium and eventually they settled down at about £3. Much money was thus made and our friends were pleased.

It was the first major issue done with Morgan Grenfell and the harbinger of much future co-operation.

Hornby himself, who had come to Cazenove's in 1927 on the recommendation of Bromley-Martin, was soon closely involved in a notable new issue scheme. His father was a partner in W. H. Smith & Son, the owner of which, the second Lord Hambleden, died early in 1929 at the age of forty-five leaving large death duties to pay. Almost all his fortune was tied up in the business and there was a real possibility of the family losing control. Hornby's father consulted Serocold and told him that he was reluctant to disclose W. H. Smith's profits. The upshot was the formation of a new company, Hambleden Estates, to hold Smith's leasehold and freehold properties, valued at £1.7 million, and lease them back to Smith's as the operating company. Hambleden Estates would then raise money on the open market, while keeping its equity shares in the hands, directly or indirectly, of the partners of Smith's. Altogether it was, in the words of the historian of that company, an 'ingenious essay in borrowing'. Consequently, Cazenove's in March 1929 sponsored a public offering by Hambleden Estates of £1 million 6% mortgage debentures and undertook a private placing of £500,000 in 7% cumulative preference shares. To the relief of those concerned, the only necessary disclosure concerning Smith's profits was that they covered at least fourfold the service of the debentures and preference. The issue went very smoothly, which was especially gratifying for the young Hornby, who had largely handled the deal: 'I was called in to the partners' room and given a cheque for £500 – my first taste of blood.'

How did Cazenove's compare with other company brokers in relation to the new issue boom that, by the time of the Hambleden issue, was starting to draw to a close? What is striking is the firm's admirable restraint at a time when there was a great deal of easy money to be made. Thus in 1928, the total of nine issues with which it was associated was exceeded by as many as sixteen other firms, all members of the Stock Exchange. It is perhaps invidious to give examples, but these firms included such now forgotten names as T. Gordon Hensler & Co (twenty-five issues of generally poor quality, like Selecta Gramophones Ltd and Continuous Gramophones Ltd); Moy, Smith, Vandervell & Co (fifteen issues, including the notorious Anty-Sag Parent Co, supposed manufacturers of a patent mattress support); and Gibbs (John), Son & Smith (fifteen issues, featuring Worldecho Records Ltd and Colour Snapshots (1928) Ltd). When Cazenove's did do a 'popular' issue, such as a cinema one, it was a sound concern like Denman Picture Houses in April 1928. The sponsors for this were Ostrer Brothers, who in the persons of Isidore and Mark Ostrer were notable pioneers of the British film industry, above all in the form of the Gaumont-British Picture Corporation. There was a connection through one of Micklem's brothers and the firm had much to do with them over the years. Cazenove's in the late 1920s clearly possessed the capacity to say 'no', and one particular example stands out. This was when Clarence Hatry, the leading financier of the boom and a flawed character of genuinely creative ability, approached the firm with a perfectly respectable prospectus that already had the name of Cazenove's printed on it as brokers. But Micklem did not appreciate this and, in Hornby's crisp phrase, 'sent him packing'. It was, as events transpired, a crucial instance of quality control.

Taking the business as a whole, it was steadily rather than vastly profitable during the first post-war decade. In only two years (1919 and 1921) did the net profit fall below £50,000, while only in another two (1927 and 1928) did it rise above £150,000. In the best year, 1927, the profit of £171,710 would have been less than that earned by several other firms; though at a time when an eight-bedroom house in Belgravia cost less than £5,000 and a seven-bedroom house in Wimbledon less than £2,000, it was a tidy enough sum to be divided among eight partners. On the income side the great variable was inevitably commission, while the annual amount earned by the money-broking operation soon settled down at around £25,000. Business expenses were for several years only just above £10,000, but by 1927 had climbed to over £21,000; and the staff bonus, normally about £4,000, roughly doubled during the boom years of the late twenties. Together they continued to comprise a scale of expenses that, to modern eyes, seems utterly negligible.

In fact, the firm remained essentially small and intimate, even though it was gradually growing. Indeed, as early as March 1919, following the merger with Tomkinson Brunton, a change of address took place because the old office at 52 Threadneedle Street no longer sufficed. We again have Kathleen Cross's account, written some sixty years later:

Fortunately offices became vacant at No 43 Threadneedle Street. This was the Bank of Montreal opposite Finch Lane. The bank had the ground and first floor as an entirely self-contained building. The Peruvian Corporation had the second floor and Cazenove's the third floor. The offices were reached either by a staircase or a very old lift; this was worked on a pulley system by a caretaker but it was quite often out of order.

Our office was approached from the landing through swing doors and there was a corridor dividing it into two halves. First on the left was a large room for the partners. Mr Serocold had a desk on his own in the far corner and then came a large centre table. Along one side of this sat Mr Geoffrey Barnett [not yet in possession of his own room] surrounded by 'In' and 'Out' baskets as he signed the letters and contracts; opposite him sat Mr Tomkinson and Mr Micklem – they were both out quite a lot down in the House, keeping appointments with business houses etc. The next room was small and occupied by Mr Sidney Brunton. After this came a medium-sized room for the typist (a male) and filing cabinets. Lastly on this side was a fair-sized room with a desk running along under the window for three transfer clerks and in the centre a large plain deal table. On this all the bonds and transfers for delivery were placed to be dealt with by two Veteran Corps men. In the afternoon it was used for making the tea on and when this was cleared away it became the post room. Also in this room was an old-fashioned letter press; all the letters and contracts were copied into buff-coloured books – we had no carbon copies.

On the other side of the corridor, first came a room for Mr Arthur Cazenove and Mr Swainson Akroyd. Next came a room with a small old-fashioned telephone switchboard which was worked by Jack Shepherd. He was a great character whom we inherited from Tomkinson Brunton. He had been a butler in very high society; he reprimanded anyone who did not answer the telephone immediately – even the partners. The door of this room was immediately opposite that of the partners' room; he would blast their door open and shout, 'Sir, don't you know I am calling you?' In this room there was also a desk for the dealers to use when they came up from the House.

Half way down the corridor on this side was an opening with a small counter. In this room sat [among others] old Joe Mead of Tomkinson Brunton on inscribed stock and working out contracts. There was not even a comptometer in those days and all tickets and contracts had to be worked out with a ready-reckoner if you were not good at maths! I remember the first comptometer arriving in 1921. Joe refused to use the B ...... thing and it was amazing how he got the answers out as quick as the machine, no matter what state of intoxication he was in! Every day at eleven he disappeared and went to Pimms who were next door to us. When in season he had his dozen oysters and brown bread and butter, otherwise he had a sole, with his pint of Pimms No. 1.

It was now decided to cut down the high desks to table level and we were provided with chairs in about 1921. The toilet arrangements were very much improved here; there were three small suites, one each on the landing immediately below the suite of offices. Females used that at the bottom, next was for male staff, and the top one for our partners.

We did work very late hours, often until 10.00 p.m., when we were busy, including coming in on Saturday mornings to write transfers. As we were nearly opposite Finch Lane, it was useful when we were at the office late for the men to go over there for refreshments; I was left in the office and they brought a packet of sandwiches back for me. We were brokers to Martinez Gassiot, the port wine importers, and we always had some cases in the office; it was usual for port wine to be served in 'tumblers' during the evening. The first time I had it, I went to sleep over my transfers, so they called a taxi and sent me home! After that I had a special small glass.

It was greatly due to the fact that we all knew each other and worked as a family sharing the responsibilities that makes Cazenove's what they are today. After the House was closed and all our general business out of the way, we all sat down to write transfers. During the day I made out the order for the amount of stamped deeds required and the messengers collected them at the Stamp Office; the next job was to pin on the relative certificates and 'Names'. The dealers were roped into this and quite often the partners would write some. It is my belief, that for continued success you must all work and pull together, no matter who or what you are.

Part of the team spirit must have derived from the fact that soon after the war Arthur Philip Cazenove seems to have introduced a quarterly bonus system that was in effect a profit-sharing scheme rather than being dependent on the particular impulse of the senior partner of the day, which for a long time remained the case in most stockbroking firms. Then as later, the bonus was in lieu of overtime and obviously varied with the amount of business the firm was doing. Kathleen Cross's first quarterly share (in 1919) was £9, 'which seemed quite a lot to me then'. It was in general a highly popular scheme with the staff and undoubtedly did help to engender a certain special feeling at Cazenove's.

By 1926 things were again very cramped – with the growth of business, number of partners and staff – and the firm decided not to renew its Threadneedle Street lease. The new home from March of that year was 10 Old Broad Street. This was a recently-constructed building in the modern style and owned by Lazards, who had their banking hall on the ground floor. Cazenove's occupied the fourth floor, the Whitehall Trust part of the fifth, and James Capel the sixth. The premises as a whole were somewhat more spacious, though hardly palatial, as Hornby found when he arrived the following year:

It wasn't very extensive. There was one open office that housed all the staff [about forty in number]. The manager, Hanneford, had his desk in a commanding position on a dais at one end. Under him like a clerk of the court sat Albert Martin (Mart), his deputy. One little corner was partitioned off which seated about six people at one table. This housed dealers and miscellaneous attachés. A passage led to the partners' room, which housed all ten of them except for Miles Brunton who occupied a separate room on the other side of the lift with his small staff of three or four. There was a telephone room, a typist's room (Miss Cross and perhaps one other) and a waiting-room and that's about all.

As to what life was like in Old Broad Street, Hornby recalled his early days with evident affection:

I was set to work with Charles Pugh in the transfers, the traditional starting point for all trainees. We plugged away pretty hard and used to have a late evening or two around account days. Mart's younger brother, Ernie, used to write out all the contracts in his beautiful copper-plate hand and Mead used to check them miraculously and instantaneously in his head. A great character he was with a mane of grey curls and a florid complexion and we used to call him the Duke of Godstone. Hanneford presided benignly like a hen with her chickens. He'd been a tea-taster but was an excellent manager and controlled everyone calmly and firmly and as far as I can remember everyone was happy. There was a bonus scheme and one was called up to his desk to receive one's slip at the end of a quarter and he beamed at you as he handed it out.

The office manager was then a powerful figure, for the basic system that obtained in all stockbroking offices (and which lasted until well after the Second World War) was that the partners secured the business, the staff executed it and the manager acted as a bridge between the two. The notion of such a thing as an 'administrative partner' was not yet a gleam in the eye. George Hanneford had become manager at about the time of the move, and it was a reflection of his importance that between the wars he was the only person (partners included) driven daily to the office by a chauffeur. He was a large, genial man and is remembered for the way that he exercised his considerable authority over the staff with great generosity of spirit.

Some others deserve mention. There was Katie Cross herself, who ran an informal tuck shop, the proceeds of which went partly to charity and partly back to the staff in the form of a 'divvy' at Christmas. She was a renowned disciplinarian and not just a secretary. Eventually she took over the ticket account and the jobbers' ledger, which she ran with an iron will. Another person of those days who knew his own mind was Major Whittington, recalled by Hornby as 'a tall, spindly, kindly man with iron spectacles and an untidy moustache'. An Ulsterman who had seen better days, he became between the wars the firm's first statistician. He had a ticker-tape in order to follow the latest price changes and, in his beautiful handwriting, made out cards for every client and kept a record of what they had bought or sold. None, however, aroused more curiosity in Old Broad Street than Mrs Lorna Keeler, who not long after the move arrived as the firm's first female switchboard operator. The men kept coming into her room to see what she looked like, but in her own words she 'knew how to behave without being familiar'. If her lines were short and a member of staff was having a long private call, she was ruthless in cutting in to reclaim the line. A trained telephonist who relished her working life at Cazenove's, she deemed it permissible for a man to ring a girl to fix a meeting but not (as she later put it) for 'half an hour's flirting'.

Sometimes in the office but usually out of it were those who were active on the floor of the Stock Exchange itself. Hornby again provides the memories:

> The partners then mostly dealt themselves and entered their own bargains in the book, but there was one professional dealer, Bertram Crosse, a great raconteur and a staunch member of the London Rifle Brigade – he was their quarter-master. He was easy-going and very popular in the House and mostly did country brokers' orders which arrived by telegram at our stand. We had no box and dealers had to stand around watching for their number to be lighted up when they would run to the telephone room; or their name would be shouted by the top-hatted waiters perched in their pulpits.

Crosse was indeed a tremendous character and, with his fruity voice as well as choice anecdotes, was in particular demand as an after-dinner speaker.

Altogether, it was a distinctive way of life, one very different from what later generations were to know. Looking back in 1971 on those inter-war days, Hornby thought that the great change had been one of tempo: 'Everything used to be more leisurely. Communications were not so good, there was no aeroplane travel and there seemed to be more time for everything. We worked quite hard but we were always able to leave the office at five to play tennis or watch the last hour and a half at Lord's.' In short, in his rather wistful words: 'City life used to consist in leisurely visits around the City and there was time to think. The whole thing was more amateurish, as cricket used to be.'

———————

The years 1929 to 1932 were traumatic ones for most people in the square mile or indeed having anything to do with it. If there was a single villain of the piece, it was undoubtedly Hatry. In the spring of 1929 he began to attempt an enormously ambitious reconstruction of the British steel industry, but by June his money was running out and on September 20th it was revealed that he had been forging bogus share certificates. He was arrested, share prices fell sharply, and then only a few weeks later came the Wall Street crash. The next year, 1930, saw the whole of the western industrial and financial world in crisis. In Britain this culminated in the climactic episode of September 1931 when the country was forced off the gold standard, this time permanently. From the point of view of the Stock Exchange there was a distinct if bitter irony involved. For fourteen years the House had been closed on Saturdays – for some years at the request of the joint-stock banks, whose staff the war had severely depleted – but at last, following many complaints, it was decided to end 'Holiday Saturday'. The first 'open' Saturday was scheduled for September 19th – Britain's last day, as it turned out, on the gold standard. The run on sterling was at its most intense, and 'Autolycus' on the Monday morning reflected on the last day of the old order:

> While Stock Exchange members are not of those who wear their hearts upon their sleeves for daws to peck at, it is impossible for them not to feel a quiet pride in the fact of London being able and ready to stand up to the flood of selling which took place. If ever the jobber vindicated his claim to fill an essential place in the machinery of the world's financial hub, he did it in the Consol market last Saturday.

On that Saturday, Sir Archibald Campbell, chairman of the Stock Exchange Committee, was summoned with the deputy-chairman to a meeting at the Bank of England, where the deputy-governor informed them that it was no longer possible to remain on the standard. They were asked if the Stock Exchange should be open after the announcement was made, to which, as Campbell later reported to the Committee, they replied that, 'they had come to the conclusion that in the interest of the Country, the Stock Exchange should not be open'. And: 'They were then informed that the Banks shared this opinion.' The House was thus not open for business on Monday the 21st, following the previous day's announcement. That at least was the theory. The practice was rather different, as Charles Purnell, an authorised clerk who soon afterwards joined Cazenove's, subsequently recalled:

> We all assembled in the street and there was a rip-roaring market, the theory being that now there could only be runaway inflation – I suppose we had Germany in mind. I have never forgotten it because I had had two wisdom teeth out on the Sunday and it had not been my intention to come to work on the Monday, but perforce I had to.

The House formally re-opened on Wednesday the 23rd, with all bargains to be done for cash and not to be continued from day to day, a restriction that remained in force for a considerable time. Meanwhile, the market maintained its downward course and did not finally bottom out until the middle of June 1932, by which time it was entirely typical that a popular security such as Great Western Railway ordinary shares stood at a meagre 25, compared with 86¾ three years earlier.

Yet it is probably fair to say that, in two particular ways, the stock market that emerged out of these desperate years was an inherently sounder organism than at the outset. This was due partly to the Stock Exchange Committee, which in the immediate wake of the discovery of the Hatry forgeries showed a willingness and capacity to deal decisively with the wider implications of the situation that marked out for all to see that it no longer regarded its duty as regulating the activities of a private club, but rather that the authority it exercised was on behalf of the public over a major public institution. This was not enunciated as such at the time, but the manifest logic was there, representing a fundamental turning-point in Stock Exchange history. The other beneficial effect was that the collapse of the new issue boom, and the long winter that followed, drove a generation of company promoters out of existence, never to return, at least not in their traditional (and shameless) Victorian garb. For many years these promoters had been a thorn in the flesh of the Stock Exchange, no doubt enabling some members to make quick fortunes but at the same time exploiting the market's facilities in such a way as to give the Exchange itself a generally poor reputation. If the result was a duller City, most found it an acceptable price to pay for a virtual end to what had often been extreme malpractice.

The new issue market did not actually dry up during the three years from 1929 but it was reduced to intermittent issues of usually sound quality. And significantly, it was in this context of a flight to quality – the inevitable accompaniment of financial crisis – that Cazenove's now began to dominate the field of company finance in relation to its stockbroking rivals. The figures tell much of the story. In 1928 the firm had been associated with nine issues, a total putting it well down the numerical league table. But in 1930, it was again associated with nine issues, which was more than almost any other broker, certainly among those concerned with industrial finance (as opposed to government finance, whether national or local). The same was true in 1931. The Cazenove tally of five was hardly vast, but no other company broker could match it. It was, in a sense, the start of the modern history of Cazenove's, a breakthrough in the corporate domain that owed everything to the high reputation that the firm had achieved by the time the City's travails began. Again, one can hardly overestimate the importance of that policy of restraint during the bubble years, when so many other firms established connections and backed issues that they subsequently regretted.

A handful of particular flotations stand out from these difficult years. Two were for companies already becoming household names. 'The products are well known for their variety and excellence, and comprise almost every description of prepared foods', the prospectus fairly trumpeted at the time of the issue in November 1929 of Crosse and Blackwell's £1½ million 6½% debentures. The issue was sponsored by the British Trusts Association, and Cazenove's was sole broker. Seven months later it shared duties with Belisha & Co when Helbert Wagg and the Industrial Finance and Investment Corporation between them sponsored a £2 million Marks & Spencer debenture issue. 'Ninety per cent of the company's merchandise is of British manufacture', the prospectus boasted, adding that 'the goods are sold at various price ranges, with a maximum of 5s per article.' The lists were quickly oversubscribed.

That same month, June 1930, Cazenove's acted on behalf of Cull & Co in a major Chester Beatty issue, namely the Roan Antelope Copper Mines in Northern Rhodesia. 'Like all mining ventures, it contains a strong element of speculation,' the *FT* cautioned; but the issue was fully subscribed. Towards the end of the year Cazenove's, with two Scottish brokers, acted for Power Securities in finding capital for the British Aluminium Company, which had recently begun what would become a fraught and controversial operation to construct a mammoth hydro-electric installation at Lochaber in Scotland. Subsequent controversy also attended the offer for sale made by Cazenove's in July 1931 for 300,000 7% preference shares of £1 each at par and 400,000 ordinary shares of 5s each at £1 of Great Universal Stores. Abraham Rose had founded the business many years earlier and was still chairman; and the other four members of the board all belonged to the Rose family. The prospectus was bullish in the extreme, a confidence that the *FT* shared: 'Judging by the figures disclosed, the Great Universal Stores has done much towards justifying its title. It is a thoroughly progressive mail order business, radiating from Manchester, London and Glasgow.' Both market and public agreed, and the offer was heavily oversubscribed. The issue had been underwritten by Cazenove's and for the moment it all seemed very satisfactory.

Turning to the day-to-day business between 1929 and 1932, we again know precious little, apart from the story that in 1931 Serocold was called to the Bank of England to explain how it was that Tomkinson had come to reclaim tax on the coupons of more Indian 6% stock than was actually in issue. It is said that Serocold suggested to the Governor, Montagu Norman, that matters would be simplified if more stock was to be issued, but that is probably apocryphal. Certainly the business as a whole did not flourish – probably no stockbroking business did – but neither did it grind to a halt. Indeed, the net profit in 1930 was remarkably handsome, at over £¼ million, before falling sharply to just over £100,000 in 1931, partly due to a considerable loss caused by an uncovered gilt position at the time of going off the gold standard. The general mood remained quietly confident in these years, with no significant cutting back on expenses, and in February 1930 the firm held its first dinner party at the Savoy Hotel for partners and staff. It was a lavish six-course affair, complete with a cabaret of a comic man on a bike, and long remembered by those present.

The dinner was attended by forty-five members of staff, including several who would in time become partners. One was Philip Cazenove, who became a partner soon after the party. He was a great-great-nephew of his namesake and grandson of the Edward Cazenove who had briefly been a partner in the 1850s. He had come to the firm in the early 1920s, after he had been given the choice on completing his education of either travelling abroad or becoming a stockbroker after a winter's hunting. Characteristically he chose the latter. In his early years with Cazenove's he often arrived on Monday mornings limping so badly that Neal the office manager would shout at him, 'They should tie you on', and he remained thereafter a fearless rider to hounds. In due course he became a valuable element in the partnership, though at this stage he was still fulfilling largely routine tasks of dealing in the House and obtaining prices. Another future partner was Stephen de Yarburgh Bateson (later Lord Deramore). His father, a partner of R. E. Tomkinson & Co, had been a renowned City character, an immensely tall man who used to drive a carriage and four from Hatfield every day in a top hat; and for some years after the merger he had continued to come to the office. Stephen Bateson himself worked from the late 1920s with Miles Brunton on the money-broking side. Almost as tall as his father and equally well-connected, though too profligate for his own good, he fitted in perfectly, shared with Brunton a love of practical jokes and likewise was highly popular in the discount market. Ultimately, however, he was not a 'serious' figure. The same could not be said of Ernest Bedford, known to almost everyone as 'Beddy'. He had come to Cazenove's in 1928 from Seligman Brothers, where he had dealt in foreign exchange. He had been recruited by Scaramanga in order to man the firm's first 'box' (i.e. its dealing office) in the Stock Exchange, acting as the vital link between the office and the dealers on the floor. This first 'box' was literally just a telephone box, down some steep stairs in Angel Court, but even there Bedford made his qualities felt. To quote Hornby: 'He was the best telephoner I have ever encountered – calm, clear, never raising his voice. He had a quick and

orderly mind and he soon revolutionised our dealing communications.'
Quiet, loyal and wholly unassuming, he became, in the words of another
future partner, 'the centre of the sanded egg timer, with partners and clients
above and jobbers below: everything passed him.'

Beddy and all his colleagues soon faced a major event: merger. The
suitors were the stockbroking firm of Greenwood & Co, which in about 1930
seems to have made an initial approach to Cazenove's (in the persons of
Belmont and Scaramanga) with a view to a union. Greenwoods was a long-
established firm, founded in 1872, which for many years had been
dominated by the remarkable Lord Faringdon, or Alexander Henderson as
he had originally been. Self-educated, decisive and entrepreneurial, he
made himself into one of the most important and respected people in the
City, with fingers in many pies but renowned above all for his South
American interests. His stockbroking firm (based at 28 Austin Friars)
naturally specialised in that part of the world, acting as brokers to the
Central Argentine Railway, the Buenos Ayres Great Southern Railway, the
Central Uruguay Railway and others. It was also broker to most of the
British mainline railway companies. By the early 1930s the firm was perhaps
no longer in its prime, but it was certainly not moribund. Indeed, in 1930
alone it was involved in as many as fourteen new issues, almost all of which
it sponsored. The real problem was that – as the octogenarian Faringdon
perceived – the firm in its existing form lacked a plausible long-term future.

The reason was essentially dynastic, compounded by an unwillingness
over the years to bring outside talent into the partnership. Faringdon had
two sons, Alec and Arnold, who had been partners since before the war. But
for all their pleasantness as people, it was evident that neither was going to
develop into a major business-getter or City figure. Alec, anyway, died
suddenly in November 1931, leaving only Arnold for the future. Moreover,
Faringdon's younger brother, Harry Henderson, who for a long time had
been the day-to-day head of Greenwoods, had died in March 1931. Thus by
the end of 1931 the only partners were Faringdon himself, his son Arnold
and a young broker called Frank Holt, who had recently become a partner
on the basis of Faringdon's friendship with Sir Follett Holt, an important
force in the South American railways world. Holt was an able, determined
person but could hardly be expected to carry on his shoulders the burden of
the firm's future. Faringdon may have been putting out feelers for a merger
before 1931, but the two deaths that year must at the least have confirmed
him in the rightness of his policy. It was a problem that he should perhaps
have tackled earlier, but it was entirely typical that he successfully resolved
it before he died.

The firms must already have known a fair bit about each other, but during the period before the merger three people were particularly important as 'marriage brokers'. One was the leading jobber Gordon Anketell, who may well have been the person who made the initial suggestion. The other two were both from Glyn Mills, namely General Sir Herbert Lawrence and the managing director Sir Arthur Maxwell, who were the people whom both partnerships (traditionally close to Glyn Mills) consulted about the merits of the other. It was in many ways a natural marriage, and negotiations seem to have gone relatively smoothly. From the point of view of Greenwoods, Cazenove's above all had the talent at the top to recommend it, a talent that meant the particular strengths that Greenwoods had developed (above all in South America) would not go to waste once Faringdon retired or died. From the point of view of Cazenove's, merger with Greenwoods had three main attractions in addition to the new business it would bring: a certain amount of extra capital, though Faringdon had never put much of his vast wealth into his stockbroking business; a further infusion of that quality one might call 'respectability', though already the firm was much more respectable than most; and thirdly, the increase in size that would accompany merger, indubitably establishing Cazenove's as a major force. None of these attractions, one must add, would have carried any weight with Serocold, Micklem and Tomkinson if they had not also felt assured that after the merger it would be they who would be continuing to run the business and be making the key decisions. In that fundamental sense, it was not a union of equals.

The announcement was made in February 1932, and at the end of March the two firms merged, becoming Cazenove Akroyds & Greenwood & Co. The business was to be carried on in Old Broad Street and Lord Faringdon became titular head, bringing with him into the partnership his son Arnold and Frank Holt. 'An important Stock Exchange fusion', *The Times* declared, referring to how 'on the ground alike of age, wealth and prestige these two firms stand in the front rank'. Cazenove's had once again gone outside to take in fresh resources. The consequences were to be wholly beneficial, but on this occasion it was a less life-saving operation than it had been in times past.

CHAPTER SIX

Building the business
1932–1945

Especially pleased (if a little nervous) about the merger was the bulk of the Greenwoods staff, who felt that Lord Faringdon had made a good arrangement on their behalf and once again shown himself to be a shrewd man. They particularly appreciated the profit-sharing system in existence at Cazenove's, with the young clerk Charles Purnell (soon to be a dealer) recalling many years later that 'my income was certainly 50% or 60% greater in the first year of the amalgamation and accelerated quite well from that point on'. In human terms the assimilation went remarkably well, though even after the Second World War someone might still be called 'a Greenwoods man' by one of the older Cazenove people. The only significant exception to this smooth process was at the level of office manager, where William Brabner of Greenwoods was quite unable to reconcile himself to the prospect of working under George Hanneford, who had carried through the merger to his own entire satisfaction as well as that of the Cazenove partners. A joint appointment was, as far as Hanneford was concerned, unthinkable; and as a result Brabner returned to Austin Friars, which Faringdon continued to use as his personal base, never apparently entering the doors of Old Broad Street. It was a peace worth having at £150 a year, paid to Brabner for life.

There was one amusing sequel to the merger. A few months after it took place, Faringdon marked the event by giving a private dinner to the partners at his house in Arlington Street. After referring in his speech to the 'Great Universal' troubles that the country was going through, he announced that Greenwoods had not achieved its expected profit (presumably in the previous Stock Exchange year) and even suggested the possibility of readjusting the new partnership percentages. Serocold thanked him, but added that Micklem had already anticipated this and that, therefore, nothing should be changed.

Several of the Greenwoods recruits in time became significant figures at Cazenove's. One was Purnell, another was Angus Eames, a future dealer, while Charles Strangeman, a talented mathematician, helped before the war to form the nucleus of what eventually became the investment department, specialising in private client business. In broad terms, life continued to be much the same after the merger as it had been before. The loans department, for instance, still sent messengers walking to the banks with £5 million in a blue linen sack; Major Whittington still kept the press cuttings, the records of important clients' holdings and the Exchange Telegraph cards that were then the partners' main research tool; and several of the secretaries in the office were still men. Also worthy of mention in a 'domestic' context is the indispensable Higgs, who was former Royal Artillery and looked after the partners. He kept their desks tidy, filled their inkwells, squeezed oranges for the fresh juice that was Serocold's regular breakfast, and obeyed Geoffrey Barnett's great command, 'Tuck me in, Higgs'. Inevitably, the size of the staff was quite a lot bigger. Frederick Cathie, another Greenwoods man who became a Cazenove stalwart, has recalled the set-up in Old Broad Street as it existed by the mid-1930s. According to him, the female staff comprised two partners' secretaries, four or five typists and two or three comptometer operators. While as for the male staff, totalling as many as sixty or seventy, they roughly divided into the following areas: transfers (six or seven), contracts (three), inscribed stock (three), journals (two), ledgers (four), bonds (three or four), jobbers' ledgers (three or four), cashier (one), dividends (two), statistics (three or four), managers (three), loans (six or seven), messengers (fourteen or fifteen, mostly men not boys), and a handful of dealers. Everyone still knew everyone else, but office life no longer had quite the intimacy that previous generations had enjoyed.

Two major developments shortly before the war further reflected the increasing scale of the firm's ambitions. One was the start that was made in about 1936 towards mechanisation. It was, among other things, an early example of Antony Hornby's invaluable knack for talking to the right person and extracting the vital bit of information. He recalls what happened:

We were the first Stock Exchange firm to do anything in this line. It came about from a conversation I had at W. H. Smith about new accounting processes. Michael, my brother, told me they had been advised by a marvellous man called Heath Robinson! Despite his name we asked him to come and see us and he and Charles Pugh and I put our heads together and the result was we went ahead on his advice with installing the Ormig system and it stood us in good stead until we computerised in the late sixties. Pugh worked tremendously hard to adapt the system to our purposes and succeeded brilliantly but naturally with some teething troubles. The system was one of a master sheet on which all information about a bargain was entered and from this master sheet the contract was produced by impression and in the same way by a system of masks relevant information was posted to the various ledgers. There was, therefore, no manual posting and no chance of error once the right information had been fed to the master sheet and checked. This was a major breakthrough and enabled us to transact a much greater volume of business with no increase in staff.

The Heath Robinson was the cartoonist's brother and he was unmercifully ribbed because of the connection. In practice, Walter Rudge, on jobbers' ledgers, still found that he had to write up the books as he had always done, in order to check what was going on. Nevertheless, Hornby was quite correct in seeing the mechanisation – essentially a line-posting system – as an important step and one that did much to create the firm's future profitability.

The other major development was the move in 1937 out of 10 Old Broad Street and into a new home. It was an inevitable decision because the office had become increasingly cramped. The search for new premises was conducted by Holt and Scaramanga, and eventually the choice narrowed down to 117 Old Broad Street and 12 Tokenhouse Yard, with the latter finally chosen. The first putty-laid building in the area, it had been built in 1871 as the home of the merchant bank Frederick Huth & Co, which had subsequently fallen on hard times. The Bank of England kept the firm going from the early 1920s, and now in 1937 it was being taken over by the British Overseas Bank, which had no use for the building. Cazenove's took up the remaining eleven years of what was a very cheap lease, subsequently renewing it, and of course the firm remains there to the present day. Tokenhouse Yard itself was a seventeenth-century creation and appropriately it was built by Sir William Petty, the earliest English writer on political economy. In 1937 the move, supervised by Holt, took place over an arduous weekend near the end of March and it seems that early reactions to the firm's new home were mixed. A few found it something of a rabbit warren, with everyone split up into different places; but more were favourably struck by the large, unsupported banking hall, the carved mahogany originally shipped from West Africa and the fine, old-fashioned teak furniture. Hornby's words, written with the benefit of hindsight, are apposite: 'It is an office of dignity and it somehow suited our style down to the ground. I firmly believe it had a considerable influence on the growth and the continuance of the tradition of our business.' Above all, 12 Tokenhouse Yard was and is *distinctive*. Cazenove's, becoming between the wars a unique stockbroking firm, had found a home entirely in keeping.

Within the partnership itself, there were relatively few changes during the 1930s. Lord Faringdon remained titular head for one year after the merger, and Hornby recalls how he 'was told to visit him once a week, which I did and found him mellow and helpful'. In 1933 Faringdon retired and his son Arnold died suddenly, leaving Frank Holt as the only surviving partner from Greenwoods; in March of the following year, Faringdon himself died. The only other person not to remain in the partnership until the war was Ashmead Vigors who, after a particularly good year, retired in 1937 in order to hunt in Ireland, which he did until a ripe old age. He was replaced by Stephen Bateson. Otherwise, there were only three new partners during these years. One was David Shaw-Kennedy (1933), a gifted mathematician who had joined Cazenove's from the discount market and continued to do much of his business with discount companies and banks. He specialised in gilt switches and, according to Hornby, 'made the firm a great deal of money by extraordinary manipulations between the Union Discount, the jobbers, ourselves and Martins Bank'. Quiet, thoughtful and gentle, he was a stalwart worker on behalf of the Eton Manor Club in the East End. Another new partner was Derek Schreiber (1936). He was a grandson of Lord Faringdon, had only come to the firm the previous year and essentially represented the interests of the Henderson family. Formerly with the 11th Hussars, he was very tall with a soldierly bearing. Although without a City background and by no means a natural stockbroker, he is fairly described by Hornby as someone who 'knew everyone in all walks of life, had common sense and was used to taking decisions'. He was also 'a most delightful person' and became 'very popular in the firm'. The third and, in the long run, by far the most important of the new partners was Antony Hornby himself (1933). His father had made W. H. Smith into a great firm and he himself had been educated at Winchester and New College, Oxford. He had then spent a year travelling round the world with Alfred Beit and a year working in Trinidad for an oil subsidiary of Central Mining. He decided that the oil business was not for him, returned to London and secured a berth at Cazenove's via Bromley-Martin, a first cousin of his mother's. During the 1930s he was certainly not a negligible figure in the firm, but it was not yet clear that he would become a major one. Rather like Serocold before 1914, his reputation was that of something of a playboy; and, again rather like Serocold, though in a different way, war would change everything.

Meanwhile, a slightly younger generation was also coming into the firm during the 1930s though not reaching partnership level until after the war. Four people stand out as having an important long-term future. Cedric Barnett, the son of Geoffrey, was always destined for Cazenove's and on arrival was sent for six months to Francis & Praed, then the leading firm of gilt jobbers. This was to further his interest in gilts, following the interest in them which his father had displayed in earlier days. Barnett set his sights rather higher than his father and in time became a significant figure. Also specialising in gilts for a period, though in his case subsequently, was Herbert Ingram, a mathematician with a particular flair for guesswork and also, most unusually for the City, an engineering degree. He joined Cazenove's on marrying into the Palmer-Tomkinson family. The third person was Alexander Coombe-Tennant, whose mother was a Serocold. He quickly revealed a keen, fresh-minded interest in things and before long was helping Strangeman in his weekly task of preparing for clients a list of recommended stocks and shares that were currently available. Finally, there was Luke Meinertzhagen, who came to the firm in 1935 after only a year at university. He was soon working with Strangeman and Coombe-Tennant in the embryonic investment department and showing that 'feel' for City matters that in due course became his hallmark. It was especially appropriate that he went to Cazenove's, which he did because an uncle (Bernard Drake) was a friend of both Serocold and Micklem; for two years later, when the firm moved to Tokenhouse Yard, he had the peculiar satisfaction of working in the building that his grandfather had built as senior partner of Huths. The Meinertzhagen family as a whole was a famous City clan, and Luke proved to be a notable and wholly worthy representative.

Throughout this time, the dominant presences remained Serocold and Micklem, autocratically determining the partnership proportions and successfully insisting that a partnership could not prosper if any jealousies were allowed to develop within it. It was laid down that no partner had an exclusive preserve and that the more people and firms whom everyone knew the better it was. In that crucial sense, it was (and thereafter remained) a very real working partnership. Nevertheless, as Hornby recalls, the daily conduct of business in the 1930s was essentially haphazard: 'There was little concerted action. Claud and Charles were a law unto themselves – very busy and always on the move. They sat opposite each other at the same desk and sometimes they engaged in earnest whispered conversation together, clapped on their top hats with a set and determined expression and dashed out of the room.' Once out of the office, Serocold and Micklem would spend much of their day wandering about the City, seeing people and doing deals; or one of them might catch the tube to visit Crump at the Pru, or Serocold take the District Line in order to lunch at the Savoy. Between them they enjoyed a complete freedom of manoeuvre in their operations. Often, at about one o'clock, they would visit the market, question their own dealers at the firm's stand (commonly called 'the pulpit') and then go and talk to the jobbers they knew best. One of those dealers was the young Purnell, who later put his feelings simply and expressively: 'After the leisurely way in which we at Greenwoods had gone on, Claud Serocold and Charles Micklem were to me a revelation and a tremendous inspiration.'

Serocold himself, the elder man, remained reasonably fit during the 1930s, partly through taking up yoga, though in 1934 he did have to go to Switzerland to be treated by an eye specialist. That he retained all his salient qualities of crispness and decisiveness is shown in a nice cameo related by Hornby:

> Claud came round with me to the Central Mining one day to defend a scale charge that we had made for valuing a deceased estate – one of their directors, Eckstein, I think. The charge was £600. They asked for it to be reduced. Claud said we would charge nothing if they would do the liquidation through us. They paid the charge! The interview took two minutes.

Nevertheless, one has an impression that during these years Serocold was beginning to give way a little in importance to Micklem, the undisputed master of that expanding field of company finance which the firm was now occupying. Certainly, it is Micklem who dominates the collective memory of the 1930s. Many people, especially the younger element, found him somewhat frightening, or at the least forbidding. As a strong believer in self-education, he gave them little formal education, rightly trusting to the effectiveness of the occasional precept. Thus Hornby never forgot what happened after he had bought 2,000 shares for a notorious and flashy friend of his called Sylvia Ashley. He was called into the partners' room and asked if it was *the* Lady Ashley. When told it was, Micklem simply said, 'Go and sell the shares straight away and never deal for her again.' Or in the case of Purnell, when soon after the merger he proudly told Micklem that he had executed a selling order at $\frac{1}{8}$th when the shares were being offered at $\frac{1}{16}$th elsewhere, the response was again crushing and always remembered. 'I like good dealing,' he told the chastened dealer, 'but I do not like sharp dealing,' adding that Purnell must undo the bargain and do it at the correct price. Yet it is Purnell (who seems to have been a slight favourite, perhaps because he was building his career on merit alone) who also tells a story that shows the other side of Micklem, a side that not everyone saw but one that undoubtedly existed and should not be forgotten:

> It was not so long after I had been dealing and I had an order to sell 10,000 Guinness, which was quite a big order in those days. I went to Eustace Mordaunt – because he was one of the two principal jobbers, namely Bone Oldham & Mordaunt – and sort of opened the ball, but he opened me [i.e. persuaded Purnell to disclose whether he was a buyer or a seller, something a jobber was not supposed to do]. I had an idea of course what the price was elsewhere with Gayton Ellis. Having opened me he then, I thought, started to make the best of it or, from my point of view, the worst. 'Oh,' I said, 'I think I'll go on.' 'If you go on,' said Mordaunt, 'then you will have to come back – you will find the price might be somewhat different.' Naturally, the young dealer was a bit upset and I more or less said, 'I'll go and think it over.' It wasn't far off one o'clock, so I waited by the pulpit and Charles Micklem came in and I poured out my poor little soul. He looked at me and said, 'Now you go away and do the best you can, do what you think best, and it will be quite all right with me.' So I went back to Mordaunt, stuck out my chin as you might say and said, 'I spoke to Mr Micklem, Sir, and he said to carry on.' I got my price – and that was the great man, underneath this dour exterior, that Charles Micklem was.

The stock market went through three distinct phases during the seven years before the outbreak of the Second World War in September 1939: gradual recovery until about 1935; some two years of boom, though of a more measured nature than in the late 1920s; and then, from January 1937, a gradual decline, first as the economic cycle peaked on both sides of the Atlantic and later as the threat to European stability of Hitler became ominously clear. In broad terms the British economy recovered significantly during the 1930s, especially with the emergence of new growth sectors like motors and electricals, as well as buoyant housebuilding. Opportunities were therefore present in fair degree for an increasingly new issue oriented stockbroker like Cazenove's, and, not surprisingly, the firm's profits during these years mirrored the changing circumstances of the larger world fairly closely. The years 1934, 1935 and 1937 were all good ones producing net profits of over £400,000; but the best year (and arguably the best-ever in real terms in the firm's entire history) was 1936, earning for partners and staff £593,578. Then 1938 saw a sharp drop to £119,980. All this was on a capital of £500,000, as it was to remain for a long time; though as Hornby points out (applicable to the post-war as well as inter-war period), 'we effectively had much more money employed, as partners' income tax and surtax reserves, amounting to well over £1 million, were always being used.' Finance partner in the 1930s was Palmer-Tomkinson, who in conjunction with James Wannan of the accountants Spicer & Pegler performed an important, rather underestimated role for the firm, being especially effective in negotiations with the Inland Revenue. Altogether, it had become a highly profitable operation, particularly as not only was the volume of corporate business increasing, but also the number of private clients remained relatively small and the size of the average bargain relatively large – an extremely cost-effective combination. Expenses thus stayed fairly steady at a third or less in relation to income and, of course, the arrival of the Ormig system helped further. In short, the firm had found its overall direction, one which would require something cataclysmic to make it even think of changing course.

On the everyday stockbroking side, gilts retained much of their traditional dominance. Of the 5,629 securities in the Official List at the end of the Stock Exchange year in March 1938, over a quarter were industrial and commercial; but in terms of market value, the British Funds comprised almost 40 per cent, industrial and commercial securities only 14 per cent. In a non-inflationary age, gilts continued to be seen as fundamentally sounder investments than equities and few institutions included substantial holdings of ordinary shares in their portfolios. Under the able auspices of Palmer-Tomkinson and Shaw-Kennedy, the Cazenove gilts business flourished, and it is striking that the firm reputedly had as big an account with Wedd Jefferson (one of the three or four big gilt jobbers) as did the government brokers, Mullens & Co.

The great event of the decade was the conversion of July 1932, when Neville Chamberlain as Chancellor successfully converted 5% War Loan to a 3½% Stock. In what was one of the major financial operations of this century, Cazenove's distinguished itself in two particular ways. Firstly, Palmer-Tomkinson and Shaw-Kennedy, according to an understandably bemused Hornby, 'invented a method of converting it which entailed buying a Treasury stock and proffering this in exchange for the War 3½% and then selling one's War 5%.' And: 'This somehow not only earned us a good commission but benefited the converter. We dealt in millions of Stock and no-one else got the idea.' Secondly, Palmer-Tomkinson was one of the six brokers and dealers in the gilt-edged market who on the eve of the operation were summoned by H. F. Chamen, deputy-chairman of the Stock Exchange Committee, to discuss the fact that he had just received official notification, following a meeting held by the Treasury, that the banks would refuse to accept non-assented War Loan as security for loans. The upshot was that

Chamen, accompanied by the six, went to see Montagu Norman at the Bank, told him that such a decision would have a severely detrimental effect on the gilt-edged market and consequently on the conversion scheme, and in the end persuaded Norman to cancel the instructions which had been given. It is doubtful indeed if the conversion would have gone as smoothly as it did but for this intervention from the market.

Crucial to the everyday broking was the firm's 'box', which at some point before the war moved from the foot of the perilous stairs in Angel Court to a cubby hole in Shorters Court on the same level as the floor of the House. Space remained at a premium – with Beddy ensconced behind his switchboard, there was only room for two other people at any one time – but it was a much more convenient site. Moreover, private lines were now installed to Barings, Schroders, Singers and others, and these lines soon began to hum. In Purnell's admiring words, 'Beddy of course was a genius and not only did he handle the orders that came down direct from the partners upstairs, but he had established a tremendous rapport with the dealers in the various City houses and conducted a great deal of business downstairs on his own.'

As for the Cazenove dealers on the floor of the House who executed the orders sent to Beddy, there are at least five who should be mentioned, comprising between them a highly capable team. Bertram ('Bill') Crosse continued to cut a larger-than-life figure and was concerned with the day-to-day routine business, especially in the Industrial market (as the old Miscellaneous market was now called). Then there were Hugh McClure, who was also a lay preacher, and Jimmy McNaught, who specialised very effectively in foreign bonds and in particular the South American business that the merger with Greenwoods had brought. It is said that McNaught would never show his dealing book to anyone, sleeping with it under his pillow and even taking it on holiday with him. A fondly-remembered dealer was Cyril John Buttery Smith, known to everyone as 'Micky'. A great character who operated on a half-commission basis, his main income derived from a very wealthy Portuguese whose account was handled through Smith's Bank, and he also did arbitrage business between London and New York on behalf of Singer & Friedlander. Finally, there was Charles Purnell, who with his ambition and good mathematical mind was clearly the rising dealer. His main client was Culls, and as he recalls: 'They were very active and very successful, though it was really hard work servicing them as I had to do when I first started dealing, but I suppose that was a good education.' Purnell was also determined (no doubt under the influence of Micklem) not to indulge in the superficially attractive policy of 'picking up' jobbers, in other words either buying shares from one jobber and selling to another or (the lesser crime) going to a jobber who was quoting the wrong price. Both ethics and the cultivation of long-term relationships with the jobbers precluded such practices in the eyes of the better kind of dealer – and Purnell in time would be acknowledged as the leading equity dealer of his generation – in an era when it was still possible to follow these eminently practical niceties.

It was Micky Smith who, in collaboration with Gerald Micklem and Philip Cazenove, was responsible from the mid-1930s for building up the firm's business with provincial brokers to a far more substantial operation than it had previously been. Gerald was the son of Hugh and nephew of Charles and had come to Cazenove's straight from Oxford in the early 1930s. Generous, irascible and rather noisy, he possessed a lively mind and had clearly inherited much of the family financial acumen. Operating as a team, these three worked up the country business, with Philip Cazenove proving especially valuable for the way in which he made friends with many of the leading provincial brokers, playing golf with them, and generally winning their confidence. Indeed, after the trio at the outset of the operation in 1935 had been placed on a half-commission basis, they did so well that after a year the arrangement had to be altered. Provincial firms with whom a close working relationship was now established included Lawrie & Ker in Edinburgh, B. S. Stock in Bristol, E. T. Lyddon in Cardiff, Murray & Co in Birmingham, William Chapman in Nottingham, Parsons, MacLachlan & Miller and Greig Wilson in Glasgow, and David Q. Henriques in Manchester. The closest connection, however, was with the Newcastle firm of Wise, Speke & Co, which during the years up to the war actually had a partner resident at 12 Tokenhouse Yard and did its London business through Cazenove's exclusively. The instigator of this overall initiative was almost certainly Charles Micklem, and he seems to have been mindful of the double-edged nature of country business: that though on the one hand the expenses were considerable because the bargains involved were often rather small, on the other hand the forging of such close links with the better provincial firms was a marvellous way of getting into the potential new issue business emerging in the regions. The latter consideration would serve Cazenove's well in the post-war years, though ultimately it was the former, negative one that prevailed.

The 1930s also saw a significant expansion of the firm's overseas contacts. Here one of the most important partners was Algy Belmont. Previously Cazenove's seem to have bought or sold New York securities through the London brokers P. N. Kemp-Gee, whose speciality was buying blocks of tobacco shares on the New York Curb and then forming a London syndicate (sometimes including Cazenove's) to dispose of them. This changed from late 1934 or early 1935, when Belmont paid his first visit to New York where a friend of his was a partner in the small broking firm of Green Ellis & Anderson. The outcome was a close relationship until the war and, as with Wise Speke, one of the Green Ellis partners occupied a room on the second floor at Tokenhouse Yard. A rather complicated daily arrangement operated during these years. Cazenove's would buy the book of a small but flourishing London jobber called Percy Weston (run by Spencer Weston, an Old Wellingtonian friend of Micklem's) and every night, going joint with Weston, 'unmake' it in New York through Green Ellis, in other words buying the book's bears or selling its bulls. Belmont, helped by Purnell as dealer, also did a substantial American arbitrage business with Green Ellis, a form of stockbroking that by tradition Cazenove's had rarely gone in for and indeed did not often do in later years. It was still the pre-telex age and all communications across the Atlantic were sent in code, through considerations of quickness rather than secrecy. On one occasion, the encoded message to Belmont ran, 'Cable A story'. Belmont therefore got the jobbers in the American market to send their best raconteurs to the firm's box and eventually he despatched in code a short, sharp story. A pause followed, before America asked, 'Please cable in clear'. Belmont duly cabled his story in clear and at last the perplexed reply came, 'What's wrong with Anaconda?' 'A' was the ticker symbol for Anaconda, then one of the biggest copper companies in the world, and hence the misunderstanding.

Belmont also cultivated relations, through Barings, with the long-established investment banking house of Kidder, Peabody & Co. During the summer of 1936, Cazenove's and Kidder were engaged, under the overall direction of Culls, in a major and highly successful operation to sell on the London market the shares of a recently-deceased Englishman who had had a controlling interest in the Chicago Flexible Shaft Company, which then made sheep-shearing machines but was to become the Sunbeam Electrical Corporation. That autumn, Belmont was in correspondence with Frederick L. Moore of Kidder about the purchase of 32,600 Babcock & Wilcox ordinary shares. 'Our client is thoroughly satisfied, as are we, with your prompt action,' wrote Moore, 'and I wish again to express our appreciation of your fine services.' He added somewhat wistfully: 'I hope you in turn will find something of interest to us – or be able to use our stock exchange facilities. I have heard that you have some connection with Green Ellis & Anderson for this sort of transaction, but I hope you can use us in other directions if this is so.' Belmont in his reply expressed gratification that Cazenove's had been able to dispose of the whole Babcock & Wilcox block 'at a moderate profit', but confirmed the existence of the Green Ellis connection, 'so you will understand that in many ways we are rather tied to them for our New York transactions'. Over the next few months, there was a strong possibility that Belmont would buy from Moore for syndicate purposes a large block of Allegheny Steel shares that the General Electric Company was proposing to dispose of. 'If I judge your interest in American stocks correctly,' Moore wrote on December 28th, 'you prefer to purchase a block of stock in a company with a relatively small amount of capitalization where the stock is closely held and where you can, therefore, control your own market to a certain degree. This is an ideal situation from that point of view.' In the event the deal fell through, but as Belmont wrote on February 1st to Alex Bowhill of the Edinburgh brokers Bell, Cowan & Co, who would have formed part of the syndicate: 'The General Electric Company of New York have decided to retain their holding as they feel certain they will be able to sell this block at a considerably higher price than that ruling in the market today. If that is not a good tip to buy them, I do not know what is.'

There was one pre-war American transaction that stood out, the celebrated Woolworths episode. The detailed documentation is rather thin, but essentially it was a series of very large selling orders in Woolworth shares brought via Lazards to Belmont by the Woolworth family, with Cazenove's essentially acting as the market, in conjunction with the jobbers. The Green Ellis connection proved a great help, and the story is related by Purnell in an account that captures much of the flavour of the times:

Now Algy, let's face it, was not a great market man and so I handled the business from the very start, about 1936, until the war and indeed polished it off sometime just after the war. I cannot remember how many were disposed of, but it ran into millions. I used to work with Elliot D. Fox [of Green Ellis] and established a tremendously close relationship with him. The orders used to come in ¼ million lots and I used to do the business always with one firm of jobbers – not necessarily the same one – and it worked pretty well. In other words one ran a tap and it was reasonably successful. They were satisfied anyway. As a side product I had to undo the exchange, in other words sell the sterling and buy dollars, and for one glorious week I was able to get $5 to the £. Fox used to ring me up at all kinds of odd hours and one evening, quite late, he rang me up and asked if I could possibly dispose of that particular tranche, about 20,000, that evening (remembering, of course, that he was five hours back from us). So I rang the jobber at his home and he was out, but his wife said that he was in London that night. Fortunately I knew his wife to pass the time of day and I said, 'Well, could you possibly tell me, is he staying at a hotel?' She told me the name of the hotel, which I subsequently rang. I asked for his room and was put through and a woman's voice answered. I don't think there was frightfully much argument about the price!

Belmont also engaged before the war in regular arbitrage business with the Cape (another new departure), but as a main thrust it was less important than the South American connection, which now emerged to the fore as a direct result of the merger with Greenwoods. Much of it took the form of business in the capital market; but it is a striking fact that prior to the war Cazenove's issued each week, for the benefit of City institutions, detailed traffic receipt statistics on all the Argentine railway companies. Moreover, every night Alex Coombe-Tennant sent an encoded cable to the Argentine on the state of the London market; and when Serocold's young nephew, Ralph Serocold, joined the firm straight from university in 1938, he was at once despatched to South America for nine months in order to learn about the Argentine. The correspondence firm there was Roberts, Meynell; while a close link existed between John Phillimore, posted in Buenos Aires on behalf of Barings, and Frank Holt, who after the deaths in the Henderson family became the undisputed king-pin at Cazenove's on all things South American. There survives a snatch of correspondence from Holt to Phillimore in June 1938:

> There is really nothing to report from this side: markets have been better, London being better on New York and New York being better on London. I am not at all sure that we are not in for a period of better trading on this side. At any rate one's clients seem to have come to life again.
>
> From what I can gather here conditions with the Argentine Rails for next year are definitely better than at this time last year. If you have time, will you drop me a line as to what your views are? I think also it is getting about time to stir up a little interest in Alpargatas [the well-known espadrille manufacturers]. What do you think?

Hardly sensational stuff, the letter serves as a reminder that day-to-day stockbroking is an essentially pragmatic business, concerned for the most part to accrue in singles rather than hit boundaries.

The other main inheritance from the merger with Greenwoods was on the investment trust side. In particular, there was the Witan, which had been founded by Lord Faringdon in 1909 to look after his family fortune and which in 1921 had gone public. Micklem joined the board, reactivating the company (following a previous moribund period) so that it soon became the firm's best client. Then, in March 1934 following the death of Faringdon, there began under the capable hands of William Brabner the Henderson Administration, whose task was to manage the sizeable estates of not only Faringdon but also his brother and two sons, all four having died between

1931 and 1934. The day-to-day investment management of Henderson Administration passed to Micklem, who proceeded to give this aspect of his work a high priority and at noon each day walked over from his office to 28 Austin Friars. Already deeply interested in investment trusts, this was a further dimension. Moreover, Micklem in these years also seems to have established for Cazenove's what was in effect a duopoly with James Capel in the trust market as a whole. This applied equally to both new issue and day-to-day trust business, in both of which areas the two firms would go joint, though any new initiative at this stage almost always derived from Cazenove's. Thus for example the Mercantile Trust, which had always had Capel as its brokers, from about 1936 also had Cazenove's. And in general Micklem not only serviced investment trusts (inside or outside the Henderson family) as a valuable way of securing regular broking income, but also played a major role in helping to create them, subsequently giving them large participations in the firm's best deals. These trusts would obviously come to Cazenove's for the execution of the major part of their business, so altogether it was the most virtuous of circles.

What were these 'deals'? Often they took the form of syndicates, a type of business that flourished in the City between the wars. These syndicates seem to have taken three main forms. A company issuing additional capital, and not wanting to disturb the market, would gradually release its shares to a syndicate specially formed for the purpose; secondly, someone might be getting rid of a big holding and, with the company again not wanting the market disturbed, a syndicate would be formed to absorb the holding; while thirdly, a syndicate might be set up to take a position in the secondary market, often over quite a long period of time. Cazenove's was much involved in such syndicates, which it would initiate, participate in, and act as brokers to. In November 1938, for instance, the firm simultaneously sold on behalf of the Public Trustee a block of over 30,000 Imperial Tobacco ordinary shares to the market (the jobbers Hadow & Turner) and bought them back at the same price in order to resell them over the following month on behalf of a syndicate it had formed. This put through the market was a requisite of the single-capacity system and established fair value. The syndicate in this case included Hadow, while the other members were Culls, the Whitehall Trust, Robert Benson & Co, and the Henderson Administration group of investment trusts that Micklem had recently been instrumental in forming.

There were also during these years the two Trigo syndicates. They were named after the celebrated Derby and St Leger winner of 1929 and were organised by Frank Holt, who had a particular penchant for syndicates, especially if as in this case they were for the purchase of Argentine securities. The first Trigo syndicate was formed in October 1936 and distributed its profits the following January. The amount of £100,000 was subscribed by thirteen participants, with Lazards, Robert Benson and Glyn Mills taking large stakes, but also including the inevitable Sir Connop Guthrie as well as Sir Follett Holt both individually and through the British Shareholders Trust of which he was chairman. Trigo Syndicate No. 2 was formed in April 1937, with almost identical participants and for the same amount. It proved so successful that it was extended three times, not being finally terminated until July 1939, when the stocks were distributed pro rata among the participants. The stocks concerned were mostly in railway companies, and clearly Holt had picked well.

If those were the main strands of the firm's day-to-day business during the 1930s, what conclusions can be reached? Perhaps that the City of those days was a simpler world than half a century later, involving more judgement and less detail; and perhaps that both the personal touch and the personal connection remained paramount. On 7th April 1934, Claud Serocold, about to go away for eye treatment, wrote a letter to General Lawrence at Glyn Mills in lieu of their regular weekly chat. He described how he had been visited the previous day by Sir James Dunn, the well-known Canadian financial adventurer of Dunn Fisher fame and also closely connected with Loewenstein: 'He talked over a variety of matters (among others regret that we had not done business together), until he came to the real point which I guessed was the object why he had asked me to see him.' This was the fact, fairly well known in the City, that the General Electric Company of America was looking for bids by syndicate managers for about a million Associated Electrical Industries ordinary shares. Serocold wrote:

> I told him that I *did* know something about the business and in the ordinary course of events we might have been interested but that we understood that probably Rowe Swann [another prominent stockbroking firm] were negotiating and we had decided not to compete but to stand aside and watch events.
>
> He then said that he quite understood but that if we did take up the business, he and the Tobacco Trust would be prepared to come in to a very considerable extent.
>
> Of course one cannot really trust Jimmie Dunn, although his frankness and friendliness is very disarming. Micklem is inclined to think that he is trying to make himself secure on both sides and if Rowe Swann fails he is anxious to be with us, but I am of a less suspicious nature than he . . .

As Serocold well knew, a broker is liable to stand or fall by his judgement of individuals. What the outcome was of this particular episode is uncertain

(Cazenove's probably did not bid for the shares), but it does seem that over the next few years Serocold became friendly with Dunn and transacted a fair amount of speculative business on his behalf. There was an intriguing sequel, related in the biography of Dunn by his friend Lord Beaverbrook. The Second World War badly affected Dunn, who 'was relying for income at this time on realisation of possessions and on speculations on the London market.' Then in about May 1940, with France being overwhelmed and shares falling drastically in value, the stockbroker Mossy Myers called for payment of loans, and Dunn was unable to comply. At least one City friend refused to help before Dunn found some much-needed relief when Serocold 'agreed to carry the loans due to his firm'. It was a characteristically generous action, but perhaps Micklem in his more sceptical judgement had had the right of it.

The 1930s witnessed a fundamental shift in the London capital market away from foreign and towards domestic issues. In the aftermath of the 1931 crisis, severe Treasury restrictions were placed upon the making of foreign issues (outside the Empire), so that by 1935 less than two-fifths of issues that year were for overseas and the annual value of that business was under one-fifth of what it had been during the 1920s. This new predominance of domestic issuing was responsible for two significant trends in terms of mode of issuing: one was towards the offer for sale, by which the shares were issued publicly by the issuing house itself as opposed to by the company, with the issuing house having bought them from the company; and the other was towards the method of a private placing accompanied by a Stock Exchange 'introduction' of the shares. Writing in April 1935 to the Anglo-Palestine Bank (which was thinking of making an issue of preference shares), Jimmy Palmer-Tomkinson usefully summarised the procedure entailed by such a placing:

We should sell the shares to our City connections; advertise details of the shares in two London papers 'for information only and not as an invitation for subscriptions'; and obtain permission to deal on the Stock Exchange.

The publicity arising from this method is obviously less than from the broadcasting of a prospectus, but the public can become shareholders through purchase in the market.

The original purchasers must, of course, get the shares a little below the price at which they could be sold on a public issue; but, as the expenses of issue are smaller, it is possible that the price obtained by the Bank would not be materially affected.

Cost was indeed the great advantage of a private placing, especially the limited press advertising involved. Not surprisingly, it proved a highly popular (if at times criticised) method, especially when a company required a relatively small sum of capital, less than half a million pounds. It was, moreover, a method in which a handful of stockbrokers (including Cazenove's) specialised, being able to execute placings in great numbers without requiring any assistance from issuing houses as such. In his excellent study of the inter-war City that was published in 1940, Barnard Ellinger adds a helpful gloss to Palmer-Tomkinson's concise phrase about 'our City connections':

> The stockbroker, before binding himself to undertake the issue, will have consulted the business friends on his list and ascertained what amounts of shares they will be prepared to take from him at an agreed price higher than that agreed to be paid to the vendor by a sum which will cover the stockbroker's out-of-pocket expenses and payment for his services. Having arranged his placing, the stockbroker will sign the agreement to purchase the shares from the vendor. The stockbroker's list for his placing will usually include investment trusts, insurance companies, and other large investors among his clients.

To what degree Cazenove's in the 1930s consulted its 'business friends' in advance would have varied from placing to placing, but the gist of Ellinger's analysis is valid. Moreover, as he explains, a stockbroker in a placing not only secured permission to deal from the Stock Exchange Committee, but also ensured that the shares would be marketable, usually by arranging 'with one or more jobbers that they also will buy from him a block of shares, or he will give them the option of calling upon him to deliver a certain number of shares at an agreed price, and will further arrange with the jobber the price at which he will open sales on the Stock Exchange'. Sometimes, according to Ellinger, the broker would opt for a Stock Exchange introduction without having a placing, in other words 'introducing the shares on the Stock Exchange without having taken steps to place the shares in advance with his clients'. This was a riskier procedure, hinging entirely on the selling arrangement with the jobbers, and was usually only employed when it was a case of raising additional capital. Subsequently, after the war, introductions would become synonymous with 'permissions to deal' and not have a capital-raising function. All in all, however, a well-honed technique was clearly at work by the time Ellinger was writing in the late 1930s. And as Hornby recalls in his memoirs about the inter-war period as a whole: 'We did start doing issues on our own without the aid of an Issuing House. This was not very popular with them and we had to be careful to know where to draw the line. But there were many occasions where an Issuing House's services were simply not necessary and if the client didn't want to pay the extra cost we couldn't force him to do so.'

It is possible to exaggerate the extent to which the merchant banks eschewed the domestic issuing take-off of the 1930s, but undoubtedly there was a sense in which during these years they failed to respond to changed circumstances. Nevertheless, it should be pointed out that these were immensely difficult times for merchant banks and that the consequences of the German banking crisis of 1931 in particular formed a heavy millstone round their necks, hardly encouraging the vigorous pursuit of entrepreneurial opportunities. But for whatever reasons, the best-known issuing houses were fairly quiescent during the 1930s; and with the old-style company promoters having been mercifully extinguished by the events of 1929 onwards, much of the issuing slack (especially in equities, traditionally perceived as more risky) was now taken up by the leading company stockbrokers of the day. It was in this context that Cazenove's, having notably held its own when the market had collapsed after the febrile 1928 boom, proceeded to emerge as the dominant force once issuing activity in general picked up again by the mid-thirties. Quantity alone – quite apart from any other considerations – was impressive. From 1935 to 1937 inclusive, the firm was associated with at least 118 issues, of which it sponsored or co-sponsored at least 73. The range of these issues was broad, the great majority being of high quality, and most proved successful. Already in possession of a long and honourable history, Cazenove's in the 1930s attained through these activities a stature in the City it had never previously enjoyed.

The skills of Charles Micklem, abetted by Serocold and to a lesser extent Palmer-Tomkinson, Holt, Belmont and Scaramanga, contributed much to this enormous success in the realm of company finance. But the smooth-running nuts-and-bolts side under Albert Martin should not be forgotten – a side typified by the fact that Cazenove's at this time was the only stockbroking firm with a supply of allotment letters already stamped in blank. There was also the breadth of connection with high-class non-stockbroker issuing houses, which was crucial in terms of ensuring the firm's involvement with high-value issues not susceptible to the techniques of a private placing. This in turn was allied to what was now becoming the firm's widely-recognised 'placing power'. Vital to this power were not only the burgeoning links with the institutions as a whole, but also the steadfast support of a group of rich individuals (headed by Guthrie and Pope) and specific institutions (like Culls, certain merchant banks, and the various investment trusts tied up by Micklem) at a time when *most* institutions were still very wary of taking a substantial stake in industrial equities, which by the 1930s were being floated in ever-greater numbers. The cultivation of loyalty was at the heart of Micklem's approach. In terms of investors, this meant ensuring that his 'followers' usually had a slice of the most profitable action; or, in a rather wider way, it might mean distributing sub-underwriting to those who had taken up their quota in a previous issue by that company, especially if it had been a difficult one, rather than to those who perhaps were currently bringing profitable broking business to the firm. Equally importantly, Micklem cultivated loyalty on the part of the companies for whom he acted. This he did not only through the quality of his service, but also through the conscious policy of charging modest fees, knowing that there would be many earning opportunities for the firm in the 'after-market' that followed the actual issue. And significantly, when by about 1934 or soon after there was some talk (it is impossible to know how serious) of Cazenove's establishing a separate, formal issuing house in addition to the regular stockbroking business, apparently reflecting a feeling that there was even more money to be made as an issuing house outside the Stock Exchange than in it (thereby following the example of Helbert Wagg and Culls), a key factor in killing the notion was almost certainly the realisation that much of the firm's 'after-market' or secondary business might thereby be lost, quite apart, of course, from the accompanying need for substantially greater capital. Micklem knew exactly what he was doing as a company financier and it is hard not to feel that he for one would have been most unwilling to jeopardise the excellent prospects that lay ahead.

In this whole area there were so many episodes of interest and importance during the years 1932 to 1939 that it is not easy to make a selection, but an attempt must be made. The first was the inglorious but necessary business of helping to clear up the affairs of Great Universal Stores. Not long after the successful July 1931 issue, the chairman, A. H. Rose, announced that the accounts for the year to March 1932 would show a loss, as £250,000 had to be written off stock values. Much criticism ensued, the ordinary shares fell sharply and by the summer of 1932 the company agreed to bring in the accountants Deloitte, Plender and Griffiths, who proceeded to engage in thorough consultations with Cazenove's. The upshot was that Serocold, believing that such an apparent fraud risked putting his own firm's reputation at stake, not only insisted that Rose and most of his family retire from the board and repay the sum to the company, but also played an active part in reconstituting the board so that confidence be restored. A letter to A. Rae Smith of Deloittes on 1st December 1932 reflected something of his anxiety:

Do you think you can include something like the following words in the Report:

'The cash position is satisfactory and the investment of £100,000 Conversion 5% Stock remains unchanged'?

I am constantly being asked about these two items and I think that it would help if it could be stated in your Report.

Altogether it was an extremely painful episode, not least for the young Hornby: 'I had put all my few clients into GUS at £1 and they fell to 7s 6d and I was mortified and I wrote to them and told them I was disillusioned with stockbroking and was contemplating giving it up.' However, both Hornby and GUS survived to prosper, with an independent chairman (Sir Philip Nash) being appointed, the accountant Leslie Farrow joining the board and a young manager called Isaac Wolfson emerging as joint managing director. That the Cazenove connection remained strong for several more years is shown by an expressive letter from Serocold to Farrow in December 1936 after an unsuccessful issue:

We are trying to place the G.U.S. Preference Shares with which our underwriters have been landed, but we are finding it a little difficult to explain away the drop in profits for last year.

Do you think that you could give us some 'dope' on the matter and also, without divulging any secrets, give us an idea of how the business has done for the first six months of the new financial year?

It was all part of the after-market service, in this case to 'our underwriters'.

A happier venture in the first year after the merger with Greenwoods was the private placing of a substantial amount of Ansells Brewery stock. Cazenove's early in 1933 formed a syndicate with the British Trusts Association and the Birmingham stockbrokers Cutler & Lacy to purchase £400,000 5% Debentures at 99¼. On January 27th Micklem sent an early progress report to Sir Pierce Lacy, who was also a director of Ansells, telling him that he had sold that day £50,000 at 100 and £25,000 at 100½ and expressing pleasure that 'our association together has been so successful again'. Lacy replied the following day:

It is always a pleasure to me to do business with you, and I am of course delighted with the immediate success of the Ansell issue. I hope we have many more deals together. The combination of City and private placing power which we together have, should always be able to compete with the issuing house for any sound issue up to say £1,000,000.

I hope when you have got some good business you will allow us to participate with you.

Lacy perhaps slightly overestimated the capacity of that combination, but nevertheless it was striking testimony. Certainly it was not a viable method for sums in excess of a million pounds. Thus when Charringtons four months later sought to raise almost £4½ million in order to take over the brewery business of Hoare & Co, they did so through an offer for sale done jointly by Barings and Rothschilds. Each of the four brokers (Cazenove's, Messels, Panmure Gordon and Sebags) was responsible for £650,000 of underwriting and Cazenove's secured permission to deal.

Undoubtedly one of the most notable schemes involving the firm during these years concerned the turbulent finances of the Argentine. In January 1933 Lord Faringdon submitted to Barings a gloomy memorandum on the subject:

> The English Railways and other Industrial undertakings operating in the Argentine Republic are very concerned at their being unable to remit their net earnings to this country. Several of them are under advances to the Bankers in respect of Loans obtained to meet their Preferential Charges, and they are faced with the position of having very large balances in pesos in Buenos Aires, which if convertible into £ sterling, would enable them to discharge their existing liabilities on this side and meet the interest upon their Prior Charges as they mature . . .
>
> Under these circumstances it is natural that they should leave no stone unturned to improve the situation, which if allowed to continue, may mean the destruction of their credit and a decline in the credit of all Argentine securities.

The eventual upshot, after complicated negotiations between the two countries, was the formation that October of the United Kingdom & Argentine (1933) Convention Trust, which issued at varying interest rates over £7 million in 'A', 'B' and 'C' Certificates and had the crucial effect of enabling the holders of blocked pesos to exchange them for negotiable sterling securities. Almost certainly Micklem was closely involved in the creation on behalf of Barings of this ingenious and successful scheme (only baldly summarised here), which apart from relieving the City had the important effect of giving the Argentine economy a respite when it badly needed one; and in the event, Argentina was virtually the only South American country in the 1930s not to default or require a rescheduling of its debts.

There were other aspects of Argentine finance over the next few years, both public and private. Between 1934 and 1936 there were five large issues (ranging from £2.3 million to £4.5 million) of Argentine Government Sterling Bonds. They were all organised by Barings and Morgan Grenfell, were usually offers for sale, and the brokers were invariably Cazenove's,

Messels, Panmure Gordon and Rowe & Pitman. Cazenove's tended to arrange most of the sub-underwriting – a highly important matter granted that the issues were usually undersubscribed, sometimes seriously – and inevitably Micklem was prominent. Thus on the eve of the third issue, in November 1934, Howard Millis of Barings wrote to Evelyn Baring in Buenos Aires: 'We held the Brokers' meeting today and everything passed off well. Micklem had already approached the original syndicate and underwritten £2,800,000 nominal. This left £1,000,000 to be divided amongst the four broking houses for their own particular clients. The usual compliments were exchanged and all the Brokers were confident that the underwriting would be readily taken up.'

As for private capital for the Argentine, the main Cazenove thrust was the series of ten syndicates that the firm (mainly in the person of Frank Holt) organised between October 1933 and December 1936 to buy 5% Debenture Stock (usually £100,000 at a time) from the Central Argentine Railway. The composition remained fairly constant, with the hard core including Robert Fleming and Robert Benson. Occasionally the invitation to participate was accompanied by some up-to-date information about the company, such as the assurance in February 1935 to the would-be fifth syndicate that 'as regards traffics for this year, the prospects for the maize crop appear to be distinctly good'. In general, Holt emerged during these years as a specialist in the organising of syndicates, especially to buy blocks of shares which the firm had found it difficult to sell at short notice. They tended to be very successful, and he rarely had difficulty in finding participants among both jobbers and clients.

Two rather controversial issues occurred in 1934, both recalled by Hornby. The first was the flotation in February of Sir Frank Bowden's Raleigh Cycle Holdings, which included Raleigh Cycle and Sturmey-Archer Gears, with the issue being sponsored by Guthrie's Suffolk Trust:

A whispering campaign and newspaper comment indicated that Bowden was selling because he foresaw the end of the bicycle era. We formed a syndicate consisting of the Prudential, Sir Connop and ourselves to support the market at 3s discount and bought some hundreds of thousands of shares. We had to sit on them for quite a long time but when the year's results were published it was seen that the company's business was going from strength to strength at home and abroad, the shares became a firm market and the syndicate made a great deal of money. This was the first example that I had that we could make more money by failures provided our judgement of a business was fundamentally sound, as in case of successes we got no shares.

Five months later, in July, the firm was responsible for the placing of the ordinary shares of the manufacturing chemists Griffiths Hughes Proprietaries, popularly known as 'Kruschen Salts':

> They quickly went to about 15s premium – I never quite knew why but they struck the public fancy and there was much gambling in new issues at that time. We got unmercifully ragged over the Kruschen issue and were taunted with 'When are you going to float Bronco?' and suchlike jibes.

Perhaps it was innately humorous that Griffiths Hughes should have been officially described at the time as 'Manufacturers of Kruschen Salts, Radox Bath Salts, Karswood and other preparations including Wax Grape Saline, Chardox, Karsote, Veldew, Baxen and Radioliser.' Certainly the issue was well-publicised and equally certainly it was a roaring success, giving rise to considerable comment. A week after dealings began, the Manchester broker Alfred Arnold (who had brought the business to Cazenove's) wrote to Micklem: 'I never doubted success but I feel a little my inadequacy to repel an attack that the ordinary shares were sold too cheaply. I am quite satisfied, however, in my own mind that the right course was taken.' Soon afterwards the Companies' Department of the Board of Trade investigated the matter (following a Parliamentary question) and came to the conclusion that the high premium established on the shares was due simply to the willingness of the public to pay it and that the extent of the demand for the shares came as a surprise to all concerned. However, as 'Lex' of the *Financial News* pointed out, foreshadowing future controversies: 'If the method of "placing" new securities invariably involved a difference of up to 100 per cent between the price received by vendors and the initial level of public dealings, it would obviously be uneconomic.'

Cazenove's in the mid-1930s had much to do with the reconstruction of the traditional heavy industries. In March 1934, for example, Major Leslie of Yorkshire Amalgamated Collieries, contemplating the creation of new debenture stock to offer to the existing stockholders of Denaby and Cadeby Main Collieries, told Barings that Cazenove's had indicated to him a price of 97, but that for the moment he wished to stay his hand until market developments had become clearer. Two months later he returned to 8 Bishopsgate:

> Major Leslie came in and said that he had had a conversation with Mr Micklem of Cazenove's. He suggested that the new Debenture Stock should be for a total amount of £1,250,000 with a 33–year life. The Sinking Fund to be 1% and the balance outstanding to be repayable at the end of the 33rd year. The Company should have no option of repayment for the first 10 years, during the second 10 years the option might be exercised at 104, or during the balance of the life of the Stock at 103.

This was constructive finance, but significantly the Barings memorandum added: 'Major Leslie asked whether we had anything new in our minds as regards the price and we told him that a $4\frac{1}{2}$% Stock at 98 was probably the best that we could do.' Almost certainly there had already been informal consultation with Micklem, but it was Barings as the issuing house who authoritatively indicated the price. This particular issue ($£1\frac{1}{4}$ million) was done privately and Cazenove's was responsible for placing a third of the sub-underwriting.

The iron and steel industry, however, was the firm's real speciality, reflecting that sector's surprisingly sharp recovery from the world depression. Major issues were done (either as issuing house or broker for an issuing house) on behalf of Stewarts and Lloyds, United Steel and Dorman Long. Undoubtedly, though, Micklem's key steel action was for Colvilles. A memorandum in the Morgan Grenfell papers, dated 19th September 1934, provides a graphic account of the all-important preliminaries:

Micklem of Cazenove & Akroyds [sic] called of his own initiative to see C.F.W. [Charles Whigham] and began by enquiring whether we knew the firm of Colvilles. C.F.W. said that if he meant the Scotch steel makers he had known some of the Colville family quite well and also knew the Chairman of the company for whom he had great regard. C.F.W. said that while he had known a good deal about their business at one time he had not followed it much in recent years. Micklem said that that information really gave him the answer to a question he was going to ask, viz: whether Morgan Grenfell were interested in any way in a proposed issue of Preference shares by Colvilles. C.F.W. said that we were not interested in any way.

Micklem went on to say that David Colville & Sons (a holding company) were the owners of a large block (?£1,500,000) of Preference shares of the operating company Colvilles Ltd. David Colville & Sons had loans from various banks including the National Bank of Scotland and the Midland. It appeared that the National Bank of Scotland to whom there was owed about £650,000 had of its own initiative offered to accept £500,000 in complete settlement of the account. The Colvilles were rather surprised at this and consulted with Mr Reginald McKenna [chairman of the Midland and a former Chancellor of the Exchequer]. He advised them to accept the offer and at the same time suggested that Tobacco Securities Ltd would be willing to market David Colville & Sons' holding of Preference shares in Colvilles Ltd. Apparently the terms proposed by Tobacco Securities Ltd were considered rather severe, viz: a price of 19s for a $5\frac{1}{2}$% Preference share with a fee of £20,000. The Colvilles therefore discussed the matter with a firm of Glasgow brokers who in turn said that if they were to do anything they would require assistance in the London market. Thus Cazenove & Akroyds had come into the matter.

Micklem then said that while he could not feel any particular obligations to ascertain the wishes of all the members of the group which handled the United Steel Companies shares [i.e. in May 1934] he of course would not do anything that might conflict with either Barings or Morgan Grenfell. He had already spoken to Barings and his object had been to make sure that his handling the Colville business, if he decided to do so, would not conflict with Morgan Grenfell.

The Glasgow brokers were Parsons, MacLachlan & Miller, and the following month (after the Colvilles board had accepted the more attractive terms offered by Micklem) an offer for sale was made of 1,600,000 5½% preference shares at 20s 6d, with Cazenove's taking two-thirds profit on the business and Parsons one-third. The issue proved massively successful. Moreover, in the words of the historian of Colvilles: 'The way was now clear to complete the process of rationalising the Scottish steel industry.' Working in close liaison with Parsons and also the Glasgow office of the accountants Thomson McLintock, and insisting that Scotland (and in particular the local cash creditors of David Colville) receive a substantial proportion of the sub-underwriting, Micklem had once again shown himself a master of company finance.

Moving into 1935, the stand-out event of that year was the highly controversial Bristol Aeroplane issue that took place in June. On May 20th, Micklem outlined his approach to Sir William McLintock, who had brought the business to him:

> The procedure we propose to adopt is to make a public issue of the 600,000 £1 5% Preference Shares at 21s 6d, advertising the issue on a fairly wide scale both in London and the provinces and then introducing the Ordinary Shares to the London and Bristol Stock Exchanges a few days after the allotments of the Preference Shares have been posted. In this way we obtain the benefit of the advertisement of the Preference Shares for the marketing through the Stock Exchange of the Ordinary Shares.

With a view to a private placing through the usual syndicate method, accompanied by a Stock Exchange introduction, Micklem had already agreed to buy 360,000 ordinary shares from the company at 37s 6d. Then, on May 22nd, Stanley Baldwin announced in the Commons that the existing target for the RAF's front-line strength was to be doubled. By the time that permission to deal was secured the following month the aeroplane market was booming; and it was to the considerable credit of Micklem that he sold the shares to his syndicate at the modest price of 38s. In the apt words of

Hornby: 'Another fat profit for our friends and the vendors took it very well. The firm could have made much more money than it did on this occasion but took the view that generosity brings its rewards. Greed and meanness can only pay in the very short view.'

Others were less sanguine about the outcome. The *FT*'s 'The Diarist' reported the prevailing mood:

> Feeling ran high at the course of the introduction of Bristol Aeroplane Ordinary 10s shares, a block of 360,000 of which was recently acquired by a leading firm of brokers at 37s 6d each.
>
> Dealings were nominally started yesterday afternoon at 55s, but even favoured brokers on a prior list secured only 100 shares each at this price. Within a minute or so the quotation had been rushed to 57s 6d, only to relapse partially later. Independent brokers wisely advised their clients not to 'chase the shares', and some of them, I hear, went upstairs to place their grievance before the Committee. They contended that they were never given the chance of executing their orders reasonably.
>
> There is not the shadow of a suggestion that the brokers responsible for the introduction infringed any of the existing Rules of the Stock Exchange. But there is a growing feeling that a number of recent 'introductions' has shown up a defect in the Rules, which calls loudly for rectification in the interests of the whole House. Under the present system it does not seem humanly possible in the case of an embarrassingly popular introduction for everyone to be treated alike.

Even the generally uncritical 'Autolycus' agreed the next day that there was a genuine grievance, accepting that 'it may be better, possibly, for everyone to have the chance of applying for shares on a prospectus, than to put down their names on lists of orders to buy at the opening price'. Though as he added with a certain world weariness: 'If a prospective purchaser did not get all that he asked for through this method of introduction, it is reasonable to assume that, had these shares been offered on a prospectus, he would have been still more disappointed.'

Faced by a chorus of protest, from both within and without the House, the Stock Exchange Committee in July set up a special sub-committee. During the summer it sent out a questionnaire to forty-two brokers. The replies established that on the one hand there was a general though not unanimous wish for some action to be taken, but that on the other the costs involved in a private placing or introduction (ranging from £350 to £1,000) were markedly lower than those for a prospectus or offer for sale (from £3,000 to £11,500). During the winter a series of brokers was summoned to give oral evidence on the subject. The first two, on October 23rd, were Micklem and

Kit Hoare of Cohen Laming Hoare. Micklem at the outset stated firmly that 'he had not been able to think out a method of improving the existing system', before the dialogue turned to the Bristol Aeroplane issue itself:

> Mr Micklem said that the price originally suggested by the company's advisers was far less than his firm gave; it was decided to await the 1933–34 figures which improved the price of the shares considerably.
>
> He replied in the affirmative to a question as to whether the public considered they were not getting a fair deal when the shares were placed instead of the issue being made by prospectus. He said the public had, in his opinion, been voiced by the newspapers but his firm had had no complaints. He thought any restrictions would prove harmful to the public as well as the Vendors and the Stock Exchange.

It was then the turn of Hoare, who despite his firm's involvement with Hatry was emerging between the wars as a company broker second only to Micklem. His firm had acted or would soon act for several of the largest British companies and he was renowned for his robustness of approach. There was little equivocation in his evidence to the sub-committee:

> Mr Hoare said he thought the whole fault lay with the Vendors.
>
> He agreed that to a certain extent it was in the interest of the Vendors that shares were sold at a low price while they retained further shares which at a later date they saw a chance of marketing at a higher price.
>
> He did not consider this good business, but it was the purchaser's own risk . . .
>
> Asked what grievance the public had, Mr Hoare said he took the view that the only people who complained were those who had lost money – all their clients had made money up to now.

In short, neither of the leading company brokers of the day was minded to abandon the method of placings nor indeed the larger, time-honoured precept of *caveat emptor*. .

The sub-committee reported in February 1936 and soon afterwards, in accordance with its recommendations, the Stock Exchange Committee publicly declared that it was 'desirable that all issues, particularly those of Ordinary Capital, should be made by Prospectus or Offer for Sale unless from the public standpoint the necessity or advantage of a private placing is indicated by the circumstances.' However, these were words only, unaccompanied by a change to the Rules, and if anything the popularity of the method actually increased in the years before the war. In 1937, for example, 92 stockbrokers made 237 issues by means of placings or introductions; and since some 56 per cent of those issues were for sums under £150,000, the low costs involved must have been a significant factor for the vendors, perhaps even comprising a decisive argument 'from the public standpoint'. Certainly Micklem would have thought so.

On a quite different tack, it was in 1935–6 that he established the Henderson Administration group of investment trusts, comprising Witan (already of course in existence), Greenfriar and Lowland. The Greenfriar Investment Company was formed in December 1935 through the issue, sponsored by Cazenove's, of 75,000 ordinary shares of £10 each at par. The issue was not underwritten and 65,275 shares were placed firm. It was such a 'house' issue that the distribution of some of those shares makes interesting reading, reflecting the true Cazenove inner circle of the 1930s. For instance: Cull & Co (6,100); Sir Connop Guthrie (2,500); Glyn, Mills (1,000); Major M. E. W. Pope (2,000); Baring Brothers (3,500); Prudential Assurance (5,000); Isaac Wolfson (2,000); Scottish Provident Institution (2,500); William Shearer (1,000); Whitehall Trust (1,000); and the Henderson family (6,015). Among the partners, Micklem took 6,000, Serocold 1,500, and Palmer-Tomkinson and Geoffrey Barnett 1,000 each, with lesser amounts going to junior partners. The staff was not forgotten, with Hanneford leading the way on 50. Six months later Cazenove's amicably acquired control from the Ostrer Brothers of the Denman Street Trust Company, whose assets chiefly comprised large holdings in the securities of Moss' Empires, Gaumont-British Picture Corporation and Provincial Cinematograph Theatres. The Greenfriar board became the new board, and the company was in due course renamed the Lowland. Thus formed, the Henderson group was ready to become a major investment force and, through its ability to take big views, be an important weapon in the Cazenove armoury of the 1930s.

Meanwhile, a couple of issues in 1936 reflected very different facets of company business. One was for Blackburn Aircraft, with a memorandum by Palmer-Tomkinson early in April providing a succinct summary and in the process shedding important light on how far a stockbroker was prepared to go in the 'corporate' sphere:

About six months ago my firm were asked to undertake the business of changing this Company into a public concern and marketing the shares. Enquiries elicited the fact that the Company required a complete overhaul in its financial and technical department. This was clearly beyond our scope as Brokers. Lazards have undertaken this overhaul and have most thoroughly and carefully reorganised the business.

When asked by Lazards to act as Brokers we advised about a month ago that in our opinion 18s od was the highest price they should pay for the shares. We now know that the Owners are most unwilling sellers even at 20s od and that the 120,000 shares sold to Lazards produces Cash required urgently for the reduction of overdrafts.

At the present moment 75,000 shares are still in the beneficial ownership of Lazards or their clients and 45,000 shares have been allocated at 21s od to ourselves for redistribution as follows:

25,000 to Market (about 10 Jobbers)
20,000 to ourselves and special clients.

These shares together with Lazards 75,000 are all to be placed in our hands for offer to the market.

Blackburn Aircraft had badly overstretched its financial capacity in the expansionary context of re-armament, and there was perhaps a sense in which Lazards, somewhat against the objective advice of its brokers, was paying over the odds in the wider national interest.

Altogether less to the City's credit, at least in the short term, was the issue of £210,000 in ordinary shares made in November 1936 for the hat manufacturers, Itas Ltd. Chairman and managing director was Gustav Ita (Swiss, but reputedly ex-Hungarian), and two of his family were also on the board. The company, based at Aylesbury, specialised in velour and fur felt hoods and capelines and had been making modest but increasing profits since starting in Britain four years earlier. Before that, the Ita family had been running hat factories in Austria since the 1870s. The issue itself, sponsored by Cazenove's in conjunction with the merchant bankers Arbuthnot Latham, went well enough. But in January 1938 it was announced that the capital was going to have to be further increased in order to liquidate a hefty bank overdraft, prompting the *FT* to comment that 'the expansion of the business has proceeded too rapidly in relation to conditions in the hat trade, which have deteriorated during the past year'. Then in April 1938 came the hammer blow. 'Itas' Unexpected Liabilities' ran the headlines, reporting that liabilities amounting to almost £80,000 had been discovered. It subsequently transpired that Gustav Ita for several years, even before 1936, had with disastrous results been carrying on, unofficially and without telling anyone, the business of a dealer in bills. He and his relatives now left the country, and, in the words of the *FT*, 'the share capital of £210,000 is stated to have been completely lost.' Faced by an appalling situation, Cazenove's and Arbuthnot Latham dealt with it as honourably as they could, buying back all the shares from holders and putting in a big non-interest bearing debenture. In 1939 the company's assets were sold to a Luton firm of hatters. After the war protracted negotiations took place with Ita, who eventually agreed to pay 155,000 Swiss

Francs into a blocked account in Zurich in favour of the Receiver, in consideration for the transfer to him of all the outstanding debentures. Altogether, it had been a serious misjudgement as well as a painful episode, though not without its moments of black humour.

A significant set-piece occurred in April 1937 after Neville Chamberlain, in his final Budget, had proposed a new tax on business profits, the National Defence Contribution, in order to help pay for re-armament. The *Financial News* led a fierce campaign against the idea and soon the City as a whole was expressing deep concern. The Stock Exchange Committee set up a special sub-committee and the first to be called to give evidence was Micklem:

> He said that the Chancellor's proposal had checked the New Issue Market, and he thought it would now be very difficult to get underwriting of Ordinary Shares. Each prospectus would have to contain a statement by the Auditors as to the probable profit after deduction of this tax and this statement Auditors would not be prepared to give until the terms of the Bill and methods of computation were known. The New Issue Market would be checked about Budget time each year owing to the uncertainty as to whether the rate of tax would be raised. He did not think that Companies would lightly decide to transfer their domicile abroad.

City opposition continued to mount over the next month and at the beginning of June the scheme was withdrawn.

1937 as a whole marked the beginning of the pre-war downturn, but Cazenove's still undertook a fair amount of new issue business, including Roan Antelope Copper Mines (for Culls), Joshua Tetley & Son (for Power Securities), Hoover, British Aluminium (again for Power Securities), and Courage. There were also two major foreign government issues, rare indeed in the 1930s: the Kingdom of Iraq in July, done for Barings with Panmure Gordon and Messel; and the Kingdom of Belgium in December, also done for Barings, but with Rowe & Pitman added to the broking team. The latter issue, an offer for sale of £5 million 4% sterling bonds at 97, proved disastrous, with 70 per cent being left with the sub-underwriters. £250,000 had been sub-underwritten through the Cazenove private list (as opposed to the much larger joint list decided upon in consultation with the issuing house and other brokers). Interestingly, of the ninety-six names on the firm's private list on this occasion, almost half were individuals.

But if Cazenove's was as usual to the fore in the new issue market during 1937, it would be wrong to give the impression that there were no other prominent brokers in this field. Apart from Cohen Laming Hoare under the determined leadership of Kit Hoare, there was the traditionally distinguished house of Greenwells, not to mention those other firms involved in the Barings issues. There were also plenty of other reputable firms, some now long forgotten. Nevertheless, the striking fact is that if one takes 1937 (and it was in no way an unusual year) the only stockbroking firm which *sponsored* more issues was Seymour, Pierce & Co, whose twenty-five issues were wholly utilities, almost all of them under £50,000. Cazenove's sponsored sixteen (of which five were of £½ million or over) and co-sponsored three. Then came Zorn & Leigh-Hunt, whose twelve issues plus one shared were almost wholly in rubber and all under £¼ million. They were followed by Cohen Laming Hoare and Rowe, Swann & Co, who each totalled eleven plus one shared, with four and two issues respectively of £½ million or over. No other firm achieved double figures off its own bat. Such figures reflect quantity only, but they do make a point.

Moreover, if one examines the 1937 lists as far as non-stockbroker issuing houses were concerned, an even more signal pattern emerges and one of wider significance. In terms of both sole *and* joint issues, the only two firms to achieve double figures were the Investment Registry (twelve, all under £½ million) and Charterhouse Investment Trust (only one of £½ million or over). Even a well-known issuing firm like Helbert Wagg sponsored just six issues, only one of which was above £300,000. As for the more celebrated merchant banking names, the only one who managed over three was Barings, who sponsored or co-sponsored six issues – all but one of which was £1 million or over. Altogether, London brokers that year not only sponsored more issues than non-brokers (242 to 228), but were also responsible for a nominal value that was 45 per cent greater. Because that pattern was to change in later years, it is easy to forget that it existed in the 1930s. And of those brokers doubling as issuing houses, foremost was Cazenove's.

Such a position had been attained in the late 1920s through an ability to say 'no'. It was similarly retained, with decisions almost always being taken on essentially personal grounds. A memorandum by Micklem of July 1938 catches this crucial process exactly:

> On the introduction of Mr Harrison of Thomson McLintock, Mr Strauss of Strauss Turnbull & Co, the London Brokers to O. K. Bazaars [South African store proprietors], came to see us today, together with Mr Saunders, a director of the Company. They explained that the Company proposed to issue 460,000 5½% second preference shares on the London market as soon as the accounts for the year ending June '38 were published (about September). It was suggested that we might like to tackle the issue, but on consideration we decided not to do so, as we have no knowledge of the ability or financial standing of the directors.

One can but add that the name of the company alone – O. K. Bazaars (1929) Limited – was hardly Micklem's style.

In general 1938 was a nervous, troubled year on the stock market, with the threat of Hitler looming large. The firm was associated with only about fourteen issues. One of the smaller ones, but of much significance for the future, was the issue in November of 294,038 Ultramar Exploration Co shares of 10s at £1. The history of Ultramar was already a complex one, but may be briefly summarised. It began in 1929, when a London-based syndicate, organised by Culls, was responsible for the formation of the Caracas Petroleum Corporation, which in the succeeding years bought concessions and options on over 2 million hectares in Venezuela. By 1935 it was still in the exploration stage, and its shareholders established the Ultramar Exploration Co in order to acquire further oil concessions and royalty rights in Venezuela. One of the directors was Ralph Micklem, and at the first board meeting Cazenove's was appointed brokers. Large stakes were held in both companies by not only Culls but also major mining houses, in particular New Consolidated Gold Fields and Selection Trust, while Cazenove's itself had over 200,000 shares in Caracas. In 1938 the two concerns were merged, giving Ultramar the benefit of the Caracas Petroleum Corporation's cash resources as well as the very efficient organisation it had built up in Venezuela. The arrangement was that Ultramar absorbed Caracas through an exchange of shares, on the basis of four Caracas shares for one Ultramar share, but was carried out only on the understanding that in due course a listing for Ultramar shares would be secured on the Stock Exchange. It was against this background, in addition to the need for more capital in order to continue exploring, that the November 1938 issue took place. Culls acted as issuing house, Cazenove's as brokers, and the name of Ultramar for the first time became widely known in the City.

New issue business was reduced to a semi-trickle during the last months of peace, but there were two issues in 1939 that reflected something of the close working relationship between Cazenove's and Barings. In January an offer for sale was made of £7.5 million 4% debentures of the Southern Railway, the first issue for several years by an individual British main line railway company. Shortly before Christmas, a Barings memorandum recorded a preliminary meeting with Eric Gore-Browne of the Southern board (and also of Glyn Mills): 'The lawyers to the Southern Railway are Messrs Smedley & Co and the brokers Messrs Laing & Cruickshank: Mr Gore-Brown said he appreciated we might prefer to use Messrs Cazenove & Akroyds in this business but he suggested that Laing & Cruickshank should also be brought in.' The two firms thus acted as joint brokers and, rather against the odds, the issue was favourably received. Five months later Barings offered for sale £1.7 million 3½% debentures of the North Metropolitan Power Station, the company needing to buy Willesden Generating Station. As in the company's previous issues sponsored by Barings, the broking ticket was shared by W. A. Simpson & Co (as brokers to the company) and Cazenove's. On June 15th, Micklem recorded his meeting that day with Evelyn Baring: 'I told him that, in view of the present price of War Loan and of the fact that our recent private placing of similar stock had not been very successful, I felt we should have to have a public issue, the price about 90, to be underwritten and advertised in the usual way.' The following day Barings passed this on to Lord Ashfield, chairman of the company: 'Sir Edward Peacock informed him that in view of the amount required and having in mind the opinion which had been strongly expressed by Messrs Cazenove's we had decided that a public issue by prospectus would be necessary.' In difficult times it was good advice, and the issue was fully subscribed.

Such was not the case in the last issue with which the firm was involved before the war. This was Eagle Oil & Shipping, comprising an offer for sale of £3 million 4½% debentures and the placing of £1½ million 5½% preference shares. The issuing house was Lazards, which employed Cazenove's and Cohen Laming Hoare as joint brokers, presumably in order to ensure that it was not short of firepower in the market. Eagle Oil was the principal subsidiary of the Canadian Eagle Oil Company, its business was transporting and marketing crude oil and its refined products, and on paper it was an attractive concern. The placing in fact seems to have been more or less achieved, partly because the Royal Dutch Shell Group took 500,000 shares firm in advance, but the offer of the debentures was a different matter. The arranging of the sub-underwriting was arduous in the extreme, affected by the recent failure of the big Amsterdam banking house of Mendelssohn & Co as well as the larger European situation, and over thirty institutions or firms declined to participate. The prospectus itself was published on August 16th. Though noting how 'international complications tend to thwart investment enterprise', 'Autolycus' was typically optimistic: 'The Shipping market list can well accommodate a new redeemable debenture of this kind, for there is none too much stock on offer of the existing issues, and the latest comer can, therefore, rely upon favourable notice.' In fact, 79 per cent of the issue was left with the sub-underwriters, and when dealings began on the 18th the stock was immediately quoted 1¾ discount. The laborious process then began of gradually relieving the sub-underwriters, and that day's Oil share market report in the *FT* noted: 'The firm of dealers responsible for the well-known series of market slips on oil companies issued today a brochure dealing with Eagle Oil & Shipping. Copies are obtainable through stockbrokers.' It is doubtful if the process had been completed by the time the world changed.

———————

War was declared on 3rd September 1939. Less than a fortnight later Micklem received a letter from David Boyle, a director of the Anchor Line shipping company, in which Boyle recalled how 'thanks to Barings and to you, the Anchor Line was preserved to take its great share in this terrible struggle'. The reference was almost certainly to the placing in January 1936 of 50,000 unissued shares (involving Micklem himself taking 9,500 shares and Major Pope 5,000) and it must have been a gratifying memory. Over the following year, as 'total war' became a reality, the City suffered in a way it had not a quarter of a century earlier. The heavy bombing of London began during the summer of 1940 and that December the Germans destroyed the Guildhall and eight of Wren's churches. But the worst night was that of 10th May 1941, when there took place what Churchill later described as 'the most destructive attack of the whole night Blitz'. Many of the City's finest, most historic buildings were destroyed, and whole areas were left in ruins. Thereafter the bombing eased, but the damage had been done. Overall, the *Luftwaffe* during the war reduced to a bomb site some 225 of the City's 675 acres; and those working at Cazenove's never knew, as they turned into Tokenhouse Yard in the morning, whether they would be greeted by their office or a pile of rubble.

Not surprisingly, quite apart from any other problems, wartime life was disruptive for most firms. For example, London Trust (whose brokers Cazenove's had become) had to move twice, following a land mine at Austin Friars in October 1940 and then again in 1944 after Old Jewry had been bombed, at which point the firm received temporary accommodation in 12 Tokenhouse Yard. Nor was travel for City workers easy. George Durno, who joined Cazenove's in 1941, recalls the problems of coming in from Redbridge in Essex and having to hitch from Mile End; while in the heart of the square mile, it was necessary for about a year to use a Bailey bridge in order to traverse the vast crater in front of the Royal Exchange. The whole experience was one that those who lived through it would never forget.

For a time there was the possibility that the Stock Exchange itself would move out of London. During the summer of 1939 the option had been obtained on a lease of the Denham film studios in Buckinghamshire; and by that autumn, with a fair number of member-firms having expressed willingness if necessary to go to Denham, the Committee was seriously contemplating such a transfer of the floor of the House and attendant Stock

Exchange administrative departments. In the words of its communication to members: 'The physical difficulties of a general concentration of Members at Denham are obvious, but it is essential that as effective a Market as possible be established at the earliest possible moment after the City has been evacuated.' The Trustees of the Stock Exchange, however, virtually refused to countenance the idea and in November 1939 gave four main reasons: the Stock Exchange's immunity thus far from air raids; inadequate telephonic communications with Denham; the present tendency for evacuated business firms to return to London; and (perhaps the most important consideration) 'the attitude of the Gilt-Edged Market and its declared intention to make arrangements of its own'. It was clear that the gilt-edged dealers and brokers (including presumably Palmer-Tomkinson) would rather perish than be divorced from the Bank of England (which was not moving) and its transfer facilities. The Committee backed down and in May 1940 informed the membership that it 'would not order a move so long as Banking facilities are available'. Over the next seven months the Stock Exchange's immunity from air raids continued, and in December it informed its solicitors that 'while we are bound to have an option, which we can in fact exercise at any time, we are not likely to exercise it arbitrarily'. The option was retained for some time, but during 1941 the threat of an immobilised City gradually receded and it became clear that the House was not going to stray from its familiar environs.

In fact, far from removing to leafy Bucks, the Stock Exchange managed to achieve a surprising degree of normality in adverse conditions. A major problem was the transaction of business during the frequent air raid warnings, and by the autumn of 1940 a strong feeling had developed on the part of both members and press that either the floor or the settling room should be allowed to remain open during 'Alert' periods. The Committee, however, was compelled to announce that experts from the Home Office had advised that 'owing to the large unimpeded area of the House and in view of the great weight of masonry and the nature of the floors of the House and the Settling Room, the building was unsuitable to the construction of extensive shelters such as would be needed to house our Members'. Moreover: 'The effect of a direct hit or the collapse of part of the building might well be to cause so many casualties among Members as to render it impossible for the Stock Exchange to function as an organisation in which accumulated experience is so important a factor.' The best solution, therefore, was for members to continue to use their offices during air raid warnings and to deal over the phone, a method anyway 'widely used by Members under normal conditions'. An obstinate streak seems to have persisted, for in February 1941 the Trustees and Committee had to post a notice in order to 'once again impress on Members the importance of leaving the House as quickly as possible on the sounding of "the Alert"'.

There were, of course, many difficulties concerning personnel, even though it was calculated in October 1940 (on the basis of a questionnaire returned by 608 firms) that only 6,260 partners and staff were travelling to the City daily, as opposed to 13,329 in April 1939. A piquant episode occurred in August 1941 when the sub-committee on clerks reported that it had 'received an application by a firm of Brokers for the admission of a woman to the Settling Room' and asked the Committee 'to approve in principle the admission of women, to the Settling Room only, as a temporary war measure'. By seventeen votes to eight the Committee decided against. Another problem surfaced in June 1942, when 'Mr Palmer-Tomkinson drew attention to cases of hardship to clerks serving in the Forces which might arise owing to their firms discontinuing business and the consequent withdrawal of their names from the List of Clerks'. The Committee took the problem on board and the solution, suggested by Palmer-Tomkinson, was a register of such clerks. Yet overall, continuity was the great domestic theme, at least among those who remained in the City. The hours of business might shorten (with at one stage the Stock Exchange closing at 2.00 pm), but there remained the traditional ban on smoking until it was almost time for members to make their way from the floor; and when that 'lighting-up' moment was about to come each afternoon, a group of dealers in the Consol market would still fill Miles Brunton's pipe with leaves, rubberbands and suchlike and wait expectantly for him to reach for his matches.

The share market itself inevitably reacted closely to the fortunes of war. At the start of 1940 prices were higher than they had been a year earlier; but a major sell-off accompanied the disasters of the spring of 1940 and on June 26th the *Financial News* (later *Financial Times*) 30–Share Index, which had started at 100 in 1935, hit an all-time low of 49.4. Gilt-edged securities were almost alone in not slumping. But then in 1941, following the imposition in April of income tax at 10s leading to a search for higher yields than those obtainable from Government securities, there took place the start of a fundamental shift towards other sections, especially Industrial equities. Wartime economic controls continued to affect dividends, but by 1943 the 30–Share Index had climbed above the 100 mark and only once again would fall below it.

Business, however, remained on a restricted scale and was still mostly done for cash and by negotiation with the jobber. It was a problem that a major gilts operator like Palmer-Tomkinson was acutely aware of and it helped to govern his attitude when in 1941 a specially appointed sub-committee considered the proposition that henceforth the broker would have to mark all bargains done on behalf of non-members. His viewpoint was typically trenchant:

> Through all Stock Exchange history (except during the last war, when the Government imposed legislation which we got rid of at the earliest possible moment) a bargain has been the private concern of the firms who do the bargain. No-one in the world has the faintest right to know even that a bargain has been done, unless one or both of the parties concerned like to publish the fact. If we accept and enforce compulsory markings we make a fundamental change; we say in effect that if a bargain is done in the Stock Exchange, the world in general has a right to know, not only that a bargain has been executed, but the price at which it was done.
>
> In most cases this will not matter to the parties who dealt and the knowledge gained by those who see the mark will be of little value. In the few cases where important business takes place, one principal at least will frequently be most unwilling to broadcast the knowledge which might well be exceedingly interesting.
>
> Will Dealers be prepared to 'take on' big lines at 'outside prices' if they are compelled to mark the bargains?
>
> This is more than a Jobber's private trouble. I believe that the accept- ance of the objective [i.e. to provide the public with a more complete picture of business done] will tend still further to turn the Jobber into a mere negotiator of business, and that any accentuation of this tendency (already apparent) will be to the detriment of our institution.

Over the ensuing months many member-firms gave evidence and in March 1942 the sub-committee reported:

> From the evidence received from Brokers, it appears that the general practice is to mark all bargains. It is estimated that at least 90% of bargains done for Non-Members are already marked. With regard to the Compulsory Marking of Bargains and its attendant problems, the principle was accepted by a majority of the Brokers consulted. As to the Jobbers it was accepted by one-third and would be acquiesced in without enthusiasm by the majority. There was, however, strong opposition from a small but influential minority.

The sub-committee therefore decided that 'it would be a mistake to adopt compulsory Marking now' and this was unanimously accepted by the main Committee.

Even so, the debate itself was clearly a reflection of the Stock Exchange's increasing pre-occupation with outside opinion. Soon afterwards, in July 1942, the Committee submitted a revealing memorandum to the Treasury

Committee under Lord Kennet that was considering the question of releasing manpower from the financial sector. The Stock Exchange Committee's basic argument was that 'no further reduction can be made in the number of members without causing most serious harm', but the opportunity was taken to address wider concerns. After making the point that 'we find in our experience a lack of knowledge and consequently of appreciation of the part we play in the Nation's life', the memorandum went on:

> We have not failed to move with the times. To a far greater extent than most public Institutions we have retained our flexibility of organisation and our ability to adjust ourselves to ever changing circumstances. We have been successful in avoiding that rigidity which in so many directions has clamped a dead hand on enterprise. The standard of service rendered by stockbrokers has been revolutionised during the last generation, and several major contributions to the development of our financial system have originated from amongst its members, one of the latest examples being the intervention of minimum prices for Gilt-Edged securities in times of National crisis, which in itself proved an enormous strength to the whole credit structure.
>
> In the United States for the last ten years there has been almost open warfare between the Government of the day and Wall Street with a resulting paralysis in many forms of enterprise, and a tremendous waste of labour and effort and money for the community. In this country there has been no such crisis, and because of the co-operation between the City and the Government of the day – in which co-operation The Stock Exchange played its full share – we had an era of satisfactory business during the years between the 1931 crisis and the outbreak of war.

After a comparison between the adaptability of the Stock Exchange and that of the British Constitution, the set-piece defence continued:

> With our long experience of international trading, our unrivalled legal system and our immense prestige for honest dealing, we ought to be able to re-create great markets in London in the future, and in this work The Stock Exchange has a vital part to play. Such markets bring to this country directly and indirectly very large earnings in the aggregate, and we shall need every penny of such earnings in the New World after the War.

What sort of world would that be? The previous year George Orwell had looked ahead to the post-war social revolution, perhaps under a socialist government, and made a confident prediction: 'The Stock Exchange will be pulled down, the horse plough will give way to the tractor, the country houses will be turned into children's holiday camps, the Eton and Harrow match will be forgotten.' It was hardly surprising if a certain nervousness now began to permeate the hitherto largely private, intimate world of Capel Court.

It was in this broad context, together with the specific one of the Cohen Committee beginning its fundamental deliberations on company law, that the Stock Exchange Committee in 1944 once again tackled the vexed question of private placings. After receiving the usual quota of evidence, the special sub-committee this time recommended, among other proposals, 'that dealings subject to permission to deal (as distinct from placing arrangements with the Market) should not be permitted in Equity Stocks'. The reason given stressed the wider constituency: 'It was almost universally agreed by witnesses that, in the case of a placing, Members and clerks can and do sometimes obtain an advantage which results in the Public paying a higher price for securities. Consequently the Public (as opposed to professional and institutional investors) do not have a fair and sufficient chance to acquire securities at the first market price.' The sub-committee's report was accompanied by a forceful minority report from Palmer-Tomkinson:

> I cannot see in what way these proposals will make it less likely that members and clerks will keep for their own accounts shares on which an immediate profit is visible; or how they are likely to enable a firm like my own, which values the goodwill of the market, to offer the jobbers a bigger share; or to compel a firm which deliberately does the bulk of the business outside to offer more to the jobbers. Nor will they prevent a jobber from dealing with shares either sold to him or left with him as he thinks fit.
>
> The Committee has power, if it thinks right, to refuse permission to deal if the broker has not made sufficient shares available. It can invoke the penalty clauses of our rules against a jobber who does not ration the shares available fairly among all brokers who wish to buy them. Either course seems to me completely contrary to the real interests of the Stock Exchange.
>
> I am well aware that the hope and objective of those who framed this report is to prevent further 'Introduction scandals' of which Kruschen and Bristol Aeroplanes are regarded as the classic examples. My firm were responsible for both, and even now I don't know how the trouble could have been mitigated. I am quite sure the recommendations of this report will not help when some similar introduction is made on similar markets. Such cases are most infrequent, and I am sure it is impossible for us to frame rules or regulations to meet them.

This time Palmer-Tomkinson's strongly non-interventionist arguments failed to sway opinion, and the Committee accepted the majority report's recommendations by an overwhelming twenty votes to two.

Meanwhile, away from these lofty issues, what of wartime life in Tokenhouse Yard? Many familiar faces were missing, with over half the partners and staff away in the Forces or engaged in war work. The firm did its best to keep them informed (the first Christmas card featured a photograph of sandbags outside the front door of No. 12) and also ensured that their overall earnings did not drop below pre-war levels. There were few outstanding military achievements, though Angus Eames won a Military Cross in Malta and Colin Huttenbach, who had joined the firm in 1938, a Distinguished Flying Cross in Italy. Ironically, the highest rank, that of Brigadier, was achieved by a comptometer operator, Miss Clark, and one day Frank Holt in uniform found himself having to salute her. As for No. 12 itself, an unexploded shell did fall on it and go through each floor to the basement, but fortunately without bursting; and the only real damage it caused was a 'barrel hole' through Albert Martin's desk. Almost every night there was someone on the roof fire-watching, which mostly meant keeping an eye on the Bank of England to see if they had an alarm. If so, his job was to ring the bell and everyone would then go down to the shelter in the basement. Equipment there included the safe, a camp bed, plentiful Ovaltine tablets and sundry miscellaneous items, most of which gradually disappeared in the course of the war. With so many away on active service, inevitably there was a tendency towards the staff being either distinctly old or distinctly young. One of the latter was Godfrey Chandler, who was to become an immensely important figure in subsequent years. Through various chance connections, he came to the firm in 1941 at the age of sixteen, having recently achieved the highest mark for the whole of England in the commercial mathematics examination set by the London Chamber of Commerce. Martin, who had succeeded Hanneford as manager shortly before the war, had the young man interviewed by Pugh, and together they showed the foresight to give him a job until he was old enough to go in to the Army. Chandler from the start warmed to the family atmosphere of Cazenove's and could not help but think of the Cheeryble brothers from *Nicholas Nickleby*.

Of the triumvirate, Serocold had been moving towards semi-retirement even before the war and spending increasing periods of time abroad. June 1940 found him trapped in Vichy France and, after a dramatic sequence of events, he had to be 'lifted' back to England. During the rest of the war he was in and out of the City but was no longer the vital force he had been, at least in the life of Cazenove's. Instead, day-to-day control of the firm rested wholly in the hands of Micklem and Palmer-Tomkinson, with the principal help coming from Bedford on the dealing side and Martin as manager. For both Micklem and Palmer-Tomkinson it was an onerous burden conscientiously discharged, especially as each lost a son in the conflict. Micklem, moreover, not only had important Home Guard responsibilities in addition, but also by this time had become a diabetic and needed daily injections. From a staff point of view, much hinged on Palmer-Tomkinson, with his highly-developed paternalistic streak. The story goes that one day, coming to the office in plus-fours and not wishing to lunch at his club in them, he made inquiries that led to him realising the problems that staff had in eating out cheaply. Accordingly, in liaison with Martin, he initiated a system by which two nearby restaurants accepted Cazenove luncheon vouchers, a pioneering step on the part of a City firm.

Within the partnership as a whole there were two significant events during the war. The first was the admission of two people 'from the ranks', for the first time in the history of the firm. One was 'Beddy', who in 1940 was asked to be a partner by Micklem in the street – in other words, not in front of the others in the box. Five years later Martin joined him, the just reward for not only an excellent office manager and acknowledged master of the new issue mechanics, but also the person who had helped design the D form which the authorities introduced for the transfer of securities during the war. The other event was the tragic death in 1944 of Algy Belmont, killed by a motor accident in the Hyde Park black-out while doing a tour of inspection of his anti-aircraft batteries. Had he lived he would eventually have become senior partner.

Inevitably the day-to-day business dwindled to a mere shadow of its former self, though soon after the market had reached its 1940 nadir, Micklem and Culls did put together a notable syndicate of some £$\frac{1}{2}$ million, instructing the two principal investment trust jobbers to buy any leading investment trust equity stock coming on offer until the money was exhausted. At that point the jobbers were told to sell the same stocks at 25% profit and they completed the whole operation within four months. As for the companies part of the business that had become the very cornerstone during the 1930s, it was a mixed picture. On the one hand, the capital market as a whole was strictly controlled and to make a public issue required Treasury sanction as granted by the Capital Issues Committee. Savings instead were channelled into War Loan issues. But on the other hand, within that broad constraint governing the new issue market, Cazenove's did manage to retain its leading position in relation to other company brokers. Thus, taking the span September 1939 to July 1945, no other firm was associated with more issues than the Cazenove total of forty-seven; then came (excluding British government stock and utility specialists) Hoare

& Co (as it was now called) on twenty-nine, Myers & Co on twelve, Laing & Cruickshank on eleven, and Rowe Swann on ten.

The value of Micklem's contacts at the highest level was exemplified by the way in which he developed during the war a very close liaison with the Bank of England, partly through Ruby Holland-Martin, who was an executive director there. When the war started he was consulted about selling the overseas assets of British residents; and thereafter he was prominent in the often tricky business of disposing of Government shares acquired in the industrial depression between the wars. Typical was the case of the Lancashire Cotton Corporation, which by 1940 had stabilised its business and was paying dividends, so becoming the first of the Bankers Industrial Development Corporation protegés to leave the nest. Organising overall matters, and seeking to ensure that the B.I.D.'s massive shareholding was sold to a wide number of British investors, was Sir Edward Peacock of Barings. On January 19th he wrote to Montagu Norman:

I cleared up a good deal with Tod [a director of the Corporation] and Micklem today and got Micklem to sound a couple of his most confidential people.

He says what he would like to do is to have the Bank tell him, say, at 4 o'clock on Tuesday evening that they would be prepared to do a deal on agreed terms. By Wednesday at the same time he would hope to be able to hand in his contract for the business, having completed his syndicate.

Peacock added, with regard to the forthcoming statement for the press:

The public inclusion of the names of one or two Lancashire brokers will not help the business and will rather prejudice it in the eyes of all the other Lancashire brokers, whereas what is wanted is that they should all take a little bit and thus spread the net much more widely in Lancashire. This Micklem is quite confident he can arrange.

The sale duly went ahead, and on February 8th Norman wrote to the Government broker, Ted Cripps of Mullens: 'Will you please assure Charles Micklem of my gratitude and admiration for the way in which he has carried out his recent purchase of L.C.C. shares.' The next day Micklem wrote to the Governor:

We have received from E.S. Cripps this morning your message of congratulation – a message which we value most highly.

As far as our end of the business is concerned, everything has gone through with the greatest smoothness, and I know I can say the same for the dealers in the Stock Exchange through whom a large proportion of the shares has been placed.

The shares in question have so far been registered in the names of about 700 investors; I should expect this number to be increased during the next few weeks.

This was hardly on a 'tell Sid' scale, but it was nevertheless a highly gratifying outcome for what was a forerunner of privatisation.

The other reasonably well-documented comparable case was that of the Belfast shipyard, Harland and Wolff. Under the scheme agreed in May 1937, the creditors of that company (comprising the Treasury, the Northern Ireland government, and some of the British joint-stock banks) had been allotted in part repayment of their loans 5.2 million 'A' ordinary shares, each carrying a 4% non-cumulative preferential dividend. By November 1941, with markets generally improving and in particular the company's 'B' shares, Micklem felt in a position to sound out a possible syndicate (Culls, Helbert Wagg, Barings, the Whitehall Trust and the Prudential) and to write to John Morison of Thomson McLintock, agents on behalf of the creditors, with the prospect of starting a market in the 'A' shares:

> I think we are justified in saying that we could now form a syndicate to take, say, half of the available Harland and Wolff 'A' Ordinary Shares at 15s 6d net, provided we have the call on the other half for three months at 16s net.
>
> I believe that, provided market conditions remain about the same as they are today, these shares when they are placed should stand somewhere between 17s and 18s, but in order to sell something like 4,000,000 shares I think we should want all that margin to make a success of the placing. I do not think that in this case it would be wise to deal in a small amount and then see how the market settled down with a view possibly to selling further comparatively small amounts from time to time. This method works in the case of ordinary shares, the price of which it is difficult to gauge at all accurately; but in the case of Harland and Wolff 'A' Ordinary Shares the market can, I think, fairly be estimated within a shilling or two.

In the event, Cazenove's took the first two million shares at 16s each and the market began at about 17s. Distributing the shares among the public proved a difficult business, largely because of the non-cumulative participating form they took, and by the time the syndicate was dissolved in June 1942 barely half a million had been sold. Accordingly, when two years later the Midland Bank indicated its willingness to part with 3 million 'A' shares, Micklem was determined that he would take the shares and attempt to distribute them only if Harland and Wolff's capital was re-organised. He therefore submitted a plan in May 1944 to divide the 'A' ordinary equally into 4½% cumulative preference shares and ordinary shares. The Treasury then put forward an alternative plan, by which the re-organised capital would still consist entirely of ordinary shares. Micklem, however, refused to budge, forcibly telling Holland-Martin on June 1st that he 'did not think it would be possible to form any syndicate to take a large block of these Ordinary shares at any reasonable price at all, as we should be cutting out a large section of investors who will take Preference shares but not Ordinary'. Twelve days later he developed his arguments to Sir William McLintock:

(1) I feel no doubt whatever that the capital structure as it is at present is not one which enables the shares of the Company to command the price in the market to which they are entitled.

(2) I am not in favour of altering the capital structure by converting the 'A' Ordinary Shares and the 'B' Ordinary Shares into one new class of Ordinary Share.

(3) With the capital structure as it is at present, I feel it is almost impossible to sell 3,000,000 'A' Ordinary Shares at anything like a fair price.

So I come back to our proposal . . .

I believe that these 4½% Cumulative Preference Shares would appeal to institutions, etc, who do not favour non-cumulative preference shares.

We should be prepared, however, to buy 3,000,000 'A' Ordinary Shares in their present form provided the profits for the year ending 31 December 1943 are not less than about £1,500,000 before Depreciation and that we approve the Board's statement to the shareholders recommending the proposals.

Cazenove's duly bought the shares soon afterwards and in October the company's capital was reconstructed according to Micklem's wishes. Over the following weeks the majority of the new preference shares were quickly absorbed by investors, but it took longer to dispose of the ordinary shares. Micklem continued to run a syndicate in them until August 1945, by which time they were all finally sold. Altogether, it had been one of the firm's more important exercises in corporate finance.

By the summer of 1942, following the removal of an embargo by the Treasury, conditions were ripe for a series of major industrial conversions to begin on the Stock Exchange. Negotiations began in May between Micklem and the brewers Courage & Company with a view to converting £324,715 5½% debenture stock into 4% stock; but it soon became clear that there was a serious problem, namely that if the conversion was a complete failure the company would be liable for the interest on both the outstanding 5½% stock and the 4% stock issued to guarantors. The Courage board took the view that it was unfair to saddle the company with what it called an 'unknown liability,' but on June 16th Micklem wrote sympathetically but firmly to the chairman with his firm's offer of guarantee:

> We suggested a modification of the terms to the Bank of England but it was over-ruled, and I am afraid you must take it from us that the terms proposed are the best we can arrange for the Company.
>
> The Bank of England's opinion is that the liability of the Company is very small in respect of double interest; it amounts to a maximum of £1. per cent less whatever interest you receive on the money involved. In our opinion, for what it is worth, we feel that the Directors would be safe in reckoning that not less than 50 per cent would be converted, and therefore their net loss in double interest would not be likely to be more than three-eighths per cent.
>
> We believe that negotiations are in an advanced stage for other conversions. If you miss the opportunity now of making your own conversion, we must point out to you that such an opportunity may not occur again for quite a long time in view of the whole national financial programme.

The board accepted this advice. Soon afterwards Micklem was writing to L. Fleischmann to apologise for being unable to offer Seligman Brothers any participation in the sub-underwriting: 'I can tell you it was not through want of trying to get into a position to offer you a participation; it was purely owing to the fact that the two or three big underwriters whom we had consulted all the way through insisted at the last moment in taking the whole lot for themselves.' These were Robert Fleming (£174,000), the Prudential (£100,000) and Barings (£50,000). Over the following weeks the conversion was successfully accomplished and in his congratulatory letter to the chairman on July 21st, Micklem noted how 'as your debenture stock conversion was the first on the list, we had between us all to bear the brunt of arranging terms satisfactory to the Bank of England, to Whitehall, to the Company and to the guarantors'.

There was no shortage of interesting or important business in the middle years of the war. In August 1942, for instance, there was a private placing for the Ozalid Company. The background to it was that the Ministry of Economic Warfare had in effect 'stolen' (for the best of motives) the German patent invention of a copying machine, put it under British management and was now bringing it to the market. All the shares were put in Albert Martin's name, and if he had been killed by a bomb the issue would have been cancelled. The following May, following the death of Lord Wakefield, Cazenove's in conjunction with Morgan Grenfell was responsible for placing among solid investors his quarter of a million shares in C.C. Wakefield, the future Castrol Oil. Also in 1943 there were large issues of British Celanese and Ultramar, the latter of which, in its arduous and still mainly unfulfilled pursuit of Venezuelan oil, needed cash in order 'to purchase $2,500,000 to carry on drilling, geophysical and other development work'. In both cases the issuing house was Morgan Grenfell, even though both companies were traditionally Cull concerns. A letter in October 1944 from R. H. V. Smith of Morgan Grenfell to his French counterpart explained why:

> You ask about Cull & Co. What happened was this. About 1½ years ago the three remaining partners [including Hugh Micklem] came in to see us and said that as they were elderly men they wished to retire from business and wondered whether we would be willing to take over their company and run it as a subsidiary. We said we were not prepared to do this but if they were willing to liquidate Cull & Co and influence their connections in our direction, we would be only too happy to co-operate . . . It was therefore arranged that we should buy all the shares and thereafter put the company into voluntary liquidation. This of course took time to carry through but the company was finally wound up last week.
>
> By taking over the business we acquired some valuable connections, the chief of which are the Chester Beatty group, Central Mining and British Celanese. None of the Cull partners of course joined the firm.

Culls had played an important part in the recent growth of Cazenove's, but this development at least had the effect of strengthening what was already a significant relationship with Morgan Grenfell.

The summer of 1944 included two unrelated but noteworthy events. In June, in the context of worries about outside competition, there was the so-called 'Grey Market Agreement', usefully described by the official historians of the Stock Exchange:

> Brokers concerned in a placing could issue shares to jobbers on the understanding that the jobbers would only sell to institutions on an approved list. These institutions in turn undertook not to sell new shares at a discount within six months, and not to buy new unquoted securities unless the issue had been approved by the Treasury. The agreement cut off would-be borrowers from the main sources of finance unless they had Treasury approval, and largely removed the incentive to go outside normal channels.

The agreement seems to have lasted for about a year and undoubtedly had the inequitable effect that shares were placed far too cheaply with a few favoured recipients. In the candid words of Antony Hornby, who returned to the firm at the end of 1944, 'for our clients it was money for jam'. The other event was in August, when Cazenove's for probably the first time acted in a new issue capacity for the New Trading Co, the precursor of S. G. Warburg & Co. Micklem had apparently been friendly even before the war with Harry Lucas and it was to become another important connection. This pioneering issue was for Woodheads Canonbury Brewery and was almost fully subscribed.

One further slice of company action – taking place after the end of the European war, but before the end of the Japanese – deserves mention. This was the complicated reverse take-over in July 1945 by which the *Financial News* acquired the *Financial Times*, but when the two papers became one that October the name of the new paper was the *Financial Times*. Hornby at last found himself coming centre stage:

> Brendan Bracken was the chairman of the *Financial News* and Garrett Moore [Lord Moore, later Lord Drogheda] was his managing director. Brendan conceived the idea of buying the controlling interest in the *FT* from Lord Camrose, whom he had reason to believe might be willing to sell, and merging the two papers so that there should only be one financial daily of really good quality. The price of *FT* shares in the market was 40s. I went to see Lord Camrose with CM and he offered us his shares at 42s. The *FN* couldn't afford to buy the lot; Camrose would sell all or nothing. So it was left to us to find buyers for the balance at above the market price. CM said to me, 'You'll be able to manage it.' Thus challenged I did and my first deal was accomplished. Very sweet it was and about twenty years after I'd joined the firm!

The new *FT* proved a great success, gaining both circulation and prestige during the post-war years, and was a source of considerable pride as the City's paper.

In general the summer of 1945 was a time for taking stock and also looking ahead to what was necessarily an uncertain future. Overall, the firm had fared well enough during the war, retaining its position as a company broker and making respectable net profits, which had grown steadily from £57,139 in 1940 to £193,391 in 1944. Nevertheless, there was by 1945 an undeniable current of pessimism at Tokenhouse Yard. It was realised that Serocold was unlikely to return as a major force, while both Micklem and Palmer-Tomkinson were in their sixties and somewhat drained by their exceptional exertions of the past few years. Moreover, the sudden death of Belmont had cruelly deprived the firm of the generally-accepted heir apparent. Put another way, there was no great confidence that the firm would be able to absorb among their replacements all the staff now returning from the Forces. In fact, a letter to them in August 1944 had suggested that some might prefer to look for a different job and announced that a demobilisation committee would be formed in order to help in that purpose; but in the event, all but one member of staff preferred to return to Cazenove's, and the committee was soon disbanded. The loyalty was indicative and heart-warming, if perhaps not wholly welcome at the time, as partners prepared to see if there would be enough business to warrant a staff almost a hundred strong.

By July 1945 all eyes turned to the general election, the results of which were due on Thursday the 26th. As ever, 'Autolycus' in the *FT* closely reflected mainstream Stock Exchange opinion. 'That Mr. Churchill and his party will be returned,' he wrote on the 19th, 'is practically taken for granted. The point of uncertainty is the sum of the majority.' Over the next few days confidence did not waver. Thus on the 24th: 'Certain it is that no sign exists in the Stock Exchange of apprehension in regard to the outcome.' By the 26th itself he was declining to make forecasts, merely referring to 'the tense atmosphere of subdued excitement which will prevail on the Stock Exchange markets today.' Across the front page, however, the main headline was 'Firm and Confident Tone of Markets', and the market report, dated Wednesday evening, began: 'The all-round firmness of markets today indicated the confidence felt that Mr Churchill will be re-installed as the country's leader by the vote of the people.' Twenty-four hours later and the mood of the House was very different. 'The Stock Markets today were like the weather – dull and overcast,' the Thursday evening report began; and 'Autolycus' began his column by noting that 'the impossibility of calculating the incalculable result of a General Election is once more demonstrated.' Labour had won a massive majority of 210, thus achieving real political power for the first time. 'It must be hoped,' said an editorial in the *FT*, 'the victors will not allow their great majority to persuade them to extremist courses such as would aggravate world anxiety.' No one in the City knew what the future would bring, but many feared the worst.

CHAPTER SEVEN

Re-building the business
1945–1959

At the end of the war the City of London was devastated not just physically. In almost every respect the outlook seemed dark: internationally the dollar reigned supreme; vast debts had been incurred in fighting the war; many foreign investments had been liquidated; the domestic industrial base was ravaged; and within the square mile itself, not only were several of the main markets (including foreign exchange and gold) likely to remain closed for several years, but the continuing existence of the Capital Issues Committee meant that for a long time to come the floating of foreign issues in London would be severely restricted. Above all, there was the threat from Westminster of a potentially hostile government entrenched with an overwhelming parliamentary majority. Charles Micklem was depressed for about a week after the General Election and with good reason; for the Labour Party's manifesto commitment to widespread nationalisation, to be reiterated in the King's Speech, represented a palpable threat to the very core of his firm's business, day-to-day broking on secondary markets as well as company finance. The promise to nationalise the gas and electricity supply industries was bad enough; still worse was the possible fate of steel; and worst of all was the prospect of the end of the private railway companies, granted that in relation to the main ones Cazenove's had achieved an almost monopoly position since the merger with Greenwoods. Moreover, in general terms, there was also the certainty that widespread nationalisation would seriously diminish the scope of the stock market as a whole, removing major categories of popular investment. Not surprisingly, the mood in Tokenhouse Yard, at least in the partners' room, was distinctly gloomy during the first winter of peace. 'It must be apparent to all that the avowed intention of the present Government to nationalise industry to an increasing extent will have a serious effect on Stock Exchange business generally,' a letter to staff in February 1946 bluntly stated, 'and it may well be that the profits of the Firm will suffer accordingly.'

Gloom was further compounded by the realisation that there could be no return to the halcyon days of the triumvirate. All three were now old men. Claud Serocold remained as nominal senior partner until 1947, but was never really active after the war. It was symbolic that, soon after the election, he sold his town house in Hyde Park Gate. The buyer was Winston Churchill and the story goes that during the negotiations Serocold feigned deafness in order not to be browbeaten by the great man. Churchill was to die there in 1965, while Serocold himself retired to his beloved south of France, knowing that he had achieved as much for Cazenove's as he possibly could. Jimmy Palmer-Tomkinson similarly remained a partner for only two years after the war. Almost certainly his staunch efforts during the difficult years of the war had taken a lot out of him, to judge by his characteristic letter in January 1947 to the chairman of the Stock Exchange Council (replacing the old Committee): 'As I am no longer able to pull my weight as a Member of the Council, I must ask you to add my name to the list of those resigning on the 25 March.' Also resigning as a partner in 1947 was Geoffrey Barnett, marking one more break with the past.

Charles Micklem, however, stayed on, becoming senior partner in the wake of Serocold. In his last years he did mellow somewhat, but he remained a formidable presence and a stickler for good behaviour, insisting on the highest possible business standards. He was the only partner to whom the bargain book was taken at the end of the day, and at least once he was heard to say to another partner, 'We don't like that name on the bargain sheet . . . We won't deal for him again.' When he rang the box with a string of orders he would still never repeat them, and more than one young dealer was saved by Mrs Keeler's kindness in always ringing in advance to warn that the great man was about to 'phone. But though still active and wholly alert he was not, indeed could not have been, the force that he had been between the wars. He was suffering from diabetes, did not attend the office usually more than three days a week, was disinclined at this stage to involve himself in the details of internal organisation, and altogether realised as well as anyone that the future rested in other hands. What would that future be? Bedford for one doubted whether, with the passing of the triumvirate, the firm would be able to maintain its ascendant position.

He and other sceptics would surely have been proved right but for two felicitous developments. The first was the emergence, during the early months of peace and under the auspices of Micklem, of Antony Hornby as a 'serious man' in his own right, willing and able to pick the whole thing up and move it into a new era. His succession to Micklem was a gradual process, but by the late 1940s it was he who was taking the key decisions that affected the future, above all rebuilding the business in the new post-war world. From then until his retirement in 1970 he was the leading partner in the firm. One of the major figures in the post-war City, he was also one of its more remarkable men.

Born in 1904, and educated at Winchester, Antony Hornby owed much to his parents. His mother was a woman of high principles, while his father, St. John Hornby, not only made W. H. Smith into a great firm, but was also the founder of the Ashendene Press and a notable connoisseur. They were well known for the private concerts they gave at their London home, Shelley House on Chelsea Embankment, one of which Virginia Woolf attended in 1918: 'How much the annual income of the audience amounted to, I should not like to guess; they wore a substantial part of it on their backs: the furs were richly dark; the stuffs of the best black.' Such a background helps to explain why Antony Hornby became a stockbroker renowned for his culture, his sophistication, and the breadth of his interests. In that sense he was more like Serocold than Micklem: a worldly urbanite in the best sense of the term. From about 1950 he began to build up a superb art collection, centred on the Impressionists and fairly described in one tribute after his death in 1987 as 'unusual, varied and subtle'. His approach to collecting was typical: to go to a reputable dealer and never ask advice from anyone. In 1961 he gave his Renoir nude to the National Gallery. When in old age his sight went, his greatest solace would be to walk round Venice in his mind, from church to church and through the Accademia, remembering almost every painting first seen during the summer tours of his boyhood.

No one who knew him would deny that Hornby was a man of strong character. Two of his most important qualities were his generosity (including much charitable work, especially in the hospital world) and his steadfastness. If one earned his loyalty, one had it for life. He was extremely good company, had the ability to charm and, with his keen sense of humour, abhorred pomposity. Once when a wealthy client had sent him a lengthy letter detailing his recent extensive travels, he replied as only he could, 'Dear Marco Polo'. At the same time he could be obstinate, a virtue as well as a fault; arrogant, adopting a dismissive tone towards people he did not think much of; and prone to occasional bursts of fearsome temper, usually when he was in the wrong, which was seldom. In this last respect, the tell-tale signs were when he began straightening his pens and pencils or his knives and forks: then was the time to stay low. But though he may have been a paternalist of the old school, who intensely disliked being crossed, the staff knew that he would protect them and take an active interest in their welfare. He had a sure personal touch and invariably would go round the different departments at Christmas. As for his role within the partnership, his attributes as leading partner were many: he was a good delegator, being much less secretive than Micklem; he was very unjealous of other partners' connections and was always willing to lend a hand, for instance in relation to a difficult client; and for a young partner, it was good to know that any excess of high spirits would probably be forgiven, because he had done it all himself in pre-war days. It has been said of him that he could be guilty of favouritism and that was undoubtedly true. Nevertheless, the objects of his partiality usually more than justified themselves in business terms; while in general he possessed the gift of being extremely encouraging to young people. His overall approach he summed up in unabashed words in his memoirs: 'Of course the firm is really far from democratic. It is a benevolent autocracy, which I have always thought can be by far the best form of government.' He would listen to the opinions of others and did not cultivate 'yes-men', but there is no doubt that for almost a quarter of a century Cazenove's continued to be an autocracy in his benevolent hands.

All this was underwritten by the fact that he was a remarkably effective businessman. He worked hard, was indeed deceptively professional; his nerves were good; despite certain prejudices, he had a broad mind and believed in the primacy of judgement and principle over fact and detail; and he had inherited from Micklem the indispensable qualities of total integrity and an ability to say 'no'. But perhaps above all, it was his complete confidence in his own judgement that lay at the heart of his and consequently the firm's success in the post-war period. Thus in a new issue, while he made a point of being generous in the sharing of commission, it was likely to be he who spoke first at the brokers' meeting to settle the pricing and other arrangements: not to have done so would, quite simply, have been unthinkable to him. From the point of view of a client, whether a company or a merchant bank, he was the most comforting of allies, always giving of his best and always positive – in his own, well-remembered words, 'merchant bankers don't want long faces'. He seemed to know everybody, he instilled confidence, he was full of humour, and most of all he was decisive, offering his considered, unequivocal opinion and very rarely having to come back with second thoughts. In April 1955 'Rufus' Smith, son of Lord Bicester, wrote a letter of introduction to a partner of J. P. Morgan & Co in New York: 'You will remember that when you were here you were in the room at the time we were discussing the price of the Imperial Tobacco issue with Rowe & Pitman and Cazenove & Akroyds. One of the partners of Cazenove's who was here at that time was Antony Hornby who is sailing for your side next Wednesday. Antony, I personally think, is the outstanding stockbroker in London of his age . . .' Smith had been managing director of Morgan Grenfell for almost twenty years and few in the City would have gainsaid his opinion.

However, Hornby could not have achieved what he did without the second crucial development in the immediate aftermath of the war. This was the arrival of Peter Kemp-Welch as a partner in the firm. He was still in his thirties but already had done much despite having no family money behind him. After school at Charterhouse he had read engineering at Cambridge. He also began to win a high reputation as a rackets player and in 1928 was selected to play for Great Britain against America and Canada. Unable to secure an engineering job after coming down, he booked a passage to Bombay with a view to becoming a cotton broker's clerk. At this point, the autumn of 1928, fate intervened: the father of his rackets partner (Duncan Cambridge, with whom that year he had reached the final of the Amateur Doubles Championship) found him a position with the tiny stockbroking firm of Read & Brigstock. It was a complete break with family tradition, for Kemp-Welch's father was managing director of Schweppes and the family as a whole had never had anything to do with the City. Over the next eleven years, first with Read & Brigstock and then at the larger firm of Foster & Braithwaite, he twice built up from scratch a substantial investment business, representing both private and institutional clients. By 1939 he was a seasoned professional, though not yet a major City figure in his own right. During the war he continued to flourish, joining the 1st Battalion of the Coldstream Guards and becoming their adjutant; while later he was closely involved first in the critical Overlord operation of 1944 for the D-Day landings and then in the crossing of the Rhine early in 1945. Soon afterwards, with the war clearly won, he was looking to return to the Stock Exchange and, if possible, build on the foundations he had laid during the 1930s.

The problem was that the family-controlled firm of Foster & Braithwaite would not allow him (or indeed any outsider who was not a Braithwaite or a Savory) to become a full partner. Kemp-Welch therefore decided he must go elsewhere; and the Government broker Ted Cripps, being aware of the situation, mentioned the matter to Serocold. He seems to have been neutral, but Micklem was inclined to be against, preferring to develop his own material. Indeed, formal mergers apart, Cazenove's in its history had hardly ever brought in an outsider in this way at a senior level. Micklem, however, left the choice to the younger partners, above all Hornby, who unhesitatingly said 'yes', recognising in Kemp-Welch someone who would stiffen the firm at a difficult time. He became a partner on 1st November 1945.

It was potentially an invidious situation for the new man, with undoubtedly some of the 'old guard' antagonistic towards his coming; but by sheer charm and force of personality he overcame any hostility and within months was a fully-accepted member of the partnership. What were his human and business qualities, still fondly remembered by many people a quarter of a century after his death? He was a very open, inviting person, with a quick mind and a bubbling sense of humour, which often took the form of the instant quip or *bon mot*, occasionally at other people's expense but usually not. He was very much a man's man, much admired for his sporting prowess, and had the enviable gift of being able to put a wide range of people at their ease, allied to a rare ability to remember names and faces. He loved talking about the things that interested him and might be seen outside in animated conversation about cricket with a taxi-driver even though the meter was still ticking away. He was immensely convivial and found it hard to decline the hospitality of his exceptionally numerous friends and acquaintances. He himself would entertain to all hours, but then ring up early next morning and say to a younger partner, 'Feel all right, old boy?', and it was as well for that younger partner to be at his desk. For beneath the conviviality lay a very hard worker, fuelled by great personal determination and fierce business-getting instincts: having made his own way in the world, these were habits he was unlikely to abandon. Nor would he have built up and now brought with him his impressive connections – which by 1945 included Equity & Law, Baillie Gifford (the major manager of investment trusts in Edinburgh) and David Wills of the wealthy tobacco family – without considerable investment skills. These were based on a close understanding of balance sheets and a willingness, in his own favourite words, to 'take a view'. He also took infinite pains with his clients, which in turn won him yet more business. One other special attribute deserves mentioning and that was his almost encyclopaedic knowledge of the brewing industry. He was on close terms with nearly all the leading brewers of the day and, building on the firm's already strong presence in that sector, was instrumental in most of them coming to Cazenove's, despite the competition between them. Altogether he brought with him all the attributes of a top-class stockbroker, and it was the good fortune of the firm to secure his services at the very moment when the enormous achievement of the inter-war years was in danger of being jeopardised.

Hornby and Kemp-Welch got on extremely well from the first. They consulted each other about almost everything, sat opposite each other at the same desk and, in Hornby's words, not only 'in course of time knew each other so well that we hardly needed to speak', but also 'could both read upside down – a useful accomplishment'. In many ways they complemented each other perfectly: Hornby was the cultured cosmopolitan, the perfect 'front man' on public occasions, and a presence of much weight in the great merchant banking houses; while Kemp-Welch loved the pursuits of the countryside and was a wonderful raconteur but no public speaker. Moreover, though very well respected by the merchant bankers, he was probably at his most effective (unlike Hornby) with both leading investment managers, many of whom were hard taskmasters, and rugged industrialists, being uniquely able to persuade them to trust the mystical doings of the City. There was also some sense in which Kemp-Welch added a crucial 'meritocratic' streak to Hornby's rather greater implicit belief in the virtues of breeding. 'Is he a good Holland-Martin?' became as important a question as 'Is he a Holland-Martin?' One other thing must be said. Hornby was galvanised after the war partly by the seriousness of the situation facing the firm, but partly also by the arrival of Kemp-Welch, who put him on his mettle and brought out all that was best in him. Together they made a splendid pair, as effective in their very different way as that earlier combination of Serocold and Micklem.

In many ways things returned to normal in Tokenhouse Yard, though some people did find it hard to readjust to civilian life after six years away. The manager after the war was the disciplinarian Charles Pugh, assisted by the more benign Charles Strangeman. Male secretaries began to give way to female ones, but it was a mark of continuity that the firm retained a wet copying machine until 1955. The system of settlement remained essentially manual. In the context of the difficult conditions obtaining in the City, Palmer-Tomkinson in one of his last, typically generous actions gave a substantial part of his profits to the staff; while for several years the staff was required to forego a third of its bonus, which was placed in individual reserve funds, in case the firm ran into difficulties and was unable to pay any bonuses at all. New partners, however, continued to be made, as was necessary as the old order passed. Cedric Barnett, Herbert Ingram and Gerald Micklem all became partners in 1946, with Luke Meinertzhagen following the next year. Also becoming a partner in 1947 was Jimmy Palmer-Tomkinson junior, who inherited from his father the charm without the obstinacy, but was not a natural businessman.

A more significant figure in the long run, though not a partner, was Peter Ashton. He was an experienced stockbroker who came with Kemp-Welch from Foster & Braithwaite in 1945, having done a superb job at keeping Kemp-Welch's business going during the war. At Cazenove's he took over the running of the private client business, introducing for the most important a 'red folder' system by which they were supplied with a regular valuation. Delightful, sensible and accurate, Ashton in time headed the investment department and became responsible for all investment advice, including that for pension funds, country brokers and bank opinions, replacing the more fragmented system by which individual partners gave individual advice to particular clients. Equally importantly, he was an early example of the 'senior executive', bridging the hitherto enormous gulf between partners and non-partners. Devoted to Kemp-Welch (though himself the older man), and often acting as his faithful deputy, especially as Kemp-Welch became increasingly occupied by company matters, he enjoyed his time at Cazenove's more than anywhere before.

As for Bedford, from soon after the war he no longer ran the box; but instead he returned to Tokenhouse Yard, where he continued with the role of buying and selling on behalf of the institutions and above all the placing of shares with them that he had begun during the war. His unique contribution in this all-important sphere was well summed up by Hornby in 1971:

> He was the most persistent and persuasive, reliable and conscientious placer of stock imaginable. He took infinite pains and he got himself respected by the investment managers of practically all the investment trusts and insurance companies. He picked up contacts which were in danger of dying out and took trouble about and made friends with the small institutions just as much as the large. He had a book in which he kept a record of those he had tried when placing a line of shares. Sometimes the first twenty people he approached refused, which would have deterred most people but not so Beddy. This was the sort of example that we needed and it set the pace for everyone else and has been the tradition of the firm ever since.

At a time when the firm was beginning to look solely to institutions to take up underwriting, and no longer to those by now heavily-taxed individuals who had featured in the inter-war period, Bedford's powers of persuasion, especially in relation to the then dominant insurance companies and investment trusts, could not have been more vital to the firm's success.

Succeeding him in the box was the sharp, terse, mathematically-endowed pair of Herbert Ingram and Gerald Micklem, who made life so hot for jobbers coming into it that eventually the jobbers complained, so that in about 1948 Charles Micklem had to withdraw them. Sensibly, conscious of his nephew's organisational ability and penchant for the more recondite theory of stockbroking, he put Gerald in charge of the just developing statistical department (building on Whittington and Strangeman), where the day-to-day work was being done by Godfrey Chandler, Frederick Cole and Harry Willmott, initially on behalf of Ashton. Now and over the next few years they pioneered several things: a fortnightly letter of investment suggestions, including a penetrating foreword by Chandler on the economic situation, the gilt-edged market or whatever; a document for internal purposes (especially for Hornby) called 'Measures of Confidence', offering a comparison of the past activity of companies, showing how the market had reacted over the years in cycles, and suggesting new areas to expand into; a trend-setting and increasingly weighty annual book for institutions and clients known as 'Investment Memoranda', with detailed information about such matters as rates of commission and methods of calculating sinking funds, as well as a section on taxation; research into convertible stocks, culminating in an annual book on the subject; graphs covering the movements of different types of stocks; and a day-to-day graph system for gilt-edged. All this was work actively encouraged by Charles Micklem, who was aware that the world was changing while being in no way willing to forfeit the sovereignty of judgement.

For a time the gilt-edged market flourished after the war, artificially stimulated by Chancellor Dalton's cheap money policy; and in Palmer-Tomkinson senior, Shaw-Kennedy and Cedric Barnett the firm had three active gilt partners. Palmer-Tomkinson indeed went out in style, with his purchase soon after the war of £150 million Exchequer Stock on behalf of the Railway Freight Rebates Board, remaining a record of size for many years despite inflation. Internationally, with the loss of many hundreds of millions worth of foreign securities (including the Argentine rail stocks, a particularly heavy blow to Cazenove's), together with the restraints of exchange control and the emerging dollar premium, there was little encouragement to do much in the way of foreign business. One notable episode, however, occurred in about 1948 when, through the offices of the Anglo-Palestine Bank, and to the annoyance of many Jewish brokers, the government of the newly-established state of Israel retained Cazenove's to sell all Israel's holdings of London-listed securities which had been commandeered from its citizens in order to raise foreign currency for the new state. These amounted to some £7 million; and checking good delivery proved a lengthy and unpleasant job, so much so that two members of staff had to visit the Hospital for Tropical Diseases as a result of contracting illness from bonds formerly sewn in Palestinian Arabs' clothing.

The post-war new issue market maintained the strong domestic orientation it had shown during the 1930s, though one significant difference was that a Memorandum of Guidance drawn up by the Stock Exchange Council in 1946 had the effect, through insisting on a more orderly market, of removing most of the criticised elements of the placing method. External control, introduced during the war, remained fairly stringent: the Capital Issues Committee scrutinised issues over £50,000 to ensure that they were for 'approved purposes', in other words would benefit the economy as a whole, while timing for issues over £100,000 rested in the hands of the Bank of England. Despite everything, the capital market was reasonably active during these early post-war years, with cheap money producing many debenture conversions and a lot of small companies coming to the market. Moreover, Cazenove's continued to lead the way. Taking the year 1946, it was associated with sixty issues, more than twice as many as any other broker. And of these sixty, the firm sponsored twenty-seven and co-sponsored three, which again in terms of quantity put it ahead of all non-stockbroking issuing houses. Next came the Whitehead Industrial Trust with twenty-four issues, as ever from that house a distinctly mixed bunch. The merchant banks (or at least some of them) would soon be beginning their all-out assault on the domestic new issue market, but not quite yet.

Various notable or interesting issues from the first two years of peace and a Labour government deserve mention. In December 1945 a preference issue for the steel concern John Summers, done jointly with Rowe & Pitman on behalf of Morgan Grenfell and Helbert Wagg, was the first post-war issue on a public prospectus. In July 1946 Cazenove's was one of the brokers for Western Ground Rents, a Cardiff property company that had bought the Bute family's reversionary properties for virtually nothing and, now brought to the market by Barings, was to prosper exceedingly. In December that year the issue of 100,000 ordinary shares in Metal Agencies was a good example of a company being brought to Cazenove's by a provincial broker, in this case B. S. Stock of Bristol. Meanwhile in 1946–7 Ultramar, under the forward-looking chairmanship of Sir Edwin Herbert, continued to look for more capital, and there were several money-raising exercises, not always easy. 'My idea would be that the syndicate should go for a net profit of about 1 per cent so that we should try and peddle the stock at about 97, free of stamp,' Micklem noted in a memo at one stage, and it was a revealing choice of verb concerning a company whose future was still in the balance. Equally problematic was the £15 million offer for sale of Steel Company of Wales debenture stock in July 1947 by a consortium of seven merchant banks. This was a newly-created amalgamation designed, in the words of the prospectus, 'to enable an old established British industry [essentially tinplate and sheet] again to make an important contribution to the country's export trade'. Cazenove's was one of the four brokers employed, and Micklem was placed in charge of arranging £9 million of the sub-underwriting, which he successfully did, even though the banks declined to follow his advice that the sub-underwriting letters be despatched a week before the signing of the contract instead of (as normal) immediately after the signing. With the convertibility crisis looming and the threat of eventual nationalisation a distinct possibility, Micklem was no doubt somewhat apprehensive, and indeed the sub-underwriters in the event had to take up a 'stick' amounting to almost three-quarters of their participations.

The year 1947 was generally difficult, some issues pulling through without causing pain to the underwriters, others faring much less well. A happy episode was the successful launch in April 1947 of Cawood Wharton, Leeds-based manufacturers, contractors and importers of solid fuels and other products. The man behind the company's rise was Eric Towler, who in the early 1930s had bought it (as a struggling coal-merchant business) for £2,000, mortgaging his house and selling his Austin 12 motor car in order to borrow the money to do so. Now he needed additional capital and had been given an introduction to Micklem by the leading steel industrialist Ellis Hunter. He was obliged by February, despite the appalling winter, to supply a profit forecast, which turned out to be almost exactly right. Accompanying Towler on that decisive visit to Tokenhouse Yard was his deputy and eventual successor, Edward Binks, who many years later recalled how, walking up the impressive main staircase, he felt he had really 'arrived'. Everything was settled in a day, with Cazenove's agreeing to underwrite a direct issue by the company of preference shares and to buy from Towler a substantial amount of ordinary shares and to place them with institutional clients. In the aftermath of the issue, Binks wondered whether the company should pay to have its shares quoted in the press, as its financial advertising agents Dorlands had suggested, but that old hand Albert Martin assured him that 'as and when the shares become an active market they will get all the free publicity that is necessary, and the papers will, in their own interests, quote them'. The company flourished thereafter, maintaining a close link with Cazenove's and in particular Peter Kemp-Welch; and when it was eventually taken over by Redland in 1982 it was valued at £137.5 million.

Altogether less propitious, and like the Steel Company of Wales caught up in the larger financial situation, was the offer for sale three months later of 200,000 shares of Bertram Mills Circus, with Cazenove's as brokers and Barings and Glyn Mills (in a rare foray) closely involved. The circus itself was a sell-out, the company had a tenancy agreement for the Grand Hall at Olympia for the next two winter seasons, and there was a marvellous list of assets; but even by July 3rd, almost three weeks before the issue, a certain nervousness was manifest, as Derek Schreiber recorded: 'Sir Edward Reid telephoned to say that Glyn Mills only wished to do £20,000 underwriting and he therefore proposed that Barings and ourselves should do £80,000 each, the balance of £20,000 being taken firm.' With market conditions starting to deteriorate (and with convertibility of sterling, with all its possible dire consequences, due on the 15th) the question of pricing became acute. The Mills brothers attended a meeting at Barings on the 7th, at which Cazenove's said that it 'considered 45s should still be all right if there was no major change in the market, and Sir Edward Reid agreed that the price should be between 42s 6d and 45s, to be decided as late as possible before the underwriting goes out.' The issue took place on the 22nd at 42s; the sub-underwriters were left with almost half; and the price of the shares soon plunged to 5s, making an effective after-market operation almost imposs-ible, in other words in terms of getting the shares off the hands of the sub-underwriters. It was the first and last circus venture with which Cazenove's was involved. As Hubert A. Meredith (a well-known merchant banker who had formerly been a jobber and then a financial editor) is said to have asked mordantly at the time: 'What security is a sea-lion?'

It was also in the summer of 1947 that Cazenove's found itself in a head-on clash with the Stock Exchange Council. The dispute, one of considerable bitterness, concerned the issue in late June of 400,000 5½% redeemable cumulative preference shares and 400,000 ordinary shares at 22s 6d per share of the Stanhope Steamship Company. This was the creation of Jack Billmeir, who had developed from an office boy in a shipbroker's office to what *The Times* in his obituary would call 'one of the most colourful personalities in British shipping'. He had made his fortune during the Spanish Civil War when his ships had been used for gun-running purposes, despite the efforts of Hitler and Mussolini to stop him trading. He now had a fleet of about a dozen cargo ships, and the business was brought to Cazenove's by Martins Bank. What then happened was that the Shipping market (which included the chairman of the Council, Urling Clark, and a prominent member of it, Charles Whittington) made a dead set against the company, refusing either to sub-underwrite or to sign the application for permission to deal. It is possible that these jobbers, comprising four firms in all, had genuine doubts about the company's viability and the terms of the issue, but it is more likely that Hornby was not far from the mark when he subsequently wrote that 'apparently some friends of Urling Clark at the Baltic had given him a bad report of Billmeir whom they regarded as an upstart' and that 'Whittington listened to Urling'. Cazenove's still managed to complete the sub-underwriting, but it then became public knowledge that the Committee on Quotations had refused quotation, an extremely rare event that prompted a perplexed full-length editorial in the *FT*; in immediate response the firm generously offered to release the sub-underwriters from their obligations, though very few did withdraw. The shares however were certain to remain unmarketable unless there was an official change of mind, quite apart from the damage caused to the reputations of the company and its financial advisers. In a grim mood, Micklem submitted a lengthy formal written appeal, while Palmer-Tomkinson and Hornby prepared to appear before a full meeting of the Council on July 8th.

At that meeting Micklem's letter was read out. He described the decision as 'a cause of great surprise and regret – regret that it could have been thought that shares which we have sponsored should be classed as in a category which cannot be admitted to the floor of the House without danger to the Public.' Micklem then defended the company and attacked the apparent view of the Shipping market that there was no proper basis for a preference issue:

> It is reasonable to ask: does the Committee accept the responsibility of deciding that the capital structure of a company is correct or incorrect? If so, are the Jobbers in any market peculiarly equipped to lay down the law on so general a question of policy? By underwriting the issue and by applying heavily for these preference shares, experienced investors showed their readiness to accept £400,000 preference shares as a first charge on the profits earned by £3,000,000 of shipping; that the City and investing Public appear to endorse our view that a preference share in this Company can properly be issued is proved by the fact that 104 out of 107 experienced underwriters accepted our offer. In all the discussions arising from the circumstances of this issue not one criticism has reached us except from the market.

In person, the jobbers from the Shipping market strongly criticised the capital set-up and also the management agreements, with Urling Clark arguing that 'very large profits had to be made before anything was available for the shareholders'. Palmer-Tomkinson, back in the Council Room after his resignation in March, was unrepentant:

> Had faulty Capital set-up ever been considered by the Council in application for Quotation? He argued that it was a matter of opinion. His partner – Micklem – was a good judge. Preference shares were a popular type of investment and 55% went in spite of the Committee's refusal. It was a 5½% Preference, because it was a fluctuating business. As to the price of the Ordinary that was a matter of opinion. He still thought the shares worth the price and on the Wednesday morning [i.e. before the Committee's decision] he left an order with his firm to apply for or buy 10,000 shares. He was prepared to back the Company because Billmeir was going on. If there had not been full enough disclosure in the

Prospectus he blamed the Share and Loan Department and the lawyers. There had been no intention to disguise anything. Mr Billmeir had offered to scratch the whole thing, but Messrs Cazenove preferred to stand by their contract. Mr Palmer-Tomkinson said he regarded refusal of Quotation as an appalling thing for the Company and for his firm.

John Braithwaite, deputising in the chair for Urling Clark, then 'reminded' Palmer-Tomkinson 'of the Council's policy in the granting of Quotations: they did not normally concern themselves with the merits of an issue – with the question of price, capital structure and so forth – but they did require that there should be full and clear disclosure of all material facts.' And Braithwaite proceeded to detail various ways in which disclosure had been inadequate, even though 'in the course of discussion on these points Mr Hornby said there had never been any question of withholding facts' and that he had 'on request from the Share and Loan Department got an undertaking from Mr Billmeir not to sell any shares when the market opened'. By twenty-four votes to one the appeal was disallowed.

The aftermath may be briefly recorded. Billmeir thought of bringing a case for libel and defamation against the Council, but was dissuaded. Eventually, the following January, a compromise was reached largely through the mediation of Braithwaite. Additional disclosures were made in the prospectus, together with some alteration in the management contract, and quotation was granted. It had been a bruising, probably unnecessary episode and Palmer-Tomkinson not only never forgave Whittington but indeed never spoke to him again, even though they had previously been great friends. The shares themselves slumped badly in the wake of the appeal's failure and Cazenove partners bought many; but they eventually recovered and Hornby for one sold his at a handsome profit.

Meanwhile, out and about in the industrial field was Kemp-Welch, in a way that probably no Cazenove partner had been before. In March 1948 he arranged for Hambros a placing in the shares of the newly public company of Le Grand, Sutcliffe & Gell, well drillers, pump makers and founders, and now doing much work in connection with Shell. The placing roughly trebled the money in the business. Soon afterwards he received a warm letter of thanks from one of the company's directors, H. M. Gell, who noted that the market situation had been 'rather difficult' and as a token of appreciation enclosed two tickets for Wimbledon, one of those occasional perquisites of a stockbroker's life. With typical energy Kemp-Welch wrote in June to his friend George Chiene of the Edinburgh investment managers Baillie Gifford, supplying details of the company and adding: 'I believe there is good scope for a company of this kind, and it will be interesting to follow their fortunes. I am going down to Rochester on Thursday and will let you know any news about the latest developments.' He duly visited the works there and soon received another warm letter from Gell: 'I feel that not only my colleagues on the Board, but the senior executives you met much appreciated your coming down. They know very well that an industry does consist of a partnership of Finance, Management, and Operatives.' In the brave new world of 1948 the relations between that triad were becoming closer and more interlocking.

One constant was the continuing heavy reliance on Micklem for new issue advice, especially in relation to fixed interest stocks. Thus in February 1948, when Nyasaland Railways were looking to make an issue at some point in the future and asked Cazenove's for its view on rate of interest and dates, an apologetic Frank Holt wrote to him at his Surrey home:

> The problem is this: at what rate, price and dates would we consider it feasible:
> (1) to do a straight Debenture, guaranteed by nobody, or
> (2) a Debenture guaranteed by Nyasaland Government but such guarantee not to constitute a Trustee security.
> I had a talk with Antony and we were thinking along the lines of $3\frac{1}{2}$% at $98\frac{1}{2}$ in the first case, and possibly $3\frac{1}{4}$% at 98 in the second.
>
> Perhaps you would give Antony or me a ring tomorrow when you have looked at it.

Micklem obliged and that same day Holt was able to put forward a suggested plan to the company, adding: 'You will, of course, understand that this is our opinion of what could be done today or in the next few days. The times are so uncertain and, if you are thinking of doing this operation, I would suggest that you waste no time.' The company seems to have heeded this advice, but unfortunately the issue was then delayed when one of the bridges on the line was washed away, causing revised figures on traffics and consequently profits. It finally took place in May, with Cazenove's sponsoring the issue of an unguaranteed £1.6 million $3\frac{1}{2}$% debenture stock at $98\frac{1}{2}$.

But in spite of this steady new issue activity, a continuous undertow of anxiety persisted during these immediate post-war years. One important cause of concern was, however, alleviated in 1946 when the firm took advantage of a change in Stock Exchange rules and on a temporary basis, which lasted for ten years, became a company with unlimited liability. Several other leading firms also did the same thing, especially jobbers, who tended to have more fluctuating profits than brokers. The thinking behind the move was that, in the context of punitive surtax rates (rising to 19s 6d in the pound), a company (unlike a firm) would be able to put money to reserve without paying surtax so long as it distributed a reasonable amount of the profits to partners (now officially called directors). It was an important and timely precaution, executed by Palmer-Tomkinson in conjunction with James Wannan of Spicer & Pegler. But net profits were still less than sparkling, settling in a range between £235,000 and £335,000 – though these are figures put in some modern-day perspective by the fact that it then cost less than £300 a year to send a boy to Eton. In 1947 both the gilts and equity markets lost all the ground that they had gained the previous year, and that August a letter from Micklem to Palmer-Tomkinson reflected something of the prevailing mood:

> You have probably seen what's been going on in the Stock Exchange in the papers, and a completely new level for gilt-edged and similar sort of securities has been reached. Whereas we were talking a few months ago of issuing £1,000,000 Surburban & Provincial Stores $3\frac{1}{4}$% Debenture Stock at par, we have now agreed with the Company to issue it in the form of a $3\frac{1}{2}$% Debenture at 98. We have underwritten it almost entirely with insurance companies. Whether it goes or not depends very much on what happens to Consol $2\frac{1}{2}$%'s over the next two or three weeks. Otherwise, we have nothing on at the moment, and our underwriting clients are a little bit congested and not anxious to take on further commitments unless the price is really attractive. The discounts on several of the new issues made a month or so ago are pretty heavy – anything from five to twenty per cent.

The next year, 1948, was almost as bad, until a belated equity recovery in the autumn. And all the time, Labour's nationalisation programme inexorably took effect, removing whole markets at a stroke: the vesting date for civil aviation was August 1946; then came the coal industry and cables and wireless in January 1947; transport and electricity in 1948; gas was due in 1949; and iron and steel likely some time thereafter. With the Conservative Party in opposition becoming incipiently 'Butskellite' (epi-tomised by its 'Industrial Charter' of 1947), there was little or no prospect of extensive denationalisation in the foreseeable future. Nor was it at all certain that the Conservatives would soon return to power anyway. In short, winds of change of an unprecedented harshness were blowing through the City.

It was against this unsettling backcloth that there took place in 1948 an episode of cardinal importance in the post-war history of Cazenove's. While on holiday in Scotland, Kemp-Welch took the opportunity to ponder on the situation and prospects of the firm he had joined almost three years previously. The result was a memorandum, together with a lengthy covering letter, that he sent to Hornby at the end of August. At the heart of both documents was a view that the partnership as a whole had become complacent during the long ascendancy of the 'triumvirate' and that if the firm was to prosper without those three it would require a much greater and more purposeful effort from the generation now rising to the top. In his memorandum, drafted in the plural so that it might represent the views of Hornby and Bedford as well as himself, Kemp-Welch stressed that the points were made in a constructive rather than critical spirit, but for all the mildness of the language their forcible drift was clear:

Competition, as we all know, is severe and in all probability is likely to increase: this may be more noticeable in the case of big firms (with more to lose) than among small ones. In the past, there have been notable examples of large firms standing still or going back, such as Panmure Gordon, James Capel, &c, through want of new blood, lack of drive, resting on their laurels, failure to maintain good service, or a host of other reasons.

Nothing has gone radically wrong yet, but there are slight indications of weakness in certain parts of our structure.

We all have probably heard whispers of outside criticism, of which a few might be:

(i) We are too much of an issuing house and are apt not to look after our stockbroking side enough. We are, perhaps, inclined, due to the volume of our new issues (particularly in the last couple of years) to give birth to a new security, and after the initial dealings of the first few weeks to lose sight of the progress of the Company, and not keep our clients informed about it.

(ii) We do not always maintain quite a regular and more or less personal contact with certain houses – eg Balfour Beatty, B.T.A., Law Debenture, Helbert Wagg.

(iii) We don't produce many 'ideas' or up to date offers, other than our own issues. Firms who have been and are extremely successful in this direction are de Zoetes, Chase Henderson, Laing & Cruick-shank, Messel &c. Pember & Boyle's service in the gilt-edged market is an outstanding example.

The memorandum candidly went on: 'We have always rather prided ourselves on being enthusiastic amateurs, and as long as CPS, CM and JET were there, this worked all right: in other words if any individual didn't do anything about some particular situation, someone else would, and whatever was required by a client was somehow achieved. This modus operandi is not going to be nearly so easy without the sheet-anchors.' In

The changing City

The Stock Exchange, c. 1844

Wyld's plan of the City of London, 1840 (by permission of Guildhall Library, Corporation of London)

Tokenhouse Yard, 1880
(by permission of Guildhall Library, Corporation of London)

Threadneedle Street,
c. 1890
(by permission of Guildhall Library,
Corporation of London)

Capel Court entrance, 1891
(by permission of Guildhall Library,
Corporation of London)

(Above) Royal Exchange, 1895 (by permission of Guildhall Library, Corporation of London)

(Below) *The Heart of the Empire* by Niels M. Lund, 1904 (by permission of Guildhall Art Gallery, Corporation of London)

The Stock Exchange, 1902
(by permission of Guildhall Library, Corporation of London)

Throgmorton Street, 1905
(by permission of Guildhall Library, Corporation of London)

The City at Dusk by Frank Armington, 1910
(by permission of Morgan Grenfell)

Capel Court entrance, c. 1930
(by permission of Guildhall Library, Corporation of London)

The flattened City: view from St Paul's Cathedral, c. 1945
(by permission of Guildhall Library, Corporation of London)

(Top left) Bank of England, 12th January 1941, the
morning after a bomb fell on Bank
underground station killing over a hundred people
(by permission of Guildhall Library, Corporation of
London)

(Bottom left) Mansion House a few weeks later
(by permission of Guildhall Library, Corporation of
London)

V.E. Day crowd at Mansion House
(by permission of Guildhall Library, Corporation of London)

Victory Thanksgiving Service in the Stock Exchange, 14th May 1945

The Stock Exchange, 1957
(by permission of Guildhall Library, Corporation of London)

Throgmorton Street, 1958
(by permission of Guildhall Library, Corporation of London)

The Stock Exchange from
Old Broad Street, 1989
(by permission of the International
Stock Exchange Photo Library)

The City skyline from
Waterloo Bridge, 1989
(by permission of the International
Stock Exchange Photo Library)

sum: 'One doesn't want to take business too seriously but there is bound to be a grave risk of losing efficiency by not taking it seriously enough: the trouble is that if we don't take it seriously enough someone else will!'

It was a convincing, remarkably objective analysis, the product of a person with a keen awareness of the fluctuations of City history; but granted that Micklem was moving towards semi-retirement there was only one partner in the firm who could effect what in essence amounted to a new cast of collective mind. As Kemp-Welch wrote in his accompanying letter: 'With regard to talking to the others and putting our ideas to them, you are the obvious person, for a good many reasons, to do this, and I am quite sure you will have everyone's confidence and support.' It was a measure of Hornby's receptiveness and lack of jealousy that he took Kemp-Welch's analysis fully on board and proceeded whole-heartedly to try to implement it. There survive the notes for a speech he subsequently gave (after consulting Micklem) to a meeting of partners, probably the six below Micklem but possibly the full partnership. In it he developed in a characteristic way the thrust of the memorandum and added a historical perspective born of personal experience:

> The main point that we're all agreed upon is that we must maintain the reputation and position of Cazenove's. It is too much to hope that we should improve upon it. We are fully conscious of our shortcomings, compared with Claud and Charles and Jimmy, but we hope to live up to their standards in time. We were lucky enough for the twenty years between the wars to have three senior partners who were quite out of the ordinary run and I won't say any more about that as one of them – and a very modest one – is, thank goodness, still our senior partner.
>
> Anyway we have now got Cazenove's as it is and it is something to be very proud of. I'm afraid there is little money incentive in business today – one is only allowed to get away with so much and no more. But obviously we in this firm would never be content to let our retainable income influence our efforts. Our incentive for the present at any rate must be our pride in keeping Cazenove's at the top.
>
> We must not assume that Cazenove's are bound to go on getting the new issues and a lot of automatic business with it and that all we have to do is to attend at the office and see what turns up. Competition is severe and I think we've got to put our heads together to see that we harness our man-power to the best possible advantage and give our clients real service.

Hornby then reiterated Kemp-Welch's point about attitude ('One doesn't want to make a burden of business but I do think there's a risk of not taking it seriously enough'), before encapsulating the case for reform in a homely nutshell: 'If you don't manure the garden the flowers won't grow next year.'

Hornby, helped by Bedford, *did* carry the partnership with him, above all those of his own generation and slightly younger; and over the next few years Kemp-Welch's memorandum palpably had a beneficial effect, in various small specific ways as well as in a larger sense concerning the whole approach to business. Many years later, an experienced investment trust manager remarked to Hornby on how his firm's relationships with Cazenove's were good all the way down their respective lists. To which Hornby replied of his own firm: 'We are a splendid bundle of professional amateurs.' It was a rare, perhaps unique blend of the two qualities, and the deliberations of 1948 had done much to achieve it. 'Amateurism' was clearly no longer enough; but nor, equally, was 'professionalism' alone the solution for the future. Above all, Hornby never lost his particular streak of arrogance, that key additional dimension (in his case handed down from Serocold) now harnessed to the new seriousness. It was perhaps the ultimate virtue of Kemp-Welch's prescription for change that it did not attempt to smooth away that supremely unegalitarian quality, without which Cazenove's would have been reduced to one of the pack, however able and however professional.

Hornby by the end of the 1940s really ran the firm, though he would always sound out Micklem before making key decisions. Micklem himself was becoming, certainly by the early 1950s, an increasingly frail, rather remote figure. On the whole these were years of continuing depression on the stock market, and 1949 saw sterling being devalued from $4.03 to $2.80 and the 30–Share Index dipping briefly below 100. It is true that the Stock Exchange Council in April that year did allow the resumption of contangoes (i.e. carrying over a bargain from one account to another), but such was the prevailing hostility towards speculation that it did so only in a very limited way. Moreover, though the City naturally rejoiced as the Tories returned to power in 1951, such were the consequences of the ending of the Korean War – with many British companies badly overstocked as international commodity markets collapsed – that the change of government heralded a distinctly nasty bear market. During the summer of 1952 it bottomed out, while 1953 was a year of quiet consolidation even though markets remained rather sluggish. 'Here we are not very busy and Philip [Cazenove] tells me that you are more or less in the same condition,' wrote Alister Mackinnon of the Aberdeen stockbrokers Horne & Mackinnon to Hornby in February 1953. The sharp climb upwards awaited 1954, when by that summer the 30–Share

Index reached 150. The City in general, moreover, was starting to come back to life by this time, with most of its traditional markets having reopened during the previous three years. During this period as a whole, Cazenove's profits were steady at about £300,000, before leaping to over £700,000 in 1954. It was the first of the great post-war bull markets.

For Cazenove's, however, the true significance of these six years 1948 to 1954 lay less in particular market fluctuations than in the application of the Kemp-Welch memorandum and, perhaps equally importantly, a crucial redefining of the firm's whole approach towards new issue business. The context was a fundamental shift in the issuing process, a shift surprisingly little discussed in the historical literature. For a variety of reasons – including expansion, amalgamations, reorganisation schemes and the increasing pressure of death duties – not only were the capital requirements of individual British companies becoming ever greater, but also their financial problems were becoming ever more complex. Predictably, companies began to look in increasing numbers to the help and expertise of the traditional issuing houses, namely the merchant banks. The banks themselves (and it is impossible to know how much in this trend was 'demand' and how much 'supply') responded for the most part with alacrity: aware that a return to the pre-1931, let alone pre-1914, world of plentiful foreign loans was more remote than ever, they stepped into the domestic issuing house business in a way that they had not attempted during the shell-shocked 1930s. Not all moved with equal alacrity, but most made that basic reorientation. Their advantages were considerable: many of the houses were great names, trusted and respected in all quarters, outside as well as inside the City; they had the resources, at least for the time being, to act as underwriters in their own right, though of course only after making careful enquiries; and they had within their ranks some notable, business-getting entrepreneurs, including Lionel Fraser of Helbert Wagg, Kenneth Keith of Philip Hill, and Siegmund Warburg (whose S. G. Warburg & Co was founded in 1946). It had taken the merchant banks a long time to make the adjustment, but once they made it the domestic new issue market was transformed.

Could the stockbrokers, the dominant domestic issuers of the 1930s and immediately after the war, have effectively resisted this challenge? That they did not – certainly in relation to the larger companies – is clear. The answer is that they perhaps could have in theory, but that in practice there were too many negatives against them. Following the 1948 Companies Act, which was probably the watershed of the whole process, they lacked the resources to cope with the vastly enlarged, infinitely more demanding prospectuses, and the massive accompanying documentation, that the new legislation required. There was also the matter of employing teams of lawyers, accountants and so on. Moreover, as issues became larger as well as more complex, most stockbroking firms lacked the capacity to make the necessary authoritative, in-depth assessments of companies, a lack (and perhaps sometimes unwillingness) acknowledged by Cazenove's even before the war in relation to the Blackburn Aircraft issue. It would be fair to say that this inadequacy of resources was human as much as financial and at least in part derived from the rather discouraging aura surrounding the Stock Exchange during these early post-war years. It was an institution very much on the defensive, a fact acknowledged by the Council's unprecedented publicity efforts, culminating in its decision to open a public gallery in 1953. With markets in a generally poor way, the political climate unhelpful and the tax situation disagreeable, there was little incentive for young people of talent and ambition coming into the City to go to the Stock Exchange. Instead, the first choice for most was Lloyd's insurance, with the merchant banks as second choice and stockbroking firms a distinctly poor third. While this should not be exaggerated, there does seem to be a consensus that it was the case. And faced by all these considerations, most company brokers from the late 1940s allowed the merchant banks to resume their historic role as issuing houses (though now domestic) in the face of little serious competition.

What of Cazenove's? The firm during these years mirrored (and indeed perhaps influenced) the larger trend, abandoning its issuing house ambitions except in relation to relatively small companies. It is impossible to know for certain why it did so, but the general considerations already mentioned must have played an important part. By the late 1940s, many companies were coming to stockbrokers *via* merchant banks; while from a capacity point of view, it was possible for a small team at Cazenove's, acting as a secondary financial adviser, to take on a lot more companies than it could have hoped to do so as a quasi-issuing house. It is also perhaps relevant that issuing fees then were not particularly handsome. Nevertheless, it is hard not also to attribute something to the emergence of Hornby: a supreme operator, he was not a master *creative* financier like Micklem, who would have passed muster among the greatest merchant bankers. Instead, he evolved an alternative, essentially two-pronged strategy. On the one hand, he aimed to cultivate, especially through Philip Cazenove's excellent connections with country brokers, the widest possible links with the better medium-sized companies, thereby rebuilding the firm's list of company clients that had been ravaged by nationalisation, sometimes sponsoring their issues but usually bringing them to the merchant banks. And on the other hand, in relation to those banks, he sought to maintain a similarly broad-based, often long-established connection and for the most part acted in a back-up role, above all in relation to pricing and underwriting; or put another way, tucking in behind their slipstream in a vital, but ultimately subordinate, role. Taken together, the two prongs complemented each other well and proved the basis for the firm's continuing success in the post-war period.

The comparison with Kit Hoare and his firm is instructive. Hardworking, tough and commercial, he had acquired as clients between the wars a clutch of giant blue-chip companies, including ICI, Vickers, Distillers and P & O; to these he added BP soon after the war. The issues for these companies tended to be of a high monetary value, though quantitatively of course Hoare & Co was well behind Cazenove's. Nationalisation when it came affected Hoare's much less severely than Cazenove's, whose response was to rebuild its list of good medium-sized company clients and to act on behalf of merchant banks. By contrast, and unlike most company brokers, Kit Hoare during the 1950s felt strong enough to stand up to the merchant banks and, as much as he could, do issues without them. This did not make him the most popular person in the great parlours of the City, but it did mean that he sometimes fulfilled a new issue function on behalf of an industrial customer more cheaply than if a merchant bank had been involved. Again the personal element was important: whereas Antony Hornby was a cultured, ultimately establishment person, Kit Hoare was a much rougher character and was not afraid of occasional blazing rows with some (but by no means all) of the famous City dynasties. He believed that he could buck the trend that was becoming apparent from the late 1940s, Hornby did not. These respective convictions perhaps determined the long-run history of the two firms.

All this assumed that Cazenove's would continue in the Hornby era to be a company-orientated firm rather than reverting to more orthodox stockbroking concentrating on the secondary market. There does seem to have been some conscious but undocumented debate on this in the late 1940s, probably in the dominating context of nationalisation. It is unlikely, though, that Hornby had many doubts in his own mind about the continuing direction of the firm: he saw himself as the inheritor of the mantle from the Serocold and Micklem era; he himself was starting to make excellent connections with the leading merchant banks; in Kemp-Welch he had a potential power-house in new issue business; and with record peacetime levels of personal taxation, it was hardly a propitious time to pin everything on private clients, who in general investment terms were still at least as important as the institutions. Accordingly, the company orientation remained. One important consequence was that, despite the impressive progress being made in the statistical department, the firm in the 1950s would not become a research-driven organisation like (most notably) Phillips & Drew; for it was quickly appreciated, and articulated at the time by Kemp-Welch among others, that writing about individual British companies was bound to come into embarrassing conflict with the firm's paramount new issue priorities. Research would take place but it would be given a low profile and remain essentially a private affair.

Much now hinged on the firm's relations with the merchant banks, where it had been clear since 1945 that this was principally to be Hornby's domain, as he later recalled:

> With some trepidation I began to go round to Barings and Morgans and Schroders, Helbert Wagg and Erlangers. Charles began to take me round with him too when there was an issue to be discussed. As luck would have it I was readily accepted in all these partners' parlours and the elder statesmen, Edward Peacock and Arthur Villiers at Barings, Vivian Bicester at Morgans, Albert Pam at Schroders, all took to me and I already knew other partners like Evelyn Baring, Francis Rodd [of Morgan Grenfell], Henry Tiarks, Lionel Fraser and so on. So this was the direction my life went and I spent twenty-five years in the close and intimate councils of these great houses.

Hornby owed a particular debt to Villiers, who 'helped me a lot when I first had to fix issue prices' and 'used to will me to say the right thing like a good schoolmaster'. His allegiance to Barings remained unswerving and in time Cazenove's became its sole issuing broker, no longer acting jointly with other firms. Second only to that with Barings was Hornby's relationship with Morgan Grenfell, which was perhaps the leading issuing house of the 1950s and where he (literally) had a key to the back door. His other main connections were with Schroders, Lazards, Erlangers (small but select) and Helbert Wagg, while through his friendship with Richard Fleming he was close to Robert Fleming, an important underwriting force because of its position in relation to investment trusts. He also developed during the 1950s a good working relationship with Warburgs, though Siegmund Warburg probably preferred Kit Hoare, like himself more of an 'outsider'. With Rothschilds somewhat moribund in these post-war years and Hambros traditionally employing Rowe & Pitman, those were the main houses with whom Hornby did business.

But there were also other houses in the City active in the new issue sphere towards which Cazenove's could not afford to stay aloof, even if they did have a rather rougher edge. Here the key figure was Frank Holt, very effective once he had made up his mind about something and still remembered for his advice about the pricing of issues: 'When you talk to the client and the selling partners keep the former thinking low, and the latter high, until the last minute. Then when you "settle" both will be pleased.' During this period he developed close relations with the leading people in Singer & Friedlander and above all Philip Hill, then under the dynamic, sometimes bruising Kenneth Keith. A kind, generous person, somewhat avuncular, and an accomplished deal-maker, Holt was regarded by these 'new men' as an establishment figure well worth having on their side, becoming indeed almost their unofficial City conscience. It was a crucial role on his part and once again showed how a partnership at its best contains individuals of widely differing attributes and inclinations.

One has only to look at the figures to see that Cazenove's during these years became even more prodigiously busy as company brokers. In the difficult year of 1949 the firm was associated with 65 issues. Next among brokers came Hoare & Co on 37, Rowe, Swann & Co on 31, and Rowe & Pitman on 28. Over the next three years the Cazenove total was remarkably steady at 85, 82 and 82. In 1953 it rose to 121. And in the boom year of 1954, the firm's tally of 165 put it numerically way ahead of all rivals, namely Hoare & Co (67), de Zoete & Gorton (59, including a lot of tea companies), Rowe & Pitman (58), Laing & Cruickshank (51), Rowe, Swann & Co (42), Joseph Sebag & Co (39) and W. Greenwell & Co (38). Most of these issues (the term as usual including placings, rights issues and conversions) were relatively small, being below £1 million and often below £$\frac{1}{2}$ million. And looking down the list, it is impossible not to be struck by the sheer range of companies, usually of the best quality, on whose behalf Cazenove's acted at this time, frequently in tandem with a merchant bank. To take only the first half of 1951, companies included Enfield Cables, East Anglian Breweries, Bollington Textile Printers, Wadkin (manufacturers of woodworking machinery), Mills and Rockleys (advertising contractors), James Rothwell (textile spinners), Lobnitz (dredgers and harbour craft), Monsanto Chemicals, Fuller's (caterers and confectioners), De Havilland Aircraft, Albert E. Reed (paper manufacturers) and Platt Brothers (textile machinery): the list is almost endless. Many of the companies in this period came to Cazenove's through the introduction of provincial brokers and most were coming to the London market for the first time, reliant on the best possible advice and assistance.

The first significant issue (in fact a private placing) in this period was in September 1948 and, as Hornby recalled, brought into play one of the City's more vivid figures:

Kit Dawnay, who was then at Dawnay Day [a good-quality issuing house], sent for me to talk about a proposition to build a plant to make

Philblack, a carbon-black strengthener for tyres. He had a good story and already some backers. I asked Charles whether I should take it on. He said I should provided we could get an interest in its success as well as a commission. Kit agreed to this and we were given an option to purchase Ordinary shares for seven years or so. I then worked like mad and had my first success with Harley Drayton of the Securities Agency, who liked the project and took 75,000 shares. With such a start I became even more enthusiastic and rapidly completed the syndicate. It was the foundation of a long and close friendship with Harley who was a remarkable, imaginative, helpful and likeable man. Philblack in time came into its own and was a great success.

A self-made financier, Drayton had first become friendly with the firm through the person of Frank Holt. He possessed considerable qualities, of which perhaps the chief was his willingness to be guided by hunch, most notably and lucratively in connection with the coming of commercial television in the 1950s; and over the years he proved a great help to Cazenove's, especially through his propensity to 'take a punt' on a company even if its share price was temporarily in the doldrums.

Stockbrokers always give particular weight to personal recommendation; and in June 1949, in the context of a placing for the worsted spinners John Smith, there appeared a name from the long-distant past, though still a client. 'We have made careful enquiries about this Company, particularly from John Fosters, and have got very satisfactory replies,' Kemp-Welch wrote to a potential placee, A. L. Brown of the Alliance Trust in Dundee. Soon afterwards the firm acted with Rowe & Pitman on behalf of Helbert Wagg in a major issue (almost £3 million nominal) for the engineering company Babcock and Wilcox. The two brokers arranged most of the sub-underwriting and, in difficult market conditions, it proved a tough process. That autumn included a typical post-war episode, with the placing of shares of Harvey & Sons, tanners and curriers. The introduction came from not the brokers but the Manchester accountants Dearden, Gilliat & Co, who wrote to Holt in July: 'This is one of the best businesses of its type in Lancashire, and has been in the Harvey family for many generations . . . Due to the fear of the operation of death duties, the family would be prepared to dispose of the £200,000 of Preference Capital.' Altogether bigger scale was the Rootes Motors issue in November, when Lazards made an offer for sale of £2 million preference shares. The issue was occasioned by the decision of the Rootes brothers, Sir William and Sir Reginald, to go public, and Cazenove's acted jointly with Hoare's. Micklem took on the business despite misgivings about the company and also (it seems) Billy Rootes, telling Lazards that it must be a $5\frac{1}{2}$% preference. To which Lazards replied, in words that had no inkling of the inflationary years that lay ahead, 'We will never give our name to a $5\frac{1}{2}$% Preference.' Thus 5% it was, and indeed the issue was oversubscribed.

However, 1949 will always be remembered in the history of Cazenove's because of W. H. Smith. The definitive 'inside' account of a major City episode comes from Hornby:

History repeated itself and Billy Hambleden, the proprietor of W. H. Smith, died [in 1948] at the age of forty-five before he'd made over any of it to his family. Enormous Estate Duty was payable and this time it would really be necessary to sell part of the business. My brother Michael [of W. H. Smith] called me in and explained the position and asked if we would undertake the operation. He was in the process of agreeing a valuation of the business with the Estate Duty Office, and immediately agreement was reached he would want the issue done as in the precarious state of the market it would be dangerous to have an uncovered liability which might wipe out the Smith fortune. Charles was keen but left the whole thing to me. I went to see Barings who were the Trustees of Hambleden Estates Debenture. They were adamant in their refusal to do the issue, keeping to their age-old rule of not issuing equity shares. But in the same breath they promised every assistance in preparing the Prospectus and in underwriting. Lord Bicester came forward with an offer from Morgans to be the issuing house, but by this time we'd decided to go it alone with Barings' help.

At length the valuation was agreed at. There was much to do and it was August (in those days a holiday time for issues). We had to get Capital Issues Committee consent and this proved a formidable task. They were all on holiday and I had to pitchfork the secretary into taking action. Then the scheme itself was rather complicated. The privately held W. H. Smith 7% Preference were to be offered partly Preference in the new [holding] company and partly Ordinary. It was necessary to get 100 per cent acceptance of the scheme from Preference shareholders. Next there was the Prospectus and one night Howard Millis [of Barings], Christopher Clarke of Slaughter & May and I sat up all night in Christopher's house in Hammersmith keeping ourselves going with Brandy and Soda.

The feature of the issue was that it was three-tiered. There were 2.5 million $4\frac{1}{2}$% Preference, 1.65 million £1 'A' Ordinary shares and 1.65 million 4s 'B' Ordinary shares. The Ordinary shares of both denominations had one vote per share. This was to give the Smith family some chance of retaining control of the company. After the issue we bought back every 'B' share that came on offer and sold 'A' shares to pay for them.

The price of issue of the 'A' Ordinary was 40s and the 'B' Ordinary 8s. The underwriting went well and the issue was a great success and the family got their money. I was exhausted and proud. No business would ever frighten me now. It was a terrific baptism. It did the firm's reputation and mine a great deal of good and I got letters and congratulations from all sides. Moreover we made about £40,000, the largest sum we'd ever made on an issue.

W. H. Smith had always been part of my life. I had been brought up to regard it as second in importance to the Christian religion and so I was glad to be able to serve it. It almost might have been preordained by fate.

Little needs adding. There is no doubt that the market situation in August 1949 was a parlous one, with speculative pressure against sterling building up and the IMF due to meet in Washington in September. With devaluation potentially in the offing, the leading sub-underwriters intimated that they would not co-operate if the sub-underwriting was not begun before the last week of August. Hornby responded with the utmost decisiveness and met the deadline. The issue was indeed a great success, being oversubscribed five and a half times – a reflection not only of the company's immense prestige, but also of Hornby's skill at judging the terms and pricing. His commitment to the issue was intense, typified by the fact that over a long week-end he attended personally to the allotment of shares; and its success made his name in the City. It was also the last really big issue that Cazenove's would do off its own bat. There could have been no finer swansong to what had been a whole epoch in the firm's history.

Soon afterwards it was back to the Ultramar saga. By 1949 there was still no significant revenue coming in, it was becoming impossible to meet the interest on loans from the Finance Corporation of Industry, and directors appointed by two of the mining houses (Central Mining and Union Corporation) resigned. At this critical point Morgan Grenfell and Cazenove's between them grasped the nettle and reached an agreement by which FCI accepted postponement of interest due and advanced a further £$\frac{1}{4}$ million provided that £$\frac{3}{4}$ million convertible debenture stock was offered to holders, the very most that the company's financial advisers thought that they could get away with. The issue took place in January 1950, sponsored by Morgan Grenfell and with Cazenove's as brokers doing the sub-underwriting for no commission, against a dismal background: the market was still shaky, and Ultramar's record was not one to inspire confidence. Cazenove partners pulled out all the stops to persuade existing equity holders to trust to hope over experience, typified by an uncharacteristically apologetic letter from Hornby on the 18th to one of his private clients:

> I am afraid that my advice to you to buy Ultramar has proved to be rather unfortunate – at any rate for the time being. We rather hope that this injection of new money will cure the sick patient and the latest news that we have from the field is of satisfactory, although slow, progress. I think that you ought to hold on to your shares, but I expect you will feel disinclined to put any more money in the Company. The new Debenture Stock, however, does have attractions because for five years it has the right of converting into Ordinary Shares on the basis of getting 200 shares for every £100 of Debenture. One hopes that within five years this option may be valuable.

That and other missives proved to little avail, for the sub-underwriters were left with a daunting 93%. Soon afterwards Union Corporation and Central Mining decided to sell their original, very substantial equity stakes, but Cazenove's managed to place them. Those who showed faith were rewarded, for within weeks the news from Venezuela was good and the company's shares rose steeply. Though it would continue being something of a roller-coaster, Ultramar's future was assured – which would certainly not have been the case but for a strong measure of faith and vision in certain quarters of the City.

All the time Micklem remained an austere force to be reckoned with. Two small, very typical glimpses survive from 1950. In January he was approached by Sir Metford Watkins of the John Lewis Partnership (for whom Cazenove's had acted before) about financing the rebuilding of the bombed-out store in Oxford Street. Watkins mentioned that a co-director had recently introduced to his board a firm of brokers called Pidgeon & Stebbing, who had offered some financial advice; and he added that 'I should like them, if, as I imagine, they are a thoroughly reputable firm, to come in at some later stage in a way that would give them reasonable compensation for the work they have done.' To which Micklem replied: 'I have nothing whatever against Messrs. Pidgeon & Stebbing, but I feel quite sure that they would, if anything, be a drag on us rather than a help. I want you, if you don't mind, to leave them out of consideration in this matter entirely.' A £½ million debenture placing took place in July and was a complete success. That same month Cazenove's acted for Lazards in the offer for sale of the newly-public company of Manfield & Sons, well-established Northampton shoe manufacturers. Micklem during the preliminary stages received various papers from Percy Horsfall of Lazards and in reply noted that the chairman's end of year report had spoken rather discouragingly about the prospects for 1950 onwards: 'It would be interesting to know what his opinion is of these prospects now that five months of 1950 have gone.' And with that streak of caution that never deserted him, he went on to stress to Horsfall: 'I have no doubt whatever that you will impress upon him that he simply must be ultra-conservative in his estimate of future profits for the prospectus. After a long period of prosperity it would be only natural if some setback were to take place, and he must be absolutely candid on this.'

October 1950 saw a giant £20 million Imperial Tobacco loan stock issue. Acting on behalf of Morgan Grenfell and Barings, Cazenove's and Rowe & Pitman were responsible for placing over three-quarters of the sub-underwriting. The Prudential took a £2½ million slice, an indication of its increasingly massive investment power during these post-war years. The issue was oversubscribed about thirteen times, with the total of £260 million being then the largest amount of money ever offered for an industrial issue. Rather less big was the £100,000 rights issue in December for a company called Metal Closures, but it again brought Cazenove's into contact with the remarkable Erskine brothers, following an issue for Associated Hotels earlier in the year. Denys Erskine was the hotelier, while Keith Erskine was a colourful solicitor-cum-businessman whom Hornby had met at the Junior Carlton Club and who eventually became chairman of Securicor, a process much helped by Cazenove's through a complex corporate evolution. That was a happy and enriching connection, but much less so was the one that began near the end of 1950 with the issue of £100,000 5½% debentures of H. & G. Thynne, a placing done on behalf of the Standard Industrial Trust. The company, based in Hereford, was a long-established manufacturer of glazed tiles, but the 1950s turned out to be a catalogue of disasters for it, involving poor management and also misfortune when a kiln was blown up. Eventually the company went into liquidation, though Cazenove's in conjunction with the Prudential managed to extract for the existing debenture holders some 60 per cent of the nominal amount of their holdings, representing roughly the current price of the stock. It was a rare example of the firm badly misjudging a business and the people running it.

Altogether more august was the £5 million World Bank issue in May 1951, organised by the leading six London merchant banks and with Cazenove's as one of the four brokers. According to Hornby, such prestige loans 'never went very well but were easy money because no underwriter dared refuse them' and 'the over-riding was never more than ⅛'. More challenging was the Bourne & Hollingsworth experience in the summer of 1951. This was an offer for sale by Cazenove's and what happened was, again in Hornby's words, analogous to Stanhope Steamship four years earlier, in that the underwriting conditions changed: 'In this case dividend limitation was announced and we'd promised in the prospectus an increased dividend. We again gave underwriters the opportunity of withdrawal but went ahead with the issue.' And: 'It did our reputation and our pocket nothing but good in the long run.' In November 1951 a name from the past was prominent with a major issue (sponsored by Morgan Grenfell) of British Celanese, in order to provide funds for the erection of a spinning and textile factory at Wrexham; but eventually the company was taken over by Courtaulds. Also at the end of 1951, Cazenove's acted as brokers in the issue of 400,000 shares of IBM United Kingdom, which had come to Helbert Wagg through Lionel Fraser's willingness to chase the half chance even though the business had seemed likely to go elsewhere – a small but telling harbinger of future change in the City.

Hornby was always on the look-out in these years for good provincial companies, exemplified in 1950–1 by Arthur Balfour, Rowntree and F. Perkins. He recalled the first connection, which took the form of a placing of ordinary shares in December 1950:

R. A. Balfour's Sheffield Steel business came to us through Dana of the issue department of the N. P. [National Provincial] – a very good friend. It was an old family business with old-fashioned accounting and stock valuation methods which were difficult to break down. However I eventually went up to spend the night with Lord Riverdale in Sheffield to buy his shares. He was a delightful old boy and I'd decided 24s was as high as I could go. He wanted 25s but I staunchly stuck to my guns and he dealt. For many years I used to go up to their annual meeting and made friends with Robert Balfour, his son, who succeeded him in the business.

Rowntree came to Cazenove's out of the blue, needing money in order to finance the high cost of cocoa beans. The result was the issue in February 1951 of £750,000 4% unsecured loan stock, with the company making it a condition that there was no quotation on any stock exchange. Hornby was mindful of the potential of the connection and in the course of the preliminaries reduced his firm's commission to three-eighths of one per cent, a gesture appreciated in York. An issue of £1¼ million 5% unsecured loan stock followed soon afterwards, again handled by Cazenove's. As for F. Perkins, Peterborough-based manufacturers of diesel engines for lorries and tractors, this came to Cazenove's in July 1951 when Barings as usual declined to put their name to an equity issue (though concurrently doing a debenture one for Perkins) and therefore handed it on. Hornby and Kemp-Welch struck up a rapport with Frank Perkins, who told Hornby that he had chosen Barings rather than Morgan Grenfell because they had fewer peers as directors.

Meanwhile, Kemp-Welch was establishing and maintaining the closest links with most of the leading breweries. In April 1951 he arranged a major debenture issue for Watney Combe Reid and in October backed up Barings and Schroders in making a big Whitbreads issue. Breweries were becoming increasingly capital hungry, the company at this time requiring money in order to establish new bottling centres to meet the increased demand for bottled beer, to modernise its licensed premises and transport fleet, and so on. Moreover, the company soon afterwards developed the idea of the so-called 'Whitbread umbrella', buying percentages in small, regional breweries in order to protect them from a take-over by a rival of Whitbreads; while Whitbread Investment Co was started for the company's own take-over purposes. Kemp-Welch, in liaison with Kenneth Keith of Philip Hill and Colonel Bill Whitbread himself, had much to do with all this; though with Whitbread eschewing the services of Barings, feeling it had too many irons in the brewery fire, this did put a temporary strain on Hornby's friendship with Evelyn Baring.

The February 1952 debenture issue of the Sunderland brewery Vaux showed Kemp-Welch in prime action. After a year of on-off negotiations and discussions, during the turbulent year of 1951, both the company and Kemp-Welch felt by January that the time had come to press the button, with Vaux urgently needing capital in order to rebuild and refurbish its public houses. After consulting other partners, he wrote a letter to the company precisely setting out the best way to proceed, a letter that in its lucid analysis and sane, level-headed judgement was typical of many others. It is worth quoting almost in full, as another reminder that successful stockbroking is about painstaking attention to detail as well as flair, hunch and other more glamorous qualities:

After giving the matter a great deal of consideration, we feel that, subject to no further appreciable change in the gilt-edged market and interest rates, it should be possible to issue, say, £1,000,000 5% Stock 1972/77 at 100, or perhaps a 4¾% Stock 1972/1977 at 97. The stock would have to be a First Mortgage Debenture, and we feel it would probably be acceptable to the institutional investors if you authorised a total amount of £1,250,000, of which under your C.I.C. consent you could issue £1,000,000, leaving a balance of £250,000 should you require some more money later on. A cumulative sinking fund of 1% would redeem about 50% of the principal amount by the final date. We feel the institutions would agree to this and would not insist on a larger sinking fund.

As regards method, we feel it would be better to place the stock rather than underwrite an offer to the public or to the shareholders. Of the two latter alternatives, the higher expenses involved in a public offer would offset a possibly slightly higher issue price, and it would take longer to prepare the additional documents required and to get the arrangements completed; whilst an offer to holders would necessitate leaving the offer open for at least two weeks, which does not appeal to underwriters at the moment except on extremely attractive terms to them.

We are, naturally, anxious to get the best possible terms for you and at the same time must avoid having another 'flop'; there have been too many issues lately where the underwriters have been left with about 90% with the result that the institutions are very 'shy' of taking on anything unless the terms are really what suits them.

Having taken all these points into consideration, we have come to the unanimous conclusion that it would be far better to try and place the stock for a placing commission of $\frac{1}{2}$%, rather than try an offer at a slightly higher price involving $1\frac{1}{2}$% underwriting and overriding commissions and $\frac{1}{2}$% brokerage, with underwriters on risk for some time as against being able to complete the operation in a couple of days or so, once the documents are ready. At the moment, I think we could manage to do this on the terms suggested, but naturally we cannot tell what the markets may be like in a few weeks.

It might be advisable to arrange for the stock to be paid up in two instalments: e.g. 50% at the time of placing and the balance after three months: this would relieve you of the short-term investment problem for the time being.

The issue took place at par and the placing went well, with only a handful of refusals. The following year there was a useful bit of Vaux 'after market' business when a major equity shareholder died and Cazenove's in conjunction with Grenfell & Co disposed of the holdings on behalf of the trustee department of Martins Bank.

The early 1950s saw some last Micklem touches. In 1950 he and Barings were asked by Dalgety to advise on a debenture reorganisation scheme, in the context of the company's 'perpetual' debentures (a legacy of the nineteenth century) making capital reconstruction impossible. Micklem went for a week's holiday in the Lake District to think it out and returned with a scheme of arrangement for the irredeemable debenture holders, who would receive new stock and cash payment for their old stock. By the end of the year the plan had been submitted to the British Insurance Association Investment Protection Committee and the Association of Investment Trusts, who both advised their members to support it. The scheme was then passed at meetings of the debenture holders in March 1951 and also sanctioned by the Court of the Bank of England. The register of the irredeemable stocks finally closed in April; and redemption of irredeemable debenture stocks and issue of the new stock took place on May 1st. The following year Micklem again made a decisive intervention when London Trust was faced by a threatened take-over from Charles Clore, the first time he had tried to take over an investment trust. Contested take-over bids were just starting to become an intermittent feature of the British corporate scene – usually reflecting the fact that the balance-sheet (or 'break-up') value of assets was well above the stock market price of shares – but the real wave was not until the 1960s. London Trust at once consulted Cazenove's, and it was not long before Micklem had devised a new capital structure, by which voting control was given to the deferred stockholders and Clore was thwarted. Finally, in 1953, it was back to Dalgety, who had recently appointed Cazenove's as its new issue brokers and now made a major equity issue in order to create a sounder balance between the company's loan and share capital. Micklem played a typically creative part during the preparations with Barings, exemplified by this snatch from one of his memoranda on the issue: 'If the market price allows of it 5s a share might be paid up, which would indicate a yield of 7%; if the market price did not allow of this, 2s 6d a share would be paid up, which would indicate a yield on the new shares of 9.3%. With this dividend the shares would obviously command a premium in the market.' It is unlikely that the City has known many more clear-minded thinkers than Charles Micklem.

No one could replace him as a creative force, but there is reasonable evidence that in the 1950s the person who came nearest to doing so was Kemp-Welch. Thus in August 1953, while on holiday in a remote part of Scotland and with a car about to go to the post, he scribbled a hasty but cogent letter to Hornby in London:

I am most interested to hear that Parsons [C. A. Parsons, the Newcastle engineering company] may want some money: of course, it depends on how much they want and how much they can or are prepared to pay out in dividends in the future. Your idea of the Williams and Williams technique [a reference to a forthcoming issue by the firm for the manufacturers of metal windows] seems the right one, but with profits tax as it is, and one thing and another, I wonder whether a Convertible Loan Stock might not be considered. I haven't got any figures so can't make any concrete suggestions – it might enable them eventually to issue less Ordinary than on the Williams and Williams line. Only Claude Gibb [the managing director] knows the answer – they have been ploughing back for years and replacing or increasing their capital assets. I imagine they are beginning to see their way now for the next few years, and should know how much permanent capital they ought to have and how much they can support easily from the dividend point of view. If you did a Convertible Stock I suppose you could do it as a rights issue? And on bonus terms if it suited shareholders? I agree it's rather taking two bites at the cherry but I have a feeling it might be worth thinking about in case the basis of Company taxation is altered and they found they didn't want quite as much money in a few years time. However as I don't know what figures Claude Gibb has in mind this may be just fruitless speculation!!

Kemp-Welch knew Gibb and so to some degree was on the inside track, but nevertheless one is struck by the vigorous, muscular intelligence at work, couching his analysis in a rather less minimalist prose than that favoured by Micklem.

Without doubt the greatest City event of 1953 was the start of the denationalisation of steel, now seen as the first full-scale 'privatisation'. By that spring, when the Iron and Steel Act became law, the basic principle was established that a consortium of the leading merchant banks, headed by Morgan Grenfell as the major 'steel house', would be responsible over the next two years or so for returning most of the main steel companies to private ownership. Many in the City were somewhat nervous: this represented perhaps the biggest collective operation it had ever attempted, fear of renationalisation by a future Labour government was widespread, and there was a certain feeling that the square mile, still recovering from the buffetings of two decades, was being 'used' by the politicians. The six leading company brokers (Cazenove's, Greenwells, Hoare's, Panmure Gordon, Rowe & Pitman and Sebags) were given overall broking responsibilities. These included the crucial preliminary task of trying to bring on side the pension funds and, far more important then, many of the insurance companies and investment trusts.

That summer was given over to detailed discussions about ways and means; and on June 29th a detailed memorandum was submitted to the consortium by Cazenove's and Hoare's. The memorandum questioned the accepted wisdom that the issues should be done as a series over a period of time:

A succession of Steel Equities separately guaranteed is only possible in an atmosphere of mounting success. It may be very difficult to overcome the attitude of 'wait and see'.

It therefore seems to us to be essential to evolve a scheme which we believe (though with little to go on at present, except our own experience) can be carried through successfully and even possibly with enthusiasm. This means a scheme which will ensure at the outset that arrangements have been made to cover the whole, or at any rate the majority, of the operation.

They suggested two possible alternative ways of achieving this. One was 'the "Package" method by which the equities of the seven or eight leading Steel Companies (amounting in money value to roughly £70,000,000) would be underwritten as a composite unit', in which case 'each Company would then simultaneously publish a prospectus and a market would develop in each individual Company's shares'. The other idea put forward was 'the principle of a revolving credit which would be available during the whole of the operation', taking the form of a Guarantor's Syndicate undertaking to subscribe for shares not applied for by the public. Neither suggestion found favour with Morgans, where the key figure was Sir George Erskine; while even more decisive was the opposition a few days later of the Prudential, whose lead all the other institutions followed. It would, in vulgar parlance, be a case of 'suck it and see'.

The first issue, involving a massive sub-underwriting operation on the part of the brokers, was for United Steel in October. Fourteen million £1 ordinary shares were offered for sale at 25s a share, and the issue was heavily and gratifyingly oversubscribed, including a considerable participation by small investors. Soon, however, United Steel shares went to a discount, largely through a shortage of buying orders from the institutions, still nervous about the financial implications of possible renationalisation. Early in 1954 the Lancashire Steel Corporation's offer engendered a disappointing response. But the turning-point came in June 1954 with the successful issue of Stewarts and Lloyds, and thereafter the success of the programme was assured. When an offer was made early in 1955 of 10 million ordinary shares of Colvilles, as many as 150,000 applications were received for a total of 130 million shares. Significantly, taking the first nine issues as a whole, Cazenove's earned more commission on dealings and allotment brokerage than any of the other five 'official' brokers, though by prearrangement had to put much of those earnings into a common pool in order to ensure parity of remuneration.

As for the overall process, the generally improving state of the markets of course helped, but much of the success was due to Erskine and his invention of a system of irrevocable applications by underwriters. It was also probably a good thing that the 'Big Bang' option was not adopted, as Hornby implicitly accepted in his memoirs when he wrote that 'the timing ensured there was never indigestion'. Yet the professional investing world never wholly enthused, as a letter from Richard Fleming to Hornby in August 1954 explained:

> I thought you might be interested in our people's calculations on the steel results to date.
>
> The profit of some £36,000 which would accrue to anyone who kept their allotment amounts to 2.7% on the amounts underwritten, and this compares with a rise in the Financial Times Industrial Index of $27\frac{1}{2}$% since the United Steel Issue, $24\frac{1}{2}$% since Lancashire, and 8% since Stewarts and Lloyds.
>
> The commission accruing to R.F. & Co [i.e. Robert Fleming] for underwriting £1,352,000 worth of stock amounts apparently to £1,385 8s 4d, or just over .1%!

Reservations would continue in the City for some time to come about such large-scale, government-inspired exercises in the industrial sphere, and during the late 1960s the institutions made it crystal-clear that they were distinctly unkeen on another cycle of denationalisation following Labour's recent renationalisation. 'The first privatisation' had, in other words, apparently been a one-off rather than a trail-blazer.

But in the closing weeks of 1953, steel was upstaged by events in the West End. This was the famous attempt by the property developer Harold Samuel, in informal liaison with Charles Clore, to take over the Savoy group of hotels, which included Claridge's and the Berkeley as well as the Savoy itself. During the autumn it became clear that they were in the process of acquiring a substantial holding in the company, whose shares rose sharply. Both men were then well outside the ranks of the Establishment; many in the City valued the Savoy for its comfort, service and friendly atmosphere; and there was a widespread sense of outrage about Samuel's plan to convert the Berkeley into an office block. In charge of the defence was the Savoy's chairman and managing director, Hugh Wontner, utterly determined to preserve control. Inevitably, Cazenove's was closely involved in the struggle. Serocold, still a member of the Savoy board, asked the firm if it would buy shares in competition to Samuel in order to prevent him getting 51 per cent, though was unable to say who would pay for these increasingly expensive shares. Hornby agreed, with the only dissenting voice being that of Holt, who had a certain connection with Clore through Philip Hill. Charles Purnell made an informal arrangement with the leading industrial jobber Sir Nigel Mordaunt (of Bone Oldham and known as 'The Baronet'), by which Cazenove's would get at least half of any shares that were offered in the market. That was one part of the Savoy defence, resulting in Cazenove's in December 1953 buying at least 100,000 Savoy shares. The other part, a source of much controversy, was Wontner's 'Worcester Buildings' scheme, by which the Berkeley would be 'hived off' to the Worcester Buildings Company, a new charitable trust whose control would be vested in the hands of the Savoy pension fund trustees. Even if Samuel acquired the majority of Savoy shares, he would still find it well-nigh impossible to alter the existing use of the Berkeley. The *FT* on December 8th described the scheme as 'revolutionary', divorcing ownership from control, and commented sternly: 'If the City accepts the Savoy Hotel directors' proposals as a precedent, the way will be wide open to the destruction of the whole company system.' But at the time, the more critical question was whether the scheme would succeed in its intention of deterring Samuel.

It did, for on the 9th he called off the battle, though by selling back his ordinary shares to Wontner at 62s 6d each he exacted a heavy price, as well as making a handsome profit for himself. The major part of the purchase (well over £1 million) was financed by Barclays Bank, though Wontner also received much help from other quarters, including great personal generosity from Serocold himself. It took Wontner some ten years to pay off the loans he had received in order to save the independence of the Savoy, but tenaciously he did so. There was also the question of the many shares that Cazenove's had bought on his behalf. By June 1954 it was clear that he would, in the circumstances, be unable to pay for them, and there took place the rare event of a partners' meeting, at which the firm decided to take them on and gradually place them with reliable holders. The following year Wontner devised a two-tier voting structure in order to give his board the best possible chance of fending off future aggressors. The whole episode had further cemented the already close connection of the Savoy and Cazenove's, between whom there would continue to exist basic shared values as well as much personal friendship.

Meanwhile, beneath the headlines and the company dramas of these years, a long-term trend was under way that was to be of fundamental importance in the evolution of post-war investment: namely, the famous 'cult of the equity', a phenomenon that still requires a proper historical study. It is clear, however, that it was a trend that had been brewing for some time. Keynes between the wars tried to persuade the board of the National Mutual to put more ordinary shares into its portfolio, an approach actually implemented in the 1930s by some leading insurance companies including Standard Life, Scottish Widows and Equity and Law; while in 1944 Hargreaves Parkinson, founder of the 'Lex' column (later transferred to the *FT*) and editor of the *Financial News*, published a treatise on *Ordinary Shares* which anticipated the post-war cult and sold very well.

Three factors after the war turned prophecy into reality. The first was nationalisation, which killed off such familiar and well-trusted securities as home railway debentures; the second was the Companies Act of 1948, which much reduced the 'risky' taint traditionally attached to industrial equities; while the third (and most important) was the economic back-ground, with a mixture of high taxation and the beginnings of persistent inflation leading to a greatly-increased investment appetite for capital gains. It is probable that the Prudential was substantially buying equities from fairly soon after the war, as well as the London and Manchester from 1953 under the direction of Lewis Whyte. But the man most commonly associated with implementing the cult was George Ross Goobey, who in 1948 was appointed as the first investment manager of the Imperial Tobacco pension fund. He put his fund into the shares of a long string of the smaller companies and in the process attracted much publicity, which in turn helped to make the cult self-fulfilling. By the mid-1950s, with the first of the post-war equity bull markets reaching a climax in 1955, it was obvious that, despite the tardiness of some institutions to make the move, ordinary shares had entered the very mainstream of investment.

There is little evidence that Cazenove's was to the fore in all this, though fairly soon after the war Chandler in the statistical department did start a panel ('Cazenove's Favourite Fifty') of reasonably safe equities, recom-mendations that necessarily were unpublished because of potential company sensitivities. Nevertheless, the firm by the 1950s was doing a considerable amount of equity business, with Charles Purnell entering his prime as a dealer in the Industrial market. Known on the floor of the House as 'The Rook', he was a much respected, even feared figure who acquired a reputation for doing only large deals and at times exercised an extraordinary dominance over the jobbers, inducing them to take on much larger amounts than they would have liked. Much of this business came from the institutions and itself fed from the firm's paramount position in the industrial new issue sphere. One should not, however, underestimate the firm's activities on the gilts side at this stage. The partners in charge during the first half of the 1950s were Cedric Barnett and Herbert Ingram, whose qualities complemented each other very well, with Ingram acting as something of a catalyst to Barnett. Gilts in general were beginning to prosper, though not as spectacularly as equities, and it is a striking fact that in 1954 the firm made a profit on gilts of over £175,000.

Overall, the day-to-day broking continued its distinctive pattern. By now firmly in charge of the country broking side was Philip Cazenove, one of the more idiosyncratic partners and very popular both inside and outside the firm. In many ways he was a pre-war broker in the post-war world and, if not quite eccentric, was relished by everyone as a 'character'. Generous to others, he could be mean to himself and tended to wear odd-fitting clothes full of holes; a prodigious eater, he once at lunch in Tokenhouse Yard took such a large helping of cherries that there developed among his fellow partners a flourishing market in the eventual number of stones, settlement eventually taking place at 54; each Tuesday he played real tennis at Lord's, with some powerful language ensuing; for visits to country brokers he would pack his guns and fishing rods as well as golf clubs; and it was somehow characteristic that when spelling out the name 'Cazenove' over the telephone, he would say 'v for veterinary surgeon'. No one would have called his a powerful intellect, but he was much loved and helped to provide that essential quality of 'bottom' without which any partnership founders. Indeed, his quality of robust common sense was shown in these years by his approach to the country broking business, where he countered the problem of expensive small orders by increasingly concentrating on about ten firms who did substantial business for large clients and thus each produced for Cazenove's annual commission of up to about £15,000; while of course the new issue spin-offs from the close links with these provincial brokers lay near to the heart of the firm's whole post-war strategy.

Also continuing, some three-quarters of a century after the advent of the telephone, was the traditional daily or near-daily broking round to the parlours of the banks, clearing as well as merchant. The brokers would collect their orders, strictly divided out so as to ensure that everyone whom the bank favoured was kept happy; while the brokers in return transmitted some market intelligence (almost invariably derived from the jobbers), often with the odd new joke thrown in. Not all the Cazenove partners shared equally in this ritual, but among those on a regular beat in the 1950s were Hornby (Barings, Morgan Grenfell and Schroders), Holt (Philip Hill, Singers and Ansbacher), Meinertzhagen (Rothschilds and Lazards), Ingram (Guinness Mahon and ubiqitious 'back-up' to most of the others), Schreiber (Lazards and others) and Barnett (Martins and Glyn Mills).

As for the institutions, which at this time mainly meant insurance companies and investment trusts, Bedford concentrated on breadth, which Kemp-Welch in his 1948 critique had implied was somewhat lacking. It was a breadth which he was able to attain to an enviable degree, helped much by his personal attributes but also by the frequent and consistently profitable sub-underwriting that he was able to offer to these institutions. A significant new addition to this institutional field was Cable and Wireless (Holding) Ltd, the investment company defiantly formed by Sir Edward Wilshaw with the compensation paid by the Treasury after the nationalisation in 1947 of his beloved Cable and Wireless. He was supported by a majority of shareholders and, in what was a controversial episode, drew on the advice of Kemp-Welch, probably his closest stockbroking friend in the City. Some wondered whether Wilshaw was cut out to be an investment man, but Kemp-Welch made it his business to get on close terms with Eric Taverner, the investment manager; and some ten years after the transformation even the *Investors Chronicle*, which had led the minority opposition to Wilshaw's action, admitted that it would have been almost impossible to have produced better results for the shareholders. Eventually, in 1977, Cables was to be absorbed into the Globe investment trust, with which historically it had major cross-holdings.

Meanwhile, regular and valuable business, serviced on the whole by, among others, Derek Schreiber during the 1950s, continued to come from the Henderson Administration; though it was a mark of Micklem's greatness that having in 1948 brought in 'Teddy' Butler-Henderson in order to (in Micklem's phrase) 'remove sentiment' out of Hendersons, he had followed this up soon afterwards by threatening Butler-Henderson with dismissal if Hendersons persisted in doing as much as 85 per cent of its business through Cazenove's, thereby not opening itself up to other influences. Only someone of Micklem's stature could have rounded on his tame house in this way. Hendersons quickly reduced the proportion to about half, doing much selling business through Cazenove's, knowing that the jobbers would make a better price in larger amounts in order to participate in Cazenove placings. It was also in 1948 that Hendersons took over the management of a new trust in the form of the Electric & General (formerly the family trust of William Shearer), which under the auspices of Kemp-Welch and David Wills (who had a room in Tokenhouse Yard), and with money put in by the Pearl and subsequently the Hambleden family, did tremendously well.

Nor was that all. Pension funds were just starting to become a feature of the investment scene, and in Hornby's eyes the jewel in the crown was (and always would remain) the W. H. Smith Superannuation Fund. He gave its portfolio the closest possible attention and even kept the relevant file in a special top drawer of his desk, occasionally bringing it out in order to run his eyes over it in a proprietorial way. There was also of course a good number of families, trusts and charities for which he and the other partners had responsibility. Especially valuable in this respect was the part played by Kemp-Welch, who in 1945 or soon afterwards brought with him the investment portfolios of five wealthy families – Wills, Rank, Morrison, Pembroke and Portal – that in a sense laid the foundations of the firm's post-war private client business. Throughout the approach of Hornby, Kemp-Welch and the others was essentially conservative: choosing sound securities, including a strong content of investment trust shares bought at considerable discounts to net asset values; taking a long view; and above all refusing to 'plough' a portfolio for the sake of generating commission. It was an approach to investment that derived from Micklem and in turn heavily influenced a future generation of Cazenove partners. Hornby in his memoirs was at pains to emphasise this whole side of his firm's work, in words which read strikingly in the present-day world of Chinese walls: 'As well as all our involvement in issuing we were doing a big investment business and this is what I really enjoy and what a stockbroker is for. Every partner in Cazenove's whatever his job should have a few lists for which he is responsible and about which he can become proud.'

Towards international business the approach in these years remained cautious, with an emphasis less on grand strategy than small-scale flexibility, deploying staff to work on areas that were flourishing or were felt to have potential, but making no long-term commitments. Alex Coombe-Tennant (who became a partner in 1951) continued to be the main person on the American side, but was now helped by Alistair Timpson, who though at Cazenove's for only seven years from 1948 made a significant contribution. American business, however, remained fitful: the 'dollar premium' was a major disincentive; British institutions preferred to talk to American brokers and do business through them; and Stock Exchange rules insisted that a London broker offer the business first to a London jobber rather than an American broker, which would have been better for the client.

Timpson was also concerned with South Africa, where he had had first-hand mining experience and which as a member then of the sterling area had definite investment attractions. The firm did a considerable amount of business there in the 1950s on behalf of British institutions, as well as running an arbitrage account with a Johannesburg broking firm. Doing this arbitrage, an extremely rough-and-ready affair, was Algy Belmont's son Michael, who on occasion found himself having to resort to bribery in order to ensure that the Post Office telephonists put his calls through before those of his competitors. In overall charge of the South African operation was Holt, who in June 1953 complained to the Stock Exchange Council about proposed new regulations for the conduct of arbitrage business. 'We were concerned last year in selling South African securities totalling in all a huge sum of money,' he stated, typically adding: 'This we were able to do to the satisfaction of our clients, and with considerable advantage to our correspondents in South Africa and ourselves, in face of intense opposition and competition from outside finance houses, who used every artifice to secure the business.' Arbitrage was still not really Cazenove's style, but it had its uses.

The other main area was Australia, the preserve of Derek Schreiber. He was perhaps an underestimated element in the partnership: a commanding presence, a good raconteur and immensely considerate as well as generous, he was very much from the old school and found it difficult to accept the modern notion of partners potentially coming from 'below the salt'; but he was a great team man, could usually grasp the big picture if not always the fine detail, and was particularly adept at picking the brains of someone he trusted. Moreover, his contacts were of the very highest quality – above all in Australia, where during the war he had been Equerry to H.R.H. the Duke of Gloucester. Earlier than most investors he saw the potential of that country and over the years, especially in the 1960s, he helped to persuade Hendersons to invest there substantially, with notably beneficial results; and he also played a large part in establishing (in 1957) the London Australia Investment Company, the first investment trust in Australian securities. Nevertheless, the fact was that the firm's day-to-day Australian business during the 1950s was still relatively unimportant, and indeed on many days Cazenove's did not deal there at all. As with the international sphere generally, expansion remained something for the future.

Stockbroking, however, is not always about buying and selling securities, or raising capital, and three times during these years the firm fulfilled an important role by providing expert witnesses in major arbitration cases. The first time was in 1952, when Peter Kemp-Welch appeared before the iron and steel arbitration tribunal on behalf of the Staveley Iron and Chemical Company, which following the nationalisation of steel in February 1951 was seeking compensation of £8.75 million, as against the Ministry of Supply's offer of £5.1 million. Kemp-Welch provided much detailed evidence about the company's high Stock Exchange reputation and value; and displaying his love of cricketing terminology he dismissed some of the companies mentioned for comparative purposes as distinctly 'third eleven'. The hearing lasted nine days (one of which ended early when, in the equally sporting words of the Arbitrator, 'Bad light stopped play') and the eventual judgement awarded compensation of £8.2 million. This was a substantial victory for the company, which then proceeded to sell the large amount of Treasury stock it received through another broker – a disappointment to Cazenove's, who had charged a modest fee for its services. Two years later Kemp-Welch was again in the witness box, in a private arbitration between Courtaulds and E. S. & A. Robinson, in the context of Courtaulds buying the latter company's 50 per cent holding in Colodense. The price was in question and, on behalf of the purchasers, he again was on the winning side, earning the gratitude of Frank Kearton, the rising star at Courtaulds. However, in an ironic aftermath, the firm became brokers to not the winners of the case but, six months later, the losers.

The other of this legal trio was the celebrated case of John Holt, a Liverpool-based company that traded with West Africa and dealt principally in cocoa. In 1950 it went public and was brought to the market by Barings, with Cazenove's acting as brokers. Three years later a dispute came to the courts concerning the value of over 40,000 shares in the company settled by Robert Holt, who had died in 1948 while the company was still private and therefore before the shares had a market quotation. Taking advice from Cazenove's, the trustees claimed that the shares in 1948 were worth 16s each; whereas the Estate Duty Office put their value at 25s, having originally estimated them at 60s. The case was heard in the autumn of 1953 in the High Court. A leading witness on behalf of the trustees was Hornby, who in an impressive appearance argued strongly that the assets of John Holt, largely comprising stocks of merchandise in West Africa, should not be made the basis of valuation. He pointed out that these assets were very vulnerable to a fall in stock prices and implied that if the assets had been in bricks and mortar in Britain, or in investments or other readily realisable property, his opinion would have been different. It was a keenly-contested case, and at one particularly heated point, under cross-examination from Sir Reginald Manningham-Buller (the Solicitor-General and later Lord Chancellor), Hornby leaned out of the witness box with a pointing finger and shouted, 'You may think you know what you're talking about – but I do this work every day!' Fully admitting the problems of assessment, Mr Justice Danckwerts eventually decided that the value of the shares was 19s. 'The clients are delighted with the result,' the Liverpool solicitors of the trustees wrote to Hornby, 'and greatly appreciate the help given by you and your Firm. Mr Chandler, in particular, was quite tireless in his supply of vital information, and we are all most grateful.' Hornby's own retrospective verdict was characteristic: 'It was a signal victory which put the E.D.O. in its place and made things easier for us in similar cases in future.'

There were of course several changes in the partnership between 1948 and 1954, though its size remained fairly constant between fourteen and eighteen; and indeed, until 1967, there remained a legal maximum of twenty partners. David Shaw-Kennedy died in 1950 while still middle aged, having rather tired of life towards the end. He is remembered by Hornby as 'an original genius, provocative and good for the firm'. Also in 1950 there retired from the partnership John Scaramanga and Jimmy Palmer-Tomkinson junior. Scaramanga had been a significant figure in the 1930s, inventing a number of investment schemes and in ingenious ways raising substantial sums of cash for corporate clients, often in liaison with Singer & Friedlander, with whose Francis Hock he was on close terms; but his period in the Air Force during the war had affected him deeply and he was never the same afterwards. Palmer-Tomkinson retired largely because he much preferred farming to stockbroking. An Olympic skier, he was tragically killed in January 1952 while marking out the danger spots of the British Championship course at Klosters. A happier sporting future lay ahead of Gerald Micklem, who retired in 1954 once he had inherited the means to take up full-time his passion for golf. He had recently won the English Amateur championship; and subsequently he captained Walker Cup teams and became one of the foremost golf administrators of the age. On his death in 1988 he was aptly described in the British press as 'the game's only authentic oracle on this side of the Atlantic'. His departure was a significant loss to the firm, for whom he had made a distinctive contribution in relation to first the country broking business, then in livening up the 'box', and finally on the research side.

Changes also took place on the money-broking side. Miles Brunton retired in 1950 after a long, honourable and enjoyable career. For the next two years Lord Deramore (the former Stephen Bateson) was in charge of the loans department, but it soon became clear that he was not really suitable. In 1952 he retired and was succeeded by David Cazenove, who became a partner at the same time. Cazenove was the great-great-grandson of the founder of the firm and the grandson of Arthur Philip Cazenove. He had come to the firm as a young man in 1946, to be told by Micklem that he would never become a partner, the name presumably being a disadvantage. After some time in different departments he was put in loans, where he found he had a knack for the work. Charming, sociable and with an agile if underused brain, he quickly achieved a rapport with the discount houses and clearing banks, being on the best possible terms with people like Arthur Trinder of the Union Discount and Peter Forrester of Barclays. The money market was still a hard-drinking, old-fashioned, congenial gentleman's club (although tolerant of other ranks if they were good company) and indeed was to change over the years much more slowly than other parts of the City. Very much left to his own devices, Cazenove ran the loans department for almost twenty years, for most of the period successfully. He was much helped by Claude Carter, a particularly able member of staff who had been on the loans side since the late 1920s. The firm during the 1950s and 1960s made a consistent profit through its money-broking activities, usually of between £100,000 and £200,000, which was probably less than that made by Laurie Milbank (and possibly also Sheppards) but nevertheless useful and regular. Few understood what the loans department did and Hornby in his memoirs referred to David Cazenove's 'mysterious rites'. They were rites that in many ways epitomised the old City, being based on personal contact, trust and hasty, scribbled calculations on the back of envelopes in order to trace a few million pounds that had temporarily gone missing.

By far the most important change in the partnership took place at the end of August 1954 with the retirement of Charles Micklem (on the same day as his nephew). His last action as senior partner carried his stamp, ultimately that of a well-meaning, stern-minded Victorian paternalist:

> I have asked Mr Pugh to add £10 to the August pay cheque of every member of the staff as a personal gift from myself; it carries with it my thanks for your loyal help and my very best wishes for the future prosperity and happiness of every one of you.

It was entirely in keeping that he let it be known that he did not want anyone to write to him. Retirement was brief, for he died the following January, aged seventy-two. His memorial service at St Michael, Cornhill, produced an impressive City gathering, with those present including Lord Ashburton, Lord Ritchie of Dundee, Lionel Fraser, Sir Eric Gore-Browne, Lord Kindersley, Sir Nigel Mordaunt, Henry Tiarks, Arthur Villiers and Richard Wilkins. Enough has been said to suggest what his great qualities were, but a final estimate comes from Hornby, who described Micklem as 'shrewd, conscientious, painstaking and a master of his craft'. That was surely true: to which one can add only that Micklem through his career not only enlarged the craft of which he was such a master, but also set standards of professional and personal conduct that would endure as long as Cazenove's itself lasted.

Upon Micklem's retirement, marking the end of an era, the firm changed its 'style' to the much more economical Cazenove & Co. Micklem had made no specific provisions for his succession and the new titular senior partner, by dint of seniority, was Geoffrey Akroyd, though everyone, including Akroyd, knew and accepted that the leading and dominant partner was Antony Hornby. In Hornby's own words: 'I fixed the partnership proportions and the special bonuses and made the speeches at the Savoy Dinners and there was never any question of this.' Akroyd was a much-liked figure, who listened to others and occasionally himself gave avuncular advice, most famously when he told a newcomer to the firm, 'You'll find the Savoy a jolly nice little place for lunch, and nice and handy because you can get there on a number 11 bus'; but in business terms he carried little weight and undoubtedly it was an anomalous situation, though not one that caused any rancour. Moreover, appearances in a sense deceived, for it was precisely in this period that it became clear that Cazenove's was not going to be lulled into the insidious trap of nepotism and that younger members of 'family' would have to show their aptitude if they were going to stay and progress in the firm. Several, unsuited to stockbroking, left for other fields then and during the 1960s, including sons of Micklem, Akroyd, Ingram and Meinertzhagen, as well as Serocold's nephew Ralph; and it became the unwritten rule that a partner could bring in only one son, and that that son had to run 110 yards to everyone else's 100 in order to prove himself. Some firms failed to apply this fundamental precept, to their considerable cost, but Cazenove's since the 1950s has not been afraid of exhibiting a necessary streak of ruthlessness in cutting out dead wood.

The new, post-Micklem order was soon commemorated by a collective portrait. It had been the custom that retiring partners had their portraits painted, but with wall space running short Hornby in 1957 took up an idea of his wife and commissioned a 'conversation piece' of the eight oldest partners. The artist was Simon Elwes, who besides portraits of the Queen and Princess Margaret had recently painted a picture, admired by Hornby, of the directors of Morgan Grenfell. The Cazenove eight are portrayed in the partners' room, where the picture was also hung when completed. The office joke was that its title should have been 'A Study in Still Life,' because of the seniority of the sitters, but in fact it was, as Hornby with his fine taste recalled, a notable, meticulously-executed piece of portraiture:

> The picture is alive and has a rhythm – things are going on – discussions taking place – D.S.S. [Schreiber] is on the telephone. The likenesses are good except for Frank [Holt] who didn't like being painted. Geoffrey [Akroyd] complained that his face was too red, but Simon said, 'I paint as I see.' He wouldn't alter the colour but he put a bright red *Directory of Directors* on Geoff's desk which took one's eye off his face. Mart died just before the picture was finished and Simon hadn't painted his shoes. We borrowed a pair from Len Martin [his son, who worked in the firm] so that every detail would be authentic.

The death of Albert Martin was sad – a last link gone with the Victorian age – but it was utterly typical that at the end of a lifetime's industry he died in harness.

Renewed confidence in the firm's future, marking the successful post-war rebuilding of the firm's business, was reflected by a flurry of new partners. Johnny Henderson, a great-nephew of Lord Faringdon and superb ADC to Montgomery during the war, entered the partnership in 1954. Two years later he was followed by Charles Purnell, perhaps rather belatedly, and Colin Huttenbach, who was related to the Akroyd family and by now coming into his own on the technical side of new issues. He was very popular within the firm and had a delightful, self-deprecating sense of humour. He much enjoyed telling the story of how, as a young member, he had given his name to a senior waiter in the Stock Exchange in order to have it called out, only for the waiter to expostulate, 'First it's Scaramanga, then Schreiber, then Meinertzhagen, and now it's bloody Huttenbach!'. Then in 1957 there were three new partners: Michael Belmont; David Wentworth-Stanley, who had fairly recently been recruited by Kemp-Welch from the excellent medium-sized brokers Vivian Gray; and Godfrey Chandler, whose talents were being increasingly applied to the companies side, earning him the just appreciation of Hornby, who was determined to keep him in the firm. Expansion was in the air, and Kemp-Welch in particular was on the look-out for youthful talent. Moreover, from 1955 newcomers with partnership prospects had to spend two years on a reasonably systematic trainee course, learning how all the various departments worked. Some found it a rather tedious exercise, but it was another manifestation of the greater professionalism beginning to permeate the firm as a whole.

This confidence in the future was underpinned by a generally flourishing stock market, despite certain 'hiccups' like the Suez Crisis of 1956 and the sharp rise of Bank Rate in September 1957, at 7% its highest level since 1920. By 1958 a remarkable equity bull market was under way, reaching a euphoric climax during the 'never had it so good' election month of October 1959. A letter from Hornby to Serocold, written in November 1958, reflected the mood:

> We have been doing a terrific business the last month or two; I think a bigger turnover than we have ever had. I expect the market has gone up too much [the 30–Share Index lay at 212, up 37 since early July], it generally does in these sort of times, but it is astonishing the new buyers for Ordinary Shares who turn up almost every day in the shape of Charities, Labour Controlled County Councils and God knows what.

Serocold himself died in 1959, two years before Palmer-Tomkinson. The triumvirate, who had done so much for the firm, left behind them a City now beginning to change faster than it had at any time during their own lengthy, distinguished careers.

Two fundamental, related changes were already apparent in the 1950s, becoming an increasing matter of discussion as the decade went on: namely, the rise of the institutional investor and the concentration of the jobbing system. Articles in the *Stock Exchange Journal* (the House magazine) considered both. In October 1955 a member bemoaned the lack of capital in the market and cited figures to show that since the war the number of jobbing firms had declined from almost 250 (itself many less than in the pre-

1914 era) to barely 130. After noting the post-war growth of institutional business and how high taxation had severely affected the private investor, he emphasised the growing size of the average bargain, which meant that the jobbing system required greater capital resources if it was 'to perform its traditional function of ironing out market movements caused by changes of sentiment.' The member then discussed the question of bringing in outside capital from insurance companies, merchant banks, investment trusts and so on, 'all of whom are interested in the existence of a market in securities', before concluding prophetically but also conservatively:

> London may eventually have to take some such steps, but there is little doubt that most Members, with their genius for improvisation, would prefer to control their own affairs for as long as they can, and manage their own business within the framework of the existing Rules, rather than adopt new methods which might in the long run threaten their independence.

Subsequent responses in the *Journal* did not challenge the basic premise that the jobbing system faced serious problems, and one jobber stressed that what really mattered to the viability of the system was the existence of a two-way market. Over the years this would become a commonly heard theme, with the implication that a small number of all-powerful institutional investors tended at any one time to drive the market only one way, putting an enormous strain on the liquidity of jobbers if they were to continue to make a market. The rise of the institutions by the 1950s should not be exaggerated: for it has been reliably computed that in 1957 personal holdings of ordinary shares amounted, in terms of market value, to 61.8 per cent; followed by banks and nominee companies (13.5 per cent), insurance companies (8 per cent), investment trusts (3 per cent) and pension funds (1.2 per cent). However, as the broker-cum-journalist Donald Cobbett noted in 1957 in the *Journal*, the 'encroachment by the institutions on the former dominance of the private investor in the field of the industrial equity' had a further significant by-product, which was that they now demanded greater professionalism and a more analytical approach from stockbrokers. Or as Cobbett put it, 'the days of the third-hand "tip", offered over a glass of sherry, are happily long past.' Two years earlier, the Society of Investment Analysts had already been founded, partly inspired by a pseudonymous letter from Godfrey Chandler to the *FT*. Some, including Chandler, would eventually become more doubtful about the benefits of heavily formal, American-style research, but at the time it seemed a necessary form of progress.

Certain developments at Cazenove's reflected these trends. In 1954 the firm recruited its first chartered accountant in the person of John Baudrier, who was hired specifically as an investment analyst. Three years later, when Chandler became a partner, the statistical department split into two: a research side run by Baudrier; and a library under the direction of Cole to back up that research. Nevertheless, the *underlying* ethos of the firm remained that, although one needed all the information one could get, in the end it would always come down to a judgement about the people involved. Nose and flair, in other words, were still valued at least as highly as back-room ability at the figures. When the young Charles Henderson (the subsequent third Lord Faringdon) spent six months at Cazenove's in 1958 prior to Cambridge and informed Hornby that he was going to read economics there, Hornby replied (misleadingly as it turned out), 'You can't come back here'.

The quality of 'nose' was in fact epitomised by Johnny Henderson, who soon after becoming a partner in 1954 emerged as a major figure in the firm and indeed the City, being a little like Serocold in the way he was known and liked by everyone. Moreover, his interests outside the square mile were many and diverse, which allied to his gregarious character resulted in much business coming to Cazenove's. Deceptively hard-working as well as very quick with figures, he was happy to be ruled by a spirit of adventure and always willing to back his own judgement, though at the same time careful to get to know about the things he touched. His particular contribution in the 1950s was to take properly in hand the pension funds, showing a knack for getting on with the investment managers, diverse and occasionally difficult though they were. Others (both brokers and merchant banks) had already begun to cultivate this field, but for Cazenove's it was enormously important in terms of new issue 'placing power' as well as day-to-day broking business.

As for the insurance companies, which still ruled the institutional roost, a significant role during the second half of the fifties was played by the confident Ingram, who for some years joined Bedford in equity sales and underwriting. The only shame was that Ingram's work on equities left Cedric Barnett more or less alone on the gilts side, which henceforth somewhat slipped as there failed to emerge another 'selling' partner to stimulate his great technical ability. This is not to say that Barnett was not a popular and well-known daily presence in the gilt-edged market, then dominated by the two jobbing firms of Wedd Jefferson and Akroyd & Smithers. He was particularly fond of playing a practical joke on young jobbers who were starting their apprenticeship by dealing in corporation bonds. An inquiry by him into the price of 'Rugby fives' would prompt a scurrying into books and anxious enquiries, as likely as not intensified by a follow-up question about the price of 'Eton fives'. There was little indication from the rather austere figure with the immaculate top-hat and dead-pan face that these were wholly fictitious securities, comparable to the mythical 'Chinese turnpikes' of the nineteenth century.

There may anyway have been two other reasons, quite apart from the cult of the equity, why the firm's gilt business now failed to match its past glories. One was the distinct if unstated feeling on the part of the institutions that since they gave Cazenove's so much of their equities business, executed by the matchless Purnell, it was only fair that they spread the gilts elsewhere. The other was Barnett's belief that because Cazenove's was also a money broker and as a result knew where the stock lay, there must therefore be certain self-imposed limitations when it came to gilts. It was a sign of more self-conscious times, as well as of the scruples of the man, that unlike his predecessors he should have felt such sensitivities.

Internationally, North America was emerging in the late 1950s as the firm's main growth area. Few London brokers had managed in recent times to penetrate it – in terms of really understanding it on the ground – so in a sense it was almost virgin territory. The Canadian expert was Cosmo de Bosdari, like Timpson something of a loner and also like him a gifted analyst with an alert brain open to new opportunities. He had made his name at Cazenove's specialising in life insurance companies, before more recently turning to Canada and making himself a master of where that country's economic potential lay. As for the United States, there were various key events. The first was Hornby's initial visit there in the spring of 1955, when he made many contacts but above all established a friendship with Kidder Peabody's Albert Gordon, a remarkable man who had been a leading figure in Wall Street for almost thirty years and would remain so for many more. Hornby asked Gordon if Kidder would like to open a London office at Cazenove's, Gordon responded positively, and a very satisfactory relationship developed between the two firms. Then, in 1957, Hornby persuaded Gordon to take Michael Belmont under his wing for three months. Belmont, who had recently gone to Coombe-Tennant on the foreign side, duly served his apprenticeship in the States and made out brilliantly, impressing everyone with his outgoing personality, willingness to learn and assiduous cultivation of the nationwide contacts abundantly provided by Kidder. He returned to London and was made a partner. Soon afterwards Hornby said something to Belmont that the young man took keenly to heart: 'Nobody in the City of London will listen to you until you're 40. They won't actually take your advice until you're 50, unless you specialise.' So Belmont decided to specialise and chose California, where hardly anyone went because of the distance, but which was starting to grow at a fantastic rate. He pumped a great deal of business to Californian brokers, they in turn introduced him to the local companies, and as a result he became aware before almost anyone in the City of the potential of a concern like Safeway, which was then just a Californian company. By the end of the decade, entirely due to his efforts, Cazenove's was recognised as *the* London authority on Californian shares. The way was pointing towards what would become a new dimension in the firm's history.

All the time during these years the new issues kept on happening, often at the rate of several a week. The capital market was exceptionally active from the autumn of 1954 through to the beginning of a post-election credit squeeze in July 1955, and Cazenove's was involved in a host of issues. Companies included Barrow, Hepburn and Gale (tanners and leather goods), Meccano (of lamented memory), Austin and Pickersgill (following an amalgamation of two Wear shipbuilders), H. J. Heinz (in the process of building in Wigan what was to be the Commonwealth's biggest tinned food factory), Rootes Motors again, Ransomes and Rapier (engineers), Church & Co (footwear manufacturers), and Sir G. Godfrey & Partners (designers and manufacturers of aircraft air-conditioning equipment, an exciting business at a time of much enthusiasm for things technological). By August 1955 the market had taken a turn for the worse; and an issue that month for the paper manufacturers Albert E. Reed, in which Warburgs joined Helbert Wagg as joint issuing house, occasioned considerable nervousness, until Hornby as ever banished pessimism by promising to make good any temporary shortfalls. Then in September there was an equity issue of the Wolverhampton company Tarmac Limited, introduced to Cazenove's by the Nottingham brokers William Chapman, who in return received a quarter of the underwriting. Capital-raising discussions usually took place in the City, but on this occasion Hornby and Meinertzhagen had travelled to the West Midlands to meet the board. The issue went surprisingly well and soon afterwards Cazenove's received Chapman's 'congratulations on the success of the issue at a time of market adversity'.

But the *tour de force* of the early post-Micklem years was undoubtedly McKechnie Brothers. Manufacturers in Birmingham of non-ferrous metals (and in particular of titanium, a new light metal starting to be used in aeroplane engines), this was a very fine family business, worth some £6 million, that had decided to go public. Cazenove's was asked to make an offer for sale of 300,000 'A' ordinary shares and during the autumn of 1955 Kemp-Welch, with support from Hornby, prepared the ground ready for action in the New Year. On November 16th, J. D. McKechnie came to Tokenhouse Yard unsure about the eventual outcome, but according to notes on the conference that day: 'Mr Kemp-Welch and Mr Hornby thought we would be all right and Equities could not go much worse. The market was firm underneath.' Equities did recover in December, but still entered 1956 in nervous mood. The sub-underwriting on January 9th was achieved, though proved hard going. Cazenove's was met with refusals from as many as forty-four institutions, a failure rate no doubt explained by a gloomy letter from the Birmingham brokers N. Lea, Barham & Brooks, who had received an underwriting participation of 30,000 shares:

> We encountered considerable Institutional resistance on three counts, (a) Non-voting Shares; (b), Yield; (c), length of time on risk. With regard to (a), there appears to be a definite movement through Institutional thought, which we have noticed before, towards the rejection of issues of non-voting shares. The Britannic, once they had heard the shares carried no votes, were not prepared to look at the Prospectus and they have asked us to pass on their reason to you. Several other Institutions took the same line.

McKechnie himself took up the theme (though one that presumably derived from the family's wish to retain effective control) in a letter to Kemp-Welch on the 24th:

> I regret to hear about the drive in certain quarters against non-voting shares. You will recall that I raised the point with you and Mr Hornby in November, but at that time neither of you thought it was material. However, I am glad to note that you think it will go all right, and wish you success.

The actual offer for sale took place at the beginning of February, against a background of what the *Evening Standard* described in a comment on it as 'see-sawing markets'. The outcome was encapsulated in McKechnie's next letter to Kemp-Welch, written on the 10th:

> I am writing to let you know how very pleased and relieved I was to learn that the issue had been over-subscribed at the finish. It was very much touch-and-go and I think we aged quite a bit at Hagley Road waiting for the results!
>
> It was particularly unfortunate that we had both a poor market and the anti-non-voting shares outcry to contend with at the same time.
>
> I know you must have worked really hard to get such a good result in the present difficult state of the market, and I do congratulate you most sincerely.
>
> If only the luck had been with us it would clearly have been an outstanding success, but, even so, it was a good effort in view of the circumstances, and clearly reflected great credit on the firm of Cazenove's and on yourself personally.

In short, following a notable achievement somewhat against the odds, the previous critical tone was abandoned, while the congratulations were warm and richly deserved. And, as McKechnie implicitly recognised, it was by no means certain that another firm would have been able to pull it off as Kemp-Welch, by dint of skill and assiduity, undoubtedly had.

1956 continued to be a difficult year, culminating in Suez and its aftermath. It brought out the best in Kit Hoare, who in early December, with other brokers but without the support of a merchant bank, successfully underwrote and got away a £40 million ICI convertible loan issue, the biggest industrial financing operation hitherto handled by the City and an immensely brave piece of company stockbroking. Cazenove's that same month placed on behalf of Securities Agency Ltd new debenture stock in Broadcast Relay Service, and writing to that company's chairman in the wake of the operation Hornby observed: 'I am glad we got on with the job. It is an unpleasant feeling in these uncertain days not to have your money in the bag.' Markets improved during the early months of 1957; and in March steel denationalisation, which had been steadily proceeding for almost four years, reached a further stage with the offer for sale of 40 million ordinary shares of £1 each of the Steel Company of Wales, a giant concern kept out of the first phase of denationalisation because of its heavy burden of debt. Lazards headed a consortium of eight merchant banks for what was then the City's biggest-ever equity issue, Cazenove's and Rowe & Pitman were responsible for placing the great bulk of the sub-underwriting, and despite better markets these sub-underwriters found themselves being allotted approximately 85 per cent.

Infinitely less momentous in the affairs of the City, but indicative of the range of responsibilities involved in being a company broker, was an episode that occurred towards the end of 1957. The context was the decision of Ceramic Holdings, a relatively small company located in Bonnybridge, Stirlingshire, to declare an interim dividend accompanied by a rather ambiguous directors' statement. Cazenove's had acted for the company in its recent new issue (the business having been introduced by the Glasgow brokers Penney & Macgeorge), and during December Hornby found himself in delicate dialogue with the chairman, W. Boyd Mitchell, who exercised a strong personal control. A well-judged letter from Hornby on the 9th set out his general position in such a situation:

My conversation with you on the telephone was in no way meant to voice criticism or to put a formal complaint but only to try and be helpful in preserving the Company's good relations with its shareholders. As brokers to the Company we regard this as part of our duty and we do expect you to repose some confidence in us.

Now we have had some comments from shareholders expressing some doubt as to what your announcement really means. You say on the one hand that 'profits to date are satisfactory although the full benefit of the new capital has yet to be reflected in the results' but on the other you reduce the interim dividend from 5% to 4%. If you consider profits satisfactory, why, a shareholder might say, should the interim dividend be decreased?

There really is in fact some ambiguity. I imagine that the position is that although profits are not unsatisfactory it is too early in the year to be certain that the full year's results will justify your paying 11% and that therefore you have reduced the interim as a precautionary measure. A perfectly reasonable thing to do; but I think the shareholders should have been told so. It is I think, always best to keep them as well and reliably informed as possible. If you take them into your confidence they will understand and support you. If you don't they can become restive. It is worth a very great deal to keep your shareholder relationships happy.

Please believe that I am only trying to be helpful.

Boyd Mitchell in reply accepted that Hornby's remarks were made in the best faith, but continued to deny that anything had been concealed from the shareholders. The role of 'honest broker' could be a thankless one, though Hornby in such matters had a pretty broad back.

However, the major Cazenove intervention of 1956–7, albeit rather poorly documented, concerned the ownership of the City's daily newspaper. The background was partly personal: Colonel Oliver Crosthwaite-Eyre, in effect the *FT*'s majority shareholder, had in recent years had an increasingly unhappy relationship with the paper's chairman, Lord Bracken. In 1956 Crosthwaite-Eyre consulted his friend and financial adviser, Luke Meinertzhagen, who told him that not only would the City take a dim view if the paper lost the services of its chairman (and probably also managing director), as seemed all too likely as a result of the conflict, but that anyhow he had too much of his capital locked up in the *FT* and would do better to spread it across a range of other investments. Crosthwaite-Eyre reluctantly agreed to take Meinertzhagen's advice. The chances are that Meinertzhagen already knew of the existence of a probable satisfactory buyer of the paper. This knowledge came through his brother Daniel, a managing director of Lazards, which in turn was part of the Pearson empire under the third Lord Cowdray. With great swiftness and secrecy a sale was made towards the end of January 1957, with Pearson paying the Eyre family something over £600,000. 'I am so glad that this deal has now been satisfactorily concluded, and I am quite sure that in the long run, and whatever feelings you may have, you and your family will not regret it,' Luke Meinertzhagen wrote to Crosthwaite-Eyre on the 30th. A week later the change of ownership became public knowledge. Perhaps in the *very* long run the Eyre interests might have benefited from continuing ownership of the *FT*, but at least they did not have to spend upwards of a quarter of a century confronting the well-nigh intractable problems of Fleet Street and the print unions; while as far as the *FT* itself was concerned, it could hardly have been in better proprietorial hands than those of Pearson.

Generally Cazenove's in this period enjoyed a good and trusting relationship with the press as a whole, though Hornby rarely forgot the importance of discretion. In March 1958, in the context of a forthcoming issue of IBM United Kingdom, he wrote to Michael Verey of Helbert Wagg: 'I am returning the top secret figures of I.B.M. World Trade Corporation in case Whitmore of the *Daily Telegraph* gets them out of me during the week-end!' Francis Whitmore was probably the leading City editor of the day, and later in the year Hornby paid him a telling tribute in a letter to Hugh Wontner following a very quietly executed placing of Savoy shares: 'Whitmore's article this morning has taken me aback. It was not difficult to guess where the shares came from, and there could be no secret about this. His other remarks were pure conjecture but he has an uncanny way of getting somewhere near the point with his guessing.'

One episode that received rather less press scrutiny was the last of the old-style syndicates. This followed the purchase from the Nuffield Foundation of over three million ordinary shares of the British Motor Corporation. A syndicate was established comprising most of the leading City houses and jobbers, and jointly with the brokers David Bevan the shares were resold at a profit over the ensuing weeks. But if that was a throwback to earlier times, 1958 also saw an important trend of the future being foreshadowed, when after lengthy negotiations and market manoeuvres Cazenove's successfully accomplished the acquisition by Lockhart, Smith & Co (a catering company operating mainly in industrial canteens) of the Associated Automatic Machines Corporation. The work was done by Charles Purnell and Johnny Henderson, the latter of whom established a good rapport with the chairman of Lockhart Smith, the Earl of Cottenham. Hostile take-over bids were becoming more common, and soon the firm would have to establish what its attitude was towards the phenomenon in general.

One of the major issues of 1958 was the Shell rights issue in February of eight million £1 ordinary shares at £5 each. Almost certainly this was the occasion, as recalled by Hornby, for a key moment in the personal history of the two titans of post-war company stockbroking:

> At the first brokers' meeting there were four firms – Rowe & Pitman, Panmure, Sebags and ourselves – and Bill Harcourt [Lord Harcourt of Morgan Grenfell] said he hoped we would agree to Kit Hoare joining us as brokers. There was a silence for some time and I then piped up (though younger than the rest) and said I thought it was quite unnecessary, that we were well able to do the job and it cast a reflection on us. The others backed me up and Bill Harcourt said he didn't realise we'd feel so strongly and withdrew the proposal. I did this because we knew that Kit had excluded us from the Anglo-Iranian issue [i.e. BP's £41 million debenture issue in December 1957]. He was terribly jealous and omnivorous and at that time was powerful and our chief rival.

This rivalry between the two firms would continue into the 1960s, usually on reasonably amicable terms, though not without a certain continuing undertow of friction between the two great men themselves.

Of course, in an era before 'league tables' and obsessive press attention on the domestic affairs of the City, few contemporary estimates were made, at least in written form, of relative standing between the main firms. All the signs are, however, that by the late 1950s the reputation of Cazenove's was as high as it had ever been, above all in the new issue sphere. One unsolicited testimonial that does survive dates from May 1957, incidentally shedding light on the American challenge that lay before Belmont. That month H. S. Morgan of Morgan Stanley in New York wrote to Lord Harcourt at Morgan Grenfell:

> We have received an inquiry regarding IBM stock from Cazenove & Ackroyd [sic] who, I think, are brokers in London. We have not done business with them before but know them by name and would normally consider offering them stock in the event we have any lay-offs.
>
> I write you to ask whether or not I am correct in thinking that they are brokers and that they are good people.

Harcourt replied:

> I have just got your enquiry about Cazenove & Co.
>
> This is the biggest firm of stockbrokers in the City of London and quite outstanding. They frequently act for us as brokers in our New Issues and we also use them very largely in our ordinary Stock Exchange business. You could not find a more high-class firm to deal with.

At the very least Cazenove's would in the late 1950s have been on almost everyone's list of the top three new issue brokers, with Hoare & Co and

Rowe & Pitman probably the most frequently included other two firms. The other significant firms in this specialised sphere were W. Greenwell & Co (though increasingly oriented towards gilt-edged and statistics), Laing & Cruickshank, Rowe, Swann & Co (though known for quantity as much as quality), Joseph Sebag & Co (a rising force), Panmure Gordon, and also perhaps J. & A. Scrimgeour. While as for numbers, the ninety-seven issues with which Cazenove's was associated in 1958 once again easily beat the field, with Rowe & Pitman coming next on fifty-eight. As the City in general approached the end of what one might call its post-war period, dominated by controls of one sort or another, it was clear that the Tokenhouse Yard strategy of the late 1940s had been amply vindicated.

Why, though, was the firm *so* successful as new issue brokers? The answer, first and foremost, was personality, above all on the part of Hornby and Kemp-Welch, with their integrity, their enterprise and their sheer hard work. Then there were the key, broad-based relationships with the merchant banks and country brokers, so good in the case of the former that the majority of them usually employed Cazenove's for their own issues. Lionel Fraser of Helbert Wagg made it clear in his memoirs what it was, apart from general support and a compatible disposition, that a merchant bank looked for from a new issue broker. Describing the breed in general, but no doubt with Cazenove's at least partly in mind, he wrote:

> It is the function of these brokers to sub-underwrite issues on behalf of the bankers or issuing houses and their judgement must be very finely drawn to advise on the price of issue. Some firms have such a following, in fair weather or foul, that they know to a flick exactly what the big investors will take, and who is on the feed for this or that type of security.

It is an excellent summary, encapsulating 'to a flick' the ability of Cazenove's to advise and then execute. It was an ability sustained by a formidable network of contacts, within and without the City, indeed within and without the market, where the firm's strong day-to-day position gave it a particular leverage. Anthony Sampson, in his celebrated *Anatomy of Britain* (first published in 1962), put it rather well in a passage about the leading stockbrokers:

> The big firms have become regarded as intelligence service for the City, at the centre of the telephone network of mmms and wells and meaningful grunts. 'Better ask Cazenove's,' a banker will mumble, and the answer will come back with the authority of the market-place.

Armed with such knowledge, as well as his invariable black homburg and umbrella on these occasions, Hornby was in a strong position when he set off to a meeting at a merchant bank.

But it was also, as Fraser emphasised, a question of how the new issue broker used that knowledge. Following in the Micklem tradition, Hornby was a resolute and skilled pricer of issues, though in his case it was pricing done essentially by character. He would make up his own mind what the price should be and never allow any doubts to cross his mind that Cazenove's would not be able to arrange the sub-underwriting at that price, even if the very occasional unholy mess resulted from this utterly self-confident approach. Nor would he consult the institutions (not even the Prudential) before recommending or fixing a price, thus ensuring that he was not talked down. As he himself wrote in his memoirs: 'Cazenove's has the name for fixing a high price for its issues. This obviously pleases the borrower and doesn't deter the lender in the long run when he knows the quality is unquestionable.' The theme of quality control remained as important in Hornby's time as it had been in Micklem's. Moreover, quite apart from the matter of quality, the institutional sub-underwriters also knew not only that loyalty would be rewarded (another Micklem principle faithfully adhered to by Hornby and his partners), but also that, in the event of an issue going seriously wrong as far as the wider investing public was concerned, then Cazenove's would give its very best endeavours, often over a period of several months, to sort out the mess. Yet of course, a new issue broker also has to keep the company happy, not just the merchant bank and the investors. Here Hornby continued the Micklem approach of giving the best possible service for the lowest possible fees, knowing that by doing so there would probably be steady post-issue earnings in the secondary market for many years. He also encouraged younger partners, like Chandler and Belmont, to make extensive tours of medium-sized companies and ensure that old or even recent contacts did not go rusty. Some industrialists were ill at ease with City gentlemen in their factories, but most welcomed the trend. Altogether, the Hornby/Kemp-Welch attitude towards the company part of the new issue triangle is perhaps best described as friendly but firm: they knew exactly what they were doing and trusted that the company would let them get on with it; aware of the unrivalled Cazenove track record, most companies were sensible enough to do precisely that.

Hornby and Kemp-Welch, together with the other partners who either specialised in new issue work or sometimes took it on board, could not have achieved the undoubted success that they did without the consistent, generally unsung efforts of the staff operating behind them. This meant not only an efficient new issue department, but also an efficient settlements side, where 'corporate' aftermath business was given a form of priority. The ability to execute, in other words, meant more than placing power alone; it also meant an effective machinery capable of continuous action. Manning that machinery were many people who frequently found themselves working flat out day and night during hectic periods, knowing that their reward lay in the sense of a job well done on behalf of the firm as well as in a richly deserved bonus at the end of the year.

During the summer of 1958 the firm sustained a major blow when Peter Kemp-Welch suffered a serious heart attack. He recovered enough to return to work in due course, and struggled on gamely for several years, but was never the same, vital force again. In less than thirteen years of intense, wide-ranging activity – his diaries for the 1950s show him regularly being in consultations with twenty people or more a day – he had made an immeasurable contribution to the post-war development of Cazenove's. The only solace lay in the fact that Kemp-Welch's son, who had been at Hoare & Co for nearly five years serving a stockbroking apprenticeship, soon afterwards accepted Hornby's invitation to move to Cazenove's. Released by Kit Hoare with some reluctance, John Kemp-Welch joined the firm on 1st January 1959 and soon showed that he was, in Hornby's words, 'a chip off the old block'.

As it happened the start of that year marked the height of the so-called 'Aluminium War', an episode legendary in City history and one that bitterly divided the square mile as never before. It was an extraordinarily complex affair, but its origins can be briefly outlined. British Aluminium was an ailing company ripe for take-over and by the end of November 1958 two possible solutions confronted its board: the 'friendly' one by which British Aluminium went into partnership with the giant Aluminium Company of America (Alcoa), though effectively this would mean a take-over by Alcoa; and the 'hostile' one by which Reynolds Metals of Virginia, in alliance with the Midlands engineering group Tube Investments, would full-frontedly take over British Aluminium. Advising BA were Hambros (replacing Power Securities) and Lazards, while on the other side Warburgs stood behind Reynolds and Helbert Wagg and Schroders behind TI. Fortunately, there survives a letter written on January 2nd by Hornby to Peter Kemp-Welch, who was convalescing at the Cape. A unique historical document, it sheds much light not only on the role of Cazenove's but also on the 'War' as a whole:

It is very remiss of me not to have written a letter to you earlier, but my Christmas and New Year has been thoroughly confused by an unpleasant fight which has blown up between British Aluminium and Tube Investments, as no doubt you have seen, even in the South African papers. We have been in the midst of it, as you can imagine, being brokers, as also are Rowe & Pitman, to both sides. For some time we were the handkerchief in the middle of the tug-of-war rope, and I think it would be best to try and tell you the story from the beginning.

The first thing we heard was that Lionel Fraser informed Arthur Anderson [of Rowe & Pitman] and me that Tubes were proposing to make a bid for British Aluminium and he realised that our position as brokers to British Aluminium might preclude us from acting in any way for Tube Investments, and that it was now necessary for Tube Investments to use brokers to put their circular before the Share and Loan [Department] to get their approval to it. At this time we had heard nothing from the British Aluminium side at all. We therefore saw no reason why we should abdicate straight off from being brokers to Tube Investments, and said that we thought it was logical for us to put the papers into the Stock Exchange. At the same time we said that we should have to take a neutral attitude about the dispute. Later we were seen formally by Lionel, Jock [Jock Backhouse of Schroders] and Siggie Warburg and asked whether we would, in fact, remain neutral in the fight that must develop. We said that this is what we should like to do, and would undertake that we would give no advice to clients or institutions one way or the other but say that our lips were sealed because of our peculiar position as brokers to both sides. Arthur and I then went round to Lazards and Hambros and told them what had transpired. They obviously were disappointed with what we had done, but I told them that they really should have taken us into their confidence sooner so that we would not have been put in the position of being entirely unprepared when the opposition told us their plans.

Well, we managed to maintain our neutrality for about a week and then [shortly before Christmas] Arthur and I were summoned to a meeting by Lazards and Hambros, at which practically all their partners were present, and we were told that in their view 'he that was not for them was against them', that they could not accept neutrality and that they must have brokers working for them, and naturally very badly wanted us. We reiterated at this meeting that they had done their best to lose us by not consulting us, because I didn't see why we should be put in the position of being 'naughty boys'. We said that we must have a little time to make up our minds, but we very soon found that our sympathies were, and had been all along, with British Aluminium, whose citadel was being stormed, and decided that we must go and tell Lionel that we must resign from being brokers to Tubes. This naturally was a sad thing to have to do, and if Tubes win we shall lose British Aluminium too, but those considerations are not important when you feel strongly about something, as we did.

I may say that all the partners of both our firms have solidly supported Arthur and I in the line we took.

Lionel Fraser and Jock Backhouse both realise the very difficult situation we were in. I think they may feel sore that we did not make up our minds earlier, and they may think that having said we were remaining neutral, we should have stuck to our guns. This was a situation without precedent and what I have learned from it is that neutrality is untenable in this sort of affair, and Englishmen are not neutral by nature, and one simply cannot sit on a fence. I told Lionel that our decision was not due to the heavy guns of Lazards and Hambros, but entirely made from the heart, and faced with the decision of supporting one side or the other I could not support Tubes, whose actions I disapproved of.

I had to go down and see [Sir] Ivan Stedeford [chairman of TI] and had an hour and a half with him. He was remarkably inarticulate, but we parted very good friends, and I think he saw our point of view.

The new brokers to Tubes are Panmure Gordon and Sebags, who have both been round to see us and apologised for unwillingly having to replace us.

In the last week events have moved thick and fast. First Lazards and Hambros formed a very strong group of City Houses [including Morgan Grenfell, Brown Shipley, Samuel Montagu and Robert Fleming] who sent out [on New Year's Eve] a circular to British Aluminium share-holders offering to buy half of their shares, if they really wanted to sell them, at a price rather above what Tubes had offered. As soon as that was sent out Tubes and/or Reynolds came in and put the price of British Aluminium above the price that the group had offered, and the shares are now 85s and we believe that in the last three days something like 750,000 shares have been bought by Sebags and Panmure Gordon.

Meanwhile the Governor of the Bank [Cameron Cobbold] has told the two sides that the battle must cease, that it is bad for the City, and meetings go on in Lazards with Stedeford and his advisers trying to come to some compromise. Our side is standing aloof from the market, as we feel that this is the only proper course while conversations are going on. Ivan Stedeford has denied that Tubes are dealing, so the finger points at Warburg and Reynolds.

Anyhow there the matter rests for the moment, and you can imagine I have had quite a lot of sleepless nights wondering whether we have done the right thing.

Four days later Hornby wrote again:

I am sorry to say that the British Aluminium battle is virtually over.

Reynolds came in as aggressive buyers and the only thing that could save the Company was that the Treasury should give consent, even at this late hour, to the Alcoa deal. This they have failed to do.

We naturally feel that it is the wrong result from every point of view, and by that I don't mean that we have lost the brokership of two very good companies, but it lays the way open to more of these piratical ventures. They don't suit us temperamentally or from a business point of view, as I fear I shall always go to the aid of the under-dog, and I suppose will generally get beaten.

Almost two months later Hornby received from Lazards a cheque for £2,500, with the accompanying letter explaining that they and Hambros had changed their minds about not asking British Aluminium (now under new management) for a fee. Hornby in reply thanked Lazards for 'a very pleasant surprise' and added: 'We certainly did suffer a good deal of mental stress and unease at the time and I am glad to think that Reynolds and Tubes are paying us all a little compensation for it.'

The 'Aluminium War' has become such a part of City mythology that some further points must be made. Commentators then and later interpreted the conflict as essentially one between the 'Establishment' (epitomised by Hambros, Lazards and BA's chairman Lord Portal of Hungerford) and the 'outsiders' (epitomised by Warburg, Fraser and Stedeford). There was indeed an element of that, but it was not the whole story. Hostile take-over bids were still a relative rarity, and undoubtedly there existed a natural disposition to support the party being attacked. Hornby's letter makes it quite clear that he was swayed not by pressure from Hambros and Lazards, but by a strong dislike of the way in which BA's 'citadel' was being stormed. Almost certainly it was a feeling shared by others who made up the City consortium. Ultimately it was an emotional reaction in an unfamiliar, disturbing situation, in effect reflecting an entrenched City belief that, within that citadel, the board knew best. Hornby's narrative also reveals (for the first time) why the consortium failed to go into the market, which was manifestly where the war was being won and lost in the early days of 1959. There is little doubt that it had the potential resources to mount a buying operation on its own account. Faced by the displeasure of the Governor, it is clear that one side was playing according to the old-fashioned rules of the game, while the other was changing them.

Some thirty years on, few would deny that the 'War' was a watershed in City history. It not only marked the arrival of Siegmund Warburg as an acknowledged master financier, comparable in his generation to Nathan

Rothschild a century and a half earlier, but also signalled that a new spirit was beginning to pervade the square mile. Lionel Fraser, in a newspaper article in 1963, described what he saw as the episode's beneficial effects: 'The merchant bankers have been more on their toes. There has been a girding of loins, resulting in more enterprise and competitiveness and less reliance on the "old boy" idea.' Put another way, the City was beginning to lose its rather cosy image and was becoming an altogether more ruthless place. The 'Aluminium War', in short, was the first step on the long, thorny road towards that bracing world formally ushered in by the 'Big Bang' over a quarter of a century later.

CHAPTER EIGHT

An international presence
1959–1970

Antony Hornby's 'Aluminium War' letter of January 1959 to Peter Kemp-Welch contained an interesting tacit admission: 'I brought John [Kemp-Welch] to the office yesterday morning and took him round and introduced him to the heads of all the Departments, and any others whose names I could remember. I found that there are a lot of young faces I couldn't put a name to at all.' Other, more tangible signs reflected the increasing size of the firm. Already it had taken out a lease on the ground floor of 11 Tokenhouse Yard and soon after Hornby's letter it acquired other floors there. Then in the early 1960s the firm acquired the lease to 9 and 10 Tokenhouse Yard, which substantially increased the available space and necessitated the construction of a 'Bridge of Sighs' to join it up with No 12. An impressive feature of the bridge was the Stock Exchange's Coat of Arms carved in stone and reproduced from the original brokers' medal struck for Philip Cazenove in 1823.

Yet for all these developments, the inevitable accompaniment of the firm's growing importance and scale of business, Cazenove's still remained (as Hornby was determined that it should) an organisation of manageable size susceptible to personal control. By the early 1960s there were little more than 150 people working in it. This sense of continuity with the past was reinforced by an unashamedly old-fashioned approach to everyday conduct, an approach that was essentially male, conservative and propounded from the top. Three aphorisms of Cedric Barnett's are still remembered with amused affection and catch something of the distinctive culture that emanated from the partners' room: namely, 'shoes have laces', 'motor cars are black' and, perhaps most tellingly of all, 'jelly is not officer food'. Cyril Jolly as general manager (succeeding Charles Strangeman at the end of 1960) implemented this approach, being a stickler for smart appearance. The 1960s may have been the decade when traditional sartorial standards began to wane in the City at large; but such was assuredly not the case at Cazenove's, where the foreigner's image of the City gentleman remained something like reality, and the suede shoe, blue or otherwise, was conspicuous by its absence.

As numbers inexorably grew, so the welfare of the staff became an increasingly systematic concern. The older partners set the tone and maintained the firm's strongly paternalist traditions. Thus at Christmas the messengers would be taken by Geoffrey Akroyd to the Victoria Palace for a party, where much beer was consumed, while Philip Cazenove would give his dealers on the country-broking side dinner at the Royal Aero Club followed by a show. Hornby himself kept a good personal contact with many of the staff, concerning himself with their difficulties or problems; while Godfrey Chandler emerged as the partner who maintained a continuous overview on staff matters. Chandler executed this task with great efficiency but also sympathy, and it was largely due to him that the post-war arrangements concerning pensions, bonuses and suchlike were further built upon and consolidated. The staff knew that he on behalf of the rest of the partnership would look after their interests, and this confidence was a crucial element in the overall harmonious atmosphere. Loyalty and respect were not key words of the 1960s, but as with things sartorial a notable exception to the rule was to be found at Tokenhouse Yard.

As ever, one needs to understand and appreciate the underlying ethos. Most members of staff were more or less left alone to get on with their work, provided they did it properly, and took pride in being part of a set-up that was recognised as the leader in its field. The organisation was small enough for them to feel that their own contribution counted and also to feel a sense of what was going on, even if they did not see some of the partners very often. The firm remained a fairly tight-knit community; almost everyone still knew almost everyone else; and there was very little demarcation or a 'that's not my job' attitude. Above all, despite inevitable periods of boredom and drudgery, it was a place where most people, at whatever level, enjoyed working. Thus when John Kemp-Welch came to the firm in 1959 from Hoare & Co, he received an encouraging letter of welcome from one of the younger partners: 'I have always enjoyed my short time here and the atmosphere, at times electric, is normally the best of fun.' Or when Anthony Forbes, another future senior partner, was doing a temporary job at Cazenove's at about the same time, the thing that made him decide to stay was the pleasure of working in the inscribed department alongside Phil Baker, a former Greenwoods man who through his cheeriness, wit and unrivalled story-telling ability was for over thirty years the life and soul of

Cazenove's. Hornby never forgot that work is pointless unless one also enjoys it and it was one of his great legacies that he passed this belief on to another generation.

All the time a fundamental principle of the partnership remained intact. As Hornby explained in his memoirs in the early 1970s:

> The continuity of the firm has been ensured by valuing the good will of a partnership at nothing. When a partner retires he withdraws his capital which is replaced by existing or incoming partners. He is a tenant with full partnership rights but has no saleable asset. This is in contrast to Lloyd's brokerage firms where a particular set of partners can sell, say, 50 per cent of the business to their own advantage but to the detriment of future generations of partners.

Traditionally, however, a problem existed in stockbroking firms that capital could be a more valuable asset to bring to a partnership than ability alone. Frank Holt in particular was determined to do something about this as far as Cazenove's was concerned, and during the 1950s he devised a scheme by which an incoming partner could be lent his share of capital. By the 1960s the scheme was working well and not only helped to ensure that no one would become a partner simply on the basis of wealth, but also encouraged the emergence of merit from within the ranks. It was an important step in the firm's modern evolution.

Within the partnership itself, Geoffrey Akroyd retired in 1962 and was succeeded on paper as senior partner by Holt. He had become a partner a year before Hornby; but it was Hornby who remained effective and undisputed senior partner. Philip Cazenove, after the best part of three decades servicing country brokers and indirectly bringing much new issue business to the firm, retired in 1963. Four new partners were made during the first half of the 1960s, beginning in 1961 with John Kemp-Welch and Rae Lyster. Lyster had come to the firm in 1955 as a result of his father's friendship with Holt and was establishing a considerable reputation on the nuts and bolts side of new issues. Kemp-Welch's speciality was day-to-day institutional broking, like his father developing a particular emphasis on the Scottish investors, in his case the fruit of early training in Scotland while with Hoare's. They were followed in 1964 by Tony Bedford and Stephen Carden, the former of whom had similarly inherited paternal selling skills, though in his case with greater emphasis on 'attack'. As for Carden, he had been recruited by Peter Kemp-Welch and come up on the Australian side under Schreiber. Among these new partners, it was a striking fact that Lyster was only the fiftieth person to enter the partnership in the entire history of the firm. A stately half century thus completed, the scoring rate would soon quicken.

The event that really affected the balance of the partnership, however, was the death of Peter Kemp-Welch in 1964, at the relatively early age of fifty-six. It was a great blow to Hornby and for several years no one sat opposite him at his desk. What it also meant was that it created a certain void at the very top of the firm, in effect the absence of someone of Kemp-Welch's stature to act as a counterweight to Hornby. It was a void that during the rest of the decade no other partner was able wholly to fill. Holt and Meinertzhagen continued on essentially parallel lines to Hornby in their respective new issue spheres; Barnett lacked the push to be a truly central player; Bedford was much respected by Hornby, but for all his wisdom and experience was not on the whole someone with whom to discuss broad strategy; Schreiber was a strong locum during holiday periods, but again was not really central; and Chandler, although increasingly perceived as the 'wise man' of the firm, was of a younger generation and had only fairly recently become a partner. The partner who came nearest to filling that void was Sir Herbert Ingram (who had succeeded to the baronetcy in 1958). By the early 1960s he had gravitated towards the new issue side and was showing a great aptitude as well as appetite for the work. There is no doubt that Hornby much admired him, particularly for his ability to grasp with speed and precision the most complicated of documents or situations; and it would be fair to say that by the mid-1960s Ingram had emerged as Hornby's natural successor as senior partner. Nevertheless, there was never quite the same rapport between the two men as there had been between Hornby and Kemp-Welch. Hornby as leading partner was always the autocrat, but in the old days he had had someone with whom he could talk on intimate terms, as between equals. Now he was much more on his own.

Antony Hornby received a knighthood in the New Year's Honours List of 1960, a gratifying moment for the firm as well as the individual. Later that year he drew up for internal purposes a memorandum that in effect was an attempt to chart what he saw as the abiding criteria by which the overall conduct of the firm should be governed during the rest of the decade. A highly characteristic document, it deserves to be quoted *in toto*:

Cazenove's have been having a successful run of business and it seems worthwhile trying to discover why. It may be a combination of the following:

1) Reliability. Secrets are safe. We do not make use of confidential information for our own ends.

2) We all work hard and full time. We know our job and most of the answers!

3) We are known not to be gamblers in private or business life.

4)   We are not unduly mercenary. Obviously one wants to make money, but we are not greedy. The amount of money to be made out of a business is not the reason for doing it.

5)   We have a reputation for being pleasant colleagues. We are considerate to smaller firms when we are working with them. We are fair and co-operative with jobbers.

6)   We keep calm when conditions for doing a business are difficult. Issuing Houses do not want long faces. We are brave without being foolhardy. We will always play our part in seeing something through when there is an initial failure.

7)   We are a happy firm at all levels and enjoy our business life and show it. We are serious but not too desperately serious.

8)   The firm is run as a benevolent autocracy, but is at the same time essentially democratic.

N.B.

a)   We must now not be afraid of saying 'No' if we are not particularly keen on a business or a client. It is not a bad thing to be rather hard to get.

b)   We must be careful to have in the partnership people who fit and who think the same way as us, and whom we are really fond of.

c)   We must never stop trying to be more efficient.

Hornby knew how far the firm had come during his own working lifetime – it is in many ways a remarkably confident, almost arrogant series of assertions – but like Kemp-Welch in the late 1940s was every bit as aware that there is nothing easier to lose than a high reputation. He now saw it as his task in his final years not just to protect that reputation, but positively to enhance it.

Hornby's memorandum was written in July 1960, soon after the end of a stirring phase in the history of the stock market. The 30–Share Index had risen from 154 in February 1958 to 342 by the beginning of 1960 – a rise made all the more impressive by the fact that during that period inflation was virtually nil. Over the next three years the equity market held its own, despite some marked if brief fluctuations, before beginning another upwards ascent (though less steep than that of the late 1950s) in response to Chancellor Maudling's expansionary policies. October 1964 saw the election of a Labour government, prompting an initial nervousness on the part of investors, but by the spring of 1966 there was a widespread feeling that there was little to fear from a further term of Harold Wilson. 'We do not regard the return of a Labour Government, with a reasonable majority, with any misgiving,' declared the *FT* on the day of the general election in

March that year; and over the next few months, with Labour handsomely re-elected, the equity market continued to rise. It seemed a long time since those dog days of 1945.

Moving into the 1960s the new issue emphasis was as strong as ever, perhaps even stronger. Taking the year 1961, Cazenove's was associated with the phenomenal total of 171 issues, in other words an average of well over three a week. It was a total over twice as many as that of Hoare & Co (81), who were followed by Rowe, Swann & Co (73), Rowe & Pitman and Joseph Sebag & Co (71 each), W. Greenwell & Co (41), Panmure Gordon (37), Laing & Cruickshank (34) and de Zoete & Gorton (30). However, the usual warning that totals are not everything is reinforced by the fact that of the four major issues that year – ICI, Distillers, Midland Bank and Royal Insurance – Cazenove's was on the ticket for precisely none. Rather, the emphasis still remained on as broad a spread as possible of the good medium-sized companies, preferably with potential for growth. Four years later, for the year 1965, the firm's total of new issues was still comfortably ahead of all Stock Exchange rivals, though there had been an interesting shift in the order below. The figures were: Cazenove's (176), Joseph Sebag & Co (109), J & A Scrimgeour (63, mostly local authorities), Rowe & Pitman (61), Rowe, Swann & Co (50), Panmure Gordon (48) and Hoare & Co (42). Sebags was becoming a major force as a new issue broker, though already was showing the lack of selectivity that was to be its undoing.

It was an extremely powerful new issue team that Cazenove's fielded during the 1960s, despite the sad fading from the scene of Peter Kemp-Welch. In particular, though Frank Holt remained a significant presence for several years, three partners now emerged under Hornby's benevolent, experienced auspices as highly capable practitioners of what was an increasingly demanding craft. Luke Meinertzhagen had been operating in the new issue sphere since soon after the war, gradually taking over from Albert Martin on the technical side; but it was in the 1960s that he established a City-wide reputation for his broader new issue skills, above all his shrewd instincts in relation to pricing. In addition to his responsibility for Lazards, he started to get particularly close to Rothschilds, closer perhaps than any Cazenove partner had been for over a century. The second partner was Godfrey Chandler, who became ever more valued, outside as well as inside Tokenhouse Yard, for the breadth of his knowledge as well as his perspicacity of judgement and quality of original thought. As one merchant banker put it, if Chandler came to a meeting it was the equivalent of having an eminent lawyer, a top-class accountant and a stockbroker all rolled into one.

Thirdly, and most importantly, there was Herbert Ingram, *the* rising star.

Quick-witted and excellent, often amusing company, though undeniably impatient and always wanting to be right (all qualities that came to the fore on the golf course), he possessed a thorough understanding of the market, allied to a natural flair for it, that gave immense authority to his work, especially in the realm of pricing. He also had a good feel for industry and industrialists, derived partly from his family's light engineering business, of which he was chairman. Thus by the 1960s it was increasingly Ingram who did the detailed business with Barings, Morgan Grenfell and Schroders, as well as establishing a close relationship with Frank Smith of Warburgs. He much preferred the telephone to the pen, worked strictly office hours, and was generally crisp in his approach, epitomised by his insistence that potential sub-underwriters must always expect him to mark them as 'Yes' if no reply was received by 3 pm on underwriting day. At least one senior investment manager, meaning to refuse, found himself being flatly overruled a few minutes after the appointed time. Ingram was also creative. Often in conjunction with Chandler he devised many schemes, of which the most important was a new method of placing debentures that met with the approval of the Stock Exchange Council and became common practice. This was the two-tranche system, which involved a 'right of recall' from the institutions if there was sufficient demand from the jobbers and effectively countered a rising groundswell of opinion that not enough stock was publicly available through traditional placings. It was an irrational criticism, granted that debentures were 98 per cent an institutional market anyway; but it is likely that without this innovation placings would have been banned. And in general it was largely through the unrivalled knowledge of Ingram and Chandler, supported by the institutions, that Cazenove's in the 1960s remained 'kings' of the debenture market.

Harnessing all these skills, and sometimes executing the resulting schemes, was Hornby himself. Although by no means involved in all new issues, he retained to a remarkable degree his enthusiasm for the work despite his many and proliferating outside interests, as well as of course his responsibilities as senior partner. Or as he accurately put it, with a nicely understated final phrase: 'Herbert and Luke and Godfrey were bearing most of the brunt of the issue work. I used to be consulted in the first place by Barings or whatever house was issuing and I took one of them along with me and everything got done.'

As usual, among the dense array of corporate activity a handful of episodes or moments stand out for particular reasons. For instance, in 1959 Bird & Co (Africa) took over Consolidated Sisal Estates. It was an agreed bid, and acting for both companies was Arbuthnot Latham as merchant bankers and Cazenove's as brokers – a situation incomprehensible to a latter-day age preoccupied by questions of 'conflict of interest'. The following year there took place one of the many brewery mergers of the period. This was between Joshua Tetley of Leeds and Walker Cain of Warrington. The key initiating figure (despite his illness) was Peter Kemp-Welch, who enjoyed a particularly warm friendship with Nicholas Herald, the finance director at Tetley. Also brought in to advise was Schroders, which at about this time was entering into merger arrangements with Helbert Wagg. For this intimate purpose, the two houses employed Cazenove's as brokers. Indeed, when Schroders was preparing to arrange a rights issue for the engineering company Wolseley-Hughes and deciding which broker to use, Henry Tiarks in a letter to the chairman described Cazenove's as 'really our closest broking friends' in the City; and the services of the firm were duly enlisted.

However, for an entertaining set-piece, though less diverting at the time, one has to turn to the offer for sale in June 1960 of just under two million ordinary shares of British Belting and Asbestos Ltd. The offer was made by ICFC (the Industrial and Commercial Finance Corporation, now called 3i), and the story is told by John Kinross, one of the Corporation's key figures, in his excellent memoirs, *Fifty Years in the City*:

We had been associated with this fine Yorkshire company for several years and I had established a close relationship with Sir William Fenton, the Executive Chairman. This was obviously going to be one of the best new industrial issues of the year and I had asked Cazenove's to act as brokers. At the final meeting at Drapers Gardens when it came to the price fixing, I asked Luke Meinertzhagen if he was content with 17s 6d, which we had virtually settled upon. He said that he was and to my surprise added that he was confident Cazenove's could underwrite the issue at 18s. After a slightly awkward few moments, the price was fixed at 18s for I felt that I could not ask Fenton to give away 6d a share, which represented £48,000.

By late Wednesday afternoon, the 29 June, it appeared that the issue was not going to be fully subscribed and Bill [Lord Piercy, chairman of ICFC] and I agreed that if the gap were to be only a small one, we could put in applications to cover it rather than call upon underwriters for a tiny percentage of their commitments.

At 10.30 am the next morning (Thursday) the Midland gave us a figure which left only a narrow gap. I authorised applications from us to cover this and agreed a press announcement for the mid-day editions which stated that the issue had been marginally over-subscribed. Then at 1.35 pm the Manager of the New Issue Department of the Midland telephoned me to say that they had just discovered that their 10.30 am total had been overstated by 180,000 shares.

It was a devastating admission. Bill was lunching in the City and I sent him a handwritten note telling him that the shortage was then 111,200 shares – or about £100,000. I asked for his agreement to our doing another £50,000 to £60,000 adding, 'Obviously there can now be no turning back.' When the messenger returned Bill had written on my note, 'Yes – agree absolutely'. Luke pulled out all the stops and before long an active market at a small premium enabled all the surplus shares to be sold. This was a one-off situation which luckily had a happy ending, but it could have been very different.

Meinertzhagen's offer of the extra sixpence was an uncharacteristic error, though one that took place in the relaxed atmosphere of this being the last ICFC issue of which Kinross was taking personal charge, and was perhaps somewhat in the nature of a 'leaving present'. The gesture backfired, but he was suitably contrite and, as Kinross says, did indeed pull out all the stops, managing to clear up the whole thing within a fortnight.

Otherwise one is left with lists, dull but unavoidable granted the nature of the business. As usual by this time, there was never a year in which Cazenove's did not act in new issues and other capital deals for a range of notable companies. Thus for instance in 1961: Liberty & Co, Elliott-Automation Ltd (early computer manufacturers), Birmingham Small Arms Co, Penguin Books Ltd (in Hornby's words, 'a romance of a company'), Twining Crosfield & Co (tea and coffee merchants), J. Gliksten & Son (timber merchants), Doulton & Co, John Waddington Ltd, Booker Brothers, McConnell & Co, and Geo G. Sandeman Sons & Co and James Robertson & Sons (of 'silhouette' and 'golliwog' fame respectively). In fact, all human endeavour seemed to be represented. 1964 was no different: Bowyers, C. T. Bowring, Higgs and Hill, Watney Mann, Thomson Organisation, Jaeger, Linguaphone, Ranks Hovis McDougall, J. Hepworth – just nine names among many. The knack was never to forget that each issue was different, requiring individual attention; that in other words company stockbroking must not be allowed to turn into something akin to the proverbial sausage factory. It was the great achievement of Hornby and his colleagues in the quarter of a century after the war to attain the width while always minding the quality.

Moving on to the day-to-day broking, there survives a memorandum that Hornby sent in February 1961 to Charles ('Dick') Troughton, the director at W. H. Smith to whom he was answerable for the managing of the company's pension fund, so near of course to Hornby's heart. The memorandum is worth quoting in full not only because of the specific light it sheds on Hornby and his investment philosophy, but also for the way it implicitly conveys so much of the Cazenove tone and ethos, those most elusive but also critical of qualities:

> I was often called upon in the United States to 'say a few words' after lunch and I have just looked up one of those speeches and quote it here:
>
> 'One last thought I would like to leave with you, and that is "Not too much investment analysis." The analyst's role is necessary and important, but I am convinced that there is duplication of effort and that reports are too lengthy for most of us to have time to read them. Let the analyst, say I, distil his thoughts and knowledge and produce a very strong potion of a page or two. Then, if I may mix a metaphor, let the potion be cross fertilised by the seed of experience; finally, add a good pinch of flair or hunch and then, I claim, a really good investment suggestion should be born.'
>
> In other words, there is more to it than figures, past profits, and projection of future profits. It is an enormous help to know the personalities involved, to become intimate with the flavour of a business and to be able to feel a sense of urgency and enterprise in the management. One wants to find a feeling of enthusiastic enjoyment as against grim endeavour.
>
> I eschew rules as much as you do and regard flexibility of mind as essential. One tries not to let advancing age make one rigid or obstinate, but one is bound to collect a few hobby horses in the stable.
>
> Whilst disliking rules I have my maxims, and these I will qualify:
>
> 1. Banish prejudice –
>   (a) One must try not to have a sentimental attachment to a stock and refuse to part with it.
>   (b) One mustn't say 'I don't like holiday camps, Jews, participating preference, etc.'.
> 2. Recognise the human element, both in the company one is investing in and the clients that one is investing for.
> 3. Don't be afraid of speculation. All investment in equities has an element of speculation, and a good speculation becomes a far sighted investment. But one must never buy blind or listen to a tip unsupported by reason. One must assess the chances on all the available knowledge and then use one's hunch and be brave.
> 4. Don't look too often at an investment list, but when doing so it ought to be possible to make one addition and one elimination, and thus there is always a tendency towards improvement.

5.   Equities should not be bought for yield but for growth. Yield will follow naturally. Dated gilt edged and debentures provide the necessary yield in the waiting period.

6.   Don't worry unduly about timing, though realise it is important. Sometimes one just doesn't feel like buying, but if an investment idea occurs when the economic climate is unfavourable don't put off a purchase, otherwise the idea may get shelved and forgotten, and good ideas are rare.

7.   Don't worry; don't be impatient; don't press; don't panic; don't fidget. Enjoy the whole fascinating affair.

8.   Whilst investment decisions must be made with the sole consideration of benefiting a fund, it is a great satisfaction when it is compatible with this to invest constructively and with vision; to play one's part in helping the country and the world.

9.   Be alive and have your antennae out. The more things you are interested in the better – politics, films, travel, anything you like. They keep you in touch; an active member of society; and all one's interests have their application to investment.

Such remained the general investment approach under Hornby and indeed beyond. As the memorandum clearly reveals, it was an approach based ultimately on a whole cast of mind, to which the question of the incompatibility of a company orientation and a research orientation was in a sense merely a technical, almost justifying annex. A little learning was not necessarily a dangerous thing, but too much probably was, certainly if unleavened by personal experience and judgement.

The gilts side continued to stagnate during the 1960s, especially as much of Cedric Barnett's time was taken up by his work on the Stock Exchange Council. In general, though, this was a highly beneficial development: considering the firm's importance, Cazenove's had been too long unrepresented on the Council; while there is no doubt that his membership of that body from 1963 brought out the very best in Barnett, who was widely valued there for his great conscientiousness as well as knowledge of the market and judicious, independent outlook. The money-broking side also remained relatively quiet. But it was still a useful earner, especially as lending money to local authorities now became quite a big business. As for the private client side, there continued to be an increasingly systematic approach in terms of the management of portfolios. New issue business often brought the firm valuable, unlooked-for spin-offs in this area, as with Sir Allen Lane after the successful Penguin flotation. Meanwhile, Peter Kemp-Welch (until his death), David Wills (though not a member of the firm) and Johnny

Henderson pursued their bold investment paths, including from about this time on behalf of the Malton Trust, which had originally been managed from Newcastle but in which in 1959 they acquired a controlling interest. The 'inner circle' of Cazenove clients, including some very wealthy families, benefited greatly from their activities, which never failed to astonish rather more staid colleagues.

But it was in terms of the day-to-day institutional broking that the most significant advances were coming. It was important that this was so, for the pattern of overall ordinary share ownership was continuing to change. By 1963 personal holdings (as measured by market value) had declined to 51 per cent, compared to 61.8 per cent in 1957; while those of banks and nominee companies were up to 20 per cent, insurance companies up to 9 per cent, investment trusts up to 3.2 per cent and pension funds up to 2.9 per cent. The individual institutional figures were not yet startling, but the trend was clear.

Behind these figures there stood out a number of individual institutional investors and investment managers – outstanding figures who deserve to be remembered for their part in the whole post-war investment scene. Standing on a pedestal of his own was Lewis Whyte, from 1953 chairman of the investment committee of the London and Manchester and from 1961 chairman of the company itself. Quite apart from his early appreciation of the potential of equities he was renowned for his ability to 'pick' undervalued investment trusts; he moved easily in many fields; and his two-volume textbook, *The Principles of Finance and Investment*, was already an unrivalled classic on the subject. Another commanding presence in the insurance world was Francis Jamieson of the Standard Life, on whose behalf he epitomised the ability that many Scottish investment managers had to take the longer view, a quality especially valuable to Cazenove's. But of course the absolutely dominant force in institutional investment at this time was the Prudential, where in the 1950s Alan Ray – high-principled, calm, sensible, much respected – seemed to encapsulate that institution's very best qualities. Insurance companies, however, were not the only institutional investors. Among the investment trusts there was no more effective pair than Freddy Grant and Teddy Butler-Henderson at Hendersons: the one practical and of a broad approach, the other more mercurial and often inspired, together making a superb team for many years. Another leading investor, this time for a merchant bank that had a particularly strong investment arm, was Michael Verey of Helbert Wagg before it merged with Schroders: crisp, incisive and always prepared to take a view, he remains a memorable, much-relished character. Finally, from this necessarily selective list, there was Jack Butterworth, investment manager from the 1940s of

BP's pension fund, a rule to himself and an almost legendary figure. He employed only three or four brokers, one of whom was Cazenove's; he was much more active than most pension fund managers and often took big views, above all in the brewery market; and he had little time for in-house research, preferring to get his feel for the market direct from Charles Purnell and particularly Durlachers the jobbers, usually over drinks in the Angel Court Club. A maverick who had real power, Butterworth was part of that 'inner' history of the old City which with the passing of the years becomes ever more difficult to retrieve.

But if these were some of the leading investors in the City at large, it would be wrong in a history of Cazenove's not also to mention, albeit briefly, some of the institutions which over the years regularly provided the firm with much of its daily commission business in the secondary market. Again, any such list is somewhat arbitrary and perhaps invidious, but three insurance companies that undoubtedly fell into this category were Legal and General, Royal, and Standard Life; while within the investment trust movement, notably steady and consistent clients included London Trust (where Lionel Rolfe was a good friend to Cazenove's for many years), River Plate & General, River & Mercantile, Mercantile Investment Trust and of course Hendersons. Also very loyal was Brander & Cruickshank, the Aberdeen-based managers of investment trusts. As for the investment departments of the merchant banks, two perhaps stood out by the 1960s from the point of view of Cazenove's: those of Barings and Warburgs, the latter starting to build up its pension fund business and become a major force. The pension funds themselves were led by BP, producing for the firm a substantially bigger commission 'take' than any other institution, while W. H. Smith stoutly and gratifyingly continued to do business solely through Cazenove's. Finally, in a category of its own, there was the Kuwait Investment Office, the fruit of that country's perception in the mid-1950s that the oil would eventually run out and that it was sensible therefore to build up an international portfolio for the future. During the 1960s and beyond the K.I.O. brought the firm consistent and valuable business across almost the whole of the broking spectrum.

Meanwhile, at the Tokenhouse Yard end of all this, 'Beddy' continued in the 1960s to play an important part in the everyday institutional business; but by now he was joined not only by his son but also by Johnny Henderson, David Wentworth-Stanley and John Kemp-Welch. Together they made a highly effective team that responded well to the increased importance of the institutions. All the time, of course, there were the firm's dealers on the floor of the House, executing the actual business. Charles Purnell led the team as a whole and imbued it with his own distinctive approach to the art of dealing, while Angus Eames in the 'box' was, in Hornby's phrase, 'a tower of strength' co-ordinating its efforts. The dealing team included Max Gilford, who had taken over the foreign bonds from McNaught, and Gerry Smith, who had taken over the country business from his father Micky; while Purnell himself continued, as at least one jobber has recalled, to dispense his orders with regal magnanimity. And again to quote Hornby: 'The Box had a great esprit de corps and was a happy place.'

If such roughly was the domestic scene in the first half of the 1960s, what about abroad? As the venue for Hornby's postprandial investment observations would suggest, much of the firm's international attentions were focused towards the United States, where Belmont was consolidating and extending his pioneering work of the late 1950s. An almost father-son relationship existed between the two, and in 1971 Hornby paid just tribute to the Cazenove partner of whom it was said (only half in jest) that he once made a mistake and dealt with a vice-president:

Michael grasped his opportunity with both hands, clicked with the Americans and today has been described to me as the best-known British Banker in the States. For a young man his achievement was remarkable. He got to know the people who mattered all over the country and on my later visits to the States I was to realise this when red carpets got laid down for me everywhere. I then used to go as an Ambassador and Michael translated it all into business. He arranged that investment managers from our insurance and investment trust companies would have a good time when they visited California and Texas; he got into intimate touch with local companies and became known as an authority in London. Our American business is now important . . .

Nevertheless, through most of the 1960s certain fundamental problems confronted the firm's American side, where in the early part of the decade Belmont received important assistance from Alex Coombe-Tennant, who always had great faith in the American economy. These problems may be briefly summarised: the introduction in 1963 of the notorious Interest Equalisation Tax for a long time severely restricted Americans from investing abroad; while on this side of the Atlantic, not only was there the continuing disincentive of the dollar premium, but there was also the inconvenient fact that a British broker had to charge his clients two commissions when dealing in US stocks, in other words one for himself and the other for the American broker who actually executed the order, since the Americans did not allow sharing of commission with overseas dealers. Moreover, many English institutional fund managers (unlike their Scottish counterparts) still felt an innate reluctance to own many American shares, beyond such obvious counters as IBM and General Motors. Belmont and his colleagues would come back from the States full of genuinely exciting buying opportunities, often having been to parts of the country where few if any British brokers had ventured before, but it could be an uphill battle selling them in the square mile and elsewhere. However, no one doubted the correctness of the strategy, even if it was – as indeed with the international business as a whole – essentially a long-term one.

But if there was a single international buzz-word in the early 1960s, it was undoubtedly 'Europe', with the British government actively (if for the time being unsuccessfully) negotiating for belated entry into the Common Market. There was already at least one European investment trust in existence – the New European and General started by M. Samuel – before Schroders and Waggs (about to merge) began in 1962 to set about forming another one, in collaboration with three continental banks, including the Deutsche Bank. The idea was that it would combine the character and status of a British investment trust with continental-based supervision of the portfolio, and in March the directors of Schroders and Waggs met to review progress:

> W.L.F. [i.e. Lionel Fraser] reported that he had spoken to Panmure Gordon about the launching of this Trust and, in view of the fact that it might prove difficult going [granted the oscillating state of the markets], he had suggested to them that it might be wise to invite Cazenove's to assist. They had readily agreed to this, as a result of which, W.L.F. had approached Sir Antony Hornby who had shown considerable enthusiasm for the project.

Following the 'Aluminium War', Hornby had quickly mended his fences with Fraser, as indeed he had with Siegmund Warburg; and in the event, he now accepted an invitation to become the third English director on the board of the Trans Europe Investment Trust. An offer for sale was made in June 1962, with Panmure Gordon and Cazenove's sharing broking duties, and received a warm welcome from the popular as well as the quality press. 'Until now investing in the Common Market has been a bit dodgy,' asserted the *News of the World*. The London equity market, however, was in the middle of a sharp fall, the continental markets were generally uneasy, and as a result the Trust fell a million short of its target of £6 million. 'We did encounter extremely adverse conditions for an issue of this sort, and private investors just "sat on their hands",' explained Fraser to the European directors, but added: 'All the same we feel that the result cannot be considered as anything other than creditable in the circumstances.' And Hornby was undismayed, writing to Charles Villiers of Schroder Wagg to thank him for the broking fee: 'It was great fun doing the job, and I shall enjoy helping this healthy baby to grow up into a strong young man.'

Cazenove's was also involved at a relatively early stage in the new Eurobond market being pioneered by Warburg. This enabled London issuing houses, acting on behalf of usually high-class companies or governments, to raise medium or long-term loans denominated in foreign currency, mainly US dollars. Although issued in London and granted a London Stock Exchange quotation, the bulk of the loans tended to be subscribed for on the Continent. It was an ingenious form of finance, which owed much to the reluctance of the United States to create a dollar empire comparable to Britain's sterling empire, and over the years played a crucial part in ensuring the international primacy of the City of London. Cazenove's in the 1960s was by no means the leading London broker in the field in these burgeoning Euromarkets – compared to the dominant Strauss Turnbull – but it was ahead of almost everyone else. In March 1964 it helped Lazards to place a $10 million loan for the Tysselfaldene Hydro-Electric Power Co; and then in June 1965 there was a £10 million placing with Warburgs for Mobil Oil Holdings, comprising $5\frac{3}{4}$% Sterling/Deutsche Mark Guaranteed Bonds. Continuing at this time to run the European side was Coombe-Tennant, who already had excellent Scandinavian connections and was constantly on the look-out for new opportunities. Helping him from 1962 was a highly capable young Swiss called Thomas Schoch, who over the years would gradually increase the firm's role in Euromarket operations: starting as part of the selling group, then moving into the underwriting, and eventually (long after the 1960s) becoming not just co-manager but on occasion even co-lead manager. The world of 'tombstones' would always be something of a mysterious world apart, not only at Tokenhouse Yard, and Cazenove's was fortunate in finding in Schoch just the right man.

Elsewhere in the world, the Australian business was building up quite well under Schreiber and Carden, mostly with Australian brokers. At the London end a useful exercise, earning the firm much goodwill, occurred in February 1965 when, on behalf of a consortium of merchant banks headed by Guinness Mahon, the firm acted jointly with Kitcat & Aitken and Rowe & Pitman in an £8 million debenture issue (with a built-in equity element) whose purpose was to enable the completion of a large building project in Sydney City Centre to be known as Australia Square. At the outset there had been considerable City scepticism, in the context of the Australian money having run out; but at the crucial meeting Hornby, to whom the unusual equity element appealed, suddenly got the wind in his sails and carried the consortium of banks with him. In the event it did prove a hard issue to sell, but it was one well worth doing, and Australia Square was an outstanding building of which the firm was later a tenant.

However, if Australia was a continuing project, altogether unfamiliar territory was Japan – so much so that in May 1960, when the president and managing director of Nomura Securities were visiting London, they received from Schroders (already well established in the Japanese market) an introduction to Cazenove's. The firm was not alone: apart from Vickers da Costa, hardly any London stockbroker then knew anything about Japan. The Cazenove partner who first saw something of the possibilities was probably Belmont in the early 1960s, following advice from Al Gordon, who had appreciated more quickly than most that a great psychological barrier to the flow of financial business no longer existed now that jets had begun to fly to Tokyo. Belmont first went there in 1963; and the following year Cazenove's helped Hambros to undertake for the Taisho Marine and Fire Insurance Co a successful placing of 2 million Deposited Units (each comprising 10 ordinary shares of Yen 50 each) at 17s 6d or $2.20 per unit, as well as securing a London quotation. The firm received the handsome fee of £12,000 for its services. These were early days, and few could have anticipated the incredible Japanese economic success story that lay ahead, but for Cazenove's it was an auspicious beginning in a new part of the world.

Senior partner from 1st May 1966 on paper as well as in practice, Hornby continued vigorously to pursue his international initiative during his last few years with the firm. It was an initiative markedly in tune with the changing circumstances of the time: finance in particular, and the corporate world at large, was becoming ever more international during the second half of the 1960s, a development well reflected by the *FT*'s decision at this time to start systematic coverage of international company news; while a crucial implication of devaluation in 1967 was to reduce the importance of the sterling area – making the non-British world as a whole a more level playing field – and in a sense thereby to push the City back towards its truly international pre-1914 role. Exchange controls of course remained, but a certain fundamental trend was becoming clear. Cazenove's under Hornby responded positively to the international theme, making a conscious decision during the decade to diversify its clients' portfolios and include in them some 25% of foreign stocks, believing that a 20 or even 30% dollar premium was a price well worth paying for getting into growth areas overseas like the computer industry that were unavailable in the generally rather disappointing (and heavily nationalised) domestic economy. Organisationally, the international side was made more cohesive, involving completely integrated settlement, with the foreign department also beginning to employ its own statisticians and experts in currency and foreign tax matters. The overall approach was still very pragmatic, even cautious, but it was nevertheless symptomatic that the foreign side in this period seems to have been able to employ much of the 'cream' of the available talent, a sure indication of the high priority that Hornby gave to its activities.

It was in this broad context that there took place in the autumn of 1967 an event of signal importance in the firm's history. The *New York Times*, in a piece headed 'British Broker Keen on Golden West', told the story:

> Cazenove & Co has strengthened its California ties by buying a seat on the Pacific Coast Stock Exchange in San Francisco for $50,000. In so doing, the London firm has become the first European member of any United States exchange.
>
> The move has caused a flutter in the London financial community, requiring changed regulations and approval by the London Stock Exchange and the Bank of England. But the precedent has been established.
>
> 'It will be simpler for the next chap,' said Sir Antony Hornby, Cazenove's 63–year-old senior partner. 'I think there are quite a few firms that will now be interested in America.'
>
> Any rush is likely to be slowed, however, by the New York Stock Exchange's prohibition of foreign memberships and by the necessity for substantial United States business to cover the cost of membership on regional exchanges. United States purchases are also deterred by Britain's foreign exchange controls.
>
> The San Francisco office, to be known as Cazenove Inc., will have an American seat holder but no salesmen and no floor trader. Orders for United States securities will still be originated in London and will be executed on the Pacific Coast by another member firm.
>
> The Pacific exchange permits a 50–50 commission split between member firms, and Cazenove will thus receive its first compensation (other than reciprocal business) for United States orders it channels through United States brokers. The New York exchange forbids split commissions as well as foreign members.

The San Francisco office opened in January 1968. The *New York Times* article correctly identified the immediate motive for membership of the Pacific exchange – namely, the commission aspect – but this pioneering move also served to cement still further the firm's connections in California, which were continuing to grow at a phenomenal rate. As Hornby correctly predicted, other London firms soon followed the Cazenove example: Rowe & Pitman and Joseph Sebag & Co both bought seats on the Pacific Coast, while James Capel & Co purchased one on the Midwest exchange in Chicago. For Cazenove's it was a very exciting time, requiring meticulous preparation. Hornby a few years later recalled the hectic social activity that accompanied membership and also the opening of a first office abroad:

> Several partners went out to San Francisco and I had to make many speeches. We gave a dinner dance at the Fairmont for 120 people from all over the States – some flew in from New York and Texas for it. We did it slap up – as Cazenove's would – and it was a fabulous party. We had told the hotel we should want the band until 1 am and were told this was quite unnecessary as there would be no one left at the party by midnight: brokers always went home early as they had to get up at six o'clock for the opening of the New York market. They were wrong. At one o'clock the party was in full swing and didn't finish until much later.

It was indeed a great occasion, its smooth running a credit to Ian Pilkington and his wife, further helped by the energy and unflappable efforts of Cedric Barnett's wife Sylvia.

The American business itself during the second half of the 1960s continued to do well. If Al Gordon had been *the* American friend during the 1950s, there is no doubt that in the 1960s and indeed beyond he was joined by Hoyt Ammidon, chairman of the U.S. Trust and one of the best connected men in the country. When he decided to start an off-shore trust based in Luxembourg for Europeans to invest in America, thereby enabling them to avoid on-shore capital gains tax, he in conjunction with the issuing house Samuel Montagu not only appointed Cazenove's to be co-manager of the fund but also asked Hornby to be a director. The United States Trust Investment Fund was successfully launched in January 1967 and involved a prospectus drafted by Rae Lyster that was a pioneer of its kind, being for one of the first offshore funds to invest in overseas securities. More close involvement in establishing offshore funds to invest in American securities followed, including the Monterey Trust in 1967 and the Aldringer Trust in 1968.

However, the ultimately more significant development in this period was the way in which the firm's involvement in America gradually began to be broadened from an essentially broking function – above all, selling American securities to British institutions – to one that also embraced a more corporate, capital-raising nature on behalf of American companies. For instance, when the du Pont Foundation decided to sell all its General Motors shares, it was Cazenove's and Rowe & Pitman acting for Morgan Grenfell which was responsible for the European tranche, obtaining a

London quotation for General Motors and, in a fairly massive operation, launching on the rather dubious institutions British depository receipts covering one-twentieth of an American share. Or again, it was Cazenove's which in 1966 acted in effect as the London issuing house in an 'introduction' of shares for Schlumberger, a large company specialising in oil services and electronic equipment. In fact, one could say that history was starting to repeat itself, as in an American context the firm began to do what it had so successfully accomplished between the wars and thereafter in a largely domestic setting. But it should be emphasised that in relation to all American business, whether in the primary or secondary market, Cazenove's went to extraordinary pains (unlike some of its British counterparts) not to antagonise potential American rivals. Granted that capital was limited and 'global' ambitions not remotely envisaged, the firm knew full well how much it needed the continuing co-operation and goodwill of the American broking community; and this it deliberately cultivated across as broad a regional base as possible, in effect swopping commission business for investment ideas, usually of a local nature. The word 'niche' had not yet entered everyday financial jargon, but if it had it could fairly have been applied to Cazenove's and its American aspirations.

Meanwhile, the Euromarket business continued to grow in the late 1960s, with the partnership enjoying an especially beneficial relationship with Morgan Stanley, a powerful sponsoring house which appreciated the firm's excellent distribution system. In particular, Cazenove's began to do a considerable proportion of the available Euro-convertibles (which were often for American companies); though the firm featured less prominently on the straight bonds, finding it rather difficult to generate interest in them among the British institutions. At the same time, Coombe-Tennant and Schoch worked hard at developing business on the Continent, in both British and European shares, and the two of them spent long periods living on the road. As for Japan, John Baudrier was deputed, at Belmont's instigation, to monitor that enigmatic country and write reports about its companies. He quickly saw that – despite the conventional wisdom perceiving its lack of raw materials as a potential Achilles heel – it was manifestly going to become a major economic power. There was still much antipathy in the City towards the Japanese, certainly on the part of some of the fund managers, but Belmont and Baudrier between them, backed by Hornby, refused to be deterred.

In the course of 1969 three new overseas offices were opened to add to the one at San Francisco. They made a strikingly contrasting trio. One office was at Beirut, then the financial centre of the Middle East, and essentially represented an ill-conceived attempt to tap into that region's money. But at the time, sited in that great international landmark of the city, the Holiday Inn, it presumably seemed a good idea. The next new office had altogether more thought behind it and future ahead of it. This was in Sydney, following a steady increase in Australian securities through the decade (culminating in that country's mining boom) on the part of the firm's British clients. It was another 'first' for Cazenove's, no other foreign broker having previously established an office in Australia, and in many ways this was the prototype for the firm's subsequent overseas expansion. As consciously formulated at the time by Stephen Carden, with the blessing of Derek Schreiber, the move had three underlying objectives: to research and generally know about the local shares, and then to sell them around the world, mainly through London; to interest Australians in investing in shares outside their own market, again mainly via London; and to pursue corporate contacts, often international, for instance securing a London listing for an Australian company. Suitably adjusted to local conditions, these objectives would be the rationale for almost all the firm's future offices abroad. In Sydney itself, Australian rules prevented Cazenove's (as a foreign firm) from acquiring a seat on the stock exchange, and Carden made it clear that he was not seeking to compete with the local brokers, but intended more to use the office as a 'listening post' for London. As it happened, the third new office of 1969 was the exception to the overall strategy. This was in Bermuda and in essence was an office of tax convenience, not seeking in its own right to generate business. It acquired an almost mythological status among the London staff as the ideal posting, and indeed for a happy few this proved to be the case.

But for most it was life more or less as usual in the damp and cold of EC2. During the late 1960s there were two main 'domestic' developments. One was the decision, due to pressure of space, to rent the top floor of a new office building, Woolgate House, where Rowe & Pitman had some spare square footage available. Several departments, including jobbers and clients ledgers as well as dividends, moved there. The building was situated in Coleman Street and, although it was only four minutes' walk away, it did break up the 'family' feel of the firm. The other development was the introduction of computerisation, ahead of almost all other stockbroking firms. Under the direction of Cedric Barnett and Claude Carter, following an early initiative on the part of Frank Holt, this was skilfully accomplished, with Cazenove's sensibly doing it a department at a time rather than all at once. The coming of the computer revolutionised the system of settlement, though for many years the firm continued to keep a written record of transactions as well as a computer record. Indeed, even after the advent of that fabled monster, the discipline of the back office still remained inherently conservative and traditional. Quill pens and high sloping desks may not actually have been in evidence, but their spirit still lingered, so that in the ledger department, for instance, balances continued to be done by hand and no one could leave until it all balanced. Yet overall, things were changing in the 1960s, epitomised by the shift in focus from personal contact on the floor of the House to the more impersonal medium of the telephone in the office. Even by 1960 the partners at Cazenove's were able to see displayed on closed circuit television the four price boards in the dealing box; while, over the rest of the decade, the jobbing system itself continued its gradual but inexorable decline. It would be wrong to exaggerate this changing balance of power from floor to office – the 1970s and beyond were to be far more dramatic – but nonetheless the writing was on the wall for the time-honoured methods of the old Stock Exchange.

Another sign of continuing growth and change was that there were several new faces in the partnership, which from 1967 was legally allowed to go above a maximum of twenty. However, as Hornby wrote at the time to all existing partners, 'you see more of your partners than you do of your wife and you should therefore pick them as carefully'. Anthony Forbes (1967) was a grandson of Arnold Henderson and first made his mark in the loans department; while Ian Pilkington (1967), who came to the firm through Geoffrey Akroyd and married a Butler-Henderson, was an increasingly valuable assistant to Belmont on the American side, in effect combining (like almost everyone senior in the foreign department) the demanding functions of analyst *and* salesman, inevitably involving a great deal of travelling. Charles Henderson (1968), great-grandson of Lord Faringdon, was closèly involved with the institutions, especially the pension funds. Robin Holland-Martin (1968), introduced into the firm by Hornby 'as some slight return for his Uncle Gran Bromley-Martin's introduction of me to Claud', shared a desk with Rae Lyster and under his auspices likewise became an expert on the mechanics of new issues. Hugh Finch (1969) came straight into the private client investment side from the Army, having been suggested to Hornby by a client, and made his reputation there with his handling of the Allen Lane account. He now became partner in charge of the department. But perhaps the most interesting of these new partners was Peter Smith (1969). Having joined the firm in 1954, he worked for a long time in the back office before being plucked out by Belmont to work under de Bosdari on the Canadian side. Smith learnt much from him and then took over when de Bosdari left to join another firm in Canada. He was a real business-getter and, as Hornby put it in 1971, 'had a genius for the American market and was so successful that Michael persuaded me that we must make him a partner'.

During the late 1960s the London equity market enjoyed distinctly mixed fortunes. The Labour government's austerity measures of July 1966 caused a temporary dip; but there then ensued almost two years of a strong bull market (despite the renationalisation of steel in 1967), with the 30–Share Index hitting in September 1968 what was until the 1980s an all-time high point (in real terms) of 521.9. This boom was fuelled by the devaluation of sterling in November 1967, which, however ignominious in one sense, did mean that there would not have to be excessive interest rates in order to defend an untenable exchange rate. The reaction came in 1969, especially when the government backed down from trade union reform, and was sharpened in the spring of 1970 on fears that Labour would be returned to power in the impending general election. With share prices showing considerable volatility, and many asset-rich companies becoming vulnerable to takeover, these were years of generally heightened financial activity, one manifestation of which was an increasing awareness of the potential problems caused by price sensitive information. An interesting sidelight on this whole area is thrown by a letter in February 1967 from Philip Chappell of Morgan Grenfell to the head of public relations at Imperial Tobacco. Describing a new procedure 'ensuring that your announcements to the Stock Exchange are available to the jobbers in the market as soon as the information is public but without involving any risks of their having privileged information', he wrote:

> With your official envelope to the Stock Exchange (which I understand is collected from Berkeley Square by one of the Stock Exchange's own messengers) it is suggested that you enclose an extra dozen or twenty copies of the statement in a separate sealed envelope. This separate envelope would have attached a covering letter asking the Quotations Department to release the contents to a messenger from Cazenove's just as soon as the official statement has been put on the notice board and the results flashed on to the 'magic lantern.' Cazenove's could then distribute the extra copies to the jobbers (who would have been told in advance they could rely on this facility) and they could all have a proper sheet of information on which to base their quotations without having to rely on a blue-button's scrappy notes from the middle of a crowd round the notice board. Security is absolutely complete and Cazenove's have confirmed to me that the Stock Exchange would be very happy with this routine.

The question of early information had traditionally preoccupied the floor of the House – sometimes taking the form of deliberately-planted false rumours or scares – but by this time the stakes were higher and the public tolerance of any malpractice appreciably lower.

In the day-to-day business of these years, Anthony Forbes was associated with two noteworthy developments. One was on the money-broking side, where his idea of lending equities as well as gilts was implemented. In what were pre-Talisman days, with no central register, this could be a tricky exercise (compared with the limited number of gilt stocks) but worth the effort. Secondly, when in about 1967 a division was made within the statistical department between long-term and short-term situations, Forbes became responsible for what was elegantly known as 'Instant Research', in effect making an analysis of company results readily available in the office as quickly as possible. This analysis remained essentially for internal purposes, so the conflict with the corporate role continued to be avoided.

Meanwhile, these were also the years when the pension funds quite perceptibly became of increasing importance within the overall scheme of things. This was so partly because they were growing in size anyway, up from 2.9% of equity holdings in 1963 to 4.9% by 1970; but partly also because it was now that the funds began to employ financial intermediaries (including of course Cazenove's) to act not merely as an agent, but actually as a fund manager, in other words making investment decisions without reference to the trustees, though within an agreed brief that was usually renewed quarterly. The actuarial profession seems to have played an important part in this, including persuading many funds, previously insured, to cash in the insurance policy and have a managed fund instead. By 1970 it was still early days, with Cazenove's being sole investment adviser to only eight funds (including the W. H. Smith one, which went way back) worth altogether a total of some £35 million; but a significant trend for the future was already clear.

If that was a growth area, however, the reverse was the case for the country broking side by the late sixties. Following computer studies which showed that, in terms of income generated per bargain, the country business was far less profitable than the private client business, Colin Huttenbach was given instructions to wind it down. This he did, with much skill and tact, over the next few years, ahead of the union in 1973 of the London and provincial exchanges into a single federation. Henceforth Cazenove's dealt for provincial firms in overseas stocks only, although of course many friendships continued. The connection had been an immensely valuable one, especially in new issue terms, but by this time the new issue thrust itself was beginning to move towards a mixture of companies abroad and large companies at home who had gone beyond their provincial origins. It was therefore an entirely logical decision, though one taken not without regret.

The same was presumably true when in the mid-1960s the Stock

Exchange Council decided to pull down the old House and replace it with a new, high-rise one. As such, it was sadly symptomatic of the decade, with many familiar City landmarks falling to the bulldozers. The money for the new Stock Exchange (eventually opened in 1972) was secured in June 1966, when Mullens invited Cazenove's to help raise the required £10 million. It was a considerable feather in the firm's cap and it did not charge a fee. A $7\frac{1}{4}\%$ debenture stock was issued at 97 and, against a fair amount of advice to the contrary from outside quarters, Hornby (abetted by Ingram and Barnett) insisted that all the money required should be raised in one go and not by tranches. This proved to be excellent advice, as money became increasingly dear in the ensuing years. The whole operation was a notable one and of course was for a very fundamental cause, prompting Hornby to write in his memoirs: 'I always regard this as the crown to all our efforts'.

Otherwise, it was business much as usual on the domestic new issue front between the summer of 1966 and summer of 1968. Companies for whom the firm acted included Rolls-Royce (on behalf of Lazards), Burroughs Machines (on behalf of Schroder Wagg), Vauxhall Motors (on behalf of Morgan Grenfell) and Allied Breweries (on behalf of Barings). In May 1967 it was employed by Hambros to help bring to the market Josiah Wedgwood & Sons, resulting in a considerable number of sales for various members of the Wedgwood family and family trusts. The following year saw in June a fine instance of Hornby in incisive action. The Mercantile Investment Trust was seeking to do a £7 million convertible and as usual employed Cazenove's as one of the brokers. At the meeting to settle the terms of the issue, the Mercantile's Paul Ledeboer expressed a hope that they might get away with a 5% coupon, but the senior partner of the other broking firm thought 7% more plausible. At this Hornby declared that instead the rate should be $4\frac{1}{2}\%$, characteristically offering to do the whole lot himself. It was a decisive intervention and the coupon was indeed $4\frac{1}{2}\%$.

A few weeks later, in July 1968, there broke out such a storm over the firm's head as completely to overshadow that and indeed practically everything else. This was the 'Gallaher affair', an episode that was not only the most public in the history of Cazenove's up to that time, but was also of considerable moment in City history as a whole. Gallaher, the Ulster-based tobacco company, had been receiving the unwelcome attentions of the American giant, Philip Morris, which at the end of June put in a bid of 25s a share. The Gallaher board rejected the bid, and there soon appeared another, more welcome contender in the form of American Tobacco. With the Imperial Group having recently sold (through Cazenove's) its controlling interest in Gallaher, it was likely that the company had become a potential takeover target. The upshot was that Morgan Grenfell, acting on behalf of American Tobacco, instructed Cazenove's to go into the market early on Tuesday, July 16th, following the announcement of a rival bid by American Tobacco at 35s a share, and make what later terminology would call a 'dawn raid'. A Morgan Grenfell memorandum, dated the 17th, relates what happened:

> He [Hornby] was instructed that, as this was a competitive situation, American Tobacco would be willing to buy all stock offered in the market provided that such purchases were at or below the offer price of 35s. Sir Antony Hornby's best guess was that if everything went very well for us we might acquire 5 million shares during the day. In a little under two hours trading, enormous numbers of shares were offered to Cazenove. In the last half hour of buying stock, the total rose from just over 4 million to what we believe to be about 10 million and by the time the transactions had all been sorted out and checked it was found that the total was in fact about 12 million.
>
> This exceptional volume of offerings must probably be attributed to the fact that following the recent Offer for Sale of 26 million Gallaher shares, a large amount of stock was still in underwriters' hands who saw a chance of an unexpected profit within a very few weeks.

This analysis of how in effect American Tobacco won the day was undoubtedly correct. The recent sale of Gallaher shares, formerly held by Imperial, had not been absorbed, and was in the hands of various institutions, over a third being with Flemings. These institutions, well known to Cazenove's, were willing sellers. From a stockbroking point of view it was a phenomenal operation, co-ordinated by 'Beddy'; it netted the firm £$\frac{1}{4}$ million commission for one morning's work, an astonishing amount for those days, though of course the subsequent settlement aspect was arduous in the extreme. Over the coming weeks there must have been moments when Hornby and his fellow partners wondered whether it was worth it.

The storm broke almost at once. Christopher Gwinner of the *FT*, speaking on BBC Radio 4 on the 17th, put the controversy in a nutshell: 'The brokers of American Tobacco entered the market early on Tuesday morning and bought about 12 million shares. And the complaint is that this was done in a way which really was in favour of big institutional shareholders and gave the small people no chance to get rid of their shares at that price.' Hornby from the start refuted any such criticism and on the same day drafted a memorandum:

> Nobody has suffered. Some have, but maybe only temporarily, done better.

I was surprised at the rate shares came in. It proves A.T.'s bid is considered more than fair.

Those who sold in the market at 34s 9d get less than offer price as they have to pay commission of 3d or more.

If one's hands are entirely tied a complete stop is put to doing any business at all.

Equality amongst investors is an illusion. We are often disappointed in missing a line of shares in the market. Someone has bought them first. He made up his mind quicker or had a better broker. This is not unfair.

A.T. are sticking to their undertaking to buy half everyone's holding at 35s. No one is worse off.

It was an unyielding document that set the tone for the public row that lay ahead.

The following day, Thursday the 18th, the Takeover Panel delivered its verdict. The Panel had only recently been established, following various controversially conducted takeovers during 1967, and was essentially the creation of the Bank of England. It now declared that Morgan Grenfell and Cazenove's had broken the Takeover Code, in particular the article declaring that all shareholders in a company being bid for should receive equal treatment. The two firms vigorously denied that they had breached the Code, stressing that its rule 29 accepted that it was undesirable to fetter the market and making much of the fact that Ken Barrington of Morgan Grenfell had received Panel approval on the 15th for the proposed course of action. That evening Hornby told Tom Mangold of BBC Television that he was most offended by the Panel's judgement and that it had given a misguided verdict, adding: 'There's a certain cut and thrust in the market that is the essence of City dealing. If you're going to wait for the amateurs then business will stop.' Press reaction was almost unanimously hostile towards the two firms, epitomised by the remarks of the financial editor of *The Times* on the 19th:

The future of the Takeover Panel hangs in the balance. If Morgan Grenfell and Cazenove's, two of the most eminent firms in their particular spheres, are to break the Code and publicly not to accept the Panel's unanimous ruling, there must be a strong reaction either from the Panel or from the bodies which constitute the Panel. If there is no further sanction against these two firms, the case against a Securities and Exchange Commission [as in America] will no longer be arguable.

'The City must act to control its members,' a leading article in the same paper declared the next day; and on the 21st the *Sunday Telegraph* called for Hornby's suspension from the Stock Exchange, a suggestion that naturally made him furious.

Meanwhile, informal discussions were continuing with the Panel. The eventual result, on the 25th, was a further announcement from the Panel, which now accepted that the two firms had on the 16th 'acted in good faith in their belief that such dealings were within the letter and spirit of the Code'. Technically, the issue turned on whether or not the Panel accepted market purchases in a partial bid situation: this the Panel did not believe it had acquiesced in, during the negotiations on the 15th, but it accepted that there had been a genuine misunderstanding. Any imputations against the integrity of the two firms were therefore withdrawn. This new pronouncement from the Panel received a generally dusty response. 'An unhappy compromise,' the financial editor of *The Times* called it, though accepting that Morgan Grenfell and Cazenove's 'are right when they say that the rules about market buying in partial bids were not clear.' The *FT* continued to maintain a studied neutrality, but the *Sunday Telegraph* was again positively savage, on the one hand laying into the City authorities ('the whole thing has been mucked up in a particularly ludicrous fashion'), on the other hand dwelling on the hostility being expressed by much of the City towards Cazenove's ('so aloof, so successful').

With the Panel having done its ill-appreciated best, the focus from the point of view of Cazenove's now switched to the Stock Exchange Council, which considered the matter for the first time on the 26th. Hornby formed a 'Defence Committee' of four, comprising himself, Ingram, Barnett and Chandler, all fortified by the opinion of Sir Hilary Scott, of Slaughter & May and a former President of the Law Society, that the firm had done nothing wrong. Ingram tended towards a compromise, complaining that the goal-posts kept being shifted; but the others took a wholly unbending line. The attitude of Barnett was particularly crucial, granted his position on the Council. Twice the representatives of the firm were summoned before the Council and both times he insisted on sitting with his partners and showing his full support. At those meetings Hornby and Chandler spoke on behalf of the firm, with Chandler emphasising that the younger partners were completely behind Hornby in his refusal to accept that the firm had acted wrongly. On August 13th the Council delivered its judgement on what it had heard. The key passage ran:

There was no evidence to suggest that Messrs Cazenove & Co knew or should have known at the time in the confused and competitive conditions of the contested bid situation that they were in danger of breaching the City Code by their actions. These conditions and the absence of precedents relating to partial bids (including the possible application of

Rule 29 of the Code) militated against a full appreciation of the dangers inherent in such a situation.

There was no evidence to suggest that their decisions were taken otherwise than in good faith.

Coupled with this acquittal on the fundamental point, the Council did censure the firm for a technical infringement concerning the way it 'put through' the market those Gallaher shares bought from its own clients. Almost certainly this censure was in the nature of a *placebo* by the Council to its outside critics, for the principle adopted by Purnell in this 'put through' was no different to that in the Council's existing rules for equity placings, giving a minuscule advantage to clients of the broker instituting the business; and it was unfortunate that he rather took the blame for something that was not his fault.

The mud continued to fly for several more days. Hornby was jubilant at what he saw as a victory and, in his statement following the judgement, as unrepentant as ever: 'We still feel we did not breach the Code as it is. We may have breached the Code as they wish they had written it.' The press for its part remained highly critical, with 'Lex' of the *FT* at last coming down from the fence and describing the Council's pronouncement as 'pitiful but predictable'. In an overall piece on the affair, Kenneth Fleet wondered whether the Takeover Panel was worth saving and asserted that the attitude of Hornby and Morgan Grenfell's Lord Harcourt 'rang with High City arrogance we thought had died with Hambros and the British Aluminium affair a decade ago'. Then on the next day, the 15th, the Governor of the Bank, Sir Leslie O'Brien, published a letter to the chairman of the Issuing Houses Association in which he supported the recent decisions of the Panel and declared that 'action in breach of the Code is not justifiable in any circumstances'. Once again, this was too much for Hornby, who told the *Evening News* the next day: 'I still say that I resent the rebuke by the Panel. There was no chance of discussion – no chance to put our case. The first announcement was bald and unkind and led to our being pilloried by the Press for eight days.' And he added, in words that perhaps only he could have used, of the need for the Panel to have a stronger secretariat: 'All new things have teething troubles. When I buy a new Rolls-Royce it tends to go wrong at the beginning when it is being run in.' It was at this point, with many of the other partners having gone on holiday, that Bedford and Belmont took Hornby to one side and convinced him that he was doing more harm than good by these continuing outbursts, especially in the aftermath of victory. Henceforth, the history books would continue the debate, but the affair itself was over.

It is impossible to deny that Gallaher was traumatic, with the firm facing sustained public criticism for the first time in its history. If events had not moved with such remarkable speed on the morning of July 16th, going far beyond the legitimate expectations of those involved, the controversy almost certainly would not have arisen. But the fact was that it did, and it did not show the firm in an altogether favourable light. In particular, many otherwise well-disposed people in the City felt that Hornby had badly over-reacted, revealing an inability to conceive even the possibility that Cazenove's could have been less than perfect. Whatever the rights and wrongs of the case itself, there is no doubt that the firm came seriously unstuck on the public relations aspect of what was an extremely high-profile episode. Many old friendships were put under strain, though in the event (as after British Aluminium) they were soon repaired. Nevertheless, the affair was not without its positive elements. It showed graphically the strengths of the partnership system as a form of mutual support against outside criticism and indeed the good feeling running through the entire firm. To quote Hornby's subsequent appreciative words: 'There was complete understanding, sympathy and community amongst partners and staff.' In a wider sense, it showed at least two important things: firstly, that people like Harcourt of Morgan Grenfell and Hornby of Cazenove's were prepared to defend to the end their clients' interests when convinced that they were in the right; and secondly, that in the rapidly changing world of corporate finance, self-regulation in the City would continue to work only if it was conducted more professionally and indeed more equitably, allowing those 'in the dock' the opportunity to mount a proper defence.

Did the affair change Cazenove's? Hornby, who throughout was concerned only with the honour of the firm, was undoubtedly disillusioned by the behaviour of the press, referring to them in his memoirs as 'hawks out for blood' who 'delight in tilting against the establishment'. The firm's relations with the press (never very close) were already becoming more distant, but Gallaher accelerated the trend. There is no evidence, however, that the episode had the effect of changing the Cazenove approach towards the conduct of business. Indeed, if anything, it confirmed it. Strong-minded, emotionally committed to his clients and utterly determined to succeed on their behalf, Hornby was not going to change at his age. And perhaps the last word should go to him, being indeed his final utterance on the whole painful affair: 'It is surprising how often a minority turns out to be right. If one is convinced of one's case one must stick to one's guns and not be deflected.'

The episode took its human toll. Herbert Ingram, who according to Hornby 'had been a worried man all through the crisis and not his usual ebullient self,' suffered a serious stroke very soon afterwards. It was sadly obvious that he would not now be senior partner, which he was due to have become the following spring. Moreover, his illness had three further important consequences. One was that Hornby very sensibly decided to delay his retirement until 1970; another was that Luke Meinertzhagen replaced Ingram as senior partner designate; and the third was that the firm filled the gap amongst the new issue partners by recruiting from outside at a senior level for the first time since Peter Kemp-Welch just after the war. The new man (suggested by a leading jobber, Jack Durlacher) was Michael Richardson. Since 1953 he had been a partner with Panmure Gordon, where he had made for himself a great business-getting reputation, one indeed not unlike Peter Kemp-Welch's before the war in the way it was based on a vigorous pursuit of the half chance. Furthermore, he too, like Kemp-Welch before him, brought a 'team' with him when he came to Cazenove's in May 1969. One of its members was Leigh Windsor, who had many private clients of his own and now became a partner at the same time as Richardson. The other newcomer, like Windsor also from Panmure Gordon, was a young cousin of Richardson's wife called David Mayhew, who began at Cazenove's on the sales side. Altogether it was a helpful infusion of new blood, at a time when the firm, though doing more business than ever, was feeling rather bruised by both public and private events.

Meanwhile, new issue fortunes continued, as ever, to be largely dictated by the state of the market as a whole. During the sharp slump that dominated the first half of 1969, probably the most spectacular victim was Alcan Aluminium, which in June made a £12 million issue of 9% convertible unsecured loan stock. Acting on behalf of Morgan Grenfell, Cazenove's shared the broking with Govett, Sons & Co and Kitcat & Aitken, and between them the three firms were able to place barely half the sub-underwriting, with Morgan Grenfell taking the balance. At the closing of the lists, only £260,480 stock had been applied for and 'accordingly', in the timeless phrase, 'underwriters were called upon to take up 97.8% of their commitments.' By August the market had bottomed out and the Meinertzhagen brothers successfully accomplished the offer for sale of £10 million ordinary shares of S. Pearson & Son, following the decision of the Cowdray family to go public and sell some of its holdings. All the time, mergers and takeovers were becoming an increasingly preoccupying theme. One of the happier variety occurred early in 1969, when the publishing firms of Chatto & Windus and Jonathan Cape came together. Cazenove's was much involved in the lengthy negotiations, which at the last almost foundered over the question of whose name would come first. Fortunately Hornby suggested 'Chatto and Jonathan Cape,' which worked because Cape, although coming second, had two names. But the firm also often found itself defending corporate clients against hostile bids, such as when General Foods of America unsuccessfully attempted to take over Rowntrees early in 1969. Hornby on the whole disliked these battles, which he thought were usually unnecessary and fuelled solely by greed, and in March 1970, shortly before retirement, he wrote to a colleague abroad: 'We are near the climax of a tussle for Cementation which I think we are going to lose but we have bought in the last few days over 3,000,000 shares, so I suppose one must be grateful for this ridiculous takeover game.' It was in many ways a new world, and he was perhaps not sorry to leave it.

During Hornby's last full year, 1969, Cazenove's continued to handle more new issues (187) than any other London broker. Next came Joseph Sebag & Co on 156. Corporate finance remained as central to the firm's business as it had ever been, perhaps even more so. Companies who had used Cazenove's once usually returned, often for a debenture placing; they might well ask the firm to advise on the investment of any surplus capital; and increasingly there were company pension funds to be managed as well. However, these and other 'spin-offs' hinged entirely on the efficient despatch of the 'primary market' new issue business itself. As they had been ever since the late 1940s, continuing good relations with the merchant banks were a crucial factor. In a memorandum putting down some thoughts at about the time he retired, Hornby usefully summed up some of these key connections.

> I think we can say we have an unassailable position with Barings, Schroders and Lazards. I believe we are Rothschilds favourites. We are very close to Morgans (though Rowe & Pitman are their first brokers) and to Hill Samuel (about equal with Sebags) . . .
>
> I would say our first loyalty of all is to Barings. We must never ever do anything hostile to them. Although it might be necessary to be on the other side in a battle if a company loyalty necessitated it. In my view, although it may be considered old-fashioned, they are in a class by themselves for quality.

For their part, the merchant banks by this time needed the services of top-class new issue brokers like Cazenove's more than ever before. With the size of issues steadily growing, as well as the risks involved, the banks could no longer afford to rely as they once had on their own resources and instead increasingly had to rely on the muscle of the investment institutions to bear the risk; and it was a firm like Cazenove's which, with its feel for the market, was supreme at judging how, on a day-to-day basis, the big institutional investors would react, in other words what the demand would be and how best to satisfy that demand. This did not mean that the broker on the whole was yet involved in high-level strategy, but it certainly did mean that his role in the pricing of an issue (especially debenture placings) was ever more critical. And after all, since the underwriting was the ultimate consideration and the broker was going to have to place most of it, that was only fair as well as sensible. Of course, there was always likely to be a keen debate, involving the company as well as the bank and broker, though in this period not usually all together; and when it came to it, Cazenove's might go along with the bank's judgement, provided that the bank supported the issue if it flopped. But either way, the message was clear by the late 1960s: in an increasingly competitive capital market, where 'antennae' were all, banks depended on brokers quite as much as the other way round.

That was one part of the story. The other was the new issue work done in Tokenhouse Yard itself. The nuts and bolts side remained indispensable, with Mark Loveday (son of a future chairman of the Stock Exchange and a godson of Hornby's) now learning the craft under Holland-Martin in a department that still had less than ten people in it. But what perhaps made even more difference between success and failure were the efforts of 'the UK institutional broking team', as it was called. These were the people who, under the continuing surveillance of Bedford right up to 1970, not only dealt on a daily basis on behalf of the institutions, which provided the main source of revenue for the firm; but they also placed the shares and sub-underwriting coming from the new issue partners. Hornby in his memoirs described them on the eve of his retirement:

> David Wentworth-Stanley headed a red-hot team of John Kemp-Welch and Tony Bedford (the two chips), Charles Henderson, Harry Cazenove (Philip's son and fifth generation) and David Barnett [the son of Cedric]. They covered Insurance companies, Investment Trusts and Pension Funds, Scotland included.
>
> When they got the smell of a business they were like hounds after a fox. It was astonishing how, as soon as they were given the 'off', the telephones started buzzing and what had seemed a big meal of several million shares was devoured in a few hours.

The remarkable success of this team (and its successors) can be attributed to many factors. Among them was the teamwork, the absence of an 'I'm not offering this to my clients' attitude if a member of the team did not care for a particular issue; there was the dogged persistence (inherited from 'Beddy') and the deliberate cultivation of sub-underwriting loyalty (inherited from Micklem); there was the almost invariable excellence of the product they were selling, usually priced to a nicety; and there was the team's daily contact with the investment managers of an ever-broadening range of institutions, which meant that it knew who wanted what, whether particular institutions were on a buying tack or a selling tack, what size of holdings they were looking for, and so on. Altogether it was an art, not a science, and one that required a great measure of skill, both to place debentures and equities and to arrange the distribution of sub-underwriting. Furthermore, it was essential to ensure that new issues were appropriately placed, which in effect meant that they were not sold immediately, thereby wrecking the prospects for an orderly after-market. This whole aspect – in a word, distribution – was crucial to the firm's new issue business, which could not have been sustained without it. Sitting in the recently-created second partners' room, the broking team performed its telephonic task with immense zest, dedication, humour and also enjoyment.

Over the years, of course, none of this could have been achieved without the existence of a core of faithful sub-underwriters, willing to support Cazenove's in thin times as well as thick. Again it is perhaps invidious to mention names, but it is a fact that on underwriting day Hendersons, Barings, the W. H. Smith pension fund and Malton Trust never had to ring Cazenove's, so sure was the firm of their abiding loyalty; while among institutions who almost always said 'yes' were London Trust and Cables in addition to those three powerful insurance names, the Prudential, Royal Insurance and Legal and General. It is worth stressing that the support of these institutions (and others) was not peculiar to Cazenove's, but that in general their steadfast attitude was crucial to that whole sub-underwriting system without which the capital-raising process on behalf of British industry could not have functioned. However, from the point of view specifically of the firm, four further points may be made. Firstly, that the bias in its sub-underwriting list towards insurance companies was not accidental, nor solely indicated that sector's great investment weight at the time, but also was governed by an appreciation of the insurance industry's ability to absorb risk, its willingness to take on board all types of issues and the fact that its investment culture, imbued by generations of actuaries, was an appropriately conservative, long-term one. Secondly, that the firm in allocating its sub-underwriting continued to be much less swayed than were many other brokers by the amount of commission business that it was doing for particular institutions – a reflection in part of the way it was rather less dependent on day-to-day secondary market broking than most firms. Thirdly, although the so-called 'cherry pickers' were sometimes the despair of the selling team in Tokenhouse Yard, the tradition was firmly maintained that institutions that sometimes said 'no' should not be struck off the firm's underwriting list, even though they might be somewhat less well favoured

Cazenove & Co, 1939–1990

Claud Serocold

Charles Micklem

Jimmy Palmer-Tomkinson

Antony Hornby

Ernest Bedford

Peter Kemp-Welch

Frank Holt

Herbert Ingram

Charles Purnell

Luke Meinertzhagen

Alex Coombe-Tennant

Cedric Barnett (right) in Throgmorton Street, 20th November 1967, when the Stock Exchange was closed the day after devaluation (by permission of the Associated Press)

Harry Willmott, a well-known figure in charge of reception at Tokenhouse Yard during the 1970s

Johnny Henderson

David Wentworth-Stanley

Godfrey Chandler

Tony Bedford

Garden party at
West Woodhay, home of
Johnny Henderson, 1979:
(above) David Wentworth-
Stanley, Michael Belmont
and Johnny Henderson
(right) Godfrey Chandler
and Claude Carter

The following group of photographs is of the 1989-90 partnership
(taken by Lord Lichfield at 12 Tokenhouse Yard)

The Joint Senior Partners
John Kemp-Welch (right) and
Anthony Forbes

The Senior Partners' Room
Anthony Forbes, John Kemp-
Welch, Stephen Carden,
Rae Lyster

Tony Bamford, Harry
Cazenove, Patrick Mitford-
Slade, Julian Cazalet,
Peter Brown
David Barnett, Michael
Belmont, David Mayhew

Corporate Finance Partners
Patrick Donlea, Michael
Wentworth-Stanley, Alex
Scott-Barrett, John Paynter,
Jim Findlay, Christopher
Smith
Malcolm Archer, Mark
Loveday, David Godwin

*Institutional Broking
Partners*
Nigel Rowe, Bob Bradfield,
Malcolm Calvert, Simon
Troughton, Peter Rylands,
Martin Wonfor
Andrew Muir, Duncan
Hunter, Richard Smith,
Tim Steel

International Partners
Thomas Schoch, Victor
Lampson, Stephen Morant,
Christian Kindersley,
Edward Whitley
Christopher Palmer-
Tomkinson, Ian Pilkington

Fund Management Partners
Patrick Dalby, David Brazier, Harry Henderson, Bernard Cazenove
Bryan Pascoe, Charles Faringdon, Nicholas Gold

Incoming Partners as at 1st May 1990
John Harbord-Hamond, Steve Daniels, Simon Dettmer,
Laurence Hollingworth, Arthur Drysdale, John Reilly, Roger Lambert
Michael Power, Richard Grubb, Richard Wintour, Jonathan Hubbard

Overseas Conference,
1988, at Eastwell Manor

Grant of Arms to
Cazenove & Co. – the first to
a Stock Exchange
Partnership, 1984

in future issues. And lastly, never to be forgotten, there was the personal touch, perhaps not often used but always there in reserve. The wry words of the investment manger of one insurance company, addressing his staff at the time of his retirement, nicely summed up how important that personal element could be: 'You can always take underwriting etc. offered in writing by Cazenove's. If they ask to come and see you TAKE CARE!'

The year 1970 marked the end of an era in the firm's history. Early in the year, 'Beddy' died of kidney trouble shortly before he was due to retire. It was unlikely that he would have enjoyed retirement much, for in Hornby's apt words 'he was a terrific enthusiast for work'. Then at the end of April there were the simultaneous retirements of Schreiber, Ingram (who had tried in vain to defy his illness and return to work) and of course Hornby himself. In his rather poignant words: 'I was really ready to go. All the people with whom I'd done business had either died or retired.' He had also become increasingly lame, the result of cerebral palsy from childhood showing itself in late age. With that characteristic mixture of emotion and realism, he wrote at the time to Peter Kemp-Welch's widow:

> I shall miss the daily contacts at Cazenove's terribly. I really love the place but I'm delighted not to have to do any more business and I never want to see a balance sheet again except those ones which are part of one's life like W. H. Smith, Savoy [of which he was a director], Witan and so on. I shall keep quite busy with Charities and picture activities but I walk like a one year old – swaying and stumbling – which is dreadfully frustrating.

Hornby certainly received a splendid send off, which was no less than his due, mainly in the form of many farewell lunches and dinners. But perhaps best of all was a handsome book (secretly prepared by Belmont and Hornby's secretary June King) containing hundreds of signatures and warm messages from friends in the City and elsewhere. One was from a future Poet Laureate, who signed himself as 'your old, though non-Wykehamical friend, grateful client and fellow art-lover'. Sir John Betjeman had been a client of Cazenove's for many years; and in the early days, when both sellers and buyers had to sign transfer deeds, he always wrote against the name of the 'other' party, 'And the very best of luck to you Sir!'. But, among many words of praise, perhaps the most telling message came from Sir Allen Lane, who wrote in the book: 'I will not forget that it was you who introduced me to the City and who guided me so surely in my first faltering footsteps in what appeared at that time to be an impenetrable jungle.'

What kind of firm did Hornby leave behind? 'I always made Americans laugh by saying I spent my time preventing Cazenove's getting too big,' he remarked in his memoirs. He did not altogether succeed to his satisfaction, but nevertheless by the time of his final Savoy party the size of the staff was still only a little over 200, excluding partners and messengers. The question of size mattered very much to Hornby, who knew in his bones that ultimately what the firm's success rested upon was a tight cohesive culture, without which it would be just another business organisation. It was a culture which had evolved under Serocold and Micklem and which he had then consciously fostered for a quarter of a century. On his retirement, in accordance with this conviction and looking ahead to the future, he drafted another series of maxims and thoughts, comparable to those of 1960. Some were of a very specific nature, but most were an attempt by him to encapsulate what he believed should be the perennial values of the firm. Once again, the general *dicta* richly deserve quotation. They not only represent a summation of the Cazenove approach to the conduct of business; but they also give us, for the last time, the authentic voice of Antony Hornby:

Our business has really been built up on trust and confidence. We are known for being able to keep secrets *absolutely* and *never* taking advantage of information given in confidence. My first senior partner said that this was the most important thing of all and I am sure it has been the basis of our business.

One cannot do all the business. Let us try and do most of the best.

One must be generous as well as competitive. One cannot prosper at other people's expense. One's friends and even competitors must be allowed to prosper as well.

Never ask for or think of commission when tackling a business. The main thing is the business should be worthwhile doing. Sometimes one gets overpaid, sometimes underpaid – generally the former.

It is harder to say 'No' than 'Yes' and very important to learn how to do so. Cazenove's should be hard to get and not available to all-comers. We must be careful to retain the 'style' of Cazenove's and the type of business that we do.

There is no rivalry and jealousy between partners and therefore no exclusive clients. In the nature of things some partners concentrate on certain clients because they like each other better and get on together. It is therefore a true partnership. Everything one does benefits the partnership and there is plenty for everybody at the end of the day.

Naturally one cannot just freewheel along on 'trust' alone. It is very necessary now to know the answers and to be professional. I don't mind admitting we used not to be. But since the war and particularly after the advent of Peter Kemp-Welch we have improved and I really think we are now pretty efficient without being professionally qualified. I would class us as high-class amateurs amongst whom are one or two who might play for England.

As regards Staff we think and hope they are happy. We try and think of their interests and do all we can to make life good for them. But we are well aware they have to work sometimes for very long hours. They share in the success of the Firm and I hope really do consider themselves as partners. But we must never cease thinking of things to do for their benefit. We depend on them enormously and we know that they percolate the Cazenove spirit at their level through the City. The tone of a firm always comes from the top.

We all enjoy ourselves. One must be happy above all things. One spends all one's life more or less in the office. It must be FUN.

CHAPTER NINE

Change and continuity
1970–1986

The City of the early 1970s was a rapidly changing place, with the emphasis sadly but inexorably moving away from personal contact. Stockbrokers no longer did their daily rounds of the merchant banking parlours – a reflection as much as anything of the increasing tempo of the square mile – and instead relied almost exclusively on the telephone to take orders. Nor did they visit the institutions as frequently as before. Instead, the emphasis was now much more on written research; and, as a former investment manager of the Prudential has ruefully recalled, it was from about this time that the real bombardment of brokers' reports began to thud down on the desks of the institutions. Moreover, brokers were increasingly less inclined to go down to the market to talk to the jobbers, once such an all-pervasive ritual. In addition to the decline of the jobbing system and the enhanced importance of more analytical research than that traditionally proffered by the market, a significant factor in this trend was the Stock Exchange's introduction in February 1970 of its market price display service. This consisted in its early stages of some twenty-five price pages, more than quintupling the amount of information available in most brokers' offices. Finally, there was the rise and rise of the Euromarkets, which not only reinforced the telephonic as opposed to face-to-face mode of dealing, but also was largely responsible for the coming to London of many foreign banks, mainly from North America. Increasingly international, impersonal and sophisticated (including in its recruitment policy), the City was beginning to lose something of its character and with it a certain underlying ethos of mutual trust.

Markets themselves had a highly febrile quality during these years: partly in the wake of the collapse of Rolls-Royce in February 1971, a traumatic event but revealing that the government would not bail out 'lame ducks'; and then especially once the inflationary 'Barber boom' was under way from that summer. It was a time of easy credit, paper empires and new-style financiers, epitomised by Jim Slater and Oliver Jessel. Things began to go sour in 1972, as industrial troubles mounted and the Heath government made its 'U' turn, but the real problems in the equity market awaited the traumatic events of 1973 and beyond. It is in this overall context that the question arises: did there exist a feeling at Cazenove's, during these first two or three years of the new decade, that in some sense the firm was being by-passed by new faces and new ways of doing things, that in short the traditional Cazenove qualities of reliability and sobriety no longer counted for quite as much as they once had? It is poss-ible that this *was* felt by some people, outside as well as inside the firm. Yet the fact was that the firm continued in the early 1970s to do its impressive share of the business, continued to regard quality as being at least as important as quantity and, in a way reminiscent of the late 1920s, was superbly poised to emerge from the inevitable crash with a yet further enhanced reputation.

Much of the credit for this was due to the firm's new leadership in the post-Hornby era. In effect it was a duumvirate, with Luke Meinertzhagen as senior partner being staunchly supported by Godfrey Chandler, these two very different men complementing each other extremely well. Meinertzhagen was the very successful business-getter, though always urbane and even a little 'laid back', but with a remarkable instinct for getting to the guts of an issue, above all in relation to its pricing. During the 1970s he emerged as a front-rank figure in the City, and at a key brokers' meeting his views about what was or was not feasible would carry enormous, usually decisive weight. Yet within Tokenhouse Yard itself he was a somewhat shy, withdrawn presence, rarely seen at lunch (preferring the City Club), and seldom concerned to communicate his views with junior partners or the staff, let alone to discuss their problems. At heart, however, he was a kind man and would always listen sympathetically if someone did go to him with a problem. Meinertzhagen had, moreover, the great quality in a senior partner of not interfering and, above all, not being judgemental if someone else had made a mistake.

Nevertheless, his apparent indifference to the concerns of others might have been a serious matter but for the wide-ranging role played by Chandler, especially after ill health forced him by 1972 to give up most of his corporate finance work. During the rest of the decade, and indeed until his retirement in 1985, his contribution was almost priceless: building on his earlier efforts in relation to staff welfare, in liaison with a series of office managers (Claude Carter, Arnold Roome, Ron Blake and John Thain);

continuing his important investment work, on behalf of pension funds, charities and private clients; taking over in 1974 from Cedric Barnett as finance partner before in due course being succeeded by Rae Lyster; and, perhaps above all, making himself readily available as a counsellor, so that within the firm there were very few during these years who did not benefit from his always perspicacious, sometimes unexpected advice on any number of matters. He also, in a period of increasing investment in new technology, began to perform an important advisory role on behalf of the Stock Exchange's Property and Finance Committee. In short, while all stockbroking firms found the 1970s a difficult decade, the uniquely matched combination of Meinertzhagen and Chandler helped to ensure that Cazenove's found the going less hard than most.

As ever the partnership continued to mutate. Between 1970 and 1974 four partners retired. Three were of an older generation: Charles Purnell, David Cazenove and Cedric Barnett; while Robin Holland-Martin decided to leave the City, subsequently returning to Hendersons. Meanwhile, there were ten new partners made. David Mayhew (1971) went to the 'box' soon after becoming a partner and for the rest of the 1970s was Purnell's successor as dealing partner, developing during these years what would become a renowned feel for the market; Patrick Mitford-Slade (1972) had been seconded to the Takeover Panel for two years following the completion of the training programme and now returned to the firm to take over the money-broking side; Christopher Palmer-Tomkinson (1972) was the third generation of his family to join the partnership and at this stage was responsible at the London end for Australian business; David Barnett (1972) continued through the 1970s and beyond to be part of the institutional sales team, as also did Harry Cazenove (1972), though in his case dealing almost entirely with pension funds; David Rochester (1972) had started on the private client side in the early 1960s, but since 1969 had been running the Sydney office; Tony Bamford (1972) was a qualified accountant who for several years had been heading the UK research team; Thomas Schoch (1973) continued to work closely with Alex Coombe-Tennant on the European side; Mark Loveday (1974) was becoming an increasing force on the corporate finance side, for which work he showed a natural affinity; and Joe Scott-Plummer (1974), who had initially come in on the research side in the late 1960s, by now was operating very effectively with Tony Bedford on the institutional sales desk. By the summer of 1974 the size of the partnership was twenty-eight, almost half as big again as the legal maximum that had obtained for so many years, but by no means as bloated as in some other parts of the square mile during the hectic early 1970s.

Moreover, turning to the business itself, within months of the new, post-Hornby era beginning there occurred a clear sign that something at least of the 'old' City persisted. This was in July 1970, when the firm again had the rare distinction of acting as broker for both sides in a merger, in this case between Pearson Longman and Penguin Books. Coincidentally it also at about the same time acted for both sides in the attempted merger between Hill Samuel and Metropolitan Estate and Property Corporation, though that came to nothing. On the other hand, a new issue later in the year saw a small but revealing sign of the changing times. This was the Pilkington flotation, which when the prospectus appeared in November featured a splendid colour photograph of glass-manufacturing in action at St Helens, a harbinger of much subsequent glossiness on these occasions. The offer for sale was undertaken by Schroder Wagg, and it was a reflection of how much some merchant banks still ran the show that at no point did either Cazenove's or Rowe & Pitman meet the Pilkington management. A few days later, Cazenove's acted jointly with W. Greenwell for Lazards in the placing of £10 million British Oxygen tonnage debenture stock. The coupon was 11%, which could not help but remind Hornby in retirement of how Lazards had once told Micklem that it would never put its name to a $5\frac{1}{2}$% preference. No one then could have imagined how interest rates would rise, and it was not very long after that 1970 placing that the new issue debenture market virtually dried up, as companies simply refused to pay the crippling rates of interest involved when borrowing for twenty or twenty-five years at a fixed rate.

Lazards was also involved in an interesting might-have-been from these years. This was the British Aircraft Corporation's ill-fated attempt to bring into production its 3–11 airbus, on which it had pinned its hopes of staying in the subsonic airliner business. Lazards was asked to devise a scheme to meet the prodigious capital needs of the 3–11, and in September 1970 it was announced that a public issue of loan stock would take place provided that the government gave financial backing to the airbus. The issue would be for £12 million, of which Cazenove's on behalf of Lazards had managed to obtain commitments to underwrite almost £8 million. Executing that task had been a chequered process, as Godfrey Chandler had found when he went to see Lord Tangley, chairman of the Trustees Corporation. Tangley was the former Sir Edwin Herbert, a long-standing friend of the firm, and a close associate of Max (later Lord) Rayne, who himself besides building up a great property-based empire as chairman of London Merchant Securities had over the years brought Cazenove's much new issue business. On this occasion, Tangley lectured Chandler for ten minutes about the mass of conjectures in the prospectus concerning the future sales and profits of the plane, adding that he was amazed that Cazenove's should have put its name to such speculative guesswork. But the punchline came as Chandler prepared to leave: 'I so much admire your partners' nerve in this that you can feel free to double our underwriting if it helps.' It did help, but in the event the government pulled the plug later that year, refusing to put £75 million of public money into the airbus, and so the issue never took place.

There is no doubt, however, about what was the stand-out 'story' of the early 1970s, certainly in terms of creative finance. A case study submitted in 1977 to the Wilson Committee on the City provides the authoritative account:

> The story of this £120 million oil exploration and production venture effectively had its earliest beginnings out of a chance meeting between Mr Michael Belmont, of Cazenove & Co, and Mr Jack Pierce, the President and driving force behind the Canadian oil exploration company, Ranger Oil, whom Mr Belmont had been asked to look after for the weekend in September 1964. He was on a fleeting visit to the U.K. to investigate the possibilities of oil exploration in the North Sea at the time of the initial opening up of that area to concessions.
>
> Mr Pierce is a geologist by training with an unerring nose for sniffing out oil. Much impressed by his expertise, Cazenove's began to recommend Ranger Oil to British investors over the next five years, while Ranger started its seismic exploration in the North Sea in earnest. By 1969 British financial interests, advised by Cazenove's, owned 55% of Ranger Oil, whose capitalisation had multiplied thirtyfold to Can$68 million, and Mr Belmont joined the board.

The Third Round of concessions was due to be awarded the following year. The question was how to ensure success in what inevitably would be a delicate political climate surrounding them:

> Mr Pierce was advised that if he could find a major international company which would add both financial muscle and credence to his own oil expertise, then Cazenove's might be in a position to produce the British element and financial capability.
>
> Once Ranger Oil found the appropriate company in the United States, International Utilities Oil & Gas Limited, who were prepared to put up 15%, the Ranger Consortium began to take shape. Ranger Oil was advised to keep 40% so that the oil expertise element of the consortium was kept at a level of just over 50%, whilst Cazenove's set about raising the balancing 45% from the British institutions. At this stage, it was felt that a large Scottish element would be helpful because the North Sea concessions to be applied for were in Scottish waters, so Cazenove's

invited Glasgow-based stockbrokers, R.C. Greig & Co, to help in approaching some of the major Scottish institutions.

The result was the incorporation, early in 1970, of the Scottish Canadian Oil & Transportation Co, generally known as SCOT. There were twenty shareholders, the bulk of them Scottish, and Cazenove's itself took a 1.67 per cent stake.

The Ranger/SCOT consortium was thus in place. It was, the case study justifiably claimed, 'unique in the oil industry on two counts':

> A host of small investors, policyholders and pensioners [i.e. all represented by the institutions] were being given the chance to have an indirect interest in a total risk venture, where the risks of failure were enormous but where the rewards for a major success should be tremendous. Secondly, this original method of participation gave the non-oil interests the opportunity for the first time to participate on an equal cost basis with the oil companies and therefore to share equally in any profit.

In June 1970 the consortium was awarded a licence for four blocks, one of which (23/27) was amongst the most sought after by the oil majors. It was a deserved reward for a sustained effort in which Cazenove's had played a key role, with Belmont receiving invaluable help from the resourceful, highly inventive Peter Smith.

But a fresh, even greater challenge soon lay ahead:

> It was common knowledge in the oil industry that additional prospective lands were expected to be made available shortly. Competition at the Fourth Round was expected to be intense.
>
> It was realised that a repetition of the SCOT formula would not have sufficient competitive edge, as several American and Canadian groups were known to be copying the 'SCOT style' in their applications for the new acreage and that it was essential to have one or two innovations for the new applications to have any chance of success against the financial muscle, power and expertise of the mighty oil majors.

Belmont and Smith accepted they would have to form a new company, partly because the investment trusts which had backed SCOT were likely to be inhibited from putting up funds for further exploration because of the '15% Rule', by which trusts lost their special tax status if they invested more than 15 per cent of their funds in one company. So another, highly secretive process of canvassing began:

> Following the success of the institutional involvement in the Third Round, Cazenove's found it slightly easier to mobilise further British

institutions, particularly from the insurance companies and investment trusts, to form another grouping which was eventually to be called London and Scottish Marine Oil Company Limited. However, it was only marginally easier and some of the institutions found it extremely difficult to reconcile such a total risk venture with their prudential responsibilities. The Chief General Manager of one major insurance company was only persuaded to put up the initial stake when he was asked by Mr Belmont by how much had the group's funds moved that day and how this compared with the total equity participation in LSMO.

LSMO was incorporated on 23 April 1971, with twenty-nine share-holders and a largely similar board and management to its sister company SCOT.

Thus strengthened, the Ranger Group made a series of applications at the time of the Fourth Round in September 1971. Not all succeeded, but enough did to give it a sizeable stake in the evolving North Sea oil story (on which, in 1972, Cazenove's produced an astonishingly comprehensive, much-admired report). Whether that story would be a triumph remained to be seen; and the firm knew from the example of Ultramar all about the forbidding financial problems likely to be caused by a lengthy period of exploration.

Meanwhile, contested takeover bids in the early 1970s were becoming even more prevalent and even more fiercely waged than they had been in the late 1960s. Cazenove's during 1971/72 was involved in three particu-larly stressful such contests. The first took place in the autumn of 1971 when, after the tile, pipe and brick makers Redland had amicably agreed a merger with Purle Brothers, it was announced by Ready Mixed Concrete that they intended to make a bid for Redland, but only if the Purle acquisition did not go through. Cazenove's was broker to both Redland and RMC; but partly through being already 'in play' over Purle, and partly because RMC had three other brokers, the firm acted for Redland, who were being advised by Barings. There followed a hard struggle between the two sides, in which, with the support of Barings and Cazenove's, Redland eventually acquired sufficient shares to ensure control of Purle and at the same time fight off the Ready Mixed bid. The episode took a heavy physical toll on Godfrey Chandler and soon afterwards he was compelled to leave corporate finance work; but in an essentially 'personal' business it was remarkable with what speed and success his companies were taken over by Rae Lyster, Stephen Carden, Anthony Forbes and Mark Loveday. At the same time as the Redland tussle, the firm was also intimately involved in the bold attempt by Allied Breweries to take over Trust Houses Forte. 'Quite ridiculous,' declared Sir Charles Forte when the initial £132 million bid was announced. Cazenove's had earlier been brokers to Trust Houses, but not to the recently formed THF; and now it naturally acted for Allied Breweries, which had been formed in 1961 out of a merger between Ind Coope, Tetley and Ansells, and for whom it had always acted. However, after a long drawn out battle for control, and heavy buying in the market, Allied had finally to admit defeat and withdraw. The third of the three contested bids was that made in the spring and early summer of 1972 by Grand Metropolitan for Watney Mann, then the third biggest British brewing group. It was at the time one of the biggest bids ever seen in the City, being eventually worth £435 million, and Cazenove's did an enormous amount of buying in the market on behalf of supporters of Watneys. In an exceedingly tight finish, marked by an unsuccessful appeal to the director-general of the Takeover Panel to appoint independent accountants to observe the counting of acceptances, what almost certainly tilted the balance towards Grand Metropolitan was the decision of the Prudential to accept the offer. Massive media attention accompanied the closing stages, and Ladbrokes even opened a book on the outcome. It was also the first time that a major brewer had been taken over by an 'outsider' and as such came as an enormous shock to established City assumptions.

All the time the firm's new issue machine worked away, as busy in these years as it had ever been before. The British Aircraft Corporation, Lucas Industries, Cable Trust, Hillards and H. P. Bulmer (of cider fame) were among the many concerns that benefited from its services. The London capital market was extremely active, and indeed 1972 saw a record number of companies being floated on it. Succeeding 'Beddy' in charge of the placing and arrangement of sub-underwriting at Cazenove's was David Wentworth-Stanley. Through the decade he showed great skill at constructing sub-underwriting lists involving a tactful feel for the sensitivities of not only the institutions but also the other, sometimes less powerful brokers with whom the firm often found itself working. He also possessed a certain streak of stubbornness, of use at times in standing up to the larger, more aggressive firms. Wentworth-Stanley found invaluable support from a whole team of people, one being David Barnett, who was especially helpful during placings: these were sometimes done under hectic conditions and Barnett's particular *forte* was the calm and accurate way in which he looked after the list, which was always kept centrally in order to ensure a proper and fair spread of shareholders.

Meanwhile, the lists themselves, particularly the sub-underwriting ones, were changing significantly in composition. For instance, whereas Ultramar issues of 1960 and even 1968 had been substantially sub-underwritten by country brokers as well as insurance companies, investment trusts and of course City houses, by 1972 the picture was beginning to alter for the £12½ million rights issue that took place in May that year. The country brokers were now a shrunken force; the insurance companies and investment trusts were both important, but slightly less so than they had been; the City houses were fairly constant; unit trusts and Continental houses (i.e. banks not represented in London) made their first appearance on an Ultramar list, though in neither case in any great number; and, by far the most striking aspect, there was a phenomenal mushrooming of pension funds, as many as forty being included on this particular list. The coming of these pension funds into prime institutional importance in the capital-raising process was not yet widely appreciated outside the City; but for the institutional broking team at Cazenove's, there was no doubting the way things were going.

Another trend of the early 1970s, much affecting the day-to-day broking, was the way in which high inflation, accompanied by higher interest rates caused by increased government borrowing, led to the virtual collapse of the debenture market as a whole. Consequently, the institutions moved into equities in an even bigger way than they had before. Private clients also found themselves having to make increasingly difficult investment decisions, and it was partly in response to this that the investment department at Cazenove's became steadily less amateur, including the putting of valuations on to the firm's computer. But perhaps the most interesting day-to-day development was in the money broking business. In 1972, as part of its policy on competition and credit control, the Bank of England decided to recognise three additional money brokers. From eighteen candidates, the three firms chosen were Hoare Govett, James Capel and Rowe & Pitman, all of them solid names with capital strength. The jobbers in the gilt-edged market initially said that they would not deal with these newcomers but after a time consented to do so. This widening of the field did not, however, have a particularly noticeable effect on the business being done by Cazenove's, which at about this time was, on Mitford-Slade's initiative, a pioneer in the lending of overseas stock. Arranging loans to Wedd Durlacher and Pinchin Denny of German, Dutch and French stock against dollar and sterling collateral and securing access to the whole of Robeco's portfolio – here was another aspect by which the firm assumed an increasingly international hue.

The activities of the foreign side itself continued to expand, with two new offices being opened in 1972. One was in New York, at 67 Wall Street.

Belmont, however, stressed to the local press that the firm's American strategy remained unchanged: 'We've generated a lot of business since we opened in San Francisco. Cazenove Inc. has become an underwriting participant in the States and hopes to participate in an increasing number of underwritings. But we never intend to and do not wish in any way to compete with our American friends for business. We want to work with them.' The other new office was in Johannesburg and reflected the firm's already good corporate connections there, including Consolidated Gold-fields and all the mines in that group, Standard Bank of South Africa, and South African Breweries. Over the years the Johannesburg office would produce relatively little in broking terms – the local market being very much an arbitrage one – but would remain a significant listening post. Elsewhere in the early 1970s, Cazenove's refrained from opening a Hong Kong office, not wanting to enter that highly speculative market at its peak, but at about this time did start a separate department in London to concentrate on the Japanese stock market and economy. In addition, the firm made the notable decision in 1972 to stay in Australia, the only London broker to retain its original business there out of the five who had opened representative offices during the latter part of the Poseidon mining boom. 'Once a jolly swagman' was *The Times* headline for this general retreat, but Cazenove's took the longer view. Finally, there was the European operation, which was still in its embryonic phase, though the firm was doing some business in Eurobonds and a certain amount in foreign equity markets (such as Belgium) on behalf of British institutions. In a piquant set-piece, moreover, the firm was responsible for a small change in French law. The occasion was the creation in Paris, shortly before Britain entered the Common Market in January 1973, of the so-called 'financial franc' and the fact that Cazenove's had some very large purchases of French oil shares unsettled. The firm 'covered' the currency for settlement day in the normal way, but the premium currency was introduced between dealing and settlement dates, involving a potentially heavy cost, as the firm had issued sterling contracts. With the encouragement of French banks, Cazenove's complained first to the Bank of England, to no avail, and then to the Foreign Office, which acted promptly. It persuaded the Chancellor of the Exchequer to take up the matter personally on a visit to Paris, and accordingly the law was changed – even more retrospectively, it might be said, than it had been in the first place.

Within a year of Britain joining the European Community, the whole of the western industrial world was turned upside down by what we now know as the first oil shock, as almost overnight the oil exporting countries quadrupled the price of crude oil. Britain suffered especially badly, its problems compounded by domestic politics and industrial relations, but stock markets everywhere slumped. The foreign side at Cazenove's was inevitably affected, but there were some bright spots. In particular, it was around this time that the firm began to make something of a speciality of securing listings on the London Stock Exchange on behalf of leading foreign companies. Manufacturers Hanover and Carter-Hawley-Hale Stores from the United States, St Gobain-Pont-à-Mousson from France, and Renown from Japan all fell into this category. Moreover, though the Beirut office was closed in August 1974, the result of an acceptance that the city was no longer the financial centre of the Middle East as well as of an awareness of impending troubles there, a few weeks later the firm opened an office in Hong Kong. Its first manager was Victor Lampson, who had joined the firm five years earlier and whose father had been British Minister in Peking (the equivalent of ambassador). The new office initially found things difficult, with the local market very flat, but gradually built up good contacts and in February 1975 on behalf of Hambros was jointly responsible for placing (mainly in Hong Kong and London) 5 million shares in Swire Pacific. Lampson was determined that the Hong Kong office should mirror the qualities of its London parent – low profile, high reputation, total confidentiality – and to a remarkable extent succeeded, though the office's range was inherently restricted by the fact that in the Hong Kong financial system the banks tend to do the distribution of new issues rather than the brokers.

Meanwhile, the square mile itself had been passing through the Slough of Despond. In February 1973, following the implementation of Stage Two of the Heath government's plan to limit pay, price and dividend increases, the monthly Cazenove letter on 'United Kingdom Investments' referred with some bitterness to how 'here in the City, disappointment with the possible changes in the economic climate has never been more marked since the advent of the first post-war Socialist Government in July 1945.' There then ensued a serious – if not yet catastrophic – bear market. The new issue market suffered badly; and when in April the firm was involved in a major corporate episode – placing (with the gallant support of Dick Wilkins of Wedd Durlacher) most of the sub-underwriting of an offer for sale made by Rothschilds in Rolls-Royce Motors on behalf of the receiver and joint liquidator in that then bankrupt company – it eventually lost almost £20,000 in a market support operation, its share of a joint effort with Lazards and Rowe & Pitman as well as Rothschilds.

Then, from the autumn of 1973, the City's situation started to become truly grave, recalling the early 1930s, as the wider drama of the oil crisis, the coal miners and eventually the three-day week was played out.

Overshadowed by all this, but of great moment in the City, was the secondary banking crisis, which came to a head shortly before Christmas and prompted the Bank of England's 'Lifeboat' operation in order to limit its consequences. One of the banks that needed rescuing was Cedar Holdings, which Cazenove's had helped to bring to the market in 1971. Its main business was in second mortgages, in other words lending to customers wishing to borrow against the equity of their own homes, then something of a novelty; and it had some strong institutional backers. But over the next two years the quality of its business declined, high interest rates caused a slump in property values, and eventually serious liquidity difficulties resulted due to the calling of short-term money which had been re-lent long-term. The episode as a whole was a considerable embarrassment to Cazenove's, which had had its name firmly on the business. Meanwhile, equities fell by an alarming 25 per cent during the six weeks to mid-December; and in this period there took place the classic example of an issue that should have been successful being blighted by its market context. Alginate Industries, a £1.7 million offer for sale made by Robert Fleming, with Cazenove's placing over two-thirds of the sub-underwriting, was a company with excellent prospects, being based on the West Coast of Scotland and engaged in the mysterious but profitable business of transforming brown seaweed into alginates for use in textile printing and food production. But on the day it was launched on the London capital market, the *FT*'s front page headlines included 'Bid to avert all-out coal strike', 'Tight situation in power industry' and 'Fighting flares in Golan Heights', not to mention 'Sunday drivers left stranded'; the sub-underwriters were left with just under 90 per cent; and dealings opened at way below the issue price. The company, however, got its money with which to finance further expansion and eventually the shareholders did very well. For a few weeks in the New Year the market rose a little, as investors cautiously anticipated a Conservative victory at the imminent general election, but at the end of February those hopes were dashed. The real storm still lay ahead.

The year 1974 has already entered City mythology. The 30–Share Index (which in May 1972 had attained a record high of 543.6) continued to slump; inflation roared ahead at over 20 per cent; a Labour government apparently committed to widespread further nationalisation was re-elected in October; and rumours continued to circulate for most of the year that many financial concerns would soon become insolvent because of the dramatic fall in the value of their investments. The most alarming rumour, fuelled by the press, concerned the National Westminster Bank. This was the clearer most closely involved in the City, being banker for most of the acceptance houses and almost all of the fringe banks; and when at the beginning of December 1974 the National Westminster's price dipped below par, Luke Meinertzhagen played an important role by going in to the market to reassure it that the bank was sound (reminiscent of Akroyd in relation to Antony Gibbs those many years before). For many London stockbroking firms it was not just rumours of insolvency, and in the course of 1974 their numbers were reduced from 362 to 297. In November the government did introduce stock relief, which in effect rescued British industry from imminent bankruptcy; but the big institutional investors remained unconvinced and, with some partial exceptions, continued to pile up cash. And then, on New Year's Eve, it was announced that Burmah Oil, one of the three great oil companies, would have to be rescued by the British government, the result of serious mismanagement as well as wider economic circumstances. Cazenove's had very recently been appointed joint and lead broker to Burmah, and it was Stephen Carden who, before the public announcement, was instructed by Barings to go to the Stock Exchange and suspend the shares. The collapse of Burmah was a profound shock, and by 6th January 1975 the 30–Share Index was down to 146, its lowest level since May 1954. Or as 'Lex' of the *FT* had written at Christmas, in a pre-Burmah piece entitled 'The equity collapse in perspective': 'Although we could foresee the general pattern of 1974, we had no real inkling of the scale of the crisis.'

Inevitably, corporate finance at Cazenove's almost ground to a halt during this traumatic year, though not entirely. Quite apart from the very occasional issue (such as the surprisingly successful placing in February of all but 70,000 of almost 2.5 million British Channel Company shares on behalf of a consortium of merchant banks), there was the continuing North Sea oil story. This entered a new dimension with the discovery in January 1974 of the Ninian Field, named after the patron saint of the Shetland Islands. Some 30% of the field underlay the block 3/8 which Ranger and LSMO shared with BP. It was soon clear that enormous sums of capital would be required in order to develop Ninian – at precisely the time that the government was making vague but threatening statements about future State participation in the whole North Sea enterprise. Moreover, it had always been a cast-iron policy that equity capital should be used to fund the exploration programme, but that development expenditure would be funded by borrowings. There was therefore no equity base. Accordingly, after rights issues had been made in December 1974, by which the shareholders in SCOT and LSMO put up a total of £10.5 million, that meant that there was sufficient to fund the cash calls on exploration for the first quarter of 1975, but with no funding on tap for any development expenditure on Ninian. With the two companies on the point of being obliged to sign the cost-sharing agreement covering that field, against a background of great uncertainty caused by the government's continuing reluctance to announce its participation terms, the situation was critical at the turn of the year.

In the domestic capital market as a whole, however, the main event of 1974 was undoubtedly the remarkable Commercial Union rights issue for £62 million that took place in the autumn. It followed barren months and comprised almost 40 per cent of the entire capital raised that year for British companies. The announcement of the issue was made barely a fortnight before the General Election and, according to the *FT*'s report, 'astonished the financial community'. The issue was underwritten by Kleinwort Benson (the lead house), Barings, Schroders and Lazards; and Cazenove's acted as brokers, taking over the job from Hoare's because of a conflict of interest there. The firm was responsible for placing the sub-underwriting of some £46 million; and it did so with some 300 institutions, of whom the life insurance companies stood out as the heroes of the hour. This was a considerable achievement, granted the size and the context, and it owed much to the firm's undimmed placing power. It was also a crucial achievement, as 'Lex' commented the day after the announcement: 'If CU had not been able to get itself underwritten then that really would have been the end of the line for the primary market.' The issue itself was a great success and, if not the turning-point in the market's fortunes, did at least put some new heart into it. Meinertzhagen himself, who was closely identified with the issue, believing that it would 'go' and above all pricing it to a nicety, later summed up the episode more laconically: 'CU took the view that it wanted to broaden its base. You cannot delay and you cannot predict.'

Yet overall, 1974 was a salutary experience for a firm which had been company-orientated for the best part of half a century. In particular, it made those specialising in corporate finance appreciate, perhaps more than they had before, that their success was dependent on the ability of the broking team to *execute* the business that they brought to it, in other words arranging the sub-underwriting, finding support for the shares and so on; and that if the broking team was unable to execute it, because of the lack of a healthy secondary market, then the corporate finance side was virtually rendered inoperative. Moreover, there was another lesson to be drawn, which was that when times were truly bad and there was no jam to be had anywhere, then it was the less glamorous day-to-day broking business that, as it had always done, provided the indispensable bread and butter – however thin it might be, as undoubtedly it was during that autumn. In fact, almost certainly unlike practically all other stockbroking firms in the City, the firm in 1974 did not make a loss in any single quarter. Moreover, again almost uniquely among its competitors (certainly the major ones), the firm refused to take the relatively easy option of laying off staff. Instead, with significantly lower profits, bonuses were reduced and holidays were lengthened; but there were no redundancies. Cazenove's at this point in its history owed an incalculable amount to its leadership, with Meinertzhagen, an optimist by nature, staying calm and refusing to get depressed; while behind him stood Godfrey Chandler as the absolute rock. His resolve never faltered, and he showed concern for the junior partners as well as the staff. He was helped by the fact that the firm had been expanding quite cautiously in recent years (the London staff had only increased by twenty-eight since 1970) and also had not taken the speculative risks of some others. But ultimately it was a matter of keeping one's nerve and believing that, in a cyclical business, better times lay ahead.

As it turned out, it was the Burmah collapse that served to lance the boil. At last more of the institutions came in as buyers and from 7th January 1975 the 30–Share Index began to rise. As early as Saturday the 11th, the *FT* in its editorial was seeing the week's recovery as 'something more than a technical reaction to the extreme gloom which preceded it'; and in particular, it cited as 'ground for hope in the markets . . . the growing feeling, throughout the week, that the Government is prepared to face up more squarely to its responsibilities.' Over the ensuing weeks the other institutions joined in the rush for equities – comprising a veritable 'buying panic' – and on a single day, January 24th, the Index rose by more than 10 per cent. By the end of February it stood at over 300, more than double its level at the start of the year. Already the first rights issue in the reviving market had been announced, on 21st February for Ranks Hovis McDougall. And as the *FT* justly reported: 'In the wake of criticism which has been levelled at the Stock Market because of its virtual inability for well over a year to operate as a fund-raising medium, the move by RHM will be watched keenly, both by industry and major investors.' The issue was for nearly £16 million and was underwritten by Morgan Grenfell, with Cazenove's placing the great bulk of the sub-underwriting. A week later the Midland Bank announced that it too was making a rights issue, for £52 million; and again Cazenove's (acting as joint brokers with Pember & Boyle) placed the sub-underwriting. Midland's advisers were Samuel Montagu, and it was the first time that Cazenove's had been involved in capital-raising for a clearing bank. Both issues were successes and, receiving much favourable press comment, were notable feathers in the firm's cap. More importantly, they showed that the market was capable of absorbing major rights issues without sinking back to 1974 price levels. After the deeply unsettling experience of peering into the abyss, unprecedented in most people's memory, the City was back on *terra firma*.

The events of the early to mid 1970s left behind a legacy of caution and sobriety. At a domestic level, this took the form of appreciably greater surveillance of member firms on the part of the Stock Exchange Council, following the painful 'hammerings' of 1974. Firms now had to provide much greater and more continuous detail about their capital ratios and suchlike; and this in turn led to much more systematic self-examination on the part of the firms themselves. To some extent this was the case at Cazenove's, which was no longer able to leave everything to the auditors as it had once done. Nevertheless, to a significant extent the firm throughout the 1970s remained an under-managed organisation where the assumption still held that the partners were concerned almost wholly with business-getting and hardly at all with administration: the sea-change in this respect, and the move towards a more professional style of management as a whole, awaited the 1980s. Sobriety, however, was not confined to capital ratios. In the wake of the excesses and then collapse of the market, respectability was back in fashion in 1975, and a firm like Cazenove's, which perhaps more than any other stockbroker combined intense respectability with unquestioned expertise, found itself much in demand. 'A flight to quality': it is possibly an overdramatic phrase, but in essence that was what was now taking place.

Following the dramatic revival of the first few weeks, 1975 continued to be a year of recovery in the equity market, especially once it became clear that the Labour government had a workable pay policy. By January 1976 the Index had almost reached (in nominal terms) pre-oil shock levels. Recovery, however, was rudely interrupted: first by a period of drift, as it sank in not only that the government's policies were in essence unfriendly to the equity investor, but also that the world economy as a whole was unlikely to resume the almost automatic growth that had characterised it since the Second World War; and then by the severe sterling crisis of September 1976, now most remembered for Chancellor Healey's dramatic about-turn at Heathrow Airport. But by the end of the year the country was taking the IMF medicine and a period of relative economic stability ensued. The market generally responded, though even by the spring of 1979 was unable to break for the first time through the 600 barrier, despite the high inflation, almost unprecedented in peacetime, that had marked the entire 1970s and much affected nominal values. The return of a

Conservative government that May was naturally welcomed in the City, but its tough industrial policies were compounded by the sudden and unexpected coming of the second oil shock, so that the market was generally on a downward course during the rest of 1979. It was the end of a bruising ten years.

In the second half of the 1970s two of the partnership died: Hugh Finch in 1976, leaving the private client side in good shape for the future, and Tony Bedford the following year; while Colin Huttenbach, Alex Coombe-Tennant and Leigh Windsor all retired. After a pause reflecting the difficult conditions of the mid-seventies, seven new partners were made towards the end of the decade. Richard Smith (1977) was a former schoolmaster who had been heading UK research for some three years and David Godwin (1977) was a qualified engineer now working under Smith; together their rise to partnership status clearly revealed the enhanced importance being attached to research, especially if good, well-informed corporate relationships were to be maintained; Julian Cazalet (1978) had an older brother at Hendersons and was part of the institutional sales team, where he developed a good connection with several City houses; Andrew Muir (1978) had come from Kitcat & Aitken and was also on the institutional sales side, as well as proving a very successful manager of portfolios; Nicholas Gold (1978) and Bryan Pascoe (1978) were both responsible for private clients, Pascoe taking over the running of the department soon after he became a partner; and Victor Lampson (1979) after completing his spell in Hong Kong now became the London partner with responsibility for the office there and investment in south-east Asia generally. All the time the Cazenove philosophy firmly remained that of making partners not by rote or by numbers, but instead only if they could pass the informal 'dual' test of technical competence and the right kind of personality. Inevitably it was not a test that everyone who aspired to partnership was able to pass.

During these years the firm's day-to-day broking ticked along unspectacularly but profitably. There was, however, a certain sense of disappointment in the 1970s about the failure to make a significant impact on the gilt-edged market, which was where (in the context of massively increasing government debt) the most profitable business potentially lay. Having once had such a commanding position there, it was undeniably galling to miss out on such a lucrative business. Any regret, however, paled beside an intensely personal sadness. This was the tragically early death of Tony Bedford in 1977, not many years after his father had died. It was not only Cazenove's that mourned, for he had enjoyed a marvellously fruitful connection with many institutional investors. Moreover, one of his most important legacies had been on behalf of Hendersons, for in 1974 he had acted as the link in its acquisition of the First Investors unit trust business that was seeking to escape the shipwrecked J. H. Vavasseur. This proved to be a wholly beneficial turning-point in the history of Hendersons. Altogether he was such an energetic, motivating person and an outstanding broker that he left a human vacuum that was not readily filled.

Meanwhile, the power of the institutional investors was ever increasing. It was estimated that at the end of 1978 the financial institutions as a whole held 50 per cent of listed UK ordinary shares and that the proportion owned by individuals had declined to about 32 per cent. Above all there were the pension funds, which by this time owned a greater share (20 per cent) of listed equity than the insurance companies (17 per cent). Moreover, it was in the 1970s that to a decisive extent trustees of the smaller and medium-sized pension funds stopped managing them, partly in the context of the increasing internationalisation of investment: fund managers on their own found it impossible to cover the world, and instead it was cheaper to employ specialist, better-resourced financial intermediaries. By 1976 Cazenove's had twenty-two pension funds under management, worth a total of some £97 million; three years later there were thirty-one and the value was £242 million. But unlike some brokers, the firm was careful not to compete directly with merchant banks in this pension fund business. The merchant banks, which in the 1960s and even earlier had been very quick at getting into this profitable and growing area, not only brought Cazenove's a great deal of remunerative day-to-day broking business, much of which, anyway, was on behalf of the pension funds; but also, it should be said, they were coming to resent the Stock Exchange 'cartel', in particular the fact that they had to charge their clients a fee and commission, whereas a firm like Phillips & Drew, which *was* openly competing with them, could charge just a commission. A certain circumspection was thus the order of the day. Nevertheless, without aggressively going out and getting this business, if Cazenove's was actually asked by a corporate client to look after its pension fund, then the firm would gladly do it; and as the figures show, it was becoming an increasingly significant responsibility.

Moving on to the domestic capital market, the dominant theme there for a time was the remarkable boom (much encouraged by the Bank of England) in rights issues, following the success of Ranks Hovis McDougall and Midland early in 1975. By the end of that year no less than £1.2 billion had been raised for British companies by this means, with major beneficiaries including Royal Insurance (£66.1 million) and GKN (£36.5 million). Altogether 166 companies had money raised for them, thereby restoring the Stock Exchange's good name for capital-raising; and top of the brokers' 'league table' in this particular contest was Cazenove's, which was broker to twenty-seven rights issues that between them netted proceeds of some £335 million. 'There must be much gnashing of teeth and gentlemanly jealousy among its fellow brokers just now,' one paper remarked perhaps rather gratuitously in the autumn. The *FT* noted how there had been 'some ribbing in the City about Cazenove's bent for marshalling would-be cash-raisers into the queue of those allotted times for making their call,' but the firm itself emphatically denied that it had been round its client companies actively seeking possible rights issues candidates. Instead, while accepting that it had been 'alert' to the possibilities, the Cazenove spokesman preferred to emphasise how the long list of clients had naturally led to this rich slice of business: 'There are a large number of companies we're brokers to, probably more than anyone else – we've built up our corporate finance side so much.'

Meanwhile, the North Sea oil saga was reaching a climax. The year 1975 proved to be nerve-wracking, with the government until almost the end of it failing to make its intentions clear and the Ranger Group's stake in the Ninian Field being kept alive only by a series of more or less desperate stop-gap financing measures. Somehow there had to be the provision of long-term finance, and it was with a view to achieving this that in June 1975 LSMO and SCOT appointed Morgan Grenfell as financial advisers. The thinking behind the choice was that Bill Mackworth-Young, who had recently gone from Rowe & Pitman to Morgan Grenfell as chief executive, would as an ex-broker appreciate that LSMO/SCOT was essentially a Cazenove creation and therefore take the firm's sensitivities into account. It was an astute evaluation, and a marvellously harmonious as well as productive relationship evolved.

The moment of truth came in January 1976, when after several months of hard work preparing a prospectus it was finally decided to raise three-quarters of LSMO's and SCOT's total capital requirement by means of a public issue of £75 million 14% loan stock. It was then the largest-ever private sector money-raising new issue made on the London stock market; and it was all the more remarkable in that American financiers said that it would have been impossible to raise via the New York Stock Exchange the equivalent sum of $150 million on what was in essence a deficit balance sheet for a company that had no assets except a few holes in the sea. The issue was a fine example of teamwork – embracing in Tokenhouse Yard corporate finance, institutional broking and fund management – and was done against the tightest of timetables, with any delay leaving the companies intensely vulnerable in relation to much bigger competitors.

Happily it was a success, helped partly by a well-orchestrated publicity campaign, but mainly by the creation of a device known as 'oil production stock', through which buyers would receive an equity stake linked directly with the profits from the oil field. It was this, the *Sunday Telegraph* reported at the time of issue, that 'has really got the fund managers excited', so that 'they came away from a meeting at Cazenove's bubbling with enthusiasm'.

A year after this crucial issue, there took place the merger of SCOT into LSMO, as heralded in the loan stock prospectus and an entirely logical move granted the similarity of their interests. In the apt words of the case study later in 1977 to the Wilson Committee: 'The progenitors of LSMO/SCOT had thus created the fourth largest oil company in the United Kingdom from scratch within the space of six years.' There were still some parlous days ahead – especially in the summer of 1978, when it was the Midland Bank that came to the rescue – but eventually in December that year the oil started flowing and all was well. It marked the end of one of the modern City's most notable forays into venture capital and of course was a proud episode in the history of Cazenove's.

During the second half of the 1970s the domestic capital market gradually picked up, and for a long time continued to be dominated by rights issues. As in 1975, Cazenove's was broker to many of the largest ones, including for Imperial Metal Industries and Chloride in 1976 and for UDS Group and Grand Metropolitan in 1979. There was also a fairly steady flow of placings – in 1978, for example, for the Bank of Ireland and British Aluminium. But by far the biggest placing that year was the one that occurred at the beginning of August, as vividly described by Patrick Sergeant in the *Daily Mail*:

A reputation for good judgement, for fair dealing, for truth, and for rectitude is itself a fortune which takes a generation to gain and a minute to lose.

At 9.30 yesterday morning, the partners in Cazenove's, the brokers whose name stands as high as any in the City, decided whether to risk their fortune on going ahead with one of the biggest share deals the City's seen, or to wait for a better day.

They had 25½ million shares in Trust Houses Forte to sell [mainly from Allied Breweries, whose chairman, Keith Showering, was close to Meinertzhagen and which needed cash quickly in order to buy J. Lyons] for about £57½ million. Even with Cazenove's unrivalled placing power among the big investing institutions, it would be touch and go whether they could sell the shares on a good day in markets. On a bad day, they would not have stood a chance.

If they misjudged the market's mood, they would drive the price of the shares down, knock the whole market, and lose a reputation they are proud of and live so well on.

By 10.30, the market was looking good with the FT Index trying to cross the 500 line for the first time since November. Knowing the law of the City – who has good luck is good, who has bad luck is bad – they breathed deeply, picked up their telephones and started selling.

By noon they were high with elation. The shares were sold and only the odds and ends had to be tied up. It was a great feat for the holiday month, a great test of the institutions' appetite for shares and a smack in the face for those who claim the London market is becoming too small and too narrow for comfort.

The firm managed to get 225p a share, a discount of only 5 per cent on the market price, and altogether the report's headline was apposite: 'Cazenove put it to the touch – and win.'

The following spring, in April 1979, there was another, even larger placing, this time of Imperial Group's 49.5 million shareholding in British American Tobacco, a holding worth some £154 million. The operation, done with Rowe & Pitman and de Zoete & Bevan on behalf of Morgan Grenfell, was the largest of its kind ever seen in the City; and, conducted with military precision, it was executed in less than two hours one Tuesday morning, involving nearly 300 institutions, led inevitably by the Prudential. 'An unrivalled triumph for Cazenove' was the verdict of the *Observer*.

Yet in retrospect, perhaps the most interesting and certainly the most ironic episode of these years was the one that took place in June 1977, when the Labour government sought to boost its revenues by selling off a quarter of its shareholding in British Petroleum. The resulting offer for sale (of over 66 million shares at over £8 each) was in a sense the beginning of the modern 'privatisation' process, though there was certainly no ideological element and the government retained a majority holding in the company. It proved an extremely taxing operation; David Scholey of Warburgs, leading the team of merchant bankers, made a name for himself through his capacity to bring all the City views together; and Cazenove's, though working with four other brokers (Mullens, Scrimgeours, Hoare Govett and Rowe & Pitman), played a useful role in allaying the doubts of the institutions. 'Privatisation' as a full-blown concept was still only a gleam in the political eye, if that, but the firm had put down an important marker.

In general, these were also the years when the corporate finance side at Cazenove's moved up a gear. Specifically, this involved partly keeping in closer, more comprehensive touch with the companies, a process helped by an expanding team; and partly using the analysts a lot more than had been the case under Hornby and, in addition, discussing the pricing with the selling room. A key figure was Michael Richardson, who achieved a close rapport with Meinertzhagen and brought to the firm, not unlike Peter Kemp-Welch a quarter of a century earlier, not only a wide range of contacts but also a certain new professional dimension. It was an important and necessary process, for the role of the corporate broker was continuing to change, becoming not just ever more vital to the merchant bank but also increasingly 'upfront': so that by the end of the 1970s it was often (though by no means invariably) he as well as the banker who would justify the price to the company, for it was he who *par excellence* had his finger on the pulse. With market conditions tending to become more and more volatile, with the large institutional investors becoming increasingly dominant, and with the larger size of transactions (partly a function of inflation) naturally making the merchant banks apprehensive of what would happen if the sub-underwriting went wrong, these were inevitable developments.

This was not all. From the turmoil of the mid-seventies, there emerged three corporate brokers – Cazenove's, Hoare Govett and Rowe & Pitman – who rapidly opened up a sizeable gap between them and the rest of the field. The 'demand' factor that lay behind this came partly from the merchant banks, acutely conscious of the key responsibilities now resting with the brokers; but also from the companies themselves, which since the 1960s had been more inclined to add another, bigger broker than had traditionally been the case. Interestingly, what quite often happened in the 1970s was that when a merchant bank asked a relatively small broker (which had usually been doing a perfectly good job) to work with a bigger broker on a particular issue, the smaller broker would choose Cazenove's as its preferred partner, being mindful of the considerate treatment it had received from the firm over the years. Hornby's precepts were thus handsomely vindicated. As for the 'big three', a table compiled by the *Investors Chronicle* in September 1979 showed that Cazenove's had more UK-quoted corporate clients (154) than its two rivals combined, revealing a spread of customers across the whole market spectrum. One must add, though, that not only were Hoare Govett and Rowe & Pitman very effective rivals, but also if the measurement had been by capital values then Hoare's in particular would have fared much more strongly. By this time such published 'league tables' were starting to become the rather insidious fashion; but the story they told was one that had been familiar in the City for over forty years.

The second half of the 1970s was also a time of increasing internationalisation of finance, perhaps most notably in the way that the Euromarkets recycled the enormous sums of money now being earned by the oil-producing countries. As for the world's securities markets, it was symptomatic that there began in 1974 the phenomenon known as global custody, itself a reflection of two developments: American legislation which enabled domestic funds to diversify their assets into non-U.S. securities; and simultaneously the growth of cross-border investment in Europe, bringing new life to continental stock exchanges that had been virtually quiescent since the war. Although Meinertzhagen himself was very much a City man, the firm as a whole responded to all this with a strongly international approach under the overall control of Stephen Carden, who succeeded Michael Belmont in charge of the foreign side and did an excellent job despite his continuing domestic corporate responsibilities. Typical perhaps of this international approach was the awareness shown by the Hong Kong office, rather ahead of conventional wisdom, of the high economic potential of the 'Pacific Rim'. Admittedly the Bermuda office was closed down in 1978; but it had always been an office of tax convenience for the firm's clients and by this time had served its purpose. One of the most interesting areas of growth (though much lower-volume than the non-convertible Eurobond business) was in European securities, after the jobbers Wedd Durlacher and Pinchin Denny had pioneered in about 1973 a market-making operation in London. Liquidity improved (though predominantly confined to French and German blue-chips), the British institutions began to feel more comfortable, and Cazenove's did a fair amount of dealing in the shares. It was also in Europe that the next new office was opened, in Geneva in 1979. From the outset it had two main functions: to be the office of Cazenove Financière, managing the investment portfolios of clients who wanted their assets to be held in Switzerland; and to serve as a regular overseas office, doing a broking business with and for the Swiss financial community. The opening of the office owed much to the firm's friendly links with Pictet (a long-established Geneva private bank with a family connection to the Cazenoves going back to the early nineteenth century) and brought the firm's total of overseas offices up to six.

Similarly there was progress on the capital-raising side of the international operation, though the business (even in the Euromarkets) was still intermittent rather than continual. In 1975, for instance, the firm was broker to a substantial Jardine Matheson issue; in 1977 there was a large rights issue for A. N. Z. Group Holdings and a big issue for Consolidated Gold Fields; while 1978 included a flotation for Novo Industri, a Danish company (manufacturing insulin among other things) that proved extremely hard to place with the British institutions, but in the event took off phenomenally a few years later. But if these were relatively occasional, though notable, involvements in the capital-raising process as such, much more frequent was the firm's role in acting as broker when a foreign company sought to secure quotation on the London Stock Exchange. By the end of the 1970s Cazenove's had almost cornered the market in this particular role, with new listings including those for Deutsche Bank and Mobil Corporation; and although such listings were essentially passive and technical, mostly involving paperwork, they did establish a connection with the company concerned that sometimes brought corporate business in later years. Indeed, the firm by 1980 was broker to as many as sixty companies in North America (including Ford, General Motors and CBS), a dozen in Europe, two dozen in South Africa, and a handful each in Australasia and the Far East. It was an impressive achievement and one which left the partnership well placed for what would become *the* international decade of modern financial times. Tribute deserves to be paid to the pioneer at Cazenove's of an international approach, Alex Coombe-Tennant: by the time he retired as a partner in 1979, after an investment career combining wisdom with world-wide vision, about a quarter of the firm's commission income came from foreign activity, let alone what it earned from overseas fees on the corporate side.

The year of his retirement was, as it transpired, a year of profound significance in the affairs of the City. That May saw the election of a Conservative government under Margaret Thatcher more committed to private enterprise and wealth creation than any administration since the war. Despite the deep industrial recession of 1980 and 1981, there gradually emerged a new, more entrepreneurial climate in which, almost as in Victorian times, the highest possible premium was placed upon creative financial skills. Moreover, five months after coming to office, the government suddenly, quite unexpectedly, announced the abolition of exchange controls. It was a decision enthusiastically greeted in the City, which in effect, again as in the nineteenth century, was given a licence to handle Britain's capital exports. Put another way, it helped to beckon a world of unfettered monetary flows, with the City of London at the centre *if* it was able to display the necessary capacity to fulfil that role. It fairly soon became clear to astute observers that the 1980s would be a 'make or break' decade – for individuals, for firms, and for the square mile itself. In short, a new era was dawning, in which no one knew whether the winds of international competition would blow warm or chill.

Luke Meinertzhagen retired as senior partner at the end of April 1980. He remained a partner for another year and died in 1984. His contribution to the firm had been a substantial one, above all in the realm of corporate finance. The same was also true of Michael Richardson, who in 1981 left the partnership after being asked by Rothschilds to lead its corporate finance side. In the course of only twelve years he had made a considerable impact. The new joint senior partners from May 1980 were John Kemp-Welch, who had made his way on the institutional broking side, and Anthony Forbes, who since the early 1970s had been in corporate finance. Both men were in their early to mid-forties and, through the partnership's decision as it were to skip a generation, were thus young enough to meet with an open mind the unpredictable challenges that lay ahead.

Between 1980 and 1986 four other partners retired – Joe Scott-Plummer, David Rochester, Johnny Henderson and Godfrey Chandler – and Peter Smith died. The contribution of Johnny Henderson, who retired in 1982, had been a notable one, in personal as well as business terms and not least in his latter years: partly through his chairmanship of Hendersons, ensuring the continuing close connection between it and the firm; partly through his seat on the board of Barclays, being responsible for Cazenove's becoming joint broker to the bank; but above all through his continuing presence, combining enthusiasm with judgement and working closely with Godfrey Chandler (as the two 'elders') to ensure that the dispensation for the 1980s was fully in accordance with the best traditions of the firm. Three years later Chandler himself retired and, on his last day at No. 12, the Chancellor of the Exchequer came to lunch and presented him with some special coins from the Mint.

Ten new partners were made early in the 1980s. Peter Rylands (1980) had joined the firm in the 1960s as a dealer and now succeeded David Mayhew as dealing partner; Duncan Hunter (1981) possessed an Oxford doctorate and combined institutional sales with a specific responsibility for advising on the pricing of fixed-interest issues; Malcolm Archer (1981) was in UK research specialising in the food and financial sectors; Michael Wentworth-Stanley (1982) was David's son and on the corporate finance side, though at this time was running the New York office; Christopher Smith (1982) was also in the corporate finance department and had gained much experience with Hill Samuel and Greenwells before being seconded for two years to the Takeover Panel; Bernard Cazenove (1982) was David's son and Arthur Philip's great-grandson, while Harry Henderson (1982) was Johnny's son, and both were part of the institutional sales team; Christian Kindersley (1982) was on the American side under Ian Pilkington; Stephen Morant (1982) had come from the mining company Foseco in order to succeed Lampson in the Hong Kong office; and Tim Steel (1982), having been an investment manager with Robert Fleming, had crossed the fence on coming to Cazenove's and become a seller to the institutions. After this burst of new partners there was then a minor pause in the mid-eighties, as the firm waited on larger City events and its own long-term plans, though three further partners were made: David Brazier (1984) had joined the private client department from Sebags and, since the abolition of exchange controls, specialised in the running of private client money offshore; Patrick Donlea (1984) had come up on the corporate finance side, doing much of his work for overseas companies; and John Paynter (1986) had made his name sorting out settlement problems in the Sydney office before returning to join corporate finance. Taking as a whole the thirteen new partners made between 1980 and 1986, it was noteworthy that nine of them had come to the firm unconnected, in other words without any particular partnership prospects, and thus had had to work their passages solely on ability allied to character. This was a far higher proportion than would have been conceivable in earlier times – certainly before 1970, when the 'self-made' partner was a rarity – and accurately reflected how the firm was changing in response to a more meritocratic world at large.

The 1980s themselves proved to be remarkable years in the London equity market, which enjoyed the most spectacular and protracted boom of its entire history. After two difficult years, a mood of bullishness set in by 1982, as it became clear that the government had at last got on top of inflation. In October that year the 30–Share Index finally made it across the 600 barrier (fourteen years after first reaching 500); while the 700 milestone was passed as early as May 1983, reflecting justified market confidence in a Conservative victory at the impending General Election. Ever onwards and upwards the rise went, usually with pauses for breath each summer, and in January 1985 the Index attained the magic four figures. Then, between the autumn of 1985 and spring of 1986, the equity market rose by a phenomenal 30 per cent. Manifestly it had become that rarest of things, a market in which it was almost impossible for investors not to make money. The figures tell an eloquent story: in the four years to December 1986, British equities produced a total return of 114 per cent in nominal terms and 78 per cent after adjusting for inflation. It was perhaps not surprising if some people came to believe that the laws of gravity could permanently be defied.

Inevitably, granted such a market background, these were immensely busy – and profitable – years for Cazenove's. Thus although the year ending April 1979 had been a reasonably profitable one, by the early 1980s (following the abolition of exchange controls) annual gross profits were running at about twice the 1979 level, by 1984 over four times it and by 1986 almost seven times it. Even allowing for inflation these were striking figures, made all the more remarkable by the fact that during the years 1979 to 1986 the number of partners increased by only five and the number of London staff by less than a third. Put another way, it was a highly remunerative period in which much was achieved and some very long, demanding hours were worked, often under considerable pressure.

In terms of the day-to-day UK operation, various specific developments warrant comment. In the loans department, the size of the book increased by much more than inflation, which to a large extent was the result of the Stock Exchange's Talisman system of settlement coming into existence from 1979: this not only made it much easier to borrow stock, but also stimulated the lending of equity stock for much shorter periods than just the fortnightly account. As for institutional broking, it continued as ever to fulfil its key twin role of unwinding corporate business and earning daily revenue. Traditionally this part of the firm had been rather handicapped by the self-imposed absence of published UK domestic research. In the early 1980s, however, a partial answer to the problem was found with the evolution of the so-called 'in-house research data base': this gave the broking team access on its screens to the analysts' (still unpublished) facts, figures and opinions about each company, enabling it to speak to the institutions with speed *and* authority. Finally, there was fund management under the original-minded direction of Lord Faringdon, who had succeeded to the title in 1977. It was the Report in 1980 of the Wilson Committee – on whose behalf the firm's David Bruce had been seconded to great effect – that really made the public aware of how important the pension funds had become; and in the 1980s they continued to grow still further, generating considerable commission for the firm's mainstream broking business. Moreover, by 1985 Cazenove's had no less than sixty pension funds under management. Even if not actively sought, this additional business was of course all to the good. But perhaps less welcome was the growing trend in this period on the part of pension funds towards monitoring short-term performance. As much as anything this was a function of computers getting more ambitious and the actuaries thus starting to make quarterly returns, as opposed to the previous annual ones; and consequently, the trustees began to want more immediate results from their managers. It was not only Cazenove's that had to alter its style accordingly, but for a firm which had always prided itself on being able to take the longer investment view it was perhaps a more painful adjustment than for most.

Internationally, the 1980s was a decade that witnessed a massive explosion of cross-border investment by the pension funds and institutions. As far as Cazenove's and its overseas offices were concerned, the traditional 'big three' areas of the United States, Hong Kong and Australia were increasingly joined by Japan, where the firm opened a representative office in Tokyo in 1981. By 1986 business in Japanese securities had increased to the point where a licence to establish a branch office, carrying a full dealing licence and an associated membership of the Tokyo Stock Exchange, was sought and granted. Another area where there was a growing volume of business was in Euro-equities, which increasingly replaced straight bonds as the flavour of the decade, reflecting the massive rise in share values not only in the London market. However, taking the firm's foreign day-to-day business as a whole during the first seven years after the abolition of British exchange controls, it would be fair to say that the international side did not benefit as much as might have been expected, granted the phenomenal amounts of money by now going overseas. This was largely because of the firm's innate preference (partly in the shadow of 1974) to do as much as possible with existing resources, rather than dramatically expanding its effort and thus cost base with perhaps uncertain results; and in consequence, the firm during the first half of the 1980s may have failed in this respect to attain a certain 'critical mass', certainly in relation to some of the American houses in London. Moreover, with ever-improving communications, there was in general a strong and natural preference on the part of the larger UK institutions to employ the big local houses in overseas transactions. It was not so much that the firm lost market share, but rather that in the new trading conditions it failed significantly to gain it. In the circumstances this was hardly surprising: for Cazenove's was still a private partnership without access to outside capital; it had always proceeded abroad in a way that mixed enterprise with caution in well-balanced proportions; and the main energies of the partnership remained concentrated on the infrastructure and machinery for the London business.

Where the international approach – one perhaps best described as developing niches with spin-offs – really paid off in the 1980s was on the corporate side. In particular, in the context of no exchange controls, Cazenove's found itself far more than it had done in the past not only arranging introductions on the London Stock Exchange, but also placing with UK institutions large quantities of shares of major foreign companies. A brief list of companies to whom the firm between 1980 and 1985 acted as broker in sizeable placings suggests something of the enviable spread that was starting to be achieved: Cardo (Sweden), Inco (Canada), Daiei and Nissan (Japan), Petroleos Mexicanos (Mexico), Comcast (USA), Source Perrier (France), Barlow Rand (South Africa), Nestlé (Switzerland) and Korea Trust. A high proportion of the companies was from Europe, including in the early years of the decade many from Sweden, where exchange controls still obtained. In addition to Cardo, there were Svenska Cellulosa, L. M. Ericsson, AGA and Volvo, among others. The firm in these Scandinavian placings often acted on behalf of Enskilda; while in general in European corporate matters, the connection with Credit Suisse First Boston proved extremely valuable, CSFB often employing Cazenove's to provide a broker's report on the company concerned and also to ensure that the shares were satisfactorily 'bedded down', in other words that they went to genuine investors. All this meant that the European side, benefiting from Thomas Schoch's marvellous range of contacts and rather like the American side ten to fifteen years earlier, was increasingly taking on a capital-raising role in addition to its conventional agency broking. But in general on the international side, however profitable much of this corporate finance work was, one should not exaggerate its significance in the firm's overall scheme of things. The core of the Cazenove corporate business remained firmly domestic; and it was within that domestic sphere that, as they had done for so long, the firm's fortunes ultimately revolved.

The long bull market of the 1980s engendered intense financial activity in the UK sector, placing particularly onerous demands upon Cazenove's as the leading corporate broker of the day. As the size and complexity of transactions continued to increase, the merchant banks leaned heavily upon the firm, as indeed did the companies themselves, which quite apart from larger questions of corporate strategy also needed to ensure that they complied with ever more stringent disclosure requirements. Moreover, simply to structure a capital deal, let alone to execute it, was by now an infinitely more complex matter than it had been twenty or even ten years before, a fact well reflected by the almost grotesquely increased size of prospectuses. In this challenging environment, Cazenove's continued to hold all the aces: it maintained excellent, broad-based relations with the leading issuing houses, with Anthony Forbes playing a key role following the retirement of Meinertzhagen and Richardson; it had the best technical corporate department in London; it understood the probable institutional response to transactions; its placing power was unrivalled; it had the ability to support companies continuously; and it could offer detached, always independent advice, seeking often to bridge the gap between industry and the institutions. The 'league tables' told the well-known story. 'King Cazenove sits loftily above all other brokers,' rather portentously declared the *Economist* in April 1984, its accompanying figures showing that at the end of 1983 the 255 British-quoted companies to which it was broker was a total well ahead of Rowe & Pitman's 143 and Hoare Govett's 133. Two years later the figures were much the same. A particular cachet came in December 1985 when, after much press speculation upon whom the accolade would fall, Marks and Spencer formally appointed Cazenove's as its corporate broker. Much had happened since the days of the 1930 issue, and there were precious few items of merchandise now to be bought at M & S for 25p or under.

The firm's corporate client list by this time included as high a proportion of the 'big' names as that of any other broker. Among the many companies for whom Cazenove's performed new issue work during the first half of the decade were BICC, Dalgety, Inchcape, Laird Group, Northern Foods, Reed International, Rowntree Mackintosh, Grand Metropolitan, Standard Chartered Bank, Standard Telephone and Cables, Allied-Lyons, McKechnie Brothers, Fisons, Reckitt and Colman, Securicor Group, Lucas Industries, and Enterprise Oil: some were familiar clients, others relative newcomers, but all were testimony to the standing of the broker they employed. One of the features of this period was the way in which the clearing banks started coming to the market at relatively frequent intervals, and Cazenove's acted for Barclays, Midland and National Westminster in a series of major loan stock issues. Not all were conducted in the easiest circumstances, and the firm earned much appreciation for the skilful and supportive role it played. More traditional was the role of Cazenove's in acting for the merchant banks in their own corporate affairs, and during the 1980s it continued to act for Barings, Schroders and Warburgs. In May 1981, moreover, it for the first time acted for Morgan Grenfell as such, co-operating with Rowe & Pitman in what was the not altogether straightforward business of placing the bank's preference shares. Five years later, when Morgan Grenfell raised £120 million of equity by tender, Cazenove's was the sole sponsor to the issue and joint broker and underwriter with Morgan Grenfell Securities.

The firm was also the sponsor in December 1981 for the £20 million share issue of Newmarket Co (1981), whose purpose was to make 'venture capital' investments in new or recently-formed companies that had been created to develop innovative products or services on a commercial scale. It was at the time a pioneering concern, seeking as it did to maximise on the high-growth potential of 'high-tech' U.S. industries through its link into Venroc (the Rockefeller venture capital family business), and over the ensuing years it would have fared better if it had not over-diversified. The Cazenove partner very much behind Newmarket was Peter Smith, and his sudden death late in 1985 was a great loss, not only in Tokenhouse Yard. More happy, in the previous year, was a fraught but ultimately successful massive tender offer of 'B' shares in Reuters Holdings. Much controversy attended the issue, and there was something of an underwriters' strike on account of the shares having only limited voting rights. It was, moreover, a highly complex deal, being the first time that a primary offering had been made simultaneously on both sides of the Atlantic; and, on behalf of Warburgs and Rothschilds, David Mayhew played an important part in helping to determine its structure. In the event the issue was over-subscribed 2.7 times in London, and accordingly 10.8 million shares were switched from New York to London.

All this was important new issue work, but is unlikely to live in the memory. Privatisation, however, will – not least on account of its labour intensity, often involving on the part of the broker 'beauty parades' in order to win the business, detailed and protracted discussions with government and industry as well as merchant banks, partners going out on 'roadshows', and in general a very substantial commitment of time and energy. Between 1981 and the summer of 1986 the Conservative government made eight initial offerings of its shareholdings and seven secondary offerings; and in all fifteen disposals Cazenove's acted as one of the brokers, a telling tribute to the firm's placing power and general reputation.

The process began in February 1981 with the £150 million offer for sale of British Aerospace, and it is easy now to forget that these were then almost completely uncharted waters. The issue was seen as a stern test of the market and its success made the City as a whole feel confident of its ability to play a major part in what would almost certainly be a continuing process. Kleinwort Benson was financial adviser and Cazenove's was joint broker; but in the autumn that year the firm acted for Kleinwort Benson as lead broker in the £224 million privatisation of Cable and Wireless. The government had recently had to postpone its plans to privatise British Airways and much hinged on this Cable and Wireless issue, which was then a record for the size of an offer of shares in a previously unlisted company. The equity market at the time was thin and jobbers generally nervous, but the outcome was wholly gratifying to those concerned. 'Rush for Cable & Wireless Shares' ran the headlines, and the press quoted a harassed official at the National Westminster (receiving bankers to the sale): 'Some people can't read instructions. We've got cheques here attached to forms with matches, hairpins and industrial staples. We asked for pins.' In other words, popular capitalism was returning.

1982 saw a piquantly contrasting pair of issues. In February the government sold Amersham International, a subsidiary of the United Kingdom Atomic Energy Authority. Rothschilds advised the government, Morgan Grenfell advised the company, and Cazenove's was sole broker to the offer. In advance of the prospectus, 'Lex' in the *FT* stressed how tricky it would be to price: 'The problem is that there is a limit to the rating at which an issue can be underwritten, but there is no telling how the market will value a share like this. However glamorous Amersham's activities in diagnostic products, research chemicals and radiation sources may be, the profit record is not especially exciting.' In the event, the 50 million ordinary shares were offered at 142p each, capitalising the company at £71 million, prompting 'Lex' to remark that 'this has all the making of a lively issue'. He was certainly right: the issue was oversubscribed by 23.6 times and, amidst a scrimmage on the Stock Exchange floor, the shares opened at a premium of 48p. It was a field day for the stags and the Labour opposition called the sale 'a scandal'. Richard Lambert in the *FT* offered a judicious retrospective. After noting that the financial advisers had distanced themselves from the government's clearly mistaken decision to make an offer for sale rather than a tender, apparently reached on the grounds that a tender would have disadvantaged the small investors, he went on:

> The Amersham issue was pitched at a very high price relative to the general run of share prices, and the initial reaction in the financial press was not wildly enthusiastic.
>
> What the bankers badly underestimated, though, was the current rage in the stock market for anything with a technological tag. Stockbrokers who would not know a radioisotope if one landed on their nose started to talk knowledgeably about Amersham's glittering prospects.
>
> The Amersham bandwagon began to roll . . .

Observing that the issue had 'left a lot of red faces in its trail', Lambert looked ahead with some misgiving to the next offering in the privatisation programme, which was the oil exploration and production interests of the British National Oil Corporation, due in the late autumn: 'It would be a terrible irony if as a reaction to Amersham, the Government insisted on a tender offer for Britoil – and then had a flop on its hands.'

The Britoil issue took place in November, with Warburgs and Rothschilds as financial advisers and Cazenove's as joint broker. It was indeed a tender offer – the biggest such ever made in the UK, being a tender of 51 per cent of Britoil shares (with a minimum tender price of 215p) that would raise at least £548 million. The tender option was correctly perceived from the outset as an attempt by the government to prevent stagging and, even more importantly, not to be accused of underpricing a national asset. 'Lex' expressed the view of the square mile: 'The exercise is being conducted at a price and on terms which will stretch the goodwill between Whitehall and the City. The prospectus groans with devices designed to prevent unscrupulous investors from making a fast buck.' But, after noting that 'the full muscle' of the City had been applied in order to get the issue underwritten, he added: 'There is virtually no danger that Britoil will flop.' The following week was selling week, and by then the equity market had the jitters and the prospects for the oil price were fading. The result was an almost entirely negative reaction on the part of the institutions, who made it plain that they disliked tender offers; and the sub-underwriters were left with 73 per cent, causing a lot of work for the brokers in tidying up the after-market, especially with the shares having opened at a 20 per cent discount. Inevitably the inquests followed. 'In opting for a tender method the government ignored the views of its City advisers,' declared 'Lex'; while the *FT* itself summed up the whole sorry year by wistfully remarking that 'if history could be rewritten, it would have been the Amersham issue which would have been mounted on a tender basis rather than Britoil'. The City did not quite feel pawns in a larger game, but there were perhaps shades of 1953 and steel denationalisation.

As with steel, the situation soon righted itself, and over the next two years the privatisation process enjoyed more plaudits than otherwise. Then, in the late autumn of 1984, came the remarkable British Telecommunications flotation, bringing privatisation to a far wider public than had hitherto been the case. Cazenove's was asked by Warburgs to represent the company, which was an important role in terms of helping to influence the post-privatisation capital structure, and of course the firm also took part in what was a formidable placing operation. The size of the issue was unprecedented – almost £4 billion – as was the hard-sell marketing that accompanied it. The government undoubtedly wished to broaden the share-owning base, but it was also apprehensive that the institutions by themselves would be unable to absorb such a vast amount of stock in what was easily the biggest act of denationalisation up to then. The fears proved groundless, for on all sides the issue was a runaway success, helped by a degree of underpricing as well as an exceptionally bullish market, and shares were allocated to some 2.3 million private individuals. There were no further primary offerings in 1985, but instead three more secondary (for British Aerospace, Britoil and Cable and Wireless); and in the course of the year Cazenove's was appointed lead broker for the government in the British Gas privatisation due in 1986 and likely to be of an even bigger size than British Telecom. In financial terms at least, it was difficult to deny that privatisation was an idea whose time had come.

During the second half of the 1970s the takeover scene had been fairly quiet, and this remained so in the early 1980s, though Cazenove's was closely involved with Warburgs in the successful defence of the House of Fraser against Lonrho. All this changed between 1983 and 1986, as the market reached dizzy heights and the mega-bids started to flow. Inevitably, as a leading corporate broker, Cazenove's was involved in most of the ensuing takeover battles on one side or the other, though if there was a conflict of interest its general policy was to step down and act for neither side. As the size of the bids increased and the corporate atmosphere became ever more competitive, so the companies and merchant banks relied heavily on the brokers not only for execution, but also for market strategy and advice; and in practice there were only three brokers – Hoare Govett and Rowe & Pitman as well as Cazenove's – who could adequately fulfil what were becoming increasingly demanding criteria. On behalf of Cazenove's the outstanding practitioner in this field was David Mayhew, who demonstrated a conceptual as well as detailed grasp of the big deals that won him a deservedly high reputation in the City. Many of these takeover battles were long and bruising, and almost invariably the firm found itself getting emotionally close to the clients concerned, whether they were aggressors or defenders. Contested bids may not have been Antony Hornby's idea of stockbroking, but for those concerned in the mid-1980s they were exciting experiences that undoubtedly got the adrenalin flowing.

This most hectic of phases began in the spring of 1983 with BTR's successful £600 million bid for Thomas Tilling, a contest that in several ways set the trends for the future. It featured a dominant individual (Owen Green); an aggressive tone (embodied in widespread press advertising); unprecedentedly large offers financed through the equity market (with Cazenove's twice placing the sub-underwriting of 83 million shares, worth almost £400 million); and a hard sell to the institutions (involving flip charts and slide shows, though temporarily defeated by round plugs in the visit to the Prudential). It was also the contest that further advanced the takeover reputation of Morgan Grenfell, with whom Cazenove's acted, overcoming an excellent defence by Warburgs of a holding company that had become a ripe target for a bid. In terms of size, however, the biggest bid of 1983 was that made by BAT for the insurance company Eagle Star, which it eventually acquired early in 1984 for £1 billion. Cazenove's was jointly in Eagle Star's corner; and the company, which for several years had been pursued by Allianz, felt the outcome to be the lesser of two evils. There was a minor pause in 1984, though towards the end of the year the Cazenove placing power did much to thwart the attempted takeover by Robert Maxwell's BPCC group of the games manufacturer John Waddington. Then in 1985 there were three major contests involving the firm, which on each occasion acted with merchant banks (Warburgs once and Morgan Grenfell twice) on the side of the aggressor: the Burton Group's successful bid for Debenhams, in which Cazenove's together with

Scrimgeours played an important part all the way through and particularly at the last minute in securing support for the winner; the successful bid by Guinness for Arthur Bell, involving a full-scale underwriting operation in order to provide the cash alternative; and, completing a hat-trick of victories for the firm, the acquisition by Dixons of rival electrical retailers Currys, an achievement rather against the odds that necessitated heavy buying in the market.

In any other era this might have marked the apogee of the takeover boom. But times were different in the mid-1980s, for 1986 topped everything that had gone before. Cazenove's continued through the year to be much involved. During the spring and early summer it was on the losing side in the unsuccessful attempt by Dixons to take over Woolworth Holdings; soon afterwards it acted for Standard Chartered when that bank (a long-standing corporate client) was rescued at the eleventh and a half hour from Lloyds Bank by Sir Y. K. Pao, Robert Holmes à Court and Tan Sri Khoo Teck Puat, the so-called 'white squires'; and in September it acted with Hill Samuel in helping the British engineering company AE to ward off an unwelcome bid from Turner & Newall, a defence that subsequently earned a mild censure from the Takeover Panel. But without a doubt the two great takeover contests of 1986, running from just before the start of the year through to the spring, were those for Imperial Group and Distillers, won respectively by Hanson Trust for £2.6 billion and Guinness for £2.5 billion. All the subsequent attention was to focus on the battle for Distillers, in which Guinness (for whom Cazenove's acted as joint broker) defeated Argyll; but at the time the contest for Imperial was very significant, if less dramatic. Cazenove's acted with de Zoete & Bevan for Imperial, for whom a reverse takeover by United Biscuits was the much-preferred option. That was not to be, but the defence under the overall direction of Hambros waged a valiant struggle, worthy of the long association between the firm and the company. Both takeover battles aroused considerable public attention, and for good reason: the offers made were of an unprecedented scale; frequent recourse was made to the Takeover Panel; and until the rules were changed the press advertising became ever more intensive, ever more aggressive. There were indeed to be other takeover battles later in the year, but in a sense these two marked the culmination of a phase that few in the City were likely to forget.

As if all this was not enough, the square mile was also much preoccupied in the mid-1980s by what would come to be known – without hyperbole – as 'the City revolution'. Its immediate origins went back to 1979 when the Office of Fair Trading referred the Stock Exchange's rule book to the Restrictive Practices Court. The main 'target' was to be the system of minimum commissions, especially on the gilt-edged side, which had become an increasing source of institutional criticism. As both sides began to gather evidence for the eventual legal show-down, the Stock Exchange pinned most of its hopes on the so-called 'link' argument, which in essence asserted that the maintenance of minimum commission was necessary in order to ensure the maintenance of the greater good, ethical as well as functional, of single capacity. The problem the Exchange faced, however, was that the jobbing system itself was continuing to decline in viability. The Wilson Report of 1980 gave the facts: whereas in 1959 there had been 104 jobbing firms in the London market, by now there were only thirteen, of which five accounted for some 90 per cent of total turnover; and inevitably, the upshot was restricted competition in some markets. The Report rehearsed the usual reasons for this decline of the system, familiar since the 1950s but exacerbated in the 1970s by high inflation and interest rates (to a point indeed where by the late 1970s three of the leading firms, Smith Brothers, Pinchin Denny and Bisgood Bishop, had all received valuable, more or less *gratis* help from Cazenove's about addressing their capital needs). The Report also, equally pointedly, expressed concern that 'in certain leading UK domiciled equities' (such as BP) the London Stock Exchange was being by-passed by foreign exchanges and brokers, a process facilitated by technological developments. In short, the Report presciently concluded: 'There is cause to doubt whether the present system will be able to continue without substantial change irrespective of the Court's decision.'

Wholly aware of the need to maintain and strengthen the international position of the London securities market, and sensible of the extent to which firms historically had been undercapitalised, the Stock Exchange Council (of which Patrick Mitford-Slade was about to become deputy chairman) made the crucial decision in June 1982 to allow outsiders to take a stake of up to 29.9 per cent in member firms, brokers as well as jobbers. Thereafter, events moved at a pace faster than anyone could have imagined possible. In the early part of 1983, with the Stock Exchange pessimistic about its chances in the looming Court case, the Bank of England came to feel that it was vital the Stock Exchange reformed itself rather than leaving it to the less flexible legal process. The result, following the Conservative victory in the June General Election, was the famous 'accord' of July 1983 by which the government called off the case in return for the Stock Exchange promising to dismantle minimum commissions by the end of 1986. During the year that followed this agreement, three further cardinal things became clear about what would be the post-1986 character of the Exchange: that single capacity was incompatible with negotiated commissions, since brokers would be forced to take principal positions and jobbers would have to respond by dealing direct with clients; that changing technology, as well as the imminent demise of the traditional jobbing system, demanded a screen-based rather than a face-to-face market; and that the pressure to maintain London's competitive edge as an international financial centre was such that the member-firms of the Stock Exchange would further have to open themselves up to outside capital.

It was within this overarching framework, one of a completely new trading environment due to come into operation towards the end of 1986, that there began in the autumn of 1983, under the informal auspices of the Bank, what many observers could not help but call the 'sale of the century'. Over the ensuing months, in an astonishingly rapid series of purchases, almost all of the leading Stock Exchange firms were bought by outside organisations, mainly banks. It was the end of a proud tradition of independence going back almost two centuries. Most people saw it as an inevitable process, but there was a certain tinge of scepticism. 'There is a risk of going too far in the vogue for financial supermarkets', commented the *FT* as early as December 1983, adding that 'in terms of style, structure and corporate culture, a clearing bank has very little in common with, say, a jobber.' Moreover, as Wall Street had found in recent years, 'company treasurers are interested in seeking out the best people rather than in one-stop shopping.' In sum: 'For the majority of City firms, organic growth is likely to be a more satisfactory course than indiscriminate merger activity.' These and similar words were little heeded, and by 1985 vast, high-tech trading floors were being put in place for the new conglomerates, the personnel for new operational structures was being recruited at notorious cost, and the 'Big Bang' of 27th October 1986 was drawing daily nearer.

What of Cazenove's? It was a great advantage to the firm that the profoundly transforming events of 1983 and beyond did not come as a complete surprise. As early as July 1980, the new joint senior partners, John Kemp-Welch and Anthony Forbes, circulated an important internal memorandum:

We have become increasingly aware of the feeling of change that exists in the City and in the Stock Exchange today. No one can know what changes there will be during the 1980s nor whether they may come about as a result of the reference of The Stock Exchange rule book to the Restrictive Practices Court or from natural evolution or from the rapid development of communication techniques. We hope very much that there will be no major change in the market system but we must nevertheless be prepared if it comes. In any event, we must expect competition to become even more intense than it is at present.

Change was still felt to be some way off, but the new order at Cazenove's did recognise that it was coming, albeit seen through a glass darkly. As a result, there began in May 1982 a major internal reorganisation. The central object was to create a larger and better-equipped stockbroking room, in response to the firm's business having become increasingly competitive as well as international; and it went into service in May 1983. Nevertheless, although the firm in 1980 had acquired extra space in the form of 16 Tokenhouse Yard (once the home of Hoare & Co), there was at this stage no great expansion in numbers. Thus between 1979 and 1983, although the size of the partnership increased from 30 to 34, the total number of staff (including those in overseas offices) only went up from 378 to 405. And in general, Kemp-Welch was determined that change should take place at Tokenhouse Yard gradually and by evolution, wherever possible bringing people along with the process rather than into conflict with it. His father had been the prime architect of harmonious change soon after the war; now he was preparing to inherit the mantle.

By 1985, as the 'marriage market' between banks and brokers became even busier and the sums involved ever more fantastic, the question began to be raised insistently: what would Cazenove's do? *The Times* perhaps exaggerated in August when it declared that the firm's future 'inspires the same kind of fascinated curiosity with which Europe watched the later careers of Louis XVI and Marie Antoinette,' but undoubtedly it was a topic that aroused widespread interest and much speculation. For Cazenove's itself, which had received and would continue to receive a variety of 'approaches', including one from a clearing bank and several from merchant banks, it was a fundamental decision to be made, certainly the most important in the firm's history to date. In March 1985, at the quinquennial office party (held at the Hilton, the firm having outgrown the Savoy), Kemp-Welch in his speech gave a strong indication about the way in which the thinking of the partnership was shaping:

We are on the threshold of a period of great change and we do not know – nobody knows – precisely what lies ahead.

All of our major competitors – indeed all of the other major Stock Exchange firms – have decided to become part of large financial groups dominated by a clearing, an overseas or merchant bank.

We do not believe it right for us to do so. We do not believe it right to sell the goodwill of the firm to a big brother. I can assure you that there has been no lack of opportunity to do so and that opportunity still remains today.

In many ways it might have been a safer choice, a softer option, a less demanding, less challenging position to take. But we do not see Cazenove's becoming part of the securities division of some large bank only to lose our identity a few years hence. We do not believe our clients and our friends see it either, and we have had tremendous support and encouragement from them to retain our independence.

This support and encouragement is, of course, music to our ears, but it will be worth nothing if we are not able to supply what they require and what will be available elsewhere.

Make no mistake, we face a fiercely competitive and challenging future and I do not wish for one moment to underestimate the risks and difficulties of the path we have chosen to take.

But it is also a path of great potential and great opportunity for us. I believe that securities markets will continue to expand as the mobility of capital increases, and that the services of a strong and independent firm of integrity which has market judgement and market capability of the highest order will be in great demand.

We start with enormous advantages – we have the reputation, we have the clients and we have the ability. Methods will change, competition will increase – but the need for these three essentials will never change and we must make sure we never lose them.

I further believe that as markets become even more international we are particularly well placed to benefit because we have been steadily building our overseas connections and reputation for a very long time.

To succeed we will need adaptability and resilience; enthusiasm and hard work; we will need to do well some things which at present we do not do at all – but above all we will need to retain an uncompromising determination to achieve excellence in all we set out to do. Nothing less will be good enough.

Ultimately, what underlay the decision to remain independent – a decision that all the partners supported – was the concept of partnership as a form of trusteeship. Years earlier in 1969, in the context of the Stock Exchange Council proposing to allow stockbroking firms to adopt a form of limited liability, Luke Meinertzhagen had in essence expressed that same belief: 'We will never go public,' he told the *Daily Telegraph*. 'It is not fair on the future partners if the existing ones sell their goodwill once and for all.' Now in the mid-1980s, the partners felt just as strongly that to sell out to an outside organisation would be a betrayal of trust, not only of future generations but also of those past generations who had worked so hard to establish and then maintain the firm's high reputation. There were of course other powerful considerations, including a strong feeling that the firm could serve its clients better by remaining on its own; confidence in its ability to continue to prosper independently; and an obstinate dislike of the notion of not being master of one's own destiny. But at the very deepest level, it was a sense of history – seeing past, present and future as one indivisible whole – that determined the outcome.

That fundamental decision reached, though for the time being not made public, the question then for the firm and its advisers was how to implement it. The most critical area was capital, which, quite apart from increasingly tough capital adequacy rules, the firm would clearly need more of if it was to operate successfully in the new market place. It was a need heightened by the decision to operate, though initially on a limited scale, as a 'market-maker' (i.e. new-style jobber) once single capacity was abolished in October 1986. The solution arrived at in the course of 1985/6 was that of raising fixed capital through a fifteen-year £32 million variable-rate subordinated loan, carrying a return linked to the firm's profits (subject to a minimum rate of 8%), though with no equity stake as such. This capital was to be provided by twelve leading institutions, of which all but one were life insurance companies, the exception being Witan Investment Trust. They were to have no say in the running of the firm and would not be able to see the firm's balance sheet, profit and loss account, or attend a formal meeting. It was, in other words, truly an arm's length investment.

This apparently simple solution in fact involved considerable creative thinking and also painstaking work over many months: at Cazenove's primarily on the part of John Kemp-Welch and Rae Lyster, including what inevitably was a somewhat detailed 'selling programme' to the institutions, who were being offered what essentially was a novel proposal; at Spicer & Pegler, where Nigel Davey in particular was invaluable to the plan's success; and at Slaughter & May in helping to resolve the sometimes formidable legal complexities. As for the choice of backers, the partnership as a whole fully accepted Kemp-Welch's preference for giving a predominant role to the life insurance companies, of which the lead participant in the group was the Royal, where David Malcolm was a long-standing friend of the firm. All the insurance companies that were approached knew Cazenove's well and, in addition, equally well understood the ups and downs of economic cycles and thus securities markets: in other words, they *par excellence* would be able to take the necessary long-term view of their prospective investment. As for the terms of that investment, Cazenove's was determined to borrow at a lowish basic rate, in order to prevent any millstone round the firm's neck in difficult times, while nevertheless ensuring that in flourishing times the lending syndicate would enjoy a proper share of the firm's good fortune. Trying to achieve a coincidence of interest between the partners, the staff and the lenders was the aim throughout, and to a remarkable extent the new arrangements managed to embody that desired fairness of balance.

But if that capital was for general purposes, there was also the need to have extra capital available in the post-1986 new issue market, which at this stage looked likely to be dominated by integrated houses possessing the capacity to distribute as well as the traditional strengths of merchant banks. Such capital would enable Cazenove's to take a principal's position, if it was desirable for competitive reasons to do so. For that highly specific function, although one that it was impossible accurately to be prophetic about, the firm at the same time as it arranged its subordinated loan also put together an underwriting syndicate. Much of the work for this was done by Anthony Forbes, helped informally by the Bank of Scotland; and it comprised seven institutions (several of them the same as in the other arrangement) as well as the firm itself. Cazenove's would be given a free hand to manage the syndicate, thereby ensuring that the firm had the resources to underwrite issues as and when required. No one knew how important this second syndicate would be, but taken together the two arrangements deftly cut the Gordian knot of combining independence with capital and in the process showed just how keen the institutions were to have an independent broker of the status of Cazenove's still in the market place when the new era dawned.

Simultaneously, there was also much else to be done during the run-up to the 'Big Bang'. Between 1983 and 1986 the firm committed a considerable sum out of its own resources to an ambitious development programme, involving people, premises, communications systems and computer power. By the spring of 1986, although the size of the partnership had remained more or less constant, the number of staff employed in London had increased significantly, from 357 to 436 in the space of three years. This development programme, led on the information services side by Peter Brown, had two main purposes: to enable the firm to be able to compete effectively and, almost as important in the new world, to satisfy both clients and regulators of the firm's ability to deal with conflicts of interest. The programme took many forms. On the international side, as early as April 1984 the firm had established an international dealership, Cazenove Securities, which following more liberal Stock Exchange rules for dealing in overseas securities was able to act as a principal, matching share deals on overseas securities and taking a position in a particular stock. In corporate finance, the existing department was strengthened and relocated as well as given its own research support; and there was also set up (modelled on

American lines and a 'first' in London) a small syndicate department to give the corporate finance team advice on issue structure, capacity and pricing while remaining separate from the day-to-day broking and dealing. Early in 1986 the broking, dealing and research departments all moved into a building in Telegraph Street (immediately adjacent to Tokenhouse Yard) that the firm fortunately had been able to take over, fully commissioned, in the previous year, allowing Cazenove's physically to keep together at this time of unprecedented expansion. Included in the new premises was a new, highly sophisticated dealing room, the construction of which inevitably had been a large and complex process, partly in order to operate within the impending new rules, but also to provide effective means of communication. Then there was the prospect of market-making, which was wholly new terrain, both at the front end in terms of doing the business and the back end in terms of settling it; but the firm was able to recruit internally and prepare for it in a controlled way, much helped by the limited initial ambitions. Following discussions with the Bank of England in the autumn of 1983, it had become clear that the post-1986 gilt-edged market would be extremely capital intensive and competitive; and the firm wisely decided to eschew it, concentrating instead on building up gradually as an equity market-maker. As for the loans department, this in September 1986 was incorporated as Cazenove Money Brokers and, completely rehoused and re-equipped, was ready to face the challenging but potentially profitable post-manual age that lay ahead in providing money-broking services to the substantially increased number of gilt-edged and equity market-makers. All in all, it required superhuman efforts to get everything ready in time for October 1986, while continuing to execute a large volume of immediate business. It could not have been achieved without a new approach to management, which was now not only properly manned and structured, but also benefited from a much greater input from the partnership as a whole than had ever been the case before. Or put another way, a firm renowned for its conservatism could be said to have moved in the course of a few years from the 1950s to the 1990s: not everyone relished the changes, which marked the end of a way of life, but in the end they accepted that there was no alternative.

On 10th September 1986, displaying an unprecedented willingness to be open to press questioning, Cazenove's formally unveiled its plans for the future, in particular the arrangements it had made for the additional capital that would ensure continuing independence. 'We have always been convinced that there is a major role for a strong, independent broker able to give unbiased advice and execution,' John Kemp-Welch told the *FT*. And he went on: 'We are also distinct from our competitors, which will be advantageous. It gives continuity to clients at a time when great change is taking place and when, we believe, personal relationships will become of increasing importance within the new City.' Reaction was both full and favourable, typified by the remark of 'Lex' that 'Cazenove's seems likely to enjoy the best of both worlds: getting the capital without surrendering control'; and there was general admiration for the way it had so distinctively bucked the trend towards large and potentially impersonal financial conglomerates. But, as everyone at Tokenhouse Yard knew, only time would tell whether the firm was capable of meeting the stiff challenge it had set itself. Some six and a half weeks later, on the penultimate Friday of October, the old Stock Exchange played out its last day, complete with some boisterous, perhaps rather self-conscious jokes on the floor of the House. It was a time for sentiment and nostalgia, but also for wondering what the fates would deliver the other side of that crisp autumnal weekend.

POSTSCRIPT

An independent firm

T he first few weeks after 'Big Bang' were hectic in the extreme, involving not only the inevitable teething problems of a new trading system but also particularly demanding responsibilities in a massive privatisation issue. And then, quite suddenly, the firm found itself in the public eye to a greater extent than at any time during its entire history. The focus of attention was its involvement in the so-called 'Guinness affair', consumer of even more acres of newsprint than the City revolution itself. Although Cazenove's had had connections with the Guinness family over many years, its official relationship with the company dated back only to 1985, when it had accepted an invitation from Morgan Grenfell to act as joint brokers with Wood Mackenzie in the context of the imminent takeover bid for Arthur Bell. After the acquisition was successfully completed, Guinness turned its attention to Distillers and from January to April 1986 engaged in a ferocious battle with the Argyll supermarket chain for control of that company specialising in the production of Scotch whisky. The Guinness offer for Distillers was mainly in the form of shares and by April 18th it was in a position to declare victory.

There matters rested until November 1986, when information began to leak out which suggested that the share price of Guinness had been artificially manipulated in such a way as to give shareholders in Distillers a misleading impression of the value of the bid. This information came primarily from the fallen Wall Street arbitrageur Ivan Boesky, in the course of questioning by the American securities authorities. On December 1st the Department of Trade and Industry sent inspectors in to Guinness to begin an investigation of the company; and immediately a mass of rumours started to circulate in the press, in the course of which several names were mentioned, amongst them David Mayhew of Cazenove's. These rumours

319

culminated, from the point of view of Cazenove's, in the House of Commons on 28th January 1987, when an Opposition spokesman on Trade and Industry directly accused the firm of having been accomplices in a concert party that had bought Guinness shares on a temporary basis during the bid in order to drive up the price and thereby increase the bid's value.

The next day, January 29th, Cazenove's issued a press release, part of which read:

In view of the intense interest surrounding the circumstances of the Guinness bid for Distillers and subsequent events, we have decided to depart from our practice of refraining from public comment, in order to make a statement about our role.

Cazenove acted as joint brokers to Guinness at the time of the bid for Distillers. As brokers, we gave advice to Guinness on market reaction to the bid; on market activity, so far as known to us, in the securities of all the companies involved; and on the timing and pricing of the bid. We were also involved in arranging sub-underwriting and played a part in visits to institutional shareholders. It was part of our responsibility to explain to investors the advantages of the merger of Distillers with Guinness and to encourage investment in the shares of Guinness where this could legitimately be done.

As soon as we became aware of the allegations of wrong-doing in connection with the bid for Distillers, we started our own internal investigation. On 15th December 1986 we appointed Simmons & Simmons as our solicitors in these matters, and shortly afterwards asked them to supplement our internal investigations by enquiries of their own into potential breaches of the law and the Take-over Code. Simmons & Simmons' enquiries have been intensive and have taken the form of interviews with our partners and a review of documents. Their findings have now been made available to The Stock Exchange, the Bank of England, the City Panel on Take-overs and Mergers and the inspectors appointed by the Department of Trade and Industry to enquire into the affairs of Guinness.

Simmons & Simmons' main conclusions can be summarised as follows:
—nothing in their enquiries has led them to believe that Cazenove was involved in, or aware of, any illegality;
—in the light of subsequent events and speculation, it would have been better if Cazenove had not relied on the assurances it received that there was no association between Guinness and Schenley Industries Inc., for whom Cazenove bought shares in Guinness and Distillers, but had made its own enquiries of Schenley.

We were pleased, but not surprised, by the first conclusion and, although we have always conducted our business in the City on the basis of trust, we accept the second.

By April 1988 seven people had been arrested and charged in connection with the Guinness case. The last of those arrested was David Mayhew who, on 7th April 1988, was charged with three offences relating to the acquisition of 10.6 million shares in Distillers by a subsidiary or client of Bank Leu of Switzerland on the penultimate day of the take-over battle almost two years earlier. In the face of these charges, Cazenove's stated that Mayhew would remain a partner and that it firmly believed him to be innocent of any offence. Three months later, in July 1988, Mayhew was charged with a further offence arising out of the same transaction. Cazenove's continued to express its complete support for Mayhew. By June 1991 the case had still not been brought to trial.

Inevitably the Guinness affair cast something of a cloud over Token-house Yard during these years. However, for the most part life there went on unaffected as the firm, like the City at large, began to deal with the implications of the profound transformation of the mid-1980s. One of the most palpable effects of 'Big Bang' was the rapid demise of almost all forms of trading on the Stock Exchange floor, with the main exception by the end of 1986 being traded options. A well-nigh deserted market place was a melancholy sight for anyone with a sense of history, but it was clear that the future lay with the new screen-dealing system operating from the premises of the individual securities houses. Other fundamental consequences of the City revolution were, however, temporarily masked by the booming state of equities – a happy, high-volume condition that continued through to the following summer and to an extent the autumn. Then, on 19th October 1987, came the notorious Black Monday, immediately followed by an equally dark Tuesday, as the FT-SE 100 Share Index fell by a staggering 500 points, down to 1801. Thereafter the slide in prices continued for some time, but those were by far the worst two days. London took much of its lead from Wall Street, where in the graphic words of John Phelan, chairman of the New York Stock Exchange, at the end of Monday: 'If it wasn't a meltdown it was certainly as hot as I want it to be'. Inevitably the question at once arose whether this was a rational response by the equity markets of the world, including London. A provisional verdict is that it was, in the sense that prices had reached incredible levels, creating the unsustainable phenomenon of a world-wide bull market feeding on itself; but also that technology did play a part, above all through computer trading in New York that seemed almost to go out of control. 'Modern markets', the *FT* declared with typical understatement after that first harrowing day, 'have tremendous technological capacity for gathering global information, but the process of analysis turns out to be clumsy and even alarming.'

During the three and a half years after the crash of 1987 the London stock market showed considerable resilience in terms of price levels, even after the British economy went into recession in 1990; but what it notably failed to recover were pre-crash volumes of dealing. The result, in a securities industry which had just been reconstructed along often less than logical lines, was overcapacity and, in due course, shake-out. By the summer of 1988 the press was reporting that securities firms were leaving markets and laying off staff. The following year the chairman of the Stock Exchange, Andrew Hugh Smith, estimated that securities houses in London were sustaining total annual losses of as much as £500 million. So it went on, with reports almost weekly of the continuing painful and protracted shake-out – protracted because of the often very deep pockets of the new owners of the securities houses. One of the sadder moments occurred in January 1990 when Citicorp closed down the two well-known stockbroking firms of Scrimgeour Kemp-Gee and Vickers da Costa, which it had acquired some five years earlier. It was, the *Daily Telegraph* commented with pardonable bitterness, 'a shockingly impressive achievement'. Essentially a bank-driven phenomenon, and conceived at a time when capital was widely regarded as king, 'Big Bang' was now unwinding in the messiest possible way.

Happily, the picture was very different at Cazenove's, not least, as in previous times of strain in the City, through the marked absence of redundancies. Instead, there continued the pre-1986 pattern of steady, purposeful growth – growth, it is worth emphasising, that was financed entirely out of the firm's own resources. Thus the size of the London staff increased from 488 at the time of 'Big Bang' to 620 by June 1991 and those overseas from 74 to 116. The partnership similarly grew, from 36 to 54 over that period, with two particularly large intakes in 1988 and 1990; and when Martin Wonfor joined the partnership in May 1989 he became the hundredth ever partner. Meanwhile, John Kemp-Welch and Anthony Forbes remained joint senior partners, providing important continuity of leadership during what were often turbulent times elsewhere.

A high priority continued to be given to achieving a more professional approach to the management of the business than had traditionally been the case. Tim Bishop, of Spicer & Pegler's management consultancy subsidiary, had since November 1983 been advising Cazenove's; and with his help, the firm completed a further thorough review by early 1988, in order to ensure that the management structure was appropriate in the light of the changed environment. This proved a valuable exercise and out of it emerged not only more sophisticated management accounting systems, but also a clearer identification of the firm's separate business areas and their differing needs. Unfortunately but inevitably, 'separate' was by now becoming the key word, in the context of the proliferation of regulations and regulatory authorities designed to keep the left hands of securities houses from knowing what the right hands were doing: in short, 'compliance'. This unavoidable if necessary compartmentalisation of its affairs was less than welcome to Cazenove's, which hitherto had relied in such ethical matters on an unwritten code based on good sense and trust; but the firm was lucky in having as its first compliance partner Tony Bamford, who with firmness, tact and humour brought even the more reluctant spirits on side. Moreover, though the physical segregation implicit in the new, highly regulated world could not but affect the sense of oneness at Tokenhouse Yard, the firm was soon making a conscious attempt to overcome the problem, ranging from a broadening spectrum of extra-curricular activities to lunchtime presentations by one part of the business to another. The dislike of the concept of 'profit centres' was a small but symbolic example of the determination to preserve as much as possible of the Cazenove ethos of a whole firm working in harness together.

One part of the business, of course, that had always been somewhat apart from the main body was the loans department, and this tendency continued with the establishment shortly before 'Big Bang' of Cazenove Money Brokers. Capitalised in line with requirements laid down by the Bank of England, and situated in appreciably greater comfort than hitherto in new offices in 3 Kings Arms Yard just round the corner from Tokenhouse Yard, CMB now proceeded to make steadily impressive profits during a period when, in general, levels of business could never be taken for granted. It continued its traditional main role of lending stock to the gilt-edged market, where the total of twenty-seven market makers in 1986 was, as everyone had anticipated, gradually whittled down over the ensuing years, though without quite the lurid 'bloodbath' widely predicted. For much of the time CMB was competing against nine other money brokers, and this, together with the introduction of negotiated rates for stock on loan from 1988, did lead to reduced margins. As for equity stock lending, there was a particular boom in the year or so immediately after 'Big Bang', as the result of an enormous volume of business being put through overworked and inexperienced brokers' settlement departments (the Cazenove back office being a notable exception), which in turn led to serious backlogs in the delivery of stock to market makers. Elsewhere, overseas stock lending continued to be a growing business, while the profits made from the money book – i.e. the turn made on borrowing and lending money from and to market makers and the banking market in general – tended to be at the mercy of the ever-fluctuating pattern of interest rates. Taken as a whole these were successful years for CMB, further helped by the introduction by the Bank of England of a fully-computerised Central Gilts Office. This provided book entry transfer for gilt-edged stock and a system of 'assured payments' whereby stock could only leave a CGO account against a movement of effectively cleared funds. An earlier generation of money brokers, to whom strong nerves were everything, would hardly have believed it possible.

Also based in Kings Arms Yard, in this case next door at number 4, was the firm's fund management side, brought together there in 1988 having previously been scattered round different parts of Tokenhouse Yard. Operating with renewed bite in an ever more competitive market, Cazenove Fund Management prospered to the extent that total funds under its management grew from some £2.8 billion at the end of 1986 to £5.8 billion in June 1991 – in other words, even allowing for an upward market, a significant increase in real terms. Of particular interest was the decision, against the general trend, not to jettison the private client. It was in this context that the firm in October 1988 launched, amidst considerable press interest, its first unit trust, which although publicly available was primarily designed as a vehicle for further looking after existing clients. Called the Cazenove Portfolio Fund, it was speedily followed by European, American and Japanese portfolio funds. Another straw in the wind in this direction occurred in June 1991 when the firm opened a small office in Salisbury, its first in Britain outside London. Elsewhere in CFM, a significant step was its appointment by Charities Aid Foundation in 1989 to assist in the setting up and management of two new unit trusts, under the Cafinvest name, designed exclusively for the benefit of registered charities. Indeed, against a background of wider fiscal changes, the management of charitable funds was a particular growth area during these years. But remaining at the heart of this side of the firm was pension fund management, and by the end of 1990 sufficient strides had been made that Cazenove's ranked sixteenth among pension fund managers, ahead of such names as Rothschilds, Baillie Gifford, Hill Samuel and Kleinwort Benson, though still way behind Warburgs' Mercury Asset Management. Pension fund management could be a trying business, with the increasing speed of quarterly evaluations allowing little breathing space, and this ascent up the league table was the result of hard work allied to investment ability. Two further points are worth making about CFM as a whole during these years.

One is that it was unusual in maintaining the pre-1986 tradition of charging commission as opposed to a fee: this was tax-effective for private clients, satisfied the preference of charities not to expend capital, and in general offered clients greater visibility than the fee alternative, though in turn implicitly demanding from them what was a wholly-justified trust that the firm would not succumb to the 'churning' temptation. The other aspect to highlight was the cool response to the October 1987 crash: spending a lot of time talking to clients, and emerging from those febrile days as net buyers rather than sellers, Cazenove's once more showed its propensity for taking the longer view.

Institutional broking was, of course, the part of the business always likely to suffer the greatest upheaval as a result of 'Big Bang', with the coming of negotiated commissions and dual capacity. Two weeks after that rather chaotic Monday, when the new electronic systems virtually collapsed, Barry Riley in the *FT* offered an overview of the emerging trading patterns within the new market structure: 'The main feature, market participants agree, is that trading by institutional fund managers net of commission directly with market makers has caught on much more rapidly than anticipated. There is a big question mark over the future of agency broking, for a commission.' Even though overall high market volume helped to mask such concerns, there was for Cazenove's, peculiarly among wholly or largely non-integrated houses, an additional anxiety over and beyond the loss of revenue from the seeming decline of agency broking: namely, that if the firm lost substantial agency business in the shares of the big companies for whom it acted as corporate broker, this could seriously undermine its position in corporate finance as a whole. In practice, fortunately, these worst fears were not fully realised, and during the first half of 1987 it gradually became clear that agency broking still had a considerable future, not least because the institutions learnt the hard way that by-passing the broking intermediaries was often a formula for failing to deal at the best price or even to get clean stock. Indeed, in the wake of the crash that autumn, it was institutional broking that provided Cazenove's with invaluable bread-and-butter business at a time when corporate finance work temporarily dried up. Nevertheless, commission rates were not what they once had been; and though the firm successfully held the line at 0.2 per cent, this still represented by traditional yardsticks a half-price service from the point of view of the institutions, which were also enjoying enhanced liquidity and narrower spreads in the market itself. Moreover, as far as the agency brokers were concerned, to secure that business would henceforth require greater perseverance, more carefully cultivated rela- tionships and in general a more value-added approach than had been the case in the ring-fenced pre-1986 world. Institutional broking at Cazenove's had never taken the loyalty of its clients for granted, but now it would be instant death even to dream of doing so.

If maintaining a strong agency role was intimately linked to the firm's corporate finance orientation – ultimately as the distributive hub – so too was the decision to enter the hitherto unknown, principal's function of market making, albeit in a limited way and primarily concentrating on relatively small companies for whom Cazenove's had acted as corporate broker, often from flotation, and thus felt a responsibility to provide liquidity in the secondary market. Deliberately eschewing the capital-intensive end of the equity market, let alone the drastically overcrowded gilt market, it was a carefully measured response that saw the firm acting in October 1986 as a market maker in 46 companies, fairly quickly increasing to 87 by May 1988, and by June 1991 totalling just under 100. Moreover, when at the end of 1988 a somewhat beleaguered Morgan Grenfell discarded its Pinchin Denny component, Cazenove's speedily recruited a group of those former jobbers and became a market maker in all 220 investment trusts. It was a field that had long been a Cazenove speciality, going back to the days of Micklem, and to make markets in them was a natural development. Was this unprecedented venture into market making in itself profitable? The answer was most definitely in the affirmative, or 'more thrills than spills' as one partner put it; and even though the 1987 crash left the firm somewhat exposed with an overlong book, the situation was eminently containable, unlike that facing some more ambitious market makers. The question of control was obviously important, and Cazenove's was much helped by its participation shortly before 'Big Bang' in a consortium with other prospective equity market makers to develop new technology allowing continuous, real-time monitoring of the principal's position in each stock and of the overall book position. But the human element was crucial, and it was to the firm's considerable credit that, with the exception of the Pinchin Denny intake, it was able to develop these unfamiliar skills, and a successful market-making capacity, with a team of homegrown talent.

A further evolving area of the firm was sales research. This was responsible for following companies on behalf of the institutional sales team and their clients, and from 1986 it was physically separate from analysts advising the corporate finance department. Increasingly effective and independent-minded, though still conducted on an almost entirely unwritten basis, its research effort added value so far as institutional clients were concerned. Inevitably much of the research focused on the larger companies, and this helped the firm to create in the secondary market an identity and consequent visibility in the alpha and more liquid beta securities in which it had no presence as a market maker – a critical consideration granted that the firm was broker to about half the top 100 British companies. But sales research also covered many smaller companies, including all those in which Cazenove's acted as a market maker; and during these years what became increasingly apparent was the existence of what was in effect an interdependent three-legged stool, comprising distribution, market making and sales research, in which each leg would flourish only if the other two were working well. Taken as a whole, the knowledge of the sales research department, together with that of the broker-dealing team, enabled the firm to achieve a clearer appreciation of institutional perceptions of particular companies than would otherwise have been the case. Knowledge, far more than capital, had always been king – one thinks of Anthony Sampson's characterisation of Cazenove's back in the early 1960s – and in the impersonal world of the new fragmented market it was to be even more so.

Turning to the international side of the business, there were few changes in the composition of the overseas offices: San Francisco closed in 1988, having served a useful purpose but by now no longer necessary in that the business had gravitated to New York; while small representative offices were opened in Kuala Lumpur in 1990 and Singapore in 1991. In general, the watchwords of the firm's international approach remained constant, above all the twin emphasis on the long term and the avoidance of rivalries in order to achieve acceptance by local investment communities. It was an approach that continued to pay dividends. For instance, in Australia, where the firm became members of the Stock Exchange in 1987, Cazenove's early in 1991 was one of the two primary underwriters in a large rights issue for the leading property company Lend Lease with which it had a long-standing connection. Or take South Africa: the firm had maintained an office there throughout often difficult times, and at last by the early 1990s, partly in the context of momentous political change, business was beginning to prosper. Perhaps the best example was Europe, where the firm had always avoided setting up a branch network; and the continuing reward was to be entrusted with a remarkable number of distributions of European equity, always within the United Kingdom and often wider, but invariably outside the issue's country of origin. Europe too was where Cazenove's was becoming involved in the wider privatisation process, allowing the firm to build on its pioneering British experience. This began in France in the winter of 1986–7, with the Saint-Gobain privatisation to the fore, and by the beginning of 1991 had extended to Eastern Europe, in the wake of the dramatic collapse of communism. In particular, the Hungarian State Property Agency appointed Cazenove's, jointly with Swiss Bank Corporation, to advise on the sale of HungarHotels, the country's largest hotel group. As that part of the world began its exciting if troubled journey into a wholly new era of economic organisation, it was as well for the firm, like several others in the City, to be somewhere near the financial leading edge.

Yet as had been the case for over half a century, it was British corporate finance where the pulse of Cazenove's continued to beat most strongly. Here the underlying strategy for coping with life after 'Big Bang' was straightforward enough: to continue as far as possible to be a corporate broker acting in tandem with merchant banks to meet the needs of British companies and in the process bringing to bear the firm's traditional skills of high-quality technical advice, pricing advice and distribution. That was the aim, and to a large extent it was fulfilled over the ensuing four and a half years, perhaps more so than some within the firm as well as outside had thought likely. In January 1991 the annual table published in *Crawford's Directory* confirmed that Cazenove's remained, by as large a margin as ever, the City's leading corporate broker. This fundamental and gratifying continuity – involving a considerably enhanced capability on the part of the corporate finance department – could not have been achieved without three key structural innovations. One was a syndicate department to give advice on issue structures, capacity and pricing: faced by the challenge of the regulatory separation of corporate finance and institutional broking, it was a highly effective device, imported from New York, that enabled a market-hardened team to stay physically behind the corporate finance wall; and the great gain was that not only did those in corporate finance retain their traditional feel for how something would 'go', in terms of capacity, pricing and so on, but also that the advice coming from the firm at any one time had a consistency about it. The syndicate department also played a key role during often protracted takeover battles, when tactical advice and the pricing of offers or market raids were invariably important. The second innovation was the autonomous research support given to corporate finance from early in 1986: introduced largely in order to eliminate any conflicts of interest or mistrust by corporate clients of the firm's analysts, this in practice also served as an excellent marketing tool, in the sense of helping to make for a more continuous relationship between the company and its broker. Thirdly, there was the existence of the underwriting syndicate, put into place shortly before 'Big Bang': essentially a defensive mechanism in the context of the advent of integrated houses, it was in the event used quite often, being given a good start with a £120 million underwriting for Tarmac late in 1986; and it served to ensure that Cazenove's would have 'a place at the table' in any transaction that required it to act as a principal. Taken together, these were three notable developments, each in its way pioneering.

All the time the core function remained to assist British companies in the ever more complex process of raising capital in the primary market. In 1989, for instance, Cazenove's was involved in placings or rights issues of at least £50 million each for such well-known companies as BICC, Enterprise Oil, Fisons, Foreign & Colonial Investment Trust (the oldest of all investment trusts), LASMO, Pearson, Reuters and Vaux. While in the first half of 1991, there were rights issues of over £150 million each for the Bank of Scotland, Bass, Redland and W.H. Smith, as well as a £403 million conversion and secondary placing for Allied-Lyons. Particularly striking from the second half of the 1980s, in the wider context of a reviving debt market, was the firm's increasing participation in the issue of Euro-sterling convertible bonds by British companies: within this intensely competitive, dealer-driven market, offering flexibility to companies and tax-efficient anonymity to investors, Cazenove's was able through its renowned placing power to secure a worthwhile participation, acting as co-lead manager or manager in about half the mainstream issues in the period from 1986. Flexibility was indeed the keynote of this work, as it was in another sphere of the debt market when in November 1988 the firm, working closely with the client, helped to design a novel £100 million issue for the Bank of Scotland and subsequently arranged the placement. The problem to be met in this case was the recent Basle agreement on bank capital, requiring that banks have a certain minimum proportion of Tier 1 capital; and the solution, a non-cumulative irredeemable preference stock by which capital need never be repaid and cash dividends can be interrupted in the event of difficulties, was acclaimed by 'Lex' as 'a trail-blazing issue'. Similarly ingenious was the issue, involving Schroders and Greenwell Montagu as well as Cazenove's, in June 1990 for the recently-privatised Anglian Water, whose £100 million inflation index-linked loan stock was the largest such issue outside the gilts market. Privatisation, of course, was a continuing City theme during these years; and though the firm was left out of the British Petroleum sell-off in 1987 (a blessing in disguise as events transpired), it was soon back in the thick of things, acting over the next few years for the Water Authorities Association which represented all ten water companies, the twelve regional electricity distribution companies and National Power. Yet in retrospect, there was perhaps a certain nostalgic glow about the British Gas flotation of November 1986 – so soon after 'Big Bang', so enthusiastically marketed (did anyone ever admit to being Sid?) and so redolent of that incredible, almost dreamlike bull market of the mid-1980s. Cazenove's was lead broker to the £5.6 billion offer for sale and in conjunction with other firms placed the entire sub-underwriting with about a thousand institutions.

Meanwhile, takeover battles remained for several years a leading feature of the London market. Cazenove's as ever was involved in many of these sagas, of which seven were perhaps particularly noteworthy, each involving the defence of a company and thus reflecting in part the post-war development of the firm's corporate client list. Three had a decidedly cosmopolitan character: in 1988–9 the tenacious defence of Consolidated Gold Fields from a £3.5 billion bid by Minorco, finally settled by the vagaries of the American legal system, only for Hanson to step in and take the prize; the pass-the-parcel story of Ranks Hovis McDougall, involving in its latter stages Goodman Fielder Wattie and Sir James Goldsmith, at last ending in RHM's favour in January 1991 after almost ten damaging years; and from July 1989 the successful, extremely well-organised defence of British American Tobacco against the mammoth £13.5 billion proposed all-paper bid by Goldsmith's Hoylake, an attempt that foundered following the collapse of Drexel Burnham Lambert in February 1990, making it what 'Lex' rather cruelly called 'a dinosaur from the age of junk'. Rather more parochial was the defence of Birmid Qualcast against Blue Circle, ending semi-farcically in February 1988 when victory was claimed only for a decisive counting error to be unearthed. Subsequently, though, Blue Circle did make an agreed offer at a higher price. The remaining three takeover battles each involved a defence in vain and a certain emotional load, with a widespread feeling (extending well beyond the City) that there was something wrong about the outcome. The first was in 1987, when Hillards, the Yorkshire supermarket chain, fell to Tesco amidst claims by the defeated board of institutional irresponsibility. The next year it was the turn of an even more familiar part of the northern landscape, Rowntrees, to fail to repel an invader, this time the Swiss food combine Nestlé; and again the air was heavy with recrimination. Finally, in the autumn of 1989, there was the takeover of the Bristol-based Dickinson Robinson group, makers of Sellotape and Basildon Bond stationery among other things. The successful predator was Pembridge Investments, the Bermuda-based vehicle of Roland Franklin, a veteran of the secondary banking crisis. 'It hardly reflects credit on the City', commented 'Lex' about the outcome, adding that 'the speed with which shareholders deserted the group ought to re-open the old debate about short-termism among the institutions.' Indeed it did, and these three rather melancholy episodes inevitably raise the question of whether financial intermediaries such as Cazenove's could have done more over the years to improve the lines of communication between the companies and the institutional investors. The short answer is undoubtedly 'yes' – a reflection in part of a traditionally reactive rather than proactive culture – but one should add in mitigation that companies themselves, not just these three, had often been their own worst enemies through a certain reluctance to cultivate fully the relationship with their shareholders. Further, overshadowed in the emotional debate of short-termism and the loss of well-known names of long standing from the market was the fact that in the event full value may well have been paid by the offeror. In any case, Cazenove's by the early 1990s was spending more time than ever before arranging meetings between companies and their shareholders, a contribution to the increasingly high-profile if still vexed question of effective corporate governance.

There was in the post-1986 market, as several commentators noted, an excess of capital and no shortage of participants eager to achieve a high profile. One direct result of this was the emergence of the 'bought deal' as a major type of transaction, and the perhaps surprising willingness of Cazenove's to engage in it. A much-touted term in advance of 'Big Bang', the bought deal involved securities firms buying a large line of stock from a single seller and taking it onto their own books before using their institutional contacts to distribute the shares through the market. In August 1990 it was in the form of a bought deal that there took place the largest-ever secondary market trade in Europe – namely, the sale by ICI of its 24.9% stake in Enterprise Oil for £679.6 million. The shares had been sold in a block for 600p each to Warburg Securities and Cazenove's, which immediately placed the stock among institutional investors at 607p. '"Bought deals" are for brokers with good nerves' ran the *FT* headline, and no one would have quarrelled with that. Over the next eight months, as large bull market stakes were progressively unwound, Cazenove's featured in a series of bought deals, though often with another securities house such as BZW or Smith New Court: for example, in October 1990 when General Cinema sold for £315 million its 102 million shares in Cadbury Schweppes, a sale that for 'Lex' recalled 'a whole vanished world of leverage, mega bids and the magic of brands'; or in February 1991, when the Reichmann brothers, best known as the developers of the Canary Wharf office complex, raised £403 million from the sale of a 9% stake in Allied-Lyons. In these bought deals, Cazenove's was usually corporate broker to one of the parties involved, but above all its participation was valued on account of the quality and sureness of its distribution. Nevertheless, for all its obvious profitability, the bought deal was still an inherently risky animal and involved enormous capital exposure, something that the firm had traditionally avoided. There could have been no clearer sign that, as transactional methods changed, Cazenove's was determined not to lose its place in the front rank.

Such, then, were the main strands of the firm's business during the initial testing years after the City revolution. Two further general 'business' points need to be made. The first was the continuing unbending insistence on that fundamental principle of quality control established in the era of Micklem and Serocold. The well-being of the client remained the central purpose of the firm, and that in turn depended as much as ever before on only having clients with whom the firm felt comfortable. The other point concerns the ability of Cazenove's during this period to work in co-operation with the whole range of other reputable houses, whether merchant banks or investment banks. The attraction of the firm for others lay partly in its own long-standing reputation and often historically friendly relations; partly in its renowned capacity to provide effective distribution; and perhaps above all in its continuing independence which inevitably offered a contrast with other broking firms. The apposite analogy is with a high-class freelance jockey: if able to make the weight, he tends to have the pick of the rides where freedom of choice applies. Some of the traditional assumptions may have changed, but there were compelling reasons why more than ever Cazenove's accompanied the best steeds.

If there had been any misgivings within the firm in 1986 about the distinctively independent course it was charting, building on existing skills rather than embarking in a major way on new types of activity, these were soon forgotten in the very hectic trading conditions of the first nine months of the new world. But what of outside perceptions of Cazenove's? For a surprisingly long time, the view taken by some in the City might best be summarised as 'brave but foolish', typified by a stark headline in the *Evening Standard* in April 1988: 'Cazenove's choice: a slow death or integration'. The accompanying article argued that lack of market-making power was depriving the firm of access to the markets, and it even suggested a somewhat improbable tie-up with Smith New Court. One year later, however, and the same paper was taking a very different line: 'It looks more and more as if, contrary to almost everybody's predictions, Cazenove, that most traditional of firms, is emerging as one of the two or three big winners in the post-Big Bang world'. Other assessments followed suit, and not long afterwards Ivan Fallon in the *Sunday Times* was writing appreciatively of 12 Tokenhouse Yard as 'a last bastion of the old City', with all its reassuring continuity: 'the same discreet entrance just behind Throgmorton Street, the same creaky lift to the partners' floor, and the same old-world courteousness . . .' It was, in other words, a dual perception of Cazenove's that had begun to solidify by the end of the 1980s: as an effective, highly profitable contestant in a changed environment, growing steadily while some other houses were more or less falling apart; and as a unique home of all that had been best in the old square mile.

There was also perhaps a wider sense in which this perception reflected a fundamental ill ease about the consequences of 'Big Bang', a phenomenon that City practitioners increasingly looked back on (not altogether accurately) as something thrust upon them by government. Obviously there had been gains, notably a more liquid secondary market for institutional investors and the successful establishment of Seaq International, enabling London to become the main centre for trading in international equities. Yet a strong feeling existed that much more had been lost, not all of it tangible but nonetheless important. To many the City seemed a less generous and also a less human place, where a diverse array of specialist firms had been replaced by theoretically one-stop financial supermarkets, where face-to-face trading had given way to the impersonal screen, and where old-fashioned trust no longer seemed relevant in an increasingly American-style litigious climate. Over the centuries one of the great strengths of the City had been its village atmosphere: a place where people knew each other and business was done quickly, without fuss and for the most part honestly. Imagination may not have been its strong suit, but character in the broad sense of the word undoubtedly was. Now that character, so wonderfully evoked those many years before by Charlotte Brontë, appeared to be in danger of being lost altogether. If it is true that progress always exacts a price, in this case it seemed a particularly severe one.

And Cazenove's, that firm where Antony Hornby had always insisted that life should be fun? There a rare and wonderful trick was being performed: holding on to time-honoured values and a recognisably 'family' way of life while not pretending for one moment that man can live by sentiment alone. In 1991 there emanated from Tokenhouse Yard a sense of calmness, of balance and of looking beyond the immediate; the partnership, that most mutually supportive of organisations, continued as strongly as ever; and mindful more than at any time before of the dangers of an increasingly unpredictable world, the firm felt ready to face whatever challenges the future held. It was no less than Philip Cazenove and successive generations would have expected.

APPENDICES

STYLE OF THE FIRM

Menet & Cazenove	1823–1835
P. Cazenove & Co	1835
Laurence, Cazenove & Pearce	1836–1854
P. Cazenove & Co	1855–1884
Cazenove & Akroyds	1884–1932
Cazenove, Akroyds & Greenwood & Co	1932–1954
Cazenove & Co	1954–

ADDRESSES

7 Old Broad Street	1823–1835
Auction Mart, Bartholomew Lane	1836–1854
39 Lothbury	1855–1859
52 Threadneedle Street	1859–1919
43 Threadneedle Street	1919–1926
10 Old Broad Street	1926–1937
12 Tokenhouse Yard	1937–

PARTNERS

Philip Cazenove	1823–1873
John Francis Menet	1823–1835
Joseph Laurence	1836–1854
Charles Thomas Pearce	1836–1847
Henry Cazenove	1846–1853
Sydney Laurence	1846–1854
Charles Pearce	1853–1854
Henry Cazenove	1855–1884
Edward Cazenove	1855–1857
Peter Reid	1858–1884
George John Coulson	1873–1884
Arthur Philip Cazenove	1884–1921

334

John Bathurst Akroyd	1884–1916
Swainson Howden Akroyd	1884–1925
Claud Pearce Serocold	1903–1947
Charles Micklem	1913–1954
James Edward Tomkinson (Palmer-Tomkinson)	1919–1947
Geoffrey Arthur Barnett	1919–1947
Ludlow Ashmead Cliffe Vigors	1922–1937
Algernon Spencer Belmont	1925–1944
Miles Brunton	1925–1950
Geoffrey Akroyd	1925–1962
George John Scaramanga	1928–1950
Cecil Breitmeyer	1928–1930
Philip Henry de Lerisson Cazenove	1930–1963
Lord Faringdon (Alexander Henderson)	1932–1933
The Hon. Arnold Henderson	1932–1933
Frank Follett Holt	1932–1966
Roger Antony Hornby (Sir Antony)	1933–1970
David Verner Shaw-Kennedy	1933–1950
Derek Shuldham Schreiber	1936–1970
The Hon. Stephen de Yarburgh-Bateson (Lord Deramore)	1937–1952
Ernest Reginald Bedford	1940–1970
Albert Arthur Martin	1945–1957
Peter Wellesbourne Kemp-Welch	1945–1964
Peter Cedric Barnett	1946–1974
Herbert Ingram (Sir Herbert)	1946–1970
Gerald Hugh Micklem	1946–1954
Luke Meinertzhagen	1947–1981
James Algernon Palmer-Tomkinson	1947–1950
Alexander John Serocold Coombe-Tennant	1951–1979
David Michael de Lerisson Cazenove	1952–1972
John Ronald Henderson	1954–1982
Charles Ronald Purnell	1956–1971
Colin Frowd Huttenbach	1956–1978
Geoffrey David Wentworth-Stanley	1957–1988
Michael Jeremy Kindersley Belmont	1957–1990
Godfrey John Chandler	1957–1985
John Kemp-Welch	1961–
Rae Lionel Haggard Lyster	1961–1991
Michael Anthony Bedford	1964–1977
Graham Stephen Paul Carden	1964–
Anthony David Arnold William Forbes	1967–
Ian Alan Douglas Pilkington	1967–
Charles Michael Henderson (Lord Faringdon)	1968–
Robert George Holland-Martin	1968–1974
Ralph Edmund Hugh Finch	1969–1976
Peter John Smith	1969–1985
Michael John de Rougemont Richardson	1969–1981
Evered Leigh Windsor	1969–1979

David Lionel Mayhew	1971–
Patrick Buxton Mitford-Slade	1972–
Christopher David Palmer-Tomkinson	1972–
Ulric David Barnett	1972–
Henry de Lerisson Cazenove	1972–1991
David John Rochester	1972–1981
Anthony Frederick Bamford	1972–1990
Thomas Schoch	1973–
Mark Antony Loveday	1974–
Patrick Joseph Scott-Plummer	1974–1980
Richard Barclay Smith	1977–
David Christopher Godwin	1977–
Charles Julian Cazalet	1978–
Andrew Hugh John Muir	1978–
Nicholas Anthony Gold	1978–
Bryan Edward Albert Pascoe	1978–
The Hon. Victor Miles George Aldous Lampson	1979–
Peter Dorsman Rylands	1980–
Duncan Robert Hunter	1981–
Malcolm Patrick Archer	1981–
David Michael Wentworth-Stanley	1982–
Christopher Smith	1982–
Bernard Michael de Lerisson Cazenove	1982–
Henry Merton Henderson	1982–
Christian Philip Kindersley	1982–
Stephen Peter Morant	1982–
Timothy Michael Steel	1982–
David Richard Brazier	1984–
Patrick Kevin Fitzgerald Donlea	1984–
John Gregor Hugh Paynter	1986–
Simon Richard Vivian Troughton	1988–
Edward Thomas Whitley	1988–
Alexander John Scott-Barrett	1988–
James William Findlay	1988–
Peter John Brown	1988–
Malcolm Calvert	1988–
Robert Andrew Richard Bradfield	1988–
Patrick Claude John Dalby	1988–
Nigel Rowe	1988–
Martin Robert Francis Wonfor	1989–
Richard David Wintour	1990–
Jonathan Cairns Hubbard	1990–
Richard de Cruce Grubb	1990–
Michael Richard Parkes Power	1990–
Laurence David Edgar Hollingworth	1990–
John Thomas Reilly	1990–
Stephen John Daniels	1990–
The Hon. John Edward Richard Harbord-Hamond	1990–

Roger Mark Uvedale Lambert	1990–
Simon John Dettmer	1990–
Arthur Philip Andrew Drysdale	1990–
David John Letbe Croft	1991–

STAFF

Cazenove's throughout its existence has been very fortunate in the loyalty of its staff. In so far as records are available the list below gives the names of all those who have worked with the firm for at least twenty-five years.

George Hanneford	1895–1938
Bertram (Bill) Crosse	1902–1948
Harry Young	1911–1940
Victor Warren	1912–1947
Miss Annie Tucker	1916–1961
Philip Baker	1917–1966
Walter Rudge	1918–1956
Miss Kathleen Cross	1919–1958
Joe Mead	1919–1946
Arthur Roome	1919–1947
Cyril Sturgess	1919–1954
Charles Pugh	1919–1957
Ernest Brooker	1920–1948
Charles McKenzie	1920–1967
Leonard Brent	1922–1948
Tom (Tabby) Burdett	1922–1947
Alban Hill	1922–1967
Frank Webb	1922–1970
Thomas Coole	1923–1948
Hugh Maclure	c.1923–1954
Charles Strangeman	1924–1960
Austin Sheldon	1925–1959
Cecil Newton	1925–1973
Eric (Angus) Eames	1926–1970
Cyril Jolly	1927–1970
Mrs Lorna Keeler	1927–1958
Claude Carter	1927–1977
Donald Ridley	1927–1976
Frederick (Larry) Cathie	1928–1974
Philip Perry	1928–1966
William (Jimmy) Bedwell	1928–1976
Mrs Alice Cooper	1928–1959
Harry Harmer	1929–1974
James McNaught	1929–1954
Leonard Martin	1929–1977
Miss Jane (Deena) Clark	1932–1970
Frederick Hoffman	1933–1981

Arnold Roome	1934–1981
Max Gilford	1934–1976
Arnold Dousse	1934–1969
Jack Coole	1935–1975
Clifford Crighton	1935–1962
Harry Willmott	1936–1978
Douglas Jones	1936–1981
Frank Layton	1937–1974
Frederick Bush	1937–1962
Kenneth Syms	1937–1972
Frank Drew	1937–1981
James Martine	1937–1980
Thomas Tulley	1937–1984
Frederick Cole	1940–1983
Ted Page	1940–1985
Mrs Dorothy Barry	1940–1965
George Durno	1941–1988
Dennis Appleton	1943–1979
Peter McMinn	1943–1987
Percy Skinner	1943–1987
Gerald Smith	1945–1975
James Cole	1946–1971
Frederick Smith	1946–1980
Hamilton Wilson	1946–1981
Benjamin Cole	1947–1982
Friend Cole	1947–1974
Ronald Blake	1947–1984
Norman (Jimmy) James	1947–1978
William Smith	1947–1974
James Venn	1950–1988
James Young	1951–1988
Raymond Chatwin	1952–1980
Stanley Hutchinson	1953–1986
John Shannon	1954–1988
John Baudrier	1954–1989
John Thain	1954–1988
Eric Gleave	1954–
Leonard Smith	1954–1987
Harold (Charlie) Coombes	1955–1983
Patrick Smith	1955–1990
Arthur Brown	1955–
Martin Barker	1955–1987
Robert Young	1957–
Mrs Evelyn Meredith	1958–1984
Miss Rosemary Bailey	1958–
Peter Gibbs	1958–1989
Colin Johnson	1958–
Frank Taylor	1959–

Dan Oliver	1959–1989
Eric Murray	1959–1987
Reginald Rule	1959–1991
Ronald (Don) Alexander	1959–
Geoffrey Wheatley	1960–
Peter Ackers	1960–1989
Nicholas Tweedie	1961–
Roy Woolven	1961–
Raymond Hare	1961–
Miss June King	1961–1986
Arthur Hammond	1961–1988
Melvin Wallace	1961–
Peter Wills	1961–1989
Frank Cruder	1962–
David Tanner	1962–
John Tansey	1962–
Reginald Smith	1963–
Peter Armour	1963–
David Morris-Marsham	1963–1989
Geoffrey Munt	1963–
John Connelly	1963–
Mrs Paula Gower	1964–
Michael Willmott	1964–
Mrs Valerie Seltzer	1964–
Michael Ladham	1964–
Adrian James	1964–
Hamish Woodward	1964–
John Munt	1965–
Peter Shove	1965–
Jeremy Clark	1965–
Malcolm Bain	1966–
Edward Holmes	1966–
Martin Saunders	1966–
Tony Byrne	1966–
Raymond Platts	1966–
Stanley Jenner	1966–

VALUE OF MONEY

During the nineteenth century the value of money was relatively constant. The great inflation has taken place this century, and the following table (the long-term index of consumer goods and services) gives a good idea of changing values.

	January 1987 = 100
1915	3.5
1920	7.0
1925	5.0
1930	4.5
1935	4.0
1946	7.4
1950	9.0
1955	11.2
1960	12.6
1965	14.8
1970	18.5
1975	34.2
1980	66.8
1985	94.6
1987	101.9
1989	115.2

Source: *Whitaker's Almanack* 1991

A NOTE ON SOURCES

The records of Cazenove's are patchy until the 1930s, but improve thereafter, especially on the new issue side. There is important material relating to the firm in the archives of several merchant banks: most notably Barings, Morgan Grenfell, and Antony Gibbs (kept by the Guildhall Library); and to a lesser degree, Rothschilds, Schroders, and Huths (kept by University College, London). The records of the Bank of England also shed some light. An unexpectedly prime source are the archives of the Bradford textile company John Foster & Son, mostly housed at the Brotherton Library, Leeds. Finally, for the Stock Exchange itself, there are the voluminous official records kept by the Guildhall Library.

There are several other significant sources. Among Parliamentary papers, the Select Committee on Foreign Loans (1875), the Royal Commission on the Stock Exchange (1878) and the Committee to Review the Functioning of Financial Institutions (1980) all have much useful matter in them; the contemporary financial press is of course invaluable, as are successive editions of *The Issuing House Year Book*, later *The Times Issuing House Year Book*; and P.L. Cottrell's 1974 University of Hull thesis on investment banking in England provides a pioneering account of the International Financial Society.

In terms of books, the following are the most relevant:

G. Duckworth Atkin, *House Scraps* (privately published, 1887).
George Bull and Anthony Vice, *Bid for Power* (1958).
Kathleen Burk, *The First Privatisation: the politicians, the city and the denationalisation of steel* (1988).
Kathleen Burk, *Morgan Grenfell 1838–1988: the biography of a merchant bank* (1989).
G.E. Cokayne, *Biographical List of the Members of "The Club of Nobody's Friends"* (1885).
P.L. Cottrell, *Industrial Finance, 1830–1914* (1980).
Charles Duguid, *The Story of the Stock Exchange* (1901).
Barnard Ellinger, *The City: the London financial markets* (1940).
Henry English, *A Complete View of the Joint Stock Companies Formed during the Years 1824 and 1825* (1827).
D. Morier Evans, *The City* (1845).
W. Lionel Fraser, *All to the Good* (1963).
A.T.K. Grant, *A Study of the Capital Market in Post-War Britain* (1937).
Francis W. Hirst, *The Stock Exchange* (1911).
Antony Hornby, *My Life at Cazenove's* (privately published, 1971).

A NOTE ON SOURCES

John Kinross, *Fifty Years in the City* (1982).

F. Lavington, *The English Capital Market* (1921).

Albert Martin, *Cazenove & Co* (privately published, 1955).

R.C. Michie, *The London and New York Stock Exchanges, 1850–1914* (1987).

E. Victor Morgan and W.A. Thomas, *The Stock Exchange: Its History and Functions* (1962).

Francis Playford, *Practical Hints for Investing Money* (sixth edition, 1869).

W.J. Reader, *A House in the City: A Study of the City and of the Stock Exchange based on the Records of Foster and Braithwaite, 1825–1975* (1979).

Margaret Reid, *All-Change in the City* (1988).

Anthony Sampson, *Anatomy of Britain* (1962).

W.A. Thomas, *The Finance of British Industry, 1918–1976* (1978).

David Wainwright, *Government Broker: The Story of an Office and of Mullens & Co.* (1990).

David Wainwright, *Henderson: A History of the life of Alexander Henderson, first Lord Faringdon, and of Henderson Administration* (1985).

Philip Ziegler, *The Sixth Great Power: Barings, 1762–1929* (1988).

INDEX

357